The Memoirs of Eva Gillies

An Interpreter at Large

The Memoirs of Eva Gillies

An Interpreter at Large

Eva Gillies

With an introduction by Wendy James and Douglas H. Johnson

YouCaxton Publications
24 High Street, Bishop's Castle, Shropshire. SY3 8JX
www.youcaxton.co.uk

Published in Great Britain by YouCaxton

ISBN 978-1-909644-13-7
Printed and bound in Great Britain.

The Memoirs of Eva Gillies

An Interpreter at Large

Interlude 3

Part Four: Towards Africa & Anthropology

Interlude 4

Part Five: Nigeria In Focus

Part Six: Reflections & Connections

List of Illustrations

All photographs are from the family collection, courtesy of Richard and Susie Winter.

EVA GILLIES IN HER STUDY, TAKEN BY ANDREW WINTER, HAMSEY, DECEMBER 2010.

The Memoirs of Eva Gillies
An Interpreter at Large

Introduction

Eva Gillies was born in Munich in 1930, but her birth was registered at the Argentine Consulate in order to keep her nationality open. Her mother, Margarita Elena ("Nena") Hirsch, was already part of a German Jewish family who had established themselves in Buenos Aires a generation earlier, becoming part of the cosmopolitan elite of that city. Her father, Heinrich Eduard (later "Eduardo") Krapf had visited Buenos Aires as a young medical professional from Germany in the 1920s, and it was there that the two first met, and became engaged. They made their first home in Germany, but by the early 1930s had decided to return to Argentina. Some members of the Krapf family in Germany were drawn into the Nazi movement, but Eva's father was and remained staunchly anti-Nazi.

Eva's world, and that of her family, was a product of the mass movement of peoples, products and ideas of the late nineteenth and early twentieth centuries. Her distant ancestor, Johann Ludwig Krapf, in whose footsteps she perhaps unconsciously followed, was a renowned African traveller and linguist. Argentina was a commercial Mecca for Europeans of many social classes, who settled and grew roots in Buenos Aires while still retaining links with their homeland. Buenos Aires itself was a distinctly international city, participating in European high culture at the same time as attracting Europe's working classes, including thousands of Italian labourers whom Eva later observed had imprinted so much of their manner of speech on the Spanish of Buenos Aires. It was a magnet for immigrants, with new vibrant European enclaves surrounding the old Spanish centre, and it was not uncommon for a person of Eva's generation and social class to grow up speaking several languages.

Buenos Aires, and to a lesser extent the Argentine Republic of which it was the centre, was in part the product of imported ideas, of the economic and political liberalism that so dominated the nineteenth century, yet it also had to contend with religious and social conservatism deeply-rooted in Argentine society. In the 1920s, when Eva's father arrived as a newly qualified psychiatrist from Germany's troubled Weimar Republic, Argentina still had a buoyant economy, and Buenos Aires society was still outward-looking and predominantly European. For Eva it was the foundation from which she later observed the momentous shifts of the twentieth century: the upheavals of the later 1930s and World War Two (the family of her first husband, Hasan Askari, having had to leave India for Pakistan as a result of Partition in 1947); the Cold War (with the flight of so many Eva was to meet from

Russia and Eastern Europe); the collapse of empires (her second husband, the British entomologist Mick Gillies, with whom she came to share regular trips to West Africa, would proudly boast that his was the generation that gave away the British Empire).

Eva's own account opens with her vivid description of arriving at Buenos Aires by ship at the age of three. While *An Interpreter at Large* remains at heart a personal memoir, her story from the beginning always looks out to the world of her international, or as one might put it today, "inter-cultural" encounters rather than focusing narrowly on her own life. In Buenos Aires, the family gravitated towards the Catholic faith, and part of Eva's education was at a convent school. German was of course her first language, but even from kindergarten years she started to take on Spanish and English, and a little later French. Having these languages led to a growing appetite for reading, new cultural experiences, and in due course for travelling. Eva was gifted academically and her parents sought out the best possible tuition for her. The first Part of this story offers a detailed and often entertaining record of her childhood, schooling, and friendships in Argentina, a set of memories to which she returns at many points throughout the rest of the book.

The family ambitions eventually led Eva to a place as an undergraduate at Lady Margaret Hall, Oxford, where she read English language and literature between 1948 and 1951. In Part 2 she offers us an intimate glimpse of life in the College and across the University scene from the (relatively unusual) perspective of a woman student at that time. The story is enlivened with portraits of her tutors, her struggles as a student of modern English with Anglo-Saxon, and with her adventures during the vacations, some abroad and some with eccentric relatives in England. Her degree completed, but without any immediate prospects for employment, she returned home to Argentina. Through a series of contacts there, Eva had a lucky break and arrived in Geneva in 1952 to embark on a career as a professional interpreter, mainly on a free-lance basis – which she vastly preferred to a settled job, a preference which came to colour much of the rest of her life.

The third Part of the book describes Eva's adventures over the following ten years on the international conference circuit. 1954 saw her first big posting for nine months to Hanoi, north Vietnam, in order to interpret at the Armistice Commission following the end of the French war in Indochina. Her account brings to life the way such major peace conferences then worked, socially as well as professionally – with all the intersecting ambiguities of personality, national politics, and language. She came to love the city and people of Hanoi (managing to make a return trip in the 1990s). Her conference travels took her eventually to all major continents. Part 4 finds Eva in West Africa by 1960, at first on conference duties; but then making a home there with her first husband, Hasan Askari from Pakistan. The marriage did not last, however, and unfortunately after their separation he died in an air accident.

Eva then took up academic life again, returning to Oxford for post-graduate studies in social anthropology, where she found herself in a period of continuing ferment and creative activity at the Institute which E.E. Evans-Pritchard had revitalized, and to which he had brought an unusual seriousness to the comparative study of religion across the world. Eva wanted to extend her existing knowledge about Nigeria, and her initial (pre-doctoral) thesis of 1964 was later published by the OUP as *Yoruba Towns and Cities*. Intensive fieldwork in central Nigeria then followed, Eva first basing herself in the Yoruba town of Kabba, and then among the independent community of Ogori – all described in Part 5, and enriched with memorable portraits of many local characters.

Eva returned in 1966 to complete her doctoral thesis for Oxford while taking on a teaching post at London University's School of Oriental and African Studies. We glimpse something of the excitement of those days, with the student rebellions of 1968 in particular. At this time, Eva was being extremely productive on the scholarly front, as can be seen from the list of her key publications we provide at the end of this book, reviewing new literature on West Africa in several languages, publishing articles of her own and finishing her doctoral thesis.

However, it was not long before Eva had more or less to choose between a regular academic career and accepting a proposal of marriage from Mick Gillies, a widower and a scientific specialist on mosquitoes and mayflies based at the University of Sussex, whose family came originally from New Zealand. They married in 1970, and "settled down" in the hamlet of Hamsey, near Lewes, where Mick was now based with his two school-age daughters Susie and Jackie. But this could only be described as a partial "settling down"; Eva was very keen to join Mick on his regular research visits to The Gambia. The couple kept up this pattern over several years to come.

In Part 6, we learn of their continuing life in Hamsey, where "in retirement" the couple visit and are visited by friends and family from all over the world. They are able to revisit many of the places Eva once knew well, including Hanoi. At the same time Eva managed to return to academic work on her own account, for example accepting Evans-Pritchard's invitation to take on the job of abridging his famous *Witchcraft, Oracles and Magic among the Azande;* translating Lucio Victorio Mansilla's 19th century classic travels to the Ranquel Indians in the Argentine interior; writing up the life and achievement of her own academic-explorer ancestor, the missionary-linguist Johann Ludwig Krapf, who had opened up the study of languages in eastern Africa and been the first explorer to see and record the snows of Mount Kenya.

In between the main Parts of the book, Eva offers vivid digressions on her professional specialisms and the communities of remarkable individuals she came to know through them. The first Interlude, largely rooted in her years based in Geneva, offers rare glimpses into the personal lives and social world of her colleagues in that most culturally skilled set, the interpreters who make the proceedings of international meetings possible at all. Many of her colleagues were Jews displaced from Poland, Russia, Germany and elsewhere. The second Interlude reflects on language itself, or rather specific languages and dialects and the interactions between them in practice. We have grouped a selection of photos from the family collection in the third, and in the fourth Eva provides some wonderful sketches of anthropology especially as she found it in Oxford and London in the 1960s and elsewhere, with gossipy portraits of many well-known figures, including E.E. Evans-Pritchard, Claude Lévi-Strauss, and Margaret Mead.

"I would have made a quite abominable foreign correspondent", Eva Gillies writes in her prelude to this book. "I have lived through many of the important events of the twentieth century; yet, try as I might, I have never actually managed to witness any of them." Nevertheless, she was a sharp observer of the human side of many of these events; she brought an interpreter's ear and an anthropologist's eye to some crucial turning points and many personal stories which helped define an era marked by wars, migrations, the fall of empires and the rise of post-colonial nationalisms, documenting how these momentous shifts in the twentieth century affected the lives of those touched by them in many subtle ways. Eva was a wonderful raconteur, able to evoke her own and others' experiences as often as not through the remembered (if a little re-enacted!) dramatic forms of encounter and conversation.

Although this is not primarily an "academic" book, we believe it holds it own as a document of social, educational, and political history, whether in relation to Eva Gillies's schooling in Argentina, her life as a professional interpreter on the world's conference circuits, her experience as a student in post-war Oxford or her later career as an academic anthropologist and expert on West Africa. We like to think that the entertaining style conceals a serious record of a serious life, to which we are proud to pay tribute.

Wendy James and Douglas H. Johnson
30 August, 2013

Note On The Genesis Of This Memoir, And Acknowledgements

Eva always talked entertainingly about her life, and friends always hoped she would write up her memoirs. She eventually embarked on the project herself, to some extent modelling her approach on her husband Mick's own autobiography, *Mayfly on the Stream of Time*, which she had edited after his death in 1999, and which can helpfully be read alongside her own. After she had completed the account of her childhood years which appears as Part One of the present book, she began hesitantly to draft a few further pieces. At this point Eva and I (we had originally met in 1962 as graduate students) had some conversations about how to take the project forward. After my own retirement in 2007 she was happy for me to come along to Hamsey from time to time with a tape-recorder and a few leading questions, and we made a lot of progress in this way, integrating her written drafts with transcripts from the tapes. Although Eva's health began to fail a year or two before her death in January, 2011, she was able to focus on completing the manuscript, taking into account points made by a range of friends who looked through it, including Daniel Waissbein (a fellow Argentine and former interpreting colleague) and Rosemary Davidson (an old undergraduate friend from LMH who later came to work for Cambridge University Press). In the event it fell to me to oversee the polishing up and final editing of the material. In this I have been given invaluable assistance by Eva's old friend June Stephenson, and by Richard and Susie Winter, Eva's closest relatives then still living in England. We are all most appreciative of the skill, interest, and friendly collaboration we have enjoyed in this course of this venture with Bob Fowke and his colleagues at You-Caxton.

Wendy James
Emeritus Professor of Social Anthropology, University of Oxford.
30 August, 2013

Prelude

Had we but world enough, and time....
We would sit down and think which way
To walk, and pass our long love's day.
Thou by the Indian Ganges' side Shouldst rubies find: I by the tide
Of Humber would complain....
Andrew Marvell

"Wake up!" said my husband, and I saw he was proffering a cup of tea. "Wake up. Don't miss the storm of the century!" – And indeed, if he had not woken me I would have slept right through the October 1987 Sussex hurricane.

An incident emblematic of my life. Born in 1930, I have lived through many of the important events of the twentieth century; yet, try as I might, have never actually managed to witness any of them. Wherever the revolution was happening, I always seemed to be elsewhere at the time! At one stage in my youth, I toyed with the idea of becoming a journalist; but I now realise I would have made a quite abominable foreign correspondent.

Yet I did manage some adventures in space and time and now enjoy reminiscing about them. Born in Germany, I was brought up in Buenos Aires, then further educated at Oxford. A familiarity with four different modern languages took me, as a professional interpreter based in Geneva, to Vietnam after the French colonial war and before the American one. I later had opportunities, through the spreading international conference circuit, to see something of Nigeria just after independence, Cuba before the arrival of Castro, Ghana in the days of Kwame Nkrumah, as well as India and most countries in Europe. In between one engagement and another, I have travelled – sometimes passportless – through Gomulka's Poland, and through Khrushchev's Soviet Union as far as Samarkand. And having re-encountered old friends – and family – in unexpected ways, and pursued others, I have come to feel the world an interconnected place.

With roots both in my mother's Jewish family and my Catholic upbringing, it may seem surprising that my first marriage was to a Pakistani Muslim, Hasan Askari. He was an international civil servant, and Nigeria became our home for a while. He lost his life, however, not long after this – as a passenger on a French aeroplane which crashed over Cameroon. I was already returning to academia, to pursue Social Anthropology back in Oxford, and later returned to Nigeria to carry out my field research. On the strength of this I was able to take up a teaching post at the School of Oriental and African Languages in London. My second marriage was to Mick

Gillies, an English entomologist. We spent several years moving between The Gambia, where he did his field research, and Sussex, where he worked at the University of that name. We journeyed to Thailand, Tanzania, and New Zealand, sometimes for work, sometimes for family visits, and sometimes for the pure fun of travel.

Looking back on the years of movement, and the way in which casual encounters surprisingly often became firm friendships, I realise how the business of interpreting between languages as such can only be a part of the story of interpreting the historic encounters between peoples. My own professional writings in anthropology, and my translations and commentaries on a few of those who have gone before, illustrate this. The reminiscences set down here, of my adventures in the colourful "world and time" of my own life, are not intended as sober interpretation of this kind, but I hope may serve to entertain my contemporaries in this new twenty-first century.

Eva Gillies
Whitfeld, Hamsey, Sussex
21 October, 2010

PART ONE
ARGENTINE CHILDHOOD

Chapter 1
Beginnings

"Those," said my mother, "are all your aunts and uncles."

A whole row of them standing on the dockside! There may have been a dozen in all, but they seemed more to me. I was three and a half years old, watching from the deck of the ship on which we had spent an eternal three weeks. Now, quite soon, one "Uncle Peter" came in his motorboat to fetch us ashore.

The next memory is of a small bright crowded room, a confusion of parents and aunts and uncles – how was I ever going to deal with so many? Perhaps if I told each of these new people to call me by a different name? I had plenty of those, after all. So: "You can call me Eva", "and you, Helen", "and you, Felicitas", "and you, Krapf" – but here I'd run out of names, and there were still aunts and uncles left over. But now, the inscrutable grown-ups decreed it was my bedtime: my new nanny was summoned to take me away to our hotel bedroom.

I already knew her name: Rosa – a wondrous name to me, for hadn't I been told the rose was the queen of flowers? And when, undressing me, she took off my shoes and socks, she actually let me stand *on my bare feet* on the bedroom carpet. Never had A-yee, my nanny back in Germany, allowed such a thing; indeed, when once on our travels my bedroom slippers had been packed and she had only a towel to protect me from the dangers of a dirty floor, she had vigorously denied that I was barefoot: "No, you're not! You're standing on the towel." But that had been in Germany – maybe here...

"Am I barefoot now?"

"Yes, of course you are!"

Already I had forgotten kind fussy A-yee and fallen in love with this new Queen of Flowers. And by the time she had tucked me up in bed and followed a brief prayer with a little song about a bell telling me it was time for bed and prayer and sleep, my heart was wholly hers.

That plethora of aunts and uncles were not, of course, all blood relations. Some were, like Great-Uncle Alfred, who for some years continued to address me as "Kräpfle"; but most were simply my mother's childhood friends, whom I would grow up to address, German-style, as "Aunt" and "Uncle". The port we had reached that evening was that of Buenos Aires – not a good natural harbour, which was why "Uncle" Peter had had to fetch us ashore on his boat. The date was 15 December 1933; if I am so certain, it is because Rosa – later Rosita, later still Titita – remained with us for nearly half a century, and we always celebrated the date of her arrival with flowers and presents.

But to explain why we were at what I later knew as the Alvear Palace Hotel, I have to go back a couple of generations.

On my mother's side

One strand of the story begins with my maternal grandfather. Young Gustav Hirsch is standing at Antwerp harbour looking at ships: like so many of his kind in the late 19th century, he has more than half a mind to sail to the Americas and make his fortune. On one ship he sees a flag striped in blue and white. "I like that one! Where is it from?" "Argentina!" And the young man decides to catch the next boat there. So at least runs family legend. In Argentina, Gustav Hirsch joined a Belgian-owned grain export firm, Bunge & Born and, a year or so later, wrote to his younger brother Alfred suggesting he join him.

Both young men did well in the new country; but both returned to the old for brides. Returned to their religious roots too; for, though not particularly observant, they were Jewish – not that this was the reason for their departure from the enlightened Germany of those days. Uncle Alfred (who married rather later) is said to have advertised: "South American millionaire wishes for beautiful bride from good Jewish family – dowry immaterial", but my grandfather married for love. (My source here is the typescript left by his wife, my grandmother *Oma* Lilli, to my sister Trixie and me: she starts out with the intention of rescuing her own mother, Henrietta Bloch, from oblivion, but soon goes on to narrate her romance with Gustav Hirsch.)

He saw her first playing the piano, in the music-room of an hotel in Baden-Baden; enquired after her and said, "If she be not betrothed, she must be mine!" And very soon Lilli Bloch was betrothed, albeit secretly, to this impetuous suitor. But he had to return to Buenos Aires, make some more money, buy a house, and generally put his affairs in order for marriage; so the young people corresponded, unbeknown to her family, *poste restante*. And then, on the very day Gustav Hirsch was due back to ask for her hand officially, Lilli thought all had been discovered – her formidable widowed mother and her brothers were speaking in low voices at the other end of the drawing-room.

But it was not Lilli's unauthorised romance they were discussing: Bank Bloch, founded by Lilli's father, was having a serious liquidity problem and seemed about to collapse. When Lilli guiltily confessed this to her impending suitor, two of her brothers went to meet his train. "Sir! There is no point in your coming to our house tonight. Lilli will be a penniless, dowerless girl tomorrow morning." "I am not seeking Lilli's dowry," replied Gustav Hirsch, "but Lilli herself." After which, naturally, he was welcomed.

Meanwhile, the merchants of the good city of Pforzheim were meeting in secret conclave and deciding they could not allow Bank Bloch to fail: all of them had at one time or another benefited from its loans, so now they would club together and guarantee its assets. Next day, Lilli was not a dowerless girl after all; the Bank's problems turned out to be short-lived and Lilli was allowed to marry her (clearly disinterested) suitor. Only the tradesmen dealing with the household were distressed and puzzled: "But surely, Frau Bloch, Fraulein Lilli doesn't have to go and live among the savages?" But Lilli did go and live among the savages and, as Señora de Hirsch, eventually gave birth to my mother, Margarita Elena, and twelve years later to my aunt, Ana Luisa, always known as Annele.

In the year of Annele's birth, the First World War broke out. The Hirsch brothers felt that, as Germans, it was unbecoming for them to continue working for a Belgian firm; so, in a gentlemanly way, both left Bunge & Born. Alfred returned after 1918; my grandfather, however, decided to remain an independent grain-broker. Later, Uncle Alfred came to control the whole of ever-expanding B. & B., and to be known as "the rich Hirsch". I am descended from "the poor Hirsch" (sometimes also called "the handsome Hirsch" as distinct from "the other Hirsch"); but my grandfather was in no ordinary sense of the word poor.

My mother went to an Argentine state primary school, and later to the German "Goetheschule"; she was made to learn the piano, but much preferred riding and tennis; later, in her teens, she spent some of her dress allowance on English and French lessons. She managed, nonetheless, to be elegant, and was clearly a success with young men; it was her second admirer whom she refused to marry on principle – because he, a Jew himself, firmly believed Jews should only marry each other, and she, with equal firmness, held that the future lay in assimilation and miscegenation.

On my father's side

The next strand in the story concerns my father, E. Eduardo Krapf as he was known in later life. Born in Nuremberg and originally christened Heinrich Eduard, he was the eldest son of a doctor – indeed a *Sanitätsrat* or Medical Officer of Health. There was a family tradition that in some earlier century a Krapf had been physician to a Habsburg; it was certainly true that at some stages the lineage had been entitled to a *von*, which they would usually lose in the next generation for lack of money to keep up their ennobled status. At some point in the 18th century, the lineage divided at Lake Constance: one branch remained in Austria, one went to Switzerland, and one into what is now Germany. All three still flourish.

The most distinguished member of our German branch was undoubtedly Johann Ludwig, a mid-19th century missionary who, although a Pietist pastor from Württemberg, was employed by the Church Missionary Society (CMS). It was in the name of this Low Church Anglican foundation that he set up, in 1846, the first Christian mission on mainland East Africa. As a missionary he was not a huge success; but, obsessed as he had been with Africa since boyhood, he learned some dozen East African languages, wrote the first English-Swahili Dictionary, was the first to suggest the mutual relationship of what we now call the Bantu languages, and (in his spare time) discovered Mount Kenya (I return to his story in Part Six).

In the *Sanitätsrat*'s family, all this seems to have been far away and long ago: they were simply good Lutherans of the prosperous professional class. My father was the eldest of four sons, all brought up at their parents' private clinic near Kreischa – a big house, a huge garden, paradise for small boys. "Eddy" was bookish, with a weakness for history – why, he asked himself as a twelve-year-old, had he been born into so dull a century? Why had all the really interesting things happened earlier?

The next year, the First World War broke out.

Although he lost a slightly older school friend in 1918, Eddy himself had been too young to fight; but closer involvement with 20th century "interesting times" was not long in coming. His student days were bedevilled by the galloping inflation Germany suffered in those postwar years; I have a letter in which he begs his parents not to send him any more money, as it will have lost all value by the time it arrives. But if they could spare one small silver spoon for his landlady? She's been very good to him. (She fed him, poor woman, largely on beetroot, which was all she had; for the rest of his life he couldn't stand the stuff.)

He was studying medicine. Initially, he had hesitated between history and philosophy, but had in the end decided to become a psychiatrist. But when he had only just qualified as a doctor, and before embarking on specialist studies, he was told of a job, open for a year, at the German Hospital in Buenos Aires.

He went, of course – for much the same reasons as young people later did stints in VSO or the Peace Corps. And thus it was that he found himself at a *thé dansant* at the Buenos Aires Plaza Hotel, where he met a certain Margarita Elena Hirsch, known to her friends as "Nena".

The courtship does not seem to have been long; but when he first proposed to her, in the shady garden of her parents' house in the suburb of Belgrano, Nena refused. She wasn't properly educated, she said; she'd never been to university; when he got back to Europe he'd meet lots of women with degrees, and then she'd bore him. Moreover, she couldn't cook, and didn't intend to learn. These objections overcome, the young man formally asked Nena's father for her hand (while her childhood friend, "Uncle Peter" Weil, walked her round and round the garden trying to talk her out of marrying abroad). After which Eddy thought of a tactful way of informing his own parents in Germany. Two telegrams he concocted: the first announcing he'd met a most delightful girl, the second breaking the news of his engagement. But owing to the vagaries of the Argentine telegraph system – or was it my father's absent-mindedness? – the telegrams arrived in reverse order. "Must be very hot out there," my paternal grandfather is said to have commented.

Peter was the son of wicked old "Aunt" Alice Weil, and thus a member of the other big Jewish grain-exporting family in Buenos Aires, and some kind of cousin to Anita, whose daughter Iris became my childhood friend. Later, during my adolescence, my father was always threatening to write a Balzacian four-volume novel, "The Wirschs and the Heils"; I have forgotten most of the titles, but remember the last volume was to be called (in German), "The Fruitfulness of Ruins". I suspect he believed me to be potentially part of that fruitfulness.

What does not seem, in those far-off happy days, to have occurred to either family was any objection to a Jewish-Gentile marriage. The wedding took place a year later in a German registry office (a photograph shows my mother, in a twenties' short white dress, with a veil) and the new couple departed for a Parisian honeymoon. Indeed, with a few intervals in the Berlin of Berthold Brecht, Kurt Weill and the young Marlene Dietrich, they spent the next few years largely in France, my father at the time pursuing his psychiatric studies at the Salpetrière clinic. As a child in the 1930s, when to have been born in Germany seemed to me the worst possible, quite unmerited disgrace, I used to console myself with the thought: "Yes – but at least I was conceived in Paris!"

Farewell to Germany

I have few memories of our German life, most of them connected with A-yee my Nanny. I remember, on a walk with her, meeting (probably not entirely by accident) the man she would later marry. He asked me, as grown-ups were so apt to do, first my name and then my age. I had, of course, been schooled in the proper answers: that to the second question was "*zweiundhalb*", two and a half. But afterwards it occurred to me to wonder: was this a permanent condition, as I knew my name was? It wasn't the kind of question you asked grown-ups, and anyway I had my answer soon afterwards: a third birthday made memorable by a toy dog I named Peggy, and a little basketwork handbag with a leather strap. Then, the feeling of being in a gently rocking boat, also with A-yee, but with another young man rowing us. Much later I was told this would have been one of my father's students, and that the boat was on a canal in Cologne.

For my father was now a *Privatdozent*, a junior lecturer, at that university (whose Rector was at that time one Konrad Adenauer). We had moved there from Munich, where I had been born (in the Red Cross clinic second class, my parents being at the time unable to afford first) in 1930 and had, shortly after my birth, been registered at the Argentine Consulate as the child of a native Argentine mother. Was this uncanny prescience on my parents' part? Or a desire to keep all options open for their newborn child? Or to please my mother, who disliked Bavaria? – too late to ask now.

Our stay in Cologne was to be brief. My father was a gut anti-Nazi (and would certainly have been so however Aryan a wife he might have had). He told me, many years later, that he had "looked about him" to see whether there was any hope of a civic uprising against Hitler; and only then, having decided there wasn't, set about our emigration.

This was not simple, even in 1933; indeed, at one point my parents contemplated a tactical divorce, but this turned out not to be necessary. The difficulty was, oddly, that my father was *not* Jewish: the Nazis, while wishing to purge the country of Jewish psychiatrists, were keen to keep the few Gentile ones at home. My mother and I were already in Switzerland; but my father could not leave without getting an exit permit stamped in Berlin. Having carefully ascertained what office contained the functionary wielding this hard-to-get rubber stamp, he stormed into it, bothered with neither "Good morning" nor "Heil Hitler", slammed his papers on the desk and barked:

"*Stempfeln!*"

The nervous official must have thought such high-handed behaviour surely betokened very high Party rank in one so young (at thirty-two Eddy did not yet sport the moustache he later grew to hide his embarrassing student duelling scars) and stamped the document at once. Whereupon my father, pleased with his easy victory, took himself off to a nightclub to celebrate: Berlin still had nightclubs, and surely he deserved a beer. Only, he wasn't enjoying that beer as much as he felt he should: the place was full of those disgusting brown uniforms... He looked over at the bandleader, decided he liked his face, and anyway among intellectuals one was generally safe; so at the next pause he went across.

"Tell me" – in low tones – "do your lads know how to play the *Internationale*"?

A sapient nod.

"And I suppose they could play it in ragtime, so these characters don't recognise it?"

This time the nod came with a delighted grin.

My father handed over a fattish tip and returned to his table, where he happily nursed his beer while, all around him, the brown uniforms stood up and danced with their girls to the strains of the *Internationale* in ragtime.

Childhood in Buenos Aires

My parents had contemplated emigrating, as their friend "E.G." (Dr Eric Gutmann) and many others did a little later, to England, but they finally decided that, since war was definitely coming sometime fairly soon, it would be better to bring up a family in a country at peace; and then, of course, my mother had family in Buenos Aires, and financial help would be easier to arrange. My father knew and liked the city, and spoke good Spanish from his previous visit; my mother tried to impart a few words to me, but was at once disgusted by my German accent. Clearly

A-yee (who in any case had elected to remain in Germany and marry her suitor) would have to be replaced by an Argentine Nanny. My mother duly wrote to her Aunt Lisa, Uncle Alfred's wife.

Alas, replied Aunt Lisa, no reliable Argentine Nanny could be found – but the Kellersbergers had a very good Swiss girl; they were taking a European trip that year and didn't feel like paying their nanny's passage, so would my mother like to take on young Rosa Huber for six months, which would give her time to look around? Which is how Rosita came to be waiting for us at the Alvear Palace Hotel that December.

She never did go back to the Kellersbergers. My mother was too decent a person to offer her more money than her previous wages; but at the end of three months Rosita herself said, "If you've no objection, *gnädige Frau*, I'd like to stay with you." Years later, she told me why: "Your mother *trusted* me! In all the years I was with the Kellersbergers, I was never allowed to take the children away on holiday by myself; but your mother sent me off with you to that *estancia* before I'd been with you three weeks."

I don't remember much about the *estancia* (which must have belonged to one of the aunts-and-uncles) except for the pleasure of sitting in the sun watching kittens and puppies and baby chicks. I know now that Rosita had been instructed to let me see baby animals being born; but if I did I don't remember it.

What I do remember quite vividly is the picture-book, *Das Vogel-ABC*, from which Rosita read to me in the hotel before bedtime. It was the only children's book we had (our "big luggage" couldn't be unpacked in hotel rooms) and must have been a present from some other of the aunts-and-uncles, perhaps slightly confused as to my age: I had by now just turned four. This wondrous book had, for each letter of the alphabet, pictures of *two* birds: one for the Latin character, and one for the Gothic – that self-consciously "old Germanic" print which was now, under Nazism, coming back into fashion. I was eleven before I realised, looking at German books in my bedroom, that not all of them were printed in the same characters. Now, sitting beside Rosita, I simply pored over pictures and letters. The last one that puzzled me, I remember, was the one that was "like half an O but with a stick down one side". "D" said Rosita, and I remembered.

When, sitting in my parents' car, I read out "POLO", we had in fact just passed the Polo Club, which they assumed I knew; but when I asked, after passing a film poster, what "MARLENE DIETRICH" meant, the secret was out: I had learnt to read. The grown-ups seemed curiously pleased about this. However, I had pronounced "Marlene Dietrich" as if the two words were Spanish; so this episode must have taken place a little after I began kindergarten. Although I never had a Spanish-speaking nanny, my mother had at least been lucky in finding a Spanish-speaking kindergarten: a modern one had just been opened by a *Madame* Renard in the city, which seemed of good repute.

Josefina Moyano de Renard had borne her naval-officer husband ten children before the doctor decreed she should have no more. But, as Captain Renard had just then been appointed naval *attaché* to the Argentine Embassy in Washington, his wife consoled herself by taking a course in modern kindergarten techniques. On their return to Buenos Aires, she turned the top floor of the family house into the city's first modern pre-school facility, starting out with her own three-year-old daughter Alicia and the children of two friends. By the time I joined, there may have been a dozen or more boys and girls.

We wore pink or blue *guardapolvos* (buttoned-up kirtles) over our everyday clothes and sat on child-size chairs at low square tables, colouring and cutting-out and pasting things in albums – the normal kindergarten occupations – under the guidance of the young *señoritas*, to whose title we added their pretty first names: Señorita Ana Maria, Señorita Kela, Señorita Rosa Blanca. (Only Señora de Renard and her partner Señora de Castillo wore surnames.) There was also a wooden climbing-frame, and a piano at which Señorita Rosa Blanca would teach us children's songs. Mid-morning, we got orange juice and dry biscuits, preceded by a short grace and followed by an enforced rest (which we resented) lying on our backs in rows on off-white mattresses, while Señorita Rosa Blanca played what were no doubt meant to be soothing tunes.

But best of all was the *azotea*, the flat tiled roof traditional in older Buenos Aires houses, which had been turned into a playground for us, with swings and a sandpit, and later a kind of Wendy-house with curtains in the windows and just the right kind of small furniture. At recreation – even kindergarten had recreation times – we were allowed to run about there, and on Saturdays were rather solemnly marched out in crocodile to a patriotic anthem, and made to swear allegiance to that blue-and-white flag my grandfather had liked so much. But this weekly display of an innocent old-fashioned patriotism was the only solemnity imposed on us; and also on Saturdays came the great treat of the week, a magic-lantern show – in later years occasionally a short silent film, with a hero we knew as "Carlitos Chaplín". The general feeling of the place was warm and relaxed, with grandmotherly Señora de Renard presiding over it all. I had no trouble making friends (Alicia Renard immediately and firmly adopted me as her own) and have no real memory of learning Spanish; except that a slight speech defect (which a specialist teacher, conscientiously recruited by my parents, had been unable to correct) made it impossible to roll my Rs in the proper way. This Alicia and others construed as a German accent; they tended to tease me about it. Oh, I did so want to be properly Argentine like everyone else!

Well, not quite everyone else, that was one comfort: there was soon one little girl just like me, only in a much improved version. At the Alvear Palace Hotel, another family had arrived from Germany. One Sunday morning, my mother, having summoned me to the separate suite where my parents lived, said she had a surprise for me. She opened a door: and – there before me stood the most beautiful creature I had ever seen.

And beautiful in a special way, as if personal to me. About my own height; brown hair like mine – but hers fell in long waves to her shoulders. Green eyes like mine – but hers were huge and long-lashed. And she was gazing at me with a rapture that seemed, unbelievably, equal to mine... And my mother was talking to *her*!

"Here's your present, Iris."

And *I*, it seemed, was the promised gift!

Moreover Iris, together with her grown-ups, was going to be living in the Alvear Palace like us, and her grown-ups even included a Gegga nanny to match my Rosita, and I was to teach her a bit of Spanish so she'd get on in kindergarten – yes, she was coming to kindergarten with me quite soon, and we were to be best friends, as were Rosita and Gegga... Life surely could hold no more.

Among Iris's grown-ups was her mother Anita, known to us children as "Mimi" as distinct from my "Mummy", whom in fact she resembled in features, though much darker in colouring. Anita Weil sprang from the other big German-Jewish grain merchant family of Buenos Aires; during the First World War, while the Hirschs were leaving their (still Belgian) Bunge & Born, Anita's father expressed his feelings of national identity another way, by turning a house he owned in Germany into a convalescence clinic for officers. Thence his daughter eloped with one of these officers, a Lieutenant or Captain Krummer; from that marriage was born a son whom his parents, in all innocence, named Adolf. By 1934, this no longer being an acceptable name in our circles, Iris's half-brother was known as "Fisch", which has stuck.

The Krummer marriage having ended in divorce, Anita married again, this time an adventurer gigolo called Hermann, who had added a romantic-sounding though quite invented "Gonzala" to his surname. The new marriage didn't last either; after the divorce Anita (as my mother was later to put it) "had the bad taste to carry on sleeping with the man"; she became pregnant with Iris, so there was a hasty new marriage and a new divorce.

And by 1933 Anita had just married Herbert Hoffmann, a somewhat undersized Buenos Aires German Jew, also known to my mother from girlhood; and was rather proud of having solved her financial problems by transferring all her considerable assets to this newest husband. All this, of course, I only learned much later; at the time I was only aware that, aside from "parents" and a nanny, Iris had an older brother called Fisch. There was also a chauffeur, Otto, so the whole family group was somewhat larger than mine. But I had eyes only for Iris.

Perhaps unusually, this parent-orchestrated friendship worked wonderfully well; as did that between Gegga and Rosita, especially after my mother advised the latter to be cautious in responding to over-friendly overtures from handsome

Otto... We two, the only small children in the hotel, were deliciously spoilt by all the staff, especially by the French manager, *Monsieur* Bellec. We ate together, played together. Even whooping-cough failed to separate us: we both caught it at the same time, as did Gegga, and the three of us were sent to recover at some other aunts-&-uncles' *estancia*, I think belonging to "Uncle Peter" (who, as a Weil, was genuinely a relative of Iris's). It was there I discovered my adored friend's preternatural talent for finding four-leaved clover where nobody else saw them; and also her fascination with snakes. Or had I known that earlier? I do remember my mother persuading Iris to eat green runner beans at the hotel by telling her they were *really* little green snakes.... At any rate, if Iris liked snakes, I was determined I was going to like them too (which stood me in good stead many years later in Africa); as determined as I was to enjoy the taste of the lemon-slices that Iris taught me to beg (in preference to sugar-lumps or cake) from the grown-ups' tea-table under which we sat.

Iris joined me at kindergarten that autumn; this was the best thing yet, for it meant that I was no longer the only not-quite-Argentine.

My father becomes Argentine

My parents meanwhile were themselves adapting to their new situation. There was, during those early months, some big party in the German community – a wedding perhaps – to which they were, naturally, invited. And at this party someone followed up the first greetings with: "And now, *tell* us all about the new Reich!"

Whereupon my father told them all about the new Reich.

Whereupon nobody – except a few loyal school friends of my mother's – ever spoke to each other again until the very late 1950s. And my parents began making new friends, outside my mother's German community of birth.

Not that there wasn't an anti-Nazi German community even then, though it grew considerably when more refugees appeared. Indeed, from the mid-30s until well after the Second World War, Buenos Aires had two German-language newspapers, the anti-Nazi *Argentinisches Tageblatt* (which we took at home, in addition to *La Nación* and the *Buenos Aires Herald*) and the Nazi *Deutsche La Plata Zeitung.* There were also two German schools: my mother's Goetheschule having gone Nazi, a new one was founded; it was in fact my mother who selected the name for it, Pestalozzi, after the seminal Swiss-born educator of the late 18th and early 19th centuries. People were eventually to think it rather odd of my parents not to send us to the Pestalozzischule; but by the time we children were ready for secondary school we had all moved quite far from any kind of German community.

For my father too was determined to be properly Argentine. He would, for instance, have nothing to do with the possibility (which existed in Argentine as in US law) of "revalidating" his German medical qualifications: he intended to make a career in his new country (whose citizenship he took at the earliest possible moment) and allow nobody to be able to say he'd got into Argentine medicine by the back door. He refused, too, to live in Belgrano – too many Germans and other foreigners in that leafy suburb. My mother was going to have to find us a flat in town – a good big one, so he could study for his new round of examinations. He would be as quick as possible about it – after all it merely meant revising, and putting his knowledge into proper Spanish medical terminology. But he did have to get started soon: even if money was no immediate problem, we could hardly live in the Alvear Palace forever.

Chapter 2
A Sheltered Childhood

My mother had found us a flat.

It was indeed a good big one, on the ninth (top) floor of one of the first modern apartment buildings in Buenos Aires; on the slope down towards Retiro Station, giving us from the living-room balcony a view of green Plaza San Martin and, towards the left, of Plaza Británica with its brick clock-tower, the "Torre de los Ingleses", whose chimes – the background music of my childhood – faithfully reproduced those of Big Ben; it had been a gift to the city from Great Britain in 1916, on the first anniversary of Argentine independence. Beyond the Plaza Británica was the so-called New Port (Puerto Nuevo) and the River Plate shining in the sun. "The best view in Buenos Aires" my mother would modestly say.

The living-room, accessed from the lift through a small lobby, was itself large, the front half communicating with a smaller dining-room, which itself gave onto a long narrow kitchen-and-pantry. Beyond the kitchen, a notional patio, not indeed unroofed, but with big windows for light and air and twin tubs for laundry; onto the patio gave two small servants' bedrooms and a tiny shower-room. And beyond that, communicating also with the entrance lobby, a long angled corridor, joining the "front" with the "back".

The middle section of the corridor had a side window giving onto the Torre de los Ingleses; this part was quite wide, with space for a treadle sewing-machine, and a table for children's and nanny's meals: the living and dining rooms were strictly the domain of parents (*die Herrschaften*, as Rosita called them) and we did not go there except by invitation. A further angle, and the corridor reached "the back", where a second little lobby led to four bedrooms and two bathrooms.

The biggest bedroom and bathroom were, again, sacrosanct to the *Herrschaften*; the other bathroom was ours, and at first Rosita and I shared the next biggest bedroom. The small room next to it was, just then, my father's study; in my earliest really clear memory of him he is sitting at a "desk" constructed out of packing cases, studying for those Argentine medical exams. Books littered the packing cases, the floor, the couch by the wall... The "big luggage" had now arrived and must have been distributed, along with a few new purchases, around the flat; I have no remembrance of any moving-in chaos, nor of any time before there was a stout Italian cook, Josefina, and a dark part-Indian maid from up-country, Dalinda.

The first Christmas at the new flat set the pattern for all my childhood Christmases. In the muggy heat of a Buenos Aires December, it was nonetheless kept, on the evening of the 24th, in traditional German style. All day, the big living room was out of bounds to *everybody*, including my father and the servants; the dining room, on the other hand, was forbidden to my mother, who could sometimes be glimpsed around some corner, clad only in a silk slip and trying to conceal whatever she was carrying. All the tables in the house had been commandeered by her, including the one in the corridor; we ate as best we could off working-surfaces in the long kitchen. Then, in the evening after dark, I was bathed and put into my best summer dress and we'd join my father in the entrance lobby; the heavy curtain was drawn between this and the living room, and we'd have to wait for my mother's little bell before drawing aside the curtain, and then – Magic!

The room was dark, thc tree sparkled with candles – a real fir tree and real wax candles that scented the dark room. And on the record player a disk brought over from Germany sang a little hoarsely –

Stille Nacht! Heilige Nacht!

And we all sang along, family in German, servants in Spanish – for they too had come into the room now, through their own door from the kitchen.

"*Frohliche Weihnachten!*" "*Feliz Navidad!*" and, at a later stage of my childhood, "Merry Christmas!"

That first Christmas there was an extra bit of magic under the tree: Iris herself! I imagine my mother must have invited her; the other family, having arrived in Buenos Aires later than ours, would not yet have got sufficiently organised for Christmas celebrations; at any rate, that was to be the first and only time she joined in ours.)

And then, the heat-wilted candles blown out and the electric light back on, each of us had to find his or her "own" table (later, when the Christmas party grew more numerous, perhaps half-table) marked out by the owner's name spelt out in sugar on a special big *Lebkuchen* (gingerbread) heart, itself the centre of a whole plateful of such goodies. Each of us had our own, including Josefina and Dalinda, and around the plate were heaped the presents – not from any Santa Claus figure, but from parents, aunts-and-uncles, friends, Rosita, Josefina, Dalinda, all of whom, then or later, had to be properly thanked. My parents felt strongly against bringing up children to believe in "lies", so there was never a Father Christmas, or an Easter Bunny, or indeed fairies – these, unlike the guardian angel Rosita had told me about, were firmly classified as fictional.

But where were my mother's presents? Ah! Soon now, my father would open the sliding doors to the dining room and reveal her gifts, all lovingly arranged by him on the sideboard. Most, indeed, were from him – he rather prided himself on his taste in handbags and scarves – but the rest of us had all, at one time or another that day, entrusted to him our own little parcels for her, and they too were part of the display.

My own presents, that first year, included an English teddy bear wearing a maid's white lacy apron and *cofia*, the dainty headdress, more Alice-band than cap, that girls like Dalinda wore to wait at table. I had specifically asked for these: being a maid seemed to me then the most glamorous occupation in the world. I was too big by now to ride satisfactorily on a feather duster, but loved to use Dalinda's, following behind her as she cleaned.

The apron and *cofia* had probably been run up by Angela the occasional dressmaker; but the teddy bear was a great luxury, as indeed were the *Lebkuchen* and the Christmas tree – a real live fir when all the shops, even the Buenos Aires Harrods, had to make do with artificial trees! But a real Christmas tree was, to my parents, a necessity, even at a time when I was being sent to kindergarten in dresses cut out by Angela from my father's old striped pyjamas. I was very proud of these dresses, and could not at all understand why my mother seemed to dislike my boasting of them to the other children.

Iris's family too had now moved from the Alvear Palace into a flat – a slightly bigger one than ours ("but just look at our view!" said my mother). And they had acquired a dog, a Skye terrier named Pierrot. If it had been possible for me to envy Iris, I would have envied her Pierrot; also perhaps her dressing-up clothes, so much more lavish than my mother's frugal leavings: Mimi went out a good deal, and would discard a wondrous veil embroidered with butterflies after a single fancy-dress ball! And then there were chauffeur Otto's purple silks, that he had worn as a conjurer for Iris's birthday party on the rooftop of the Alvear Palace. But if I envied anyone, it was my other friend, Alicia Renard.

Enviable origins

The Renards were considerably less well off than either Iris's family or mine; I was not aware of this, but very much aware of something I could not have defined: a greater rootedness, a solidity we somehow lacked. The Renards were still, at that early stage (most of Alicia's brothers and sisters having grown up and moved away), living on the ground floor of the kindergarten house – only half a house for them perhaps, but with interestingly odd-shaped rooms and, unlike our modern flat, proper nooks and corners. And, between the rooms used by the family and the kindergarten on the top floor, there was an *entrepiso*, a sort of middle-of-the-house attic, full of trunks Alicia and I were allowed to open and which contained real storybook treasures: dressing-up clothes that were not the discards of a single party, but had belonged to Alicia's grandmother; copies of a long-defunct family newspaper; even a little cardboard puppet theatre, in which you could move Cinderella and her fairy godmother along, using little castors supposed to be invisible from the front… And then, Alicia's father was by this time a (retired) Admiral, and best of all she had actually been born in Buenos Aires and didn't speak with that horrid German-sounding R… Iris, for all her faerie perfection was, I knew, the same sort of person as I: our families had come from Germany via the Alvear Palace. Alicia's family was different – at once more solid and more like the world of stories.

Another storybook world, yet also oddly more satisfying than everyday life in a big flat with box-shaped rooms and no attics, came to me from Rosita's tales of her own childhood in the Swiss village of Oberwyl in Canton Aargau. She too had been the youngest of a large family, her father a fairly prosperous farmer who, with his older sons, worked his own acres; as a little girl, it had been one of her chores to take mid-morning snacks out to the men – *z'Nüni* it was called, "nineses" rather than "elevenses", their day having started well before sunrise. At home, mother cooked and baked while she directed the girls' housework (and she never sliced into a new loaf without first blessing it by cutting a cross on the crust with her breadknife); on winter evenings they would all sit around the big pottery stove plaiting straw hats for sale in the shops of Zürich. In winter, too their barn would occasionally shelter a *G'lünki*, a tramp (I now think the word must be related to the German *Halunke*); he would not be allowed in the house, but sent off in the morning with a bit of bread and cheese. School was in the next village, and *Herr Lehrer* did not allow shoes in summer: winter socks and boots were deemed necessary, but *Herr Lehrer* held that wearing shoes in summer was entirely too namby-pamby for good Swiss children. (No wonder Rosita had not minded about my standing barefoot on that carpet.) Later, she had gone to a Benedictine convent-school called Marienburg; two of her sisters were nuns there now. And, some time after her return to Oberwyl (had she, I now wonder, suffered a disappointment in love?) she had daringly answered an advertisement in a church magazine offering a job as nursemaid in Buenos Aires, and had thus been engaged by the Kellersbergers.

But I wasn't interested in the Kellersbergers: what I wanted was to hear more and more about Oberwyl, about the house, the farm, the chores, the brothers and sisters. That life seemed endlessly desirable to me – as, in a slightly different way, did that of *Doña* Julia, Dalinda the maid's aunt, where Dalinda was sometimes allowed to take me for a tea-time visit. Did my mother know we got hot chocolate and *churros* there – those delectable fried cakes strictly excluded from my healthy diet at home? But it wasn't only the *churros*; *Doña* Julia's old-fashioned house in a decent working-class suburb had a big *real* patio – open to the skies, full of bright geraniums in huge earthenware pots, with an aviary taking up almost a quarter of the space, full of budgerigars and canaries. Why couldn't we live in a house like that? or even in the country? Have a proper patio – or even a garden? cagebirds? chickens? (At about this time a little chick-hatchery had been set up on the *azotea* at kindergarten, but of course the chicks had been taken away while still adorably fluffy.)

Other things were happening at kindergarten too. I vividly remember my first English lesson (these were now being offered to those children whose parents liked the idea and were prepared to pay a small extra fee). We stood with the tall new teacher around a little table –"Sit down," she said very clearly; and suited the action to the words.

Sit! Sitzen! This language was going to be *easy*. And very soon I discovered something still better about it: English had no (actually spoken) trilled letter R! In this new language, my troublesome speech defect was not going to matter. I made up my mind then and there: English was going to be *my* language, come what might.

A baby sister

It must have been that same winter my mother told me she had a new baby growing in her tummy; and I, she added, was to have a new baby too! True, mine would be a doll – but one I could bathe, and put to sleep, and it would have exactly the same baby clothes as her own. And indeed, Rosita was already knitting little caps and bootees and matinee jackets for both babies – white mainly, since one couldn't know in advance whether Mummy's baby was going to be a boy or a girl. And Rosita and I were to move out of the bedroom we had shared – we'd each get one of our own – for the new baby was to have, for the first few months, a *Kinderschwester*, a baby-nurse, to settle it in. Somehow, out of wherever the remains of the "big luggage" were still stored, the *Wickeltisch* was produced which (I was told) had been mine when I was a baby myself. This "swaddling-table" was in fact a chest of drawers, painted white, with a little mattress fitting into the top and a wooden railing on a hinge, such that it could be swung forward to prevent baby falling off if mother or nursemaid had to leave it an instant during the nappy changing process. And my own baby was to have nappies too, and a swaddling-band to keep them in place (safety-pins were considered *unsafe*).

Rosita and I were with Iris and Gegga in their flat when the news came – I had a baby sister! What were we going to call her? "Iris", obviously – I couldn't for the life of me think of another name. But our parents chose Beatriz Darcy. Darcy, an odd name for a girl, was after the wife of Brazilian President Getulio Vargas (who, now seen as having been a wicked dictator, had won approval at home for being diplomatically close to the English-speaking peoples); not a saint's name, so that my father had his troubles getting it registered on his new daughter's birth certificate. And "Beatriz", as my mother explained when I visited her at the clinic to see my little sister, would go so easily into nice diminutives: "She can be either Bea or Trix, you see." She is "Trixie" to this day to all Buenos Aires; or, depending on the social status of the speaker, "*la señora Trixie*".

Next came the christening, in the clinic chapel. Only godparents were present – Uncle Alfred's son and daughter Mario and Leonor; my mother was still recovering from the birth, my father I suppose studying for those exams. But the odd thing was, the priest did exactly the same to me as he did to the new baby – salt on the tongue, water on the forehead, sign of the cross... Nobody but me seemed to find this curious. Presumably it was all part of the mysterious universe of adults, which I understood very little and about which I was somehow reluctant to ask questions. But this time – a few weeks later, when my mother was up and about again – I did venture, albeit indirectly, to raise the subject:

"Mummy, when I was a baby, was I christened too?"

A little impatiently: "Of course you were, dear, everybody is!"

Curiouser and curiouser. But then, the grown-up world *was* very odd.

Now of course I realise my mother, growing up in a Jewish household (however non-observant) can't have been christened as a baby at all; and I imagine both my parents' conversion to the Catholic Church, which I know happened some time in the 1930s, must have taken place *after* Trixie's birth and baptism in 1935. The priest probably knew of my parents' intention, and indeed my father may well have asked him to christen me along with my baby sister.

My mother has told me since that she'd "always intended" to become a Catholic sometime: it seemed to her the proper historical continuation to Judaism. As for my initially Lutheran father, I know he had read St Thomas Aquinas's *Summa contra Gentiles* at about this time – presumably in Latin – and had found it convincing. An intellectual convert then – but I can't help wondering whether some of the motivation wasn't part of his general rejection of the background he had left behind him. I do know my mother thought him a trifle exaggerated in dragging her straight off to another church to be married to him: she had considered herself already his wife all these years. But then, he did always retain a certain Central European obsession with having his papers in order.

Primary school

The following year, Alicia, Iris and I, along with a handful of other six-year-olds, started primary school; but without leaving the kindergarten building. Already the previous year, a few parents had begged Señora de Renard to start a first form elementary ("You're so *good* with the children! I really don't want to take my little Juan Carlos away from your place...") And the Señora, herself reluctant to send her own little Alicia away, had yielded. In the end, Alicia, Iris and I went through the whole of our primary studies at what became known as the "little school", the *escuelita*.

Meanwhile, there I was in *primer grado inferior*, one among ten pupils, and the only one able to read. I know now there had been some discussion between Señora de Renard and my parents, as to whether I should perhaps skip a grade and go straight into *primero superior*; but they decided, rightly I think, in favour of keeping me with my friends. And I was not in fact bored; although I could read, and indeed do the simple addition and subtraction sums while the Señorita was slowly dictating them (good! less homework) I did have to learn joined-up writing, which I never became very good at.

What had come to bore me a little was the Saturday-morning patriotic march onto the patio, where we were supposed to salute the blue-and-white flag. On one such occasion, a rebellious thought came into my head: why on earth were we saluting what was only a piece of cloth? Immediately, unbidden, another thought followed – wasn't Jesus just a very good man? None of this particularly bothered me at the time (I suppose I dismissed it as yet another quaint feature of the world of grown-ups); but it must have lodged somewhere in my mind, for it came back to haunt me later.

A visit to the Old World

The next year was 1937. My father had acquired those coveted Argentine medical qualifications, and a trip to Europe was planned, partly in celebration and partly, I think, to persuade members of the family still there to move out to Buenos Aires while there was time. We travelled – all of us, including Rosita and baby Trixie – once again by transatlantic liner, this time to Trieste; there, Rosita would take me up to the old castle on the hill, and explain that those huge heavy stone spheres lying about were cannon balls and had once been shot from those big iron guns. And I learned to feed pigeons in the town square, but was too scared to let them settle on my wrist until the very last day, when it was too late... this regret lingered for many years.

Then, it was Zürich, where we stayed at the old Hotel Eden by the lake shore. Rosita was to have a month's holiday while we were there, to visit her family at nearby Oberwyl; so a new, temporary, Nanny was found for me. I didn't like her: I missed my Rosita. But the new one did in part redeem herself by giving me a copy of *Heidi*, which I still have, and at the time devoured with delight.

I had my seventh birthday in Zürich; and my parents took me out for the day! First, a boat trip across the lake; then, lunch in a real grown-up restaurant, where I was allowed my first taste of (well-watered) wine. We drank to my birthday, of course, and a number of other toasts; and then my parents said we should drink to those who were no longer with us: *Opa* Gustav and *Opa* Heinz. For both my grandfathers had died by now: Don Gustavo a year after my birth and the *Sanitätsrat* quite recently, in 1936: only the two *Omas* remained, *Oma* Lilli and *Oma* Ada. And that afternoon we spent in nearby woods, by a meadow where I was allowed to pick as many *Himmelschlüsselchen* as I liked – "little keys to Heaven", also known as cowslips, not yet then an endangered and protected species. Afterwards, sitting on a bench with my parents, I asked them what the *real* difference was between girls and boys; and they told me about the male organ boys had which girls didn't – I could see it, if I looked, on some statues; but often the sculptor covered it up with a leaf because some people for some reason didn't like to see it. So I was introduced to wine, death and (in a very preliminary way) sex all on the same day... though my mother did slightly spoil the effect when we got back to the Eden by saying she now wanted absolute quiet: "For the next few hours I don't even want to know I *have* a daughter." Probably she had one of her headaches – but at the time it did rather hurt.

The day after that birthday, though, a dream came true: Rosita came to fetch me to Oberwyl for the day, to visit her brother and his wife, her nephews and nieces. And all of it – timber-framed house, stove heating the one big main room, fields and woods beyond – was just as she'd told it... it didn't even bother me when one nephew, a boy around my own age, laughed at me when I stepped plump into a cowpat. Quite as good as an extra birthday, Oberwyl!

Soon after this Rosita's holiday came to an end; now she, Trixie and I were to spend some time with *Oma* Lilli in Ascona, where she had a little house called *Villa Spatz* (Sparrow Villa), while the *Herrschaften* moved on to France and England. I still had vague pleasant early childhood memories of *Villa Spatz*, mostly of the blue *and pink* forget-me-nots growing alongside stone steps outside the house: I must have spent a little time there before we ever moved to Buenos Aires. This time we were not to live with *Oma*, though – too many of us! – but at a *Pension* on the edges of the little town. But we went to see *Oma* every day, and every day the sun shone and the Lago Maggiore was blue; and there were walks along meadows bright with wildflowers – why were clover-heads here so huge and pink, not like the sparse anaemic things on the Plaza San Martín, where I was not even allowed to walk on the grass? – and afternoon coffee and cakes in a woodland glade, served by a smiling young waitress in wide flowered skirt and black velvet bodice over a white puffy-sleeved blouse that showed off bare brown arms.

One day – I must have been at *Oma*'s by myself – a young woman was standing in front of the downstairs looking glass, glamorously combing long brown hair that went all down her back. Oh, how I yearned for long hair – and this, *Oma* said, was my Aunt Annele! On a visit from somewhere called Liechtenstein, where she had her own farm and did her own housework. "She kneels to clean her floors" added *Oma* impressively. And this creature from the land of stories actually bent down to hug and kiss me. But I mustn't tell my parents, *Oma* warned – they'd be upset; and Rosita later reinforced this several times. The world of grown-ups – who could hope to understand it?

Years later, when I'd become a grown-up myself, my mother explained. In Trieste where Annele had come to meet our ship, her own mother had one day said "You should know, Annele's not actually our child. She's adopted."

"Adopted?" my mother said, "But *Mamita*, I was twelve years old when she was born! I remember perfectly, you went away to the clinic...."

"All the same, from now on she's adopted."

At the time my aunt was already running the little farm in Liechtenstein which Don Gustavo had bought her not long before he died. And she was being courted by the local *Jagdmeister*, Master of the Hunt; and, she insisted to her mother, the *Jagdmeister* must on no account know she was Jewish. She'd been adopted by Jews, not born to them! – My mother was understandably incensed, as was my father when she told him; and Annele remained unmentionable for a few years, until, just before the war, she redeemed herself by ditching the *Herr Jagdmeister* and marrying an Englishman. But that is, in Kipling's phrase, another story (to which I shall return on occasion below).

First time in England

And now came the bombshell: we had to leave Ascona! The message was from my parents: we were to join them in England. I don't know whether Trixie had any views on the subject, but neither Rosita nor I wanted to leave; nor did *Oma* Lilli want to part with us. But the *Herrschaften* had spoken: a day or so later we were off, rather tearfully, to Zürich.

But at the Eden Hotel another message awaited us – one that went far towards softening the blow: we were to *fly* to London! Rosita was to pick up our tickets from the hotel travel bureau. And *Oma* hadn't been told because she'd only worry.

The flight took over three hours in those days, including a re-fuelling stop at some French airfield, where I picked daisies to take to my mother. After that, I was mildly sick into the stout brown-paper bag provided. But, when we did get to London, I was the very first off the plane and full of my achievement; even the daisies were still fresh.

Only my mother had come to meet us; my father was in Glasgow, picking up a third, British, medical degree. In the hired car, she explained we would be living at a lovely place called the Toxova Hotel, in Dulwich just on the edge of London: the Park Lane Hotel where my parents were staying was unsuitable for small children ("but if you're good, Bundle, you can come up and stay the night with us a bit later"). Rosita was a little disconcerted – how would she manage at this Toxova place if she didn't speak the language? "Don't worry – Bundle will help, won't you, dear? And anyway, they're very kind people. Really you only need to know two things: *'Thank you'* and *'For the baby'*." She rehearsed Rosita in these two phrases, explaining their meaning. "That'll get you anything you need."

The Toxova was a long low building, set in its own spacious grounds abutting a golf course. We arrived more or less at tea-time; I was a little puzzled by a cake called a "Swiss roll", never having had such a thing in Switzerland, but devoured it cheerfully enough. "That's right," approved my mother. "You're in England now, Bundle. It's a different country. You'll find there's two meals worth eating here: breakfast and tea. If I were you, I should concentrate on those, and not bother too much about the others. Oh, it'll do her no harm, Rosita! You'll find they're very nourishing, particularly the breakfast. Oh, and a little later this afternoon Dr Gutmann will be arriving – in fact he should be here any minute now – a good friend of ours, he found this hotel for us; he lives quite near by. He'll help you with any problems you might have, though really you shouldn't have any – oh, here he is now. We're here, E.G.! Come and meet *Fraulein* Rosa and the children."

A tall man, not bulky like my father; fair-skinned, balding, spectacles, a kind face; and he clearly spoke German as well as English. "E.G." (for some reason I wasn't supposed to call this one "Uncle"), a friend and colleague of my father's, had left Germany at much the same time, but had settled here in England rather than overseas. He did live in Dulwich, having two children at the local College; and, for the two months we lived there, did indeed call and see us several times a week, occasionally taking me on a shoulder ride alongside the edge of the golf course, where – naturally – I was not allowed alone.

But the hotel grounds, at least for the first fortnight or so, offered plenty of space for exploration (they cannot possibly have been as large as I remember them); and they too contained forbidden pleasures – the kitchen-garden, where rhubarb-leaves could be filched and secretly eaten; a big patch of long grass, where Rosita feared there might be snakes... My companions on these forays were two Anglo-Belgian boys, Jack and Bobby; one or the other was generally available for such adventures. But then Jack and Bobby's parents took them away, and I was left (baby sisters not counting) alone in a world of grown-ups. Friendly grown-ups on the whole: the chambermaids (whom I was instructed to address as "Miss Ethel" and "Miss Alice") would provide me with cardboard shoeboxes and scraps of furnishing-fabric to make dolls' beds; and, I was later told, bickered with each other as to which of them could take me to feed the ducks in the park on their afternoon off. I didn't then know about the bickerings, but remember the duck-feeding, and also the street walk to the park: odd place, this England, streets and streets of little houses all exactly alike... and why wasn't the sun shining as it always did in Ascona?

There were the "ball-girls" too. The hotel had a couple of tennis-courts, and a gaggle of teen-agers in green uniforms were employed to recover the guests' tennis-balls and generally make themselves useful. They made a great pet of me; a favourite pastime was to make me, puzzled but amenable, say something – anything – in Spanish. And one day one of them, greatly daring, wanted to know – "Where you live – do tell us, do you have bathrooms like ours?"

"Oh no – *much* better!" – which indeed, in our spanking-modern Buenos Aires flat, they were. English plumbing in the 1930s was still as primitive as the food of the period at a suburban hotel like the Toxova. I remember dark green stuff that came in a thick sliceable wodge – "cabbage" they called it – and a pale grey substance known as "chocolate pudding", which did not taste of chocolate. My mother had been quite right, lunch and supper were not worth eating; but the fried breakfasts were sheer glory.

Some things, though, were more important even than food. I had fallen in love with a young woman called Valerie, staying at the hotel with her mother to recover from an appendicitis operation. I was not alone in my devotion: Valerie was beautiful and there was usually a cluster of men sitting on the lawn around her. But she was engaged to somebody in Austria, and may have found it convenient to focus her attention firmly on me. Sometimes she'd even give me my bath. And often she'd tell me stories or read to me – I remember a Walt Disney *Water Babies* and the puzzle of those enormous water-lily pads on which frogs and water babies cavorted together. And some version of *Peter Pan* – O how hard I tried, for lovely Valerie's sake as much as for Tinker Bell's, to believe in fairies! But somehow in my inmost self I knew I couldn't make the final leap of faith: a rational upbringing had put paid to that.

The promised West End evening at a grown-up restaurant with the *Herrschaften* proved, in the end, a little disappointing: I remember it chiefly as the first time I told those grown-ups polite fibs, making them believe I was enjoying it far more than I really was – since, poor dears, they clearly meant well. It gave me a pleasant feeling of superiority to be able to fool them so easily. Anyway, one hotel dinner wasn't going to change my settled opinion after two months in England: The food inedible, the climate unpleasant, the people extremely kind.

The food has improved a good deal since then.

My memories of the English ship that took us back to Buenos Aires are vague, though pleasant enough. More serious matters lay ahead: it was now September, I had missed nearly a whole school year (in our southern hemisphere, with the seasons reversed, the *escuelita* year ended in November.) So I had exams to pass, unless I was to be left behind by Iris and Alicia and the rest – unthinkable. The Señorita in charge of my form was duly persuaded to come and give me private lessons after school. These seemed to consist largely of the multiplication tables; I remember the "seven times" table as troublesome, it didn't seem to relate to anything else. But my memory was good: I learned the pesky things off by heart, and passed the November exams with no particular difficulty, as indeed was only proper for a pupil of the *escuelita.*

Chapter 3
Learnings

My mother was now trying to find me an attractive English teacher, to come twice a week in the afternoons. There was, naturally, considerable choice in the still large British community; but, in my mother's view, my teacher had to be young and attractive ("I didn't," she told me later, "want you taught by some dried-up old maid"). While she was searching, she gave me English lessons herself – delightful ones, since they consisted of our reading, together, *Little Lord Fauntleroy* and *Alice in Wonderland.* But eventually, one Miss Philpotts was found, who satisfied my mother's requirements; she came to give me English lessons on Monday and Thursday afternoons. And she too, at the end of the lesson, introduced me bit by bit to the Winnie-the-Pooh books, and later to *The Wind in the Willows.*

It was very much "English English" that I was taught; and, not being allowed cinema visits, I had no experience of American pronunciation. Once, a little American boy my own age was sent to play with me – he was in fact Igor Kipnis, nowadays a celebrated musician, whose father Alexander, equally famous at that time, was visiting my parents. I was totally thrown by Igor's accent – until, gazing at my full bookshelves, he chanced to say, "Boy! *Some* liberry!" – and that got through to me.

In Spanish, I had begun to make up "poems", and couldn't for the life of me think why the mysterious grown-ups made such a to-do about something as natural as rhyming, and even made me write the things down. The first, "*El cochecito de oro*" was inspired by a tiny gilt-filigree carriage, which I still have, the gift of a kindly antique dealer to whose shop I had accompanied Mummy.

Meanwhile, Trixie was herself beginning to discover language – in her case, the spoken word. It was decided that *Bündel,* "Bundle", my hated nickname, was too difficult for baby-talk, so to my relief I became "Eva", bad enough because it was then unusual in Argentina, but at least my given name. By the same token, Rosita became "Titita", by which name she was known ever afterwards.

Uncle Alfred's house

I think the first time I realised my mother was not the most beautiful woman in the world was when I saw her beside Leonor, Trixie's godmother and Uncle Alfred's daughter. ("And how, Alfred," asked wicked old "Aunt" Alice Weil – "how did a man as ugly as you manage to have a beautiful daughter that still looks like him?") For Leonor was truly, dazzlingly beautiful, but with a character in her face that her mother Aunt Lisa lacked; this is clearly visible in their two big oil portraits by Laszlo, now in a museum somewhere but then hanging in the "rich Hirsches'" house, always known to us as "Conde", from the name of the street it was on.

It is at "Conde" that I was first struck by Leonor's dazzling beauty. My mother and I had gone to see her; she received us glamorously in bed, resting on her return from a European trip. What I did not know until later was that, though her own travel had been private, she had there unofficially joined her lover, General Agustín P. Justo, at that time President of Argentina, himself on an official trip. Justo, by all accounts a decent man, democratically elected, could not, in the Argentine law of the period, divorce his long-estranged wife. All the Hirsch family naturally knew of the liaison, and indeed took considerable pride in it, though it was not permissible to discuss it with outsiders. Or appropriate to do so before small children.

"Conde" was a big house in Belgrano, brick-built, flanked by statues and surrounded by a small garden. Very grand: the door was opened by a footman, and there were other men-servants around the house. ("Wouldn't have one even if we could afford him," my mother commented, "or how could I wander round the flat in my slip in the hot weather?") "Conde", however, was no flat, but a spacious house on three floors. Ground floor and *piano nobile* were not just for living in; much space was, on both, devoted to Uncle's art collections: a wallful of Madonnas (plus one very minor reputed El Greco) in the big ground-floor sitting-room framed a player-piano (or "pianola") whence music could be produced from appropriately pierced rolls of paper; the Rembrandt etchings were kept in a protective glass-topped desk in the ante-room to the huge dining hall. Upstairs there was at one stage a "Chinese room" for Oriental pictures and objects, also a "Spanish" one for those seen as more at home in such surroundings. These arrangements changed from time to time as Uncle Alfred's collections grew, or Aunt Lisa had some different idea.

And at the very top of the house, the huge attic contained a real life-size theatre! Quite as good as a grown-up one, with dressing rooms behind it, where Mario, Rodolfo and Leonor had been able, as children, to put on their own entertainments before an audience which could have occupied the rest of the room. This was the part of the house I really envied; and was surprised when Leonor once told me her childhood had not been one long unalloyed bliss.

Obviously, I did not learn all these things at once. Visits to Conde, for Uncle Alfred's and Aunt Lisa's birthdays as well as sometimes on other occasions, punctuated my childhood and adolescence. The birthdays I remember as very grand occasions indeed; especially Aunt Lisa's, which often included a *Lieder* concert (Uncle Alfred had had her soprano voice professionally trained); later there were sometimes other singers as well. Altogether, Aunt Lisa became increasingly involved in music, organising as well as (in private) singing; soon, Buenos Aires nicknamed her *la madre de la música*, "the Mother of Music".

My mother had noticed how fascinated I was by the pictures at Conde, and even by the rather more modest sketches she and my father had bought during their time in Paris. At some party she met an Anglo-Argentine lady, one Ana María Berry, who was said to know about introducing children to the graphic arts. On my mother's enquiry, Ana María Berry admitted she had herself just brought out a book for this purpose: *Art for Children*, which, of course, I got the following Christmas.

Art for Children was, and remains, a delight. The author sensibly grouped her reproductions by *subjects* rather than periods or schools of painting: The Book of Animals, of Travel and Adventure, of Angels and Fairies, of Children and so on. Within each book, pictures ranged from Dürer to Picasso, China to the Italian Renaissance – but all accessible to any child who liked looking at pictures. All my life I have been re-discovering items of Ana María Berry's choice in art galleries and museums all over Europe.

Nor was our visual education neglected at the *escuelita*. By the time I was ten, we had a weekly drawing-master – not somebody who made us draw arrangements of cubes, cones and cylinders in perfect perspective, but a cartoonist who taught us how to portray people: their bodies, but above all their faces, faces with different features and expressions. I loved this.

Music, though, was a problem. My father was, I believe, musical; but he was seldom at home, and my mother took rather less of an interest. Iris and Alicia had both begun piano lessons, with different teachers; naturally enough, they often compared their experiences with each other, a conversation I could not share. For that reason, rather than any genuine longing for music, I yearned for piano lessons myself, little knowing that my mother, who had so much disliked her own enforced hours of practising in childhood, had decided that no child of hers would have piano lessons *unless he or she asked for them*. And this, in my shyness, I never ventured to do. (Trixie, later, had more sense – and was allowed piano lessons as soon as she could show she had stopped biting her nails.)

First Communion

But I must have ventured to ask for the other new lessons my two friends, and a number of other children, were having – Catechism – which took place at the *escuelita* in the evenings. Or perhaps Señora de Renard had had a word with my parents? – who were indeed very willing to have me prepared for my First Communion in December of that year, 1938.

In the beginning, I enjoyed Catechism very much. I found theology interesting (I still do) and my good memory was a help too. But, after we had learnt about Mortal Sin, I must have been absent, perhaps with a cold, when it came to the Sacraments: I was very bothered about the mortal sin I had clearly committed, all that time ago, when I had doubted the divinity of Christ. Would this mean eternal hell fire? It didn't seem fair, I hadn't known then that my doubt might be a sin, let alone a mortal one. I revved up my courage, and privately asked the gentle Señorita who took us for Catechism. Instantly, she reassured me – no hell fire at all! I need only *confess* my sin and say I was truly sorry, and all would be forgiven. And we were going to make our first Confessions very soon now. When the first Confession day finally came, I suspect the kind deaf old priest didn't really take in what I was talking about: he didn't preach at me at all, but simply gave me absolution. O the relief!

Four of us were to make our First Communion together, a girl called Babe joining Iris, Alicia and me. We would be wearing identical "bridal" dresses and veils of white organza; so at home, dressmaker Angela came to make mine. And on the side, as a special gift, she also made a First Communion dress for my doll.

My mother, however, was rather bothered about the extreme piety I had begun to display. Not having herself been brought up a Catholic, she couldn't know what a common occurrence this is in children – especially perhaps girls – around the time of this particular rite of passage; and she feared to lose me to a nunnery. But she did take the trouble to find out about the other material requisite for a proper First Communion in Buenos Aires: a lot of memorial *estampitas*, the little "holy pictures" that were then still in fashion; so she duly selected a picture and had a suitable number of them gold-printed on the back with my name and the date, for distribution to family and friends.

When the great day came and we made our communion at the charming little *Mater Admirabilis* chapel (since, alas, destroyed by a bomb aimed at a nearby Jewish centre) we were duly photographed in the chapel's back garden, in our white dresses and veils and flanked by two older white-clad girls dressed as angels. It then emerged that only Alicia, Babe and I had *estampitas* to distribute: Mimi had not bothered to find out about them for Iris.

"Typical" was my mother's comment. I was beginning to notice how much she disliked Anita *née* Weil.

At home, other presents awaited me – a little missal, a rock-crystal rosary from Leonor and – a bicycle! Which I promptly tried to mount, in my long-skirted First Communion dress, and ride around my parents' living-room. I was gently dissuaded, and consoled by a First Communion cake.

Blair House

I think the ensuing hot summer months (January/February 1939) – were our first in Los Cocos. Buenos Aires is steamy during those months; everyone who can – basically the women and children of reasonably well-off families – gets away, either to the seaside or to the Córdoba hills. My mother was an exception: she elected to stay with her husband. But we children, with our Titita, were sent off to Córdoba.

The hills in the north of that province were, in those days, divided rather than shared between English and German residents and holidaymakers. The village of Los Cocos and the neighbouring town of La Cumbre, were, so to speak, British territory; La Falda, a little further downhill, was German. Los Cocos had, indeed, two fairly major English places for children: the Allen Gardiner Homes (so named after an early missionary to Patagonia) for the orphans of Anglican clergy, and Mrs Hill's "Blair House", where we were bound on that and later summers.

Mr Hill, whom one occasionally saw shambling good-humouredly along the grounds, was, I now know, an alcoholic; which meant his handsome grey-haired wife had to earn the family living. This she did by turning their very sizeable property into a school, designed (in winter) for the children of English *estancia* people who, before being sent to "proper" English boarding-schools in Buenos Aires, were considered to need some preliminary English-language "3 Rs", as well as a year or two of civilising.

In summer, these children naturally returned to their homes, and Blair House became a kind of non-scholastic holiday home for unaccompanied children of every origin. A few boarding-school rules did have to be obeyed, but the only lessons were in swimming (by a Miss Gibson, in a splendidly large though permanently green-slimy pool a little further up the hill) and riding with Don Roberto, who hired out horses across the road and accompanied young inexperienced riders.

Trixie and I were not, of course, unaccompanied children: we had Titita. The three of us were indeed lodged in a large room in the "grown-ups' building" where the Hills and Miss Gibson and other adults lived. I rather resented this: I would have loved to share the girls' dormitory, or even, wonderfully, live in a tent (but only boys were allowed that). However, the *Herrschaften* had decreed otherwise.

A few years later, I once heard my mother on the telephone recommending Blair House to a friend: "It's cheap," she was saying "and perfectly healthy. Oh, your kids will come back with their clothes in rags – don't for heaven's sake pack their best things – and probably a bit thinner, the food's hardly luxurious. But in any emergency – broken bone, appendicitis – Mrs Hill will cope well. Totally to be relied upon!"

The food was indeed "hardly luxurious" – reminiscent of the Toxova Hotel, except that at breakfast and tea we got *matè* (served in cups with milk and sugar). Meals were served in the "schoolroom", and certain rules had to be observed: I can still hear the ritual shouts of "Bread please," "Butter please," and (at the end of the meal) "Excuse me please!"

But there were compensations. The "schoolroom" also contained books: Kingsley's *The Heroes*, plus an elegant little children's novel about an Athenian boy kidnapped into Sparta – so that I learned the difference between those two cultures very early in life. *The Jungle Book* was there – for some obscure reason in French. And here was my first exposure to Kipling's poem *If*; so that at some level Mowgli is forever, to me, "*un petit d'homme*" and *If* ends with "*Et, ce qui est plus, tu seras un homme, mon garçon!*"

My parents would have been horrified: they had a positively Puritanical disapproval of translations. Oh, it was permissible to read Tolstoy in English or French – but to read a translation from a language one was supposed to know was seen as a heinous crime. I never told them how, on the school bus, Alicia had introduced me to the German adventure writer Karl May *in Spanish*. But now, at Blair House, the schoolroom library utterly fascinated me: indeed, one afternoon I was so absorbed in George MacDonald's *The Light Princess* that I actually didn't go up to the swimming-pool.

Nonetheless, I learned to swim, however inelegantly, that first summer – I was always being coaxed to lend my privileged rubber ring to other children. And then there were the "riding lessons" with Don Roberto. Not lessons in any strict sense: we were, most of us, too small to grip with our knees, and anyway rode, very comfortably, on *recados* covered with sheepskin rather than on the more austere "English saddles". Anyway, riding in those parts is not the demanding European sport; horses are not fed oats, and are certainly not raring to go. Don Roberto's instructions were correspondingly simple: "If you want the horse to turn left, pull the left rein; same thing for the right. To stop it, both reins; and here's a *rebenque* (a small flat leather whip) to make it go. And you must never, never, go fast downhill." He was a big gentle man who, on the two-hour rides, kept a keen eye on the less experienced of us, while never making us feel inadequate.

And then there were the Allen Gardiner Homes, our friendly rivals. Once in the season, there would be a football match between our boys and theirs; despite our loyal cheers of "*Blair House School!*" Allen Gardiner always won. Even better, for me, was the Allen Gardiner summer charity bazaar: my first exposure to that immemorial English rite, which I confess still fascinates me. I took no part in the raffles (I've never been a gambler) but Lucky Dip was all right, at least you were sure of *something* for your money. And, even better, I could spend my pocket money on embroidered lavender bags and other such Anglo handicrafts – useful presents for grown-ups when their birthdays came around, and sometimes *even* for myself.

Also, at some stage during these Blair House summers, came my first exposures to talking movies. Mrs Hill would occasionally take us down to the La Cumbre cinema. I remember two of these films: a somewhat free but very colourful adaptation of Maeterlinck's *Blue Bird*; and, much more impressively, the American black-and white *Mrs Miniver*, with Greer Garson in the title role (which we all naturally took as a faithful representation of what was really going on in fabled wartime England).

For one week during the two months at Blair House, my mother would pay us a visit, my father joining her for the week-end. These were of course very special times, involving rather longer walks than usual (Titita staying behind with Trixie) and all sorts of ice-cream and other treats.

And then the end of February would come, time to return to Buenos Aires for the opening, first of the kindergarten and then the *escuelita*. (The Señora de Renard maintained, correctly, that at her *escuelita* we could learn quite as much in eight months as less fortunate children did in nine; so our winter term started only on 1st April and ended on 30th November. But we "big girls" took a pride in going to "help" at kindergarten when that started up on 15th March, and staying on until 15th December.

By this time the *escuelita* was beginning to outgrow the old Renard family house in central Buenos Aires. The Renards had to move to Belgrano – not the fashionable part where Uncle Alfred and Aunt Lisa lived, but enviably leafy and tranquil all the same, with a garden and even a tiny swimming pool, as well as a huge attic which put the old *entrepiso* to shame, and where Alicia and I were to spend many happy hours. And at the luncheon table, *cheese* was served – probably because of the old Admiral's French origins.

This year, Alicia, Iris and I were the *only* three pupils in our form; and I began to discover that my two companions, even when they discussed their piano lessons, were quietly at odds with one another. With hindsight, this was probably jealousy over me, each of them wanting to be my *very* best friend. At the time, it just felt uncomfortable.

French lessons

Iris was, like me, beginning to have English lessons at home in the afternoons. Alicia on the other hand was learning French. And now the Renards lived in Belgrano, she and I travelled on the school bus together.

"Mummy! Mummy! Alicia's teaching me French!" "That's nice... let's hear a bit?" And I went –

Savez-vous planter des choux
A la mode, a la mode?
Savez-vous planter des choux
A la mode de chez nous?

All this in Alicia's formidably strong Argentine accent (the old Admiral, on the other hand, had never lost his French one in Spanish).

Shock horror. "We can't *possibly* have you going around speaking French with *that* accent! Oh well, I suppose that means you'd better start proper French lessons at once; I'd really meant to wait another year. Who teaches Alicia, do you know?"

So I too began lessons with Mademoiselle Jacquard, who was Swiss not French, but did come from Neuchatel, where they take a pride in the purity of their pronunciation – no vulgar Vaudois/Genevois accent for them. Mademoiselle was white-haired – so much for my mother's reluctance to have me taught by "dried-up old maids" and was probably, even for those days, a somewhat old-fashioned teacher. She did know her stuff, however: she kept up a fiction of knowing absolutely no Spanish (how, Alicia and I used to wonder, could she possibly do her shopping?), and, after the "*Voici le crayon, voilà la plume*" stage, dragooned me firmly though verbs both regular and irregular before allowing me to learn the better-known *Fables de La Fontaine*. In later years we progressed to Corneille, Molière, and Racine. Mademoiselle having been requested, just like my succession of English teachers, to teach me everything a little French (English) girl should know, I too, like black children in the French colonies, learned that "our Gaulois ancestors were fair-haired". (I did quite soon connect these "Gaulois ancestors" with the Ancient Britons from my English lessons – all those druids and oaks, all that woad and mistletoe; my first real insight into history. Earlier, I had placed "Antiquity" at the time of the discovery of America and "the Middle Ages" at that of Argentine Independence in the 19th century.)

So now the time-table was in force that would continue till I was twelve years old: *escuelita* in the morning, English lessons at 2 pm on Mondays and Thursdays, French lessons at the same time Tuesdays and Fridays; all these involved homework. It sounds like a punishing regime for a child, but in all honesty I have to say I enjoyed it.

Another source of learning was the children's weekly *Billiken* (I now wonder – did its editor, Constancio C. Vigil, have a small son or nephew known as "Billy Ken"? or one such boy for each name?). The admirable *Billiken* provided not only cut-out pictures to fit in with primary-school syllabuses, but also cartoon strips of Laurel & Hardy (and later, Superman ("*El Superhombre*"), and (again in strip-cartoon form) Persian legends on the origin of chess, Buddhist ones on that of tea, Amerindian ones on the visits paid by Our Lord, St John and St Peter, to the Guaraní villages in northeastern Argentina.... as well as, in each issue, a short moralistic reflection, "*Vida Espiritual*", which exactly suited the rather priggish child I was.

And then there was "The Book of the Many" (officially *A Treasury of Many Wonders*), my parents' gift – a 1936 English children's encyclopaedia with end-papers mapping the British Empire and an idyllic frontispiece of the child then still known as Princess Margaret Rose. Inside this wonderful book, I was not much arrested by "The Round of the [English] Year", but much taken with the big cats and elephants of "The Wild Life of the World", the cathedrals of "God's Glory in Stone" and most of all by "World Literature" – Homer and Virgil, the Eddas and Dante, Goethe and Tolstoy; never mind a special section on English literature, where I learned not just about Shakespeare and Milton, but also that Byron, Shelley and Keats exemplified "an old Greek saying, that those whom the gods love die young".

Politics

And now, in 1939, Mummy was going to Europe again – by herself, this time. "Make sure you're back before the end of July," my father advised; "the war's almost certainly coming this year, but not before everybody's got the harvest in."

I knew, of course, that there was "the war" coming, and that the good English and French were going to fight against the bad Nazis in Germany: I was growing up a very political child. *Billiken* was approved by my parents, but I would not have been allowed its rival, *Figuritas*, which was deemed "nationalist", a code-word then for pro-Franco, and therefore quite possibly pro-Fascist or even pro-Nazi: being pro-Franco, like the old ladies living on the second floor of our apartment building (and many *bien-pensant* Catholics at that time), was nearly as bad as being overtly pro-Nazi.

My father also took it upon himself, in case I came across anti-Semitism anywhere, to tell me my mother was of Jewish descent. He was later to tell me he was somewhat surprised by my reaction.

"*Jewish!* But how *wonderful*." "Oh? And how is it so wonderful?" "Well, the Jews – they're so brave – *and they wear sheepskins*!" Sheepskins, as sold by up-country peasants at nearby Retiro railway station, were to me the utmost in glamour; and my English book of Bible stories had, of course, a picture of young David wearing just that as he aims a stone at Goliath....

Also around this time, I remember seeing on newsstands a paperback book, *Las Dos Cruces* ("The Two Crosses" i.e., as illustrated on the cover, Hitler's swastika and the Cross of Christ) by one Alberto Duhau. I didn't of course read it; but my father did, and thereby hangs a tale.

Alberto Duhau, a wealthy and devout Argentine bachelor of aristocratic French descent, disapproved of Pope Pius XII's silence on Nazi anti-Semitism. He went to Rome and obtained a private interview with the Pope. The two did not reach agreement, and it was, contrary to all etiquette, Duhau who ended the interview; by saying: "Your Holiness! There was once a king of France who, as seems to be the case with Your Holiness, was unable to make up his mind: Louis XVI – Your Holiness will have heard of him. He lost his head. It would be a sad thing, Your Holiness, were the same thing to happen to the Church of God. – I have the honour to wish Your Holiness a very good morning."

And, sweeping out, Duhau returned to his native Buenos Aires to write *Las Dos Cruces*. My father bought and read the book, thought it rather badly written, but clearly indicating the author's heart was very much in the right place. He arranged to meet Duhau, and together they started a pro-Allied Catholic weekly, *Orden Cristiano,* financed by Duhau, and in the beginning written largely by my father; who felt it was necessary to counteract another (piously pro-Franco and thus pro-Axis) weekly, at that time the only publication to enter many presbyteries and convents. *Orden Cristiano* was a success, and in fact lasted until sometime in the 1960s; it also got my father on the Nazi hit-list for Argentina if they had won the Second World War. (He was aware of this; and, good Catholic though he had become, secreted enough poison for himself and his family just in case.)

And now Mummy was back, closely followed by *Oma* Lilli and then by my father's youngest brother Rolf, who had only just finished his secondary studies. This left the two middle Krapf brothers in Germany: Günther, the archetypal "good German", a medical officer during the war, who never did anything at all nasty, but never stuck his head out either; and Fred, a card-carrying member of the Nazi party, whose name was never mentioned in our household.

Punctually on 3rd September, 1939, war broke out. As soon as I knew, I rushed to my bedroom and, on my knees, thanked God! I had always *known* this war would come, and now we would soon defeat the evil Nazis.

It was not to turn out quite like that.

The next day, my father went to the British Embassy – to offer his services to them as a medical officer in the war. This had its comical aspects – he was grievously overweight and almost blind in one eye. The Brits very sensibly declined his offer, so he went on serving the cause, as best he could, in other activities such as *Orden Cristiano*.

Wartime as seen from Buenos Aires

By 1940, France had fallen – a fall felt quite painfully by the Francophile upper class in Buenos Aires, where children (as in Tolstoy's Russia) sometimes spoke French before their native tongue. Britain now stood alone, and my parents listened to Churchill's speeches and, anxiously, to the radio news. My mother, atypically, took up knitting – comforts for the British troops ("Well, Titita can teach me – stupider women than I have learnt to knit"). And knit she did, in Air Force blue ("easier on the eyes than that horrid khaki") throughout the war; after which she never touched a knitting needle again. She would move, with her knitting, from room to room, accompanied by a small kerosene stove: it was cold on our ninth floor. This was because of a fuel shortage – our only wartime deprivation in that part of the world. There was supposed to be central heating for two hours at lunchtime, but of course not much of it reached up to us. My mother's feet, encased in slippers, also rested on newspapers. My own feet were, during those years, icy all day (I still bear the marks of the chilblains) from the time I got up in the morning to hot-bath time at night.

Petrol for driving was short, too, though not too bad for my doctor father; he also called in favours here and there. I remember, a little later on weekend trips, always stopping at a particular petrol station just outside the city boundary, whose owner had received some help from him. And while the car was filled up, so were we – with huge steak sandwiches from a passing vendor: Saturday lunchtimes tended to be late, since my father, after a full morning's work, had stopped at Retiro railway station to buy magazines: the American *Saturday Evening Post* but especially the English *Picture Post* and *Illustrated*, from which I learned about air-raid shelters and clothes rationing ("How to take the same black dress to work and out for the evening").

Of course, I had already heard from my parents about air-raids on London; and every night on my way to sleep, fantasised about rescuing people from the ruins – how brave I'd be. And of course, I'd know all about first aid. At some level I felt faintly guilty about not *being* in London: I knew my parents, unlike Eric Gutmann, had chosen Argentina in order to bring up their children – though at the time I was the only one – in a peaceful country.

"E.G.", along with other anti-Nazi refugees from Germany, had been unjustly interned at the beginning of the war; my parents pulled strings to get him out of the camp, and would have succeeded on condition he too left England. But E.G. was having none of that: he had thrown in his lot with (initially hospitable) Britain and he was going to help her fight. Again, all this I only learned later; during those early war years, the Britain I heard about could do no wrong. Indeed, no English child can possibly have been brought up more totally to such convictions.

The French were something else; there were baddies called Pétain and Laval, and a great goody called De Gaulle, who also earned the approval of Swiss Mademoiselle Jacquard; who, indeed, thought that after the war the name of France should be changed back to "Gaul" in his honour.

Meanwhile, however, life went on. For my tenth birthday ("your first in double figures") I was given a small, graceful roll-top desk: "You can write your homework on it now, and later your love-letters, and later still your household accounts!" I do still use it, but mostly as a home for postcards.

I also still have the pencil portrait of me my father commissioned that year from one Mariette Lydis. He must have been one of her first clients in Buenos Aires, where she had very recently arrived (just in time) from Paris, already having made a considerable reputation as a portraitist; a Jew, she had fled Hitlerland for France several years earlier. Later, when Trixie was herself just pre-adolescent, my father had *her* portrait done by one *Madame* Vrede; at the time I rather envied my little sister, who I felt had been made to look rather prettier than Mariette Lydis had made me, but I have since come to realise that I own the better picture.

And *then* –

There came a Sunday we were all to spend near the small town of San Miguel, at the week-end *quinta* of my parents' friend the architect Jorge Bunge (no relation, as far as I know, to the original owners of Uncle Alfred's Bunge & Born). This was a delight to me, the huge garden with its little stream, outdoor lunch on the terrace – and after lunch, back to the stream, while ladies took their siestas and gentlemen left for the fashionable amusement of attending a local land auction.

They were back by tea-time.

"Well?" teased my mother, "buy anything nice, darling?"

"Well *yes* – as a matter of fact I *did*. Come and see."

He had in fact bought two wide strips, forming an L-shape, from a very large *quinta* in the area. The end of the narrower strip faced on to the motor-road; to reach the angle where the two strips joined, one passed a thick plantation of bamboo. "Kipling!" enthused my father; but I'm not sure my mother quite shared his feelings; probably she foresaw the end of week-end social life.

But for me – total ecstasy! All that afternoon and evening, my heart felt as if it would burst with sheer joy. A garden at last. I had no trouble getting to sleep; and that night gave never a thought to those London air-raids.

My Brown Owl

My English teacher Miss Philpotts had meanwhile married and stopped giving lessons; she was succeeded by a cousin, one Miss Kathleen Ingouville – and I, once again, fell in love. The darkly handsome Miss Ingouville introduced me – at my parents' request – to the King James Bible; but I was even more impressed by the fact that she was, in her spare time, a Brown Owl. Especially as she explained to me about the troop of "Brownies" she led, away in Belgrano where I couldn't easily join them. But she made me a Brownie all the same, with a badge, and gave me a little book by Baden-Powell. A good deed every day was easy enough – but Brownies also had to learn to skip rope; and practise though I might on the *azotea* of our house, this was an art I never mastered.

And then came the blow. Miss Ingouville too was getting married! After only one year of teaching me... and married, moreover, to one Dudley Miles who didn't even live in the city of Buenos Aires, but out in the province somewhere; so she could no longer oversee Brownies in Belgrano or teach me at home.

She broke the news to me one day at the end of my lesson. An hour later, my mother found me sitting on my bed in tears, trying to say the 23rd Psalm to myself... She was extremely good about it: no expression of jealousy, only consolation and the promise of a new party frock for the wedding. A well-chosen comfort: Angela the dressmaker made me a stiff pink petticoat that *rustled*, and over it a frilly blue-and-white organdie dress... and at the wedding I not only met my fellow Brownies at last, but got my very first compliment on my appearance from a man. Not that I remember him; but I do remember tall be-spectacled Dudley Miles, who, on introduction, gazed deep into my eyes saying, "Well! And do you hate me *very* much?" and I found I couldn't.

Only later did I learn that Kathleen Ingouville had herself been quite distressed at leaving me – so much so that Dudley had said, "Well, why don't you marry Eva then?" I may have found that out when, their honeymoon over, I was allowed to go and stay with them a few days in the provincial town where they lived.

Hirsch and Krapf connections

Oma Lilli had meanwhile been installed in a small flat of her own. She saw to the furnishings herself, in the then fashionable *Provenzal* style – I don't know what connection it may have had with Provence, but my mother considered it very bad taste. But then, she did find her own mother in many ways embarrassing – she *would* blow soap-bubbles from a little white pipe, not only on her own balcony but even in the back of the car she had been persuaded to hire for visits; it quite put the driver off. And then, she didn't dress at all elegantly; and she *would* cook.... Considered as a Granny, however, she was quite perfect; and to our joy Trixie and I were now allowed, on Wednesdays when I had no English or French lessons, to be dropped off by the school bus for lunch with *Oma.* We did enjoy her cooking – I particularly remember the aubergines she had christened after her *Villa Spatz* in Ascona – but she had other skills as well; for instance, she could make (and teach us to make) tiny dolls' beds out of any small cardboard boxes handy: the bed itself was the box, the lid, upright, served for the canopy.

During those years, there were also occasional holiday visits (in March usually, the end of summer in our southern hemisphere – winter holidays did not then exist for us) to one or other of Uncle Alfred's *estancias.* The old man had, over time, bought a great deal of land and was trying, among other things, to cross-breed cattle into something that would both be resistant to the huge local ticks *and* produce as much good meat as European cattle. Now, the proper way to inspect one's *estancia* is on horseback; but this Uncle Alfred, being crippled (by syphilis, it was whispered) was unable to do. So, next best thing, he progressed by carriage. He would buy up old state carriages from the government, have them painted a decent black and, if they needed it, put back into proper order; and there he would sit, behind a coachman and a well-matched pair. Sometimes I would accompany his progress on horseback; at others, sit beside him in the carriage (which I think he preferred) and have him explain things to me as we went.

On one of these family visits, I think in 1940, there were three new Hirsch boys – a bit too young to be interesting to me – and their mother. Born Countess Agnes zu Eulenburg, the lady inevitably had brothers who were officers in the German Army; my mother had initially sent a message saying that, as she herself prayed for their defeat every day of her life, she thought it best they did not meet. Agnes replied that she sent up her own prayers for exactly the same thing. After which the two of them became the best of friends.

Agnes Hirsch had in fact come, not just for the sake of her half-Jewish sons, but to ask Uncle Alfred to buy her husband Conrad out of Germany; which was in fact still possible at the time, even though Conrad was in some kind of transitional concentration camp, pretending to be tubercular. How tall, broad-shouldered, athletic Conrad ever managed to persuade anyone of this was always a mystery to me; but that was the story we were told. So, by some combination of "compassionate grounds" and hard cash, Conrad was indeed brought to Buenos Aires very soon after this. And, as happened to all rescued (male) Hirsch relatives, even my young Krapf uncle Rolf, he was duly found a slot (initially modest) in Bunge & Born. My mother used to say she was so glad she'd married a doctor, so she didn't have to be part of that nest of mutual intrigue.

Rolf, my father's youngest brother by a number of years, had, after completing his German secondary education, decided that he too would come to Argentina; whether this was from youthful political ideals or simply from a desire to see the world (with perhaps some protection from an elder brother) I don't know, nor does it matter. Being qualified for nothing in particular, he was slotted into Bunge & Born, initially on travelling jobs around the country; and he too, as soon as possible, took on Argentine nationality.

More reading matter

All these years I read and re-read voraciously those novels regarded as suitable for young girls: Angela Brazil school stories – a gift from Uncle Alfred these, my parents rather disapproved – but also Louisa May Alcott, *Rebecca of Sunnybrook Farm* and *Uncle Tom's Cabin*. I soon realised that, outside the school stories, these books had only two sorts of heroine: the blonde kind (Beth, Little Eva) who died about a third of the way through, and the dark rebellious ones who survived all odds (Jo March, Rebecca). And decided I was definitely not the blonde kind.

I also read, largely on the school bus, my Spanish-language *Petit Larousse Illustré* (I still own the French original, but that was for French lessons): my main interest was in the second half of that admirable manual, that devoted to proper names, including those of the Olympian deities. They were in their Latin, not their Greek forms; I was mildly teased by my fellow travellers on that bus for going on and on about Jupiter and Juno.

At home, and as I grew older, my reading was rather less intellectual. I spent some part of my afternoons in the servants' patio, with the new cook, Danish-descended Ana Rasmussen, and a succession of maids who were usually ironing. (Cooks tended to be of foreign origin, and stay a long time; maids were younger, from the provinces, and left to marry after two or three years.) And there I was lent, and devoured, what my parents contemptuously called *novelitas* (little novels), generally about aristocratic maidens who, after escaping various perils, married to live happily ever after.

Of the *Herrschaften* we saw in fact very little. My father was away working; my mother worked too, for him, at her typewriter on the dining-room table; she used only two fingers, but typed fast and accurately. Their mealtimes were very different from what was regarded as suitable for children: a very late lunch, and an evening meal which, though early by Buenos Aires standards, would still have made us unacceptably late for bed. Just before we retired, we would go in our dressing-gowns to spend a few minutes with our parents, who would then be drinking a small vermouth and soda in the living-room; never, rather oddly for Argentina, wine at meals, unless there were dinner guests and my father couldn't work after the meal. Trixie and I ate, with Titita, at "proper" hours, from the small table set up in the broadest bit of the corridor. Except, of course, on birthdays, when we did have lunch with our parents, and were allowed to choose the menu! Among my own favourite dishes I remember roast duck and also *lechón,* the milk-fed stuffed piglet that my sister still likes to feed me when I visit her. At those dining-room meals I used to envy my parents the availability of both bread and water, neither of which we children were allowed at meals: my mother did not consider them "real" food, and didn't want us to fill our stomachs with them. (I also envied the prisoners in novels, who actually lived on these forbidden delicacies.)

Summers at San Miguel

Meanwhile at our new San Miguel *quinta,* work was proceeding: a gardener's house was, my father decreed, more urgent than one for us; and indeed we had acquired a gardener, Basilio, a Polish immigrant whom for some reason we knew as José. A motorable road was also driven through the bamboo, against the day when our own house would be built.

In local politics, General Justo's term had come peacefully to an end. He was succeeded by one Ortiz, a decent enough man, but sickly; which was soon to leave the field open to his pro-Fascist Vice-President Castillo. Cousin Leonor, Justo's long-standing mistress, at about this time left him to marry a younger man, José Caraballo, more generally known as "Pepet". My mother was indignant: she had liked and admired Justo, and had, like the rest of the family, seen the liaison as rather an honour. "And what a way to leave somebody like that. Nothing but a note on his dressing-table!" I got the impression that she regarded some love affairs, however adulterous, as more respectable than certain marriages. Now, I imagine Leonor's main and urgent desire was for children.

At this time, we went on spending two months every summer at Blair House in Los Cocos. The population there varied: one summer, we had three boys named

Enrique, whom we distinguished as "*Enrique Primero*", "*Enrique Segundo*" and "*Enrique Tercero*"; my school friend Alicia Renard grew up to marry *Enrique Segundo*. Another summer, "Aunt" Hella Berneke, staying nearby at another resort, invited Titita, Trixie and me to tea to meet two boys just arrived from England! Bernie and Harry Ingham (*nés*, in Germany, Iggelsheimer), were very thin, but disappointingly silent about their doubtless thrilling air-raid experiences – in fact, they had none to tell, their boarding school having been evacuated to Forest Row in Sussex. And we none of us knew that Bernie would one day marry Trixie.

That year or another, I made friends with three French girls, the middle one about my own age. I greatly admired Marie-José, especially her command of new and fascinating slang; but when we got back to Buenos Aires and I told my mother, in all innocence, that I had leant new words like *puta* and *mierda*, she firmly told me to forget them, they weren't nice words; took my hands and swung me round thrice: "There. All forgotten now!"

How could one forget interesting words just like that? Really, grown-ups were very odd.

Then, there was "Mr Bunny's" year. That is how he was known to us Blair House children; his grown-up name was Mr Bensusan. Mr Bunny was, I now suppose, bored by the Blair House adults and felt happiest amusing the children. Not that Titita allowed me to stay up to listen to his ghost stories; but he invented other forms of pleasure. Best of all was The Wedding: we were all sub-teenagers now, and beginning, though still in a rather childlike manner, to pair off (my own "boy friend", Carlos de Elía, an "older man" of fifteen to whom I owe my first very innocent kiss, actually gave me a doll he had won at the Allen Gardiner Homes coconut-shy). So Mr Bunny decided that one of the oldest and best-established couples should get "married". He himself officiated, in the "schoolroom", as parson; the bride wore a white nightie and mosquito-net veil; the rest of us girls were bridesmaids; and Carlos, who owned a mouth-organ as well as a small battery radio, was confined inside an empty chest-of-drawers to provide the music. And afterwards, there was the party to end all parties – a barbecue up by the swimming-pool, into which, at one point, *Mr Bunny threw Mrs Hill!* And she didn't seem to mind!

Back in Buenos Aires, my mother approved of my friendship with Carlos – a "nice boy" who'd given me that doll, attended a most reputable secondary school and lived with a widowed mother across the Plaza San Martín in the Kavanagh Building. Both of us being at school, we hardly saw one another; but I was allowed a telephone call from him every day. My mother would occasionally listen to my side of the conversation; she said it amused her.

At San Miguel too things had moved on. The Polish gardener known to us as José had been told he couldn't have all the new plants he wanted, because *el patrón es pobre* (the boss is poor); so he went around the district, begging plants from other gardeners for his poor boss. The money was in fact needed for our own week-end house. The architect, naturally enough, was Jorge Bunge; there were amicably furious arguments between him and my father: "Who's the architect here, you or I?" "Oh? and who's going to live here, you or I?" The client's views prevailed in the end.

The house, when built, was imitation South American colonial – low and white, with a big colonnaded verandah which would allow us to be out of doors in rainy weather, and, on one wall, a colour-tile mosaic – designed by Jorge's daughter Cecilia – of the traditional image of Our Lady of the Good Winds (*Nuestra Señora de los Buenos Aires).* Buenos Aires was named after her by its founding Spanish sailors, in gratitude for the good winds she had sent them: she carries the Child on her right arm and, on her left hand, a small sailing-ship. For our *quinta*'s official name was "Buen Aire", though this was later changed to "Atilí", Trixie's baby version of the German "*ich hab' Dich lieb*" ("I love you").

Elsewhere, the house incorporated several other ideas of my father's – he had thought long and hard about what sort of house he would have built for himself when the time came – such as a thick layer of sacking on the flat roof for insulation (overlaid with pitch to keep off the rain) and, inside, a pull-out desk from a cupboard. This was in fact never used, my father doing his week-end writing, and I my French and English homework, on the big heavy dining-room table of *quebracho* hardwood from the Chaco. We also used this hardwood for fuel, both in the "English" fireplace and to heat our water; the smaller branches were sliced into ashtrays.

We began to spend every week-end at San Miguel. My mother had been right, we didn't have social life there – not even a telephone. My father said he saw quite enough neurotics during the week; if there was a patient he was specially concerned about, he would ring for news from next door. And if anyone new went mad over the week-end – well, there were other psychiatrists in Buenos Aires!

The only one of my friends I was occasionally allowed to invite for the week-end was Iris – my parents loved her, and probably pitied her as well because of her home background. She was happy in San Miguel, anyway – plenty of the plants she loved to look at and ask about; and after every meal, "What can we eat now?" – by which she meant medlars (in their season) straight from the trees, or tiny young peas, or tomatoes from the vine: José had by now created a notable vegetable garden, from which we took fresh produce back to town on Sunday evenings. His wife Sofía kept chickens, and these too we would occasionally harvest; I learned, if not to kill them, to pluck the carcases without disgust.

Every evening, and often late into Saturday night, my parents would anxiously listen to the radio for news of the war (as no doubt they also did during the week in town). And, one Sunday morning in June 1941, my father announced at breakfast that Hitler had invaded Russia. And this, he said, would be the long-hoped-for turning-point. "They're savages," I well remember him saying. However anti-Fascist, he was no friend to Communism – "And like savages they'll fight that German invasion!"

And it was at the end of that same year, on 7th December, that, on our way to San Miguel, we heard on the car radio that the Japanese had attacked Pearl Harbor, thus allowing Roosevelt to launch his long sought-for attack on the Axis. The jigsaw was now complete: the picture of Allied victory was, to our eyes at least, clearly visible.

End of escuelita education

The following year, 1942, was to be my last at the *escuelita*; and just now, when primary-school years were ending with the most important exam of all, we began to realise we had an incompetent teacher. I suspect Señorita Eloísa had been given her job for compassionate reasons; in any case we children decided, halfway through the school year, that at this rate we would never complete the syllabus by the end of November. We had, for a few years, been four now: the Iris-Alicia-Eva triangle had been joined by a boy called Julio. "I didn't", Señora de Renard was to confess to him many years later, "really want to take you on at first – I was so fond of that tiny little class of mine – but when I found out you'd already been expelled from three schools – well, I couldn't resist!" And all the time Julio was with us he behaved like the most perfect of gentlemen.

Julio was best at arithmetic, I at language, Iris at natural history, Alicia at imparting knowledge in general. It never occurred to any of us twelve-year-olds to complain about Señorita Eloísa to our elders and betters; instead, we divided up the different subjects among ourselves, and taught each other, quite successfully, for the rest of the year. Clearly, the *escuelita* had educated us properly.

And so we went our separate ways into secondary education. I'm not quite sure what Julio's was – or indeed whether his parents didn't take him straight out to their land, to learn to manage an *estancia*. Iris and Alicia were both hived off to a teacher-training secondary establishment known as *Lenguas Vivas*, which, as its Spanish name implies, specialised in modern ("living") languages: Iris to the English-teaching section, Alicia to the French. For me, a different future had already been prepared.

Chapter 4
The Way Out is Through

That year, 1942, my last at the *escuelita*, my mother had once again found me a new English teacher.

Not a young pretty one this time, but a middle-aged, rather dowdy Englishwoman she'd met in a lift coming down from a ladies' tea-party. My mother detested such gatherings – "Don't ever learn to play bridge," she would advise me later; "then you'll be fairly safe" – but had for some reason felt obliged to attend this one. In the lift, both women simultaneously exhaled a loud sigh of relief; my mother looked at her fellow-sufferer and, on impulse, said, "Come and have a decent drink! I live quite near here."

Her new friend was one Dorothy Johnston, not a member of the local British community but a real proper Englishwoman, married moreover to a Commander now serving in the British Navy. Mrs Johnston, left to cope with three children on a less than adequate income, was making ends meet by giving "advanced" English lessons to adults; but she consented to take me on that winter.

A little earlier, I had been given two books that would greatly contribute to my general education: Hendrik Willem Van Loon's *The Arts* and, slightly later, his *History of Mankind* – both written, by that refugee from Nazi Europe, to educate his new fellow-citizens in the USA; much permeated by Dutch-Protestant prejudice, but replete with information and delightfully illustrated by the author. Between them, both books gave me a useful insight into the history of civilisation; for instance, it was Van Loon that first introduced me to the Etruscans. (My newly acquired knowledge also produced some embarrassment at *Mademoiselle* Jacquard's 1941 Christmas gathering, where I innocently asked her to explain Louis XIV's reign to me really thoroughly next winter, since I gathered there had been several secret marriages...)

But now, Mrs Johnston was teaching me, like her predecessors but in a far more grown-up manner, English literature and rather more of the history of England. I vividly remember a book that brought that history *up to* the Battle of Hastings, and said, in its final paragraph, something like: "You will later read a good deal about events *after* 1066, of which much more is known; but you must never forget that just as much time elapsed between Julius Caesar's arrival in Britain and that of William the Conqueror, as between that and now." And indeed, I never have forgotten it.

She also told my parents that, by the end of the year, I would be ready to sit for an exam, current at that time in British communities overseas under the name of "Junior Cambridge". Everybody was pleased about this – my father had already decided that, when the war (which "we" now seemed much likelier to win) was over, I would go to university in England; this was one *Herrschaften* decree I never rebelled against. But what my parents didn't know (perhaps Dorothy Johnston didn't either) was that Junior Cambridge was, in our part of the world at least, generally taken by young persons at least two years older than I – something that would cost me dear the following year.

Thus it was that after the final *escuelita* exam I was sent off to an English school, Northlands, to take my Junior Cambridge. This was no hardship: I liked exams, and was good at them – even though, during those war years, all answers for overseas exams had to be written, in indelible pencil, onto a top lined sheet of paper, with carbon paper beneath it, over another sheet of writing-paper. This was in case the ship carrying the first lot of answers to England was sunk in the Atlantic. On this occasion, it wasn't; and, to no one's surprise, I passed very nicely.

Michael Ham

There were, at that time, five English-language girls' schools in and around Buenos Aires (there are many more now). Northlands was the best of them; St Hilda's was regarded as being strictly for hockey-playing girls from Patagonian *estancias*. A third school, Michael Ham Memorial College, was run by the Passionist Sisters, initially for the Irish-*porteño* community.

I should perhaps explain that in Argentina, unlike the USA, Irish immigrants had very rapidly risen in the social world, the combination of English language and Roman Catholicism having proved irresistible to the local upper class: much intermarriage had resulted in names like Lynch and Cullen being seen as aristocratic. And after the fall of France in 1940, the upper classes began to want their daughters taught English – but *not*, in most cases, at Northlands where they might get corrupted by nasty Protestant ideas! So Michael Ham had become *the* snob school – and was, naturally, my mother's choice for me. She had conscientiously visited them all, and *said* her reason was the girls at Michael Ham were prettier (and, years later, "Well, you had to get your Catholic tradition from *somewhere*, and Heaven knows I was in no position to give it to you"); but I still suspect that the main attraction were those distinguished "society" surnames. Another attraction would have been the Principal, slender and impossibly ladylike, with a languid cool handshake I instantly disliked. Mother Superior – her name in religion was Scholastica – was very old and not often visible; fierce Mother Aquinas was in charge of boarders.

And it was at my own request that I was to go to this new school as a boarder – O Angela Brazil! O dreams of midnight feasts and climbs onto the roof! My mother was, I think, quite pleased at my choice: she was beginning to find an untidy adolescent daughter at home a bit much. But she and my father did negotiate for me a dormitory in the "New Building", where I would share the bathroom with only four other girls.

One thing I very soon found out was that boarders had to attend early Mass – fully dressed, though our navy veils were sometimes bumped out with curlers – on three separate weekdays; another, rather worse, was that we were supposed to dress and undress "modestly", which meant keeping one's dressing-gown over the shoulders throughout the process. This takes some doing! and I had had no practice at it.

But being a boarder was not the worst of it. Having passed that Junior Cambridge exam, I was catapulted straight into the "Senior Cambridge" 8th form. I was thirteen years old, with short straight hair, clearly still a child; my classmates ranged from fifteen to seventeen, teen-agers already glamorous and seriously interested in boys (and vice versa). Even worse, my reputation had preceded me from that previous exam – "they had a *genius* at Northlands last year, and she's coming here next!" – which, understandably, did not make for popularity among my new classmates.

And I did so want to be just like the others. But my surname, Krapf, was neither Hispanic nor Anglo-Irish – and were my parents even the "good Catholics" my prayer book said I should thank God for? Certainly they didn't go to Mass on Sundays.

Some time later came the day when, walking with them both down some country lane near our San Miguel Quinta, they began to discuss the possibility of emigrating once again if the political situation here in Argentina got any worse.

"Canada?" suggested my father. "Sounds like quite a nice country."

"And just think," enthused my mother. "We'll be able to walk along the streets of Ottawa or wherever, and *nobody will know us!* Won't it be *wonderful?*"

I think that was the moment I realised that my parents would never be just like other people's parents. And that I'd better love them for being what they were, even if it meant that I too was fated never to be like "the others".

I was also, for my present environment, dangerously naïve. The *escuelita* had left me with no sense of teachers as a class enemy. True, we had disliked some of the *señoritas* – but it was individually, not as members of a class. And there had been no notion of "swotting", or shame about learning more than was strictly required. I had a good memory, and loved anything in verse; when our infamous literature teacher "Golly", having told us to learn 16 lines of a long poem in our *Anthology of Modern Verse*, added "Of course, you can learn the whole thing if you want to", I did not recognise sarcasm, but simply did what I thought I had been encouraged to do – and was fool enough not to conceal it. This made me one or two dangerous enemies in the 8th form.

Not all the teachers felt comfortable with my ways either. Dorothy Johnston had believed that every one of those nuns had a university degree; but I don't think this can have been true. Certainly Sister Cecilia hadn't – the youngest nun had only recently "entered" and had been, we all knew, one of the local Nolan girls; and, with the war on, no new Sisters were coming from the other side of the Atlantic. The last one to have arrived before the war was one Sister Margaret Mary; and she, undoubtedly, did have a degree: a double one, in English and Geography, from Cambridge; and she had, we knew even then, taken those degrees *before* ever she took the veil.

Sister Margaret Mary, whom I later came to call "Sister Peggy", remained my friend throughout her life; so I now know a good deal more about her. *Née* Pauline O'Neill, a doctor's daughter from Northern Ireland, her initial vocation had been as a teacher; and she had "entered" initially because, as a laywoman, her social life grievously interfered with her teaching! The specifically religious vocation came only later. In our Senior Cambridge form she taught geography. Short, plump, snub-nosed, she was hardly impressive to look at; yet, standing there in front of us, always balancing a pencil between her fingers (replacing the cigarette of her lay teacher days) she taught quite unforgettably.

Sister Peggy was also, as it happened, in charge of the New Building where I slept; and, there, quite a firm disciplinarian. We girls called her, behind her back, *la Chanchita*, "Piggy" – and indeed, bundled up in her habit, her plumpness and snub nose did point to a certain resemblance. She was not particularly popular among her boarders; and it took me a while to realise she had a soft spot for me. Initially I suppose it was part of an all-too-human teacherly preference for her brighter pupils – the other nuns were mostly interested in our being "good Catholic girls", but Sister Peggy, I came to realise, liked even naughty ones as long as they were intelligent.

My father, who felt strongly about the intellectual value of mathematics, wanted me taught that form of thought to Senior Cambridge standard. Arithmetic I had done for my Junior Cambridge exam, but now there would be Geometry and Algebra as well, none of them subjects offered by Michael Ham. To fit Mathematics tuition into the school time-table, I had to give up the Biology classes – a pity this, since that subject was (apparently) well taught by one Sister Gerardus; but, even worse, the person deputed to take me on for Maths was by far the worst teacher in the Senior School – the only laywoman, Miss Gwendoline McGonnigall, known to us as "Golly".

Sister Peggy told me many years later of her suspicion that Golly wasn't, strictly speaking, a "Miss" – there was a husband somewhere in the background. And when I asked, "But *why* did Golly have it in for me?" she said, "Isn't it obvious? She was dead scared of you!" "*Scared*? Of a thirteen-year-old schoolgirl? What on earth... "Don't you see? You could have asked her a question to which she didn't know the answer."

Oh.

In class, Golly taught us, not only English Literature and Language – which even she could not spoil for me – but also History, and a curious subject that existed in those days under the name of Hygiene. Hygiene gave us some notion of the human skeleton and of the digestive, respiratory and circulatory systems (sex, naturally, did *not* arise), interspersed with advice about diet, vitamins, water-closets and other such practical matters. But the worst was History. The Sisters did not feel we should learn English history, which contained a troublesome thing called the Reformation; so what we got was "History of the British Empire" (like Hygiene, also an accepted exam subject then). In later days, when I began to study Anthropology, I very much wished I did know something about British imperial history; but even now I can hardly think of a subject less likely to appeal to Argentine schoolgirls in their teens.

And then there was Golly's teaching method. We each had a rather worn red-covered history book, presumably handed down from before the war. "Open your books at page 163, girls, and start underlining at the second paragraph. Second and third, you may skip the fourth. Turn over the page and start again at the fifth..." and so it went on, until "That is your lesson for next time, children." On some themes – I remember "Causes of the loss of the North American colonies" – Golly had produced notes of her own, and dictated these to us. I also remember what seems to have been an obsession with the "Black Hole of Calcutta", which appeared not only in the History of the British Empire, but also in Hygiene, and was later elaborated as a paragraph for parsing.

Religious studies were, naturally enough, to be our main strength for Senior Cambridge. The Gospels were taught by old Sister Marie de Lourdes, who looked exactly like Grumpy in Disney's *Snow White* film; the Acts of the Apostles by our Principal, Sister Redemptus. Neither taught particularly well, but they were didactic marvels compared to Golly. We were also taught "Apologetics", a kind of primary theology said to be useful in defending our faith when required to do so, which did have the merit of introducing us to such concepts as the syllogism. Initially, the teacher here was an American priest whose accent we found distinctly comical; later, when he moved on, we were taught by Sister Peggy, who made a rather better job of it.

Spanish we were not taught; it was assumed we knew it well enough to pass an English exam. But a few of us, including me, had, at our parents' request, French lessons with a bearded Monsieur Lenoir. The lessons were well chaperoned by Sister Marie de Lourdes; but Monsieur Lenoir, while an excellent teacher, did imbue us with such heretical notions as "the top-of-the-class student is often not the one that does best in later life".

And then there was Latin – another subject in which my father felt I should have a good grounding. This I was taught, during the first school hour on Friday mornings, by Sister Peggy.

Revolutions

And then one morning, as I was making my way back to the Senior Cambridge classroom, I was met by a great stream of my classmates, and other girls from the upper school, all shouting –

"Revolution! Revolution!"

My first notion was that we had started a revolution against the school authorities; I was all in favour of that. But no. The revolution in question was a national one, which had started at a military academy not far from Michael Ham; the school authorities were still very much in control. Daygirls were bussed home at once; we boarders were assembled in the Great Hall, the large space normally devoted to ballet lessons and (with its vulgar devotional plaster statues) to assembly prayers. But this time, an impromptu entertainment took place: we older pupils were encouraged to "keep the little ones from being frightened" by standing up in front of them leading them in song or if need be singing solo.

This was my chance! I had already been politely requested to leave the school choir ("You'll have a *lovely* voice in Heaven!" "If I ever get there, Sister"); but now, after the ritual "When Irish eyes are smiling" I got up and sang an English army ditty I had learnt at Blair House:

"There are mice, mice, mixed up in the rice In the Quartermaster's store..."

And, on this day of days, it even seemed safe to add

"There are ants, ants, wearing ladies' pants..." which got me no worse than a frown from Mother Aquinas – plus, of course, rapturous applause from most of my audience.

In the evening, we were all escorted to the chapel "to pray for this new good government" – which neatly summed up the nuns' attitude to national politics at that time (things were to change later, when Perón began to persecute the Church).

Thus ended my first Argentine revolution. It will be obvious that our "revolutions" then were nothing of the kind, but peaceable *coups*, in the tradition of the first, the 1810 May Revolution against Spain, aiming quite simply to bring about a change of government. (When, a few years later, *one* student was killed in a "revolution", there was such an outcry all over the city that his name, Salomon Salmún, is engraved forever in my memory; his people, "Turks" as all Middle Eastern immigrant families are still called, owned a dress-materials shop in central Buenos Aires.)

And indeed my parents, and other people who had detested pro-Fascist President Castillo, tended to agree with the nuns about "this new good government". We had at that time no particular reason to fear military take-overs, which never lasted long anyway, and it was felt in 1943 that the new lot might be better disposed towards the Allies. I have forgotten the several generals who thereupon followed one another in quick succession; it took us all a while to notice one Juan Domingo Perón, who very cannily never took over as President, but stayed in the Vice-Presidency, thus enabling himself to stand as a candidate when elections finally did take place.

The next excitement was that year's school play. Sister Peggy was, as always since her arrival, in charge of this; the previous year she must have had help, for the play had been a dramatisation of the Argentine national epic *Martín Fierro* (about how a good *gaucho* becomes an outlaw); and the year before she had very bravely produced a version of *Macbeth.* This year, however, was to be rather less intellectually demanding: a kind of musical called *Pearl the Fishermaiden*, complete with happily-ever-afterwards ending.

Because the nuns were collectively somewhat in love with my father ("Just like G.K. Chesterton!" – I couldn't see the resemblance myself, except that both were rather stout), I, as one of the supporting cast of fishermaidens, was given a small speaking part. Two lines – *"And how does it feel to be sweet seventeen?"* and *"What woman wouldn't?"* Unfortunately, the part also came with a garish red-and-green striped "fishermaiden" costume... and, at the actual performance, I managed to put my foot into a bit of the background scenery.

"That has to have been our daughter," my father is reported to have said from the audience; he hadn't actually seen me make the hole, but somehow he was quite certain. Clearly, I was not made for a dainty fishermaidenly stage appearance.

New friends

Had I made any friends among my fellow-boarders? Well yes, I had. In the first instance, others who, like me, didn't quite fit in. The best was big warm Elaine, daughter of some Scots who ran, but did not own, an *estancia* in the flatter part of the province of Córdoba, well south of the hills of those Blair House childhood holidays. Elaine didn't fit in for more than one reason. Not only were her parents not well off (she was not alone in that) but also, she was a Protestant, and in general felt uncomfortable with what she called "the rich Argentine set". I found out later that the nuns were a bit worried about our close friendship, not for religious reasons, but because they feared it might become somewhat too physical. My father, quite rightly, reassured them on this point; and indeed, gave his permission for me to accept Elaine's invitation to spend the following Christmas with her family, the Campbells, on the *estancia.*

And then there *were* two members of that rich Argentine set, though neither exactly came across as such. Betty Cárdenas Lynch had, she told me years later, actually prayed for a friend; what she got was me. Margaret Llamosas, on the other hand, had no need to pray for friends, and I don't suppose it ever occurred to her – any more than to take her studies seriously. She was tall and beautiful, a glamorous sixteen-year-old. She is also an inherently kind person; in that first difficult year and later, she made sure

I was included in every school group, party, outing (such as the bazaar held mid-town on the afternoon of St Joseph's day, which to us was a great treat).

Oddly, both Betty and Margaret, having complied with their society's requirements by marrying (in both cases men of great charm) soon after leaving school and borne children soon after that, were at a later stage forced to earn most or all of their families' living: Betty's husband took to drink, Margaret's fell seriously ill. And both these grievously under-educated young women did exactly the same thing: each took to teaching English (the one thing they did know) to girls of a lower social class. Both did quite nicely: in the socially-mobile, languages-obsessed Buenos Aires of that day, if you couldn't afford to send your daughters to Michael Ham you at least improved their chances in life by having them taught English by a Michael Ham alumna. Betty's "Institute" still exists, now run by her own daughters and nieces. Margaret never quite made it to an institute; indeed, she told me, she had to buy a grammar book and struggle to keep one lesson ahead of her pupils! Instead, she put together such pennies as she had and bought a second-hand coach, in which she herself drove assorted children to assorted schools. In time, she had a small fleet of the things and was able to hire drivers; but if one of them fell sick, Margaret would take his place. All this while nursing her sick husband, as well as doing the cooking and housework for which they could not afford help – and always managing to look fashionable and with her usual ear-to-ear smile.

And now the end of the year was coming and with it the dreaded Senior Cambridge exams. Not in general dreaded by me – but I was, I remember, a bit scared of the maths tests; which, of course, I took alone. Arithmetic I could manage, and for some reason was fairly good at algebra; my bugbear was geometry. I could and did learn axioms and theorems by heart; but the exercises utterly defeated me. I could, after a fashion, do the required diagrams, and had been trained in the "Given", "To prove", "Proof" sequence; but, that once done, all I could write was a mendacious "Lack of Time..." which naturally meant I had finished what I could do about three quarters of an hour before the official end of the time allotted to the paper. The kindly person invigilating – a stranger from out of school – came to ask me whether I'd finished? Yes, I confessed, I had; but my maths teacher was outside in the corridor and would ask me angry, embarrassing questions if I emerged too early. The invigilator immediately understood my problem, and left me alone until time was up and I could face Golly. This may be the time to say that, when our results eventually reached us from England the following year, I found I had achieved "Credit" in Elementary Mathematics.

The results did, indeed, take a long time to arrive. This time, the ship carrying our papers really *was* sunk by the Germans in mid-Atlantic, so we were only informed of our results the following August. My friend Margaret, surprised and delighted at having passed, asked permission to ring home with the news. "Mummy, Mummy! I've *passed the exam*!" "What exam?" Mrs Llamosas understandably wanted to know.

The exams over, and after a few days at home, I was off to southern Córdoba province to spend Christmas with Elaine Campbell's family – my first English Christmas, which I found quite pleasant, but odd. Nothing on Christmas Eve! And that curious festival on 26th December, which these people called "Boxing Day". But there was a tree, and there were presents – my father had sent me Henry Fielding's *Tom Jones*, which I think slightly shocked Mrs Campbell. Other than that, it was a delightful holiday. A good deal of riding – Elaine was distinctly "horsy" and there were plenty of animals to choose from – and, on hot nights except at full moon, we slept out of doors in hammocks (Elaine had, among other local country superstitions, absorbed the belief that the full moon shining into one's face sent one lunatic). Naturally enough, I fell in love with Elaine's tall elder brother David; equally naturally, he took no notice of me – but that was not enough to spoil my time at the *estancia*.

The rest of the hot summer months I spent with Trixie and Titita across the River Plate, near Punta del Este, not yet fashionable and over-built with hideous modernity, but a pleasantly modest resort with superb beaches. An elderly Frenchwoman owned the *Grillon*, hotel of choice for people like my parents, who appealed to her to find a nice, safe, not too expensive place for their daughters; thus it was we came to stay with a married niece of hers, just beyond "Pine Beach", already a Punta del Este residential suburb, where my mother's cousin Rodolfo Hirsch and his Uruguayan wife Sarita had a house. I would look in at Rodolfo's and Sarita's on my way to a 4 pm tennis lesson my mother had duly arranged for me, and find them still engaged in pre-lunch drinks – Uruguayan holiday mealtimes being even later than fashionable Buenos Aires ones.

My mother herself came to Punta for a few days, rather as she used to visit us halfway through at Los Cocos; she stayed, of course, at the *Grillon*, but spent long mornings on the beach with us. She confided to me that she was expecting another baby; which emboldened me to ask exactly *how* did the process of pregnancy start? But this clearly embarrassed her; she replied evasively that perhaps I was still a bit young to be told that.... The wrong thing to say to a thirteen-going-on-fourteen!

I was to find out soon enough.

The Higher Cambridge year

In March 1944, it was time for school again. My parents had by this time discovered the existence of a further English exam known as "Higher Cambridge", which would facilitate entrance to a university; and my father naturally decided I should take this. Higher Cambridge corresponded more or less to later A-levels, as Senior Cambridge had done to O-levels; it was thus a rather more specialised exam. I seem to remember I chose to take English Literature (now to be taught by Sister

Peggy) at "advanced" level, French Literature and Spanish Language at "ordinary". My parents had also, well in advance, acquired the necessary books – in English Literature two copies of each – in case other girls' parents might wish their daughters to join.

There were in the end six of us, segregated in the small office/classroom where Sister Peggy had earlier given me Latin lessons; Sister Redemptus used to present us to distinguished visitors as "our novices" – her idea of a joke, I think; though one of us, Gemma Harrington, actually intended to join the order.

The bond between us six was, initially at least, quite close – close enough to confess to each other that we *none of us* knew how babies came to arrive in their mother's tummies. "And" Gemma added "if I don't find out now I don't suppose I'll ever know!" Fortunately one of us, Doris, did have a married cousin she was able to ask; so we did find out, pretty much accurately and in a non-traumatic way – Doris's cousin having even added that the sexual act was an expression of love. Which seemed odd to us, but we took it on board. And I decided that, my mother being so foolishly shy about such things, when Trixie got to the right age I'd have to tell her myself (when I did try to do so I found she'd already been enlightened by the gardener's daughter).

Gemma's vocation to the religious life naturally made me wonder whether I shouldn't be thinking of the same thing. But when I wondered aloud to Sister Peggy, she just laughed: "O for Heaven's sake, Eva. Think of the poor community!" – and I couldn't help feeling she was right.

Gemma did eventually enter (and has been known as "Sister Gemma Harrington" ever since, since nobody can remember her "name in religion"). She was always serenely sure about her own vocation, but a bit worried about her several younger sisters: "How are they going to manage? Of the lot of us, I'm the only one that knows how to talk to boys." For Gemma, though not conventionally pretty, was attractive. Years later, when nuns went into "civvies", she was nicknamed "the nun with sex appeal". Her own view was different; she once said to me "It's a bit difficult to explain to anybody why one should want to be a nun; but I'll tell you one reason I *didn't* have, and that's to be stared at in public! I've got to be out and about a good deal on convent business, and while I still wore the habit I got lots of curious glances, and didn't like them. Now, in ordinary dress, I can catch a bus like any other woman."

About halfway through the school year, and as far as I remember a bit before we got those long-delayed Senior Cambridge results, my mother gave birth to a boy, who was christened Thomas Andrew, after my father's much-venerated St Thomas Aquinas, and St Andrew of Scotland, because news of the birth reached him, apparently, just as he was about to address the St Andrew's Society of the River Plate on some mental-health subject. (This was reported in the *Buenos Aires*

Herald as a talk given by "Doctor Daddy Krapf" – Buenos Aires has not kept its nickname *la Gran Aldea*, "the Great Village", for nothing.) I was Tommy's Godmother; Godfather was no less a person than Alberto Duhau, the co-founder of *Orden Cristiano*. I remember too that when my classmate Doris produced, with kind regards from her parents, a couple of suitably tiny garments "for the son and heir", my mother said they would indeed come in useful when the baby was exposed to winter sun and air on the balcony.

My father, however, was clearly thrilled at the idea of a son and heir; indeed, as I later learned, my mother had wanted to have this late baby precisely to give him this joy. Work soon commenced on an extension to the house at San Miguel – a small extra room beside the large one shared by Titita, Trixie and me, but with its own door to the outside world "for later", it was mysteriously explained. And over what was still his cot in that room, was hung, at his father's behest – *an illuminated copy of Kipling's "If"* – and no French translated nonsense.

Studies continued apace, and I think all of us enjoyed being taught English literature by Sister Peggy. For French literature I was taught by elegant Jeanne Pavageau. An odd syllabus, I seem to remember – *Lorenzacchio*, Beaumarchais's *Mariage de Figaro* (so at least I know what a very iconoclastic, revolutionary play Mozart managed to smuggle into the Habsburg operatic repertoire), and *Cyrano de Bergerac*, with whose hero I naturally fell in love, to the extent that I can still quote a number of his speeches. I still have the first edition of Edmond Rostand's play my father gave me that year

The English Literature syllabus was rather more mainstream: a couple of Shakespeare plays, Books I and II of *Paradise Lost* and the *Lyrical Ballads*, plus a Thomas Hardy novel and a book we nicknamed "the frog" from the green of its dust-cover; it was called, I think, *England from Wordsworth to Dickens*. I have, since, often wished I had read it properly.

Trixie, Tommy, Titita and I spent that summer at San Miguel, together with the housekeeper-cook Marianne, a Bohemian refugee who had joined that household a couple of years earlier. The *Herrschaften* had gone off to explore a new seaside resort, Pinamar, which their architect friend Jorge Bunge was starting up at the time. I was bored, sullen, resentful and on a diet – my mother still worried about my puppy fat, which had considerably increased during that unhappy first year at Michael Ham, and not melted away since. For once, I was quite glad when it was time for school again.

I was to turn fifteen in that year, 1945; it was felt I should spend another year at boarding-school. My father thought it might also be useful to me, at some future time, to have Argentine secondary studies under my belt; these normally took five years, but surely I must be able to do it in two? Especially as, with his usual pleasure in tactically defeating the authorities and their red tape, he had secured for me an exemption from the first three years' maths, most of the geography and – reasonably enough – the foreign languages. And had found me a teacher, Aida Canclini, who apparently specialised in getting dumb society girls through those secondary exams.

Secondary exams were generally agreed to be a series of rather high hurdles. The system dictated that any pupil worth his or her salt got a good enough teacher's assessment to make exams unnecessary, so that these were strictly for the useless students, and those who, like myself, had somehow got themselves outside the system.

I was prepared to give it a try. "The Cancli" as I called her to myself, had the good sense to explain to me, at our very first session together, that she was good at maths and sciences, but in history and literature I'd have to be on my own. Suited me. And here I have to pay due homage to *one* aspect at least of this curious educational system. For the "first three years" (in my case, that first year) "history" was *world history*. First year: the Orient and Greece. Second year: Rome and the Middle Ages. Third year: the Renaissance and everything since. This was the least successful of the three (too much material to cram into a single textbook?) but at least everyone emerged from secondary education having been introduced to the idea that China, Egypt and a few others had had a literate and sophisticated culture many centuries before us poor Western savages... I don't know whether all this was copied from the French *bachot*; if so, I wish many more countries copied it.

The War ends

I cannot now remember how, at Michael Ham, the news came very punctually through of the end of the war; we had never been allowed newspapers or radios, so the nuns must have found it important enough to tell us. I do know that it had long been agreed between them and my parents that, on that day I was to be allowed home.

So, by the very next suburban train, home I went. The rest of the day is, in my memory, a single confused and many-coloured joy. My parents and I joined the crowds on the streets; I have one clear memory of a couple of Free French sailors in uniform at what was then still the Buenos Aires branch of Harrods... and that is strictly all; except I did later become aware that, though my father had presumably listened to the beginning of Beethoven's Fifth Symphony, he had not kept his vow of shaving off the moustache that hid those embarrassing student-duelling scars.

Argentine Secondary exams

Back to school, and to prepare for those first, second and third year exams. These I had to take at a *Colegio Nacional* (an official secondary school) several suburbs further out at San Isidro, travelling there daily by train. The San Isidro railway station was quite a distance from the *Colegio Nacional,* a distance I would walk in the December morning sun. One day, though, I was followed by a total stranger, who was trying to get me to respond to his flirtatious "good morning". I was not then yet quite accustomed to the *piropo*, the local custom that allows a man to utter a compliment to any passing woman; moreover, this one insisted on getting an answer. "Proud, that's what you are. A proud girl. Proud girls never have any luck! Too proud to say good morning to me – you'll have bad luck all day." With hindsight, it's quite clear the man knew where I was going, and why – my school uniform must have been a dead give-away; but at the time, and despite the broad daylight, I was scared. But *bad luck all day*! I couldn't risk that – I had exams to pass, one in the morning, one in the afternoon. So, just as we reached the gates of the *Colegio Nacional*, I quickly turned round towards him and said "Good morning, then." A good-humoured laugh: "That's better! Now you'll be lucky all day." And I was.

That first day, I was amused by my fellow-candidates: not the expected classroom dunces, but a large contingent of tall blond German-speaking students from what had, all those years ago, been my mother's *Goetheschule*, the one that had in the thirties gone Nazi. For Argentina, pro-Axis throughout most of the war, had rather disgracefully joined the winning side three days before the end – just in time for the atom bomb! – and now these young people, their school demoted, were just as much outside the system as I was.

It was funny to watch them, formally shaking hands with one another every morning, heels together, head slightly bowed. Naturally, I took good care not to let anyone see that I understood what they were saying to each other.

The exams themselves were a new experience to me, though the Cancli had taken care to instruct me in the form they took. Most subjects involved both a written paper and a further oral test; and each was subdivided into so-and-so-many segments, known as *bolillas*, (marbles), corresponding I imagine to the chapters of some official textbook. For the written paper, a number was drawn out of a box and loudly announced; for example "Number Eight", whereupon we all had to write out as much as we knew of *bolilla* No. 8 – a test rather more of memory than understanding. My own memory was fortunately excellent, and I was both articulate and grammatical; so these written exams gave me no trouble. My real problem was the rather odd subject known as "Calligraphy and Linear Drawing": calligraphy I could make some sort of a stab at, but linear drawing involving as it did compasses, set-squares, specialised writing implements and a great deal of Indian ink, was my nightmare. And I did have to pass the damn subject, in both its first-year and second-year avatars, so I could reach (and pass) third year and complete my course. I can't quite remember how I managed.

Calligraphy and Linear Drawing didn't, in the nature of things, involve an oral test; other subjects did. For these, each candidate, faced usually by a single examiner, had to pull out his or her own *bolilla.* Here, I got lucky: for first-year ancient history I drew China! A civilisation I actually knew a little about, thanks to an exquisitely illustrated book my father had given me, *The Wisdom of Confucius*; and it so happened my examiner, a scholarly man, had been Argentine consul in China in his younger days. He was as delighted as I was, especially when he found out I had even heard of Mencius.

But neither of us was as delighted as the German student who, for his geography oral, drew Germany. "*Alemania!*" he announced to the world at large, the open vowels widening a joyous grin. He too got a very high mark for that particular exam.

And in the evening, I'd return to Michael Ham, to eat delicious "angel food" and other such treats dear Sister Peggy had prepared for me. "Because I do know" she said, "that when you're doing exams you don't want just ordinary food." And thus it was I completed my "first three years" of Argentine secondary education. For the remaining two, generally agreed to be more difficult, the Cancli was to teach me at home – or rather, in my father's consulting-rooms.

At some point in the 1940s, my father had carried further his interest in psychoanalysis. He had been interested in it already. I own two very short notes to him, signed by Sigmund Freud, thanking him for some papers. But now my father thought he would do a didactic analysis, which is what a doctor or psychiatrist (or in some countries, to his regret, a lay person) has to do before they're allowed to analyse other people. And he did this with the only extant psychoanalyst in Buenos Aires, one Ángel Garma, a Spanish refugee from Franco.

I have a feeling he told me about it before ever he told my mother: I recall a weekend conversation on a walk along the roads around our San Miguel house. My mother rather resented the whole psychoanalysis involvement, calling its practitioners the "psychoanalytic new rich", meaning not just financially but intellectually. These days it is said (and I am prepared to believe it) that Buenos Aires is the capital of psychoanalysis, having overtaken even New York.

During the week, now that I had left Michael Ham I pursued my studies with the Cancli in my father's consulting-rooms, which he did not use in the mornings. He kept his scientific library there; in addition to works of psychology, psychiatry, psychoanalysis, there were the works of Margaret Mead! – which at the time I read with avidity on mornings when the Cancli wasn't coming.

The studies themselves, for this next two-years-in-one, presented considerable difficulties. A lot of what I was supposed to learn was science, which she regarded as her speciality, but even she could not get physics or chemistry to make sense to me. History and literature, it had been agreed between us, she would let me study by myself; which should have been all right, but I had already then a very low boredom threshold, as well as the usual Buenos Aires snobbery that preferred all things European. So I neglected both Argentine history and Argentine literature, something I came to regret.

That December, 1946, I did in fact muddle through the exams in those easier subjects. I had developed a low cunning: I remember, during a history oral, finding I knew nothing whatsoever about the particular few years of our 19th century anarchy that had come out of the hat for me, I gazed adoringly at my (in fact rather handsome) examiner: "*Ay, Señor Doctor!* This is something I've *never* understood... I suppose you couldn't explain it to me?" Which he did – and gave me a (low) pass mark.

But such techniques did not work for physics or chemistry: I simply failed both subjects, and had to spend a few hours (of a three-month summer holiday) mugging them up. Which I did, mostly by heart and still not understanding what on earth it was all about; and duly passed renewed examinations in March.

I gradually slipped into going out with young men, and had acquired a boyfriend of kinds, who asked me to the Caledonian Ball. (Scottish dancing is immensely respectable and upper class in Argentina, so going to the Caledonian Ball was all right by my parents!) My mother had a dress made for me – she worried perennially about my figure, I was overweight and she hated it, certain I would never make a good marriage that way. So she had a becoming dress made for me, at considerable expense, in the form of a Grecian tunic, long and rather narrow in the legs. Imagine trying to do Scottish dancing wearing that.

The way out

So much for my Argentine education; the next thing was to get me into Oxford (since Cambridge was not contemplated). Oxford, it was known, consisted of Colleges: one was supposed to apply for a place, not to the University as such, but at one of these, and – my parents were advised – it was best to apply for a scholarship at one of the five women's Colleges: the candidate would almost certainly not get it, but beneath it, as a sort of academic safety-net, lay the possibility of at least a *place* there. And what would be the best College to ask for this notional scholarship? Well, said their informant, Somerville was the most intellectual, Lady Margaret Hall (appropriately) the most ladylike... "Ah!" my mother decided. "That's the one for Eva then!" I was, in her view, quite intellectual enough, but could certainly do with being rather more ladylike.

Once again, a teacher had to be found.

The one recommended (by whom, I wonder?) as the likeliest to get me into LMH was one Miss Myrtle Moore, herself a recent Oxford graduate; the snag was, she worked at Northlands – that other English girls' school where I had, so long ago, sat for Junior Cambridge; and it was against Northlands rules that any of their teaching staff should give private lessons – on pain, if it became known, of losing their job. So Miss Moore was approached (again, by whom?) in the utmost secrecy; and agreed, under the pseudonym of "Pauline", to take me on. So I was to work very very hard, to repay my parents for all the trouble they'd been taking about all this.

I did work very hard, and with great pleasure. Sister Peggy, in on the secret, was amused at the "Pauline" bit, Pauline having been her own first name before she took vows. I myself always addressed my teacher as "Miss Moore". She and I got on extremely well, even though she made fun of C.S. Lewis, and talked down what was at that time my favourite novelist, the now forgotten Charles Morgan. But she introduced me to Marlowe, to Webster, to Beaumont and Fletcher and I think to John Donne, and I loved all of this. And in my spare time I was reading Erich Kästner's verses, as well as his one novel for adults, the skilled and very political *Fabian*, gazing at my parents' photographs of Marlene Dietrich, and generally wondering about Berlin in the twenties, and the Germany they'd left behind a very few years later.

Then, at the end of that academic year came that scholarship examination. The only rule appeared to be that I must not write my answers in my own home; so every morning I would take the train to Miss Moore's suburban flat and sit at her dining-room table as she opened the envelope containing my exam papers. After the allotted time-span she would give me a light lunch, and then sit me at that table again and open the day's second envelope.... In the evening, she would seal all my answers back into their envelopes, write the address, and give them to me to mail at Retiro post-office on my way home. I remember thinking how trustful and English all this was, how easily I could have cheated – with hindsight, not as easily as all that, since I'd have needed to fake quite long answers to rather open-ended literary questions.

And then, three weeks later, the telegram came:

"LADY MARGARET HALL OFFERS SCHOLARSHIP...."

I rang Miss Moore at once with the news – and had to say, twice, "Miss Moore! Miss Moore! Are you *there*?" before she could manage an audible answer. I found out later that a friend had told her it was asking a bit much of an Oxford college to award a scholarship to a girl with a German surname, in Argentina of all places! But LMH was never like that – they had after all kept both their German tutor and the German Christmas carols going all through the war.

PART TWO

DISCOVERING OXFORD - SEEKING A LIFE

Chapter 1
Oxford, 1948-51

Before I came up as an undergraduate, I had once visited Lady Margaret Hall with my parents. It was vacation time, so we were shown around by the German tutor, a respectable refugee who had been kept on, as had her subject, throughout the war. She was still there in my undergraduate days, and at the end of each Michaelmas term organised a session of German Christmas carols.

Now, she took us around and showed us a study-bedroom. My mother said (I hope in Spanish) "I think you will be quite happy in this shabby little room." I was rather cross with her – why must she always spoil everything for me? LMH, clearly, was not what she had hoped for.

First-year scholars and exhibitioners were supposed to arrive at Lady Margaret Hall a day before the rest of the student body. This was in order to welcome us, give us a little talk about our special responsibilities, and invite us to make some kind of vow to uphold the ideals of the College.

It was 1948: I was eighteen years old. I remember arriving that first term, with two enormous trunks. These had come with me from Argentina, because (not having a home in Britain) I had to have sheets and winter clothes and the like with me. These two trunks, one cabin trunk and one wardrobe trunk, therefore had to live in my room for the rest of the time I was at LMH. My parents had also kindly bought me a bicycle, but this was not a great success. I had no sense of balance; someone had attempted to teach me to cycle in Buenos Aires, but I never learned properly. My bicycle was fairly soon stolen, and I never bothered to inform the police, or tried to acquire another one, but simply walked everywhere. Quite far sometimes – not just to lectures at the Examinations Schools in the High Street, but also to the Catholic chaplaincy, at the other end of nowhere beyond Christ Church.

My first-year room was in the Deneke Building, then the newest part of LMH. The money for this had been gathered by the Misses Deneke, who had some old connection with the college and were clearly quite wealthy. They had also endowed a scholarship in Modern Languages, which they thought I held. This was not so – I had a College scholarship – but there was a mix-up for several weeks, before they sorted out that the holder of the Deneke scholarship was one Rosemary Davidson, who lived a couple of doors away from me in the Deneke Building and has remained a friend. But for a couple of weeks or maybe more, I was a bit puzzled by the fact that the Misses Deneke were forever asking me to tea and drinks: they kept an eye on their Deneke scholar. After that it was Rosemary they had to tea and drinks. They lived in Norham Gardens, not very far from College.

Also up the corridor, a little further, lived a very remarkable woman, a few years older than the rest of us: she had served in the war. Her name at that time was Brigitte Heinsheimer and she was doing, as far as I remember, French and German. German by origin, she and her parents were refugees. Her secondary education had thus been interrupted, but at the end of the war, having served in the WAAFs, she found herself at some desk organising places at university for various ex-service people; and her father, old Professor Heinsheimer, had said to her "While you are about it, my dear, why don't you organise yourself a place at Oxford?" She had, naturally, no such thing as any secondary certificates from either Germany or England; LMH, to its eternal credit, took her on in spite of that. She was at that time in her second year, and is another who has remained a friend ever since.

Brigitte's room, unlike everyone else's, was always tidy. There were flowers in a vase and she always seemed to have coffee and biscuits. You could knock on Brigitte's door at any time and be well received. More or less opposite there was a pantry, where we not only washed up our tea things, but also ironed our clothes. I am told that I once forgot I was ironing something and just left the hot iron on it and everything caught fire – but then, I didn't have very much experience of this kind of thing! We also had, in each room, a fireplace, for which we got two rather small buckets a week of what was mostly coal dust. I had been cold in Buenos Aires as a child, and I was cold again at LMH that first winter. I soon found, however, that the answer to my problems, at least twice a week, was to invite a young man to tea, because he could then make up my fire!

Joining things

Fortunately there was no shortage of young men, seven or eight to every girl; so this was not a problem. I was permitted male visitors between the hours of one (or possibly two) in the afternoon, and seven in the evening. (Presumably no hanky panky could possibly take place before 7pm.) I was also allowed to go out in the evening, as long as I returned by ten-thirty. Or I could get late leave, in which case I should be back by eleven-fifteen. All this seemed to me absolutely dazzling freedom.

Initially I went to Mass at the Catholic chaplaincy, even though the chaplain of the period was totally unsuited to his job: he had served in the Navy during the war, and had no idea how to deal with intellectuals. Later I moved to the Dominican church at Blackfriars, where I was much happier, and which indeed I have continued to frequent when in Oxford.

However, I did meet some interesting people through the chaplaincy. The first time I emerged from Mass in my exotic South American fur coat (also provided by parents – the cheapest available fur, to protect me against the dreaded English climate), there was a large vehicle with quite a number of people in it, and one tall young man said "Come and join us!" So I did, sitting on his knees. His name was Galvin Whitaker; he was long to remain a friend. Galvin and a few others had organised something they called the Festive Collective for the sole purpose of having parties together.

They were all northerners. (I was then just beginning to understand that the history of England consists of new things coming in from the south east, and older things, including Roman Catholicism, being displaced to the north and west.) And they teased me unmercifully about my lah-di-dah accent. But I did have the wit to say "Look, I learned English as a foreign language! This is the way I was taught it, and I'm not changing my accent for all of you" – as good northerners they accepted this and I was then left in peace.

I was also besieged at college by people trying to get me to join the most various university societies. I did join a vast number, including – since I was interested in politics – both the Labour and the Conservative Clubs. This was not actually very useful, because their meetings happened on the same day of the week, so I couldn't attend both – a disappointment.

University Vacations

My first Christmas vacation I was still able to spend with my parents. I was supposed to join them, via a series of trains, in Switzerland, somewhere up in skiing country near Davos. My mother was very worried about my travelling arrangements: "Eva is bound to take the wrong train somewhere and end up the wrong side of the Iron Curtain!" My sister Trixie, aged thirteen at the time, tried to comfort her: "Oh don't worry about Eva – if she's in any difficulty, she'll meet some man and borrow money off him!" – which did nothing to reassure my poor mother. In point of fact, after a few days staying with my friend Rosemary Davidson's parents, I did take the right trains and ended up in the right place. If I'd asked, I suppose I could have had skiing lessons; but it just didn't occur to me. After a snowy Christmas, we spent a few days in Zürich at the delightful Hotel Eden facing the lake, which I believe no longer exists; then I returned to Oxford for Hilary Term.

Problems might well have arisen, however, during later university vacations. I couldn't, like other undergraduates, go home to my immediate family; and I wasn't allowed to stay in College for more than a week or so, because they needed my room in order to hire out the building for conferences. So I always had to pack up my belongings into my trunks and remove myself.

Some of the time, I went to stay with my Aunt Annele – now simply known as Ann, whom I had last seen at *Oma* Lilli's Ascona house when I was seven. The following year, the two of them – mother and daughter – had travelled to the

United States for a holiday; and on the boat, Ann had met a Merchant Navy officer, Billy Tanner. Not long after, she had married Billy and come to live with him on his native Isle of Wight.

Early in the war, Billy had been involved in Dunkirk – "a bloody hero" my father pronounced, perhaps to reassure me as well as himself that we did have one of those in the family. Billy had, however, been quite badly wounded during the operation, and had to spend the rest of the war at home, making wooden toys for children who otherwise would have had none.

This marriage had, in my parents' eyes, redeemed all Annele's anti-Semitic sins; so that, after the war, they were only too happy to ask the Tanners for hospitality for their children – in particular for me during those University vacations – at the farm they were gradually establishing on the Island. True, Ann was still very chary of anyone knowing about her Jewish origins; I found this puzzling since I, if anything, tended rather to brag about mine; but she did ask me not to make it obvious to anyone that it came to me from my mother's side, and that my mother was her own sister.

Ann and Billy were by now living at a place called Rookley Manor, just about in the exact middle of the Island: you could just, by straining your eyes, distinguish the sea from the very highest down on their land. I think the house already came with a field or so; soon, they bought another couple of fields, then two or three cows, then more land and a very tame and gentle bull named Toby. All the cattle were Dexters, an odd little breed no taller than a large dog, but very useful, being hardy in the Isle-of-Wight climate and also giving both milk and meat. Their milk she had, in those days, to sell to the Milk Marketing Board; so she also kept a few goats for the family. She devoted every hour of daylight to her animals; I remember once arriving on a visit and being greeted with "Oh hello, dear! Sorry I can't stop and talk to you now, my poor Billy's got something stuck in his hoof and I've got to get disinfectant for him at once!" I thought she meant her husband, but it was the billy goat whose wound concerned her.

As for Bill Tanner, he still made a few toys as well as dealing with breakfast and other domestic matters; there was also a Mrs Russell from the nearby village to clean the house, thus leaving my aunt to concentrate on what really mattered.

Ann named her cattle the Atlantic Herd, and they won prizes at shows all over southern England with monotonous regularity. She attended the shows herself, disguised in overalls as her own farm worker; if anyone asked her who she worked for, she did not reveal her identity, but simply replied "Farmer Tanner".

The one person who was not at all pleased about Aunt Ann's cattle farm was Uncle Alfred – my Great-Uncle Alfred, Ann's actual uncle. This was because she insisted on moving her very considerable share of my grandfather's money to

England, where there were all these taxes to pay. "This money my brother worked so hard to earn, she's wasting it in England. What for? To buy *cows.* Now tell me, are her cows any better than my cows?" I should say that Uncle Alfred was at that stage a very much larger landowner in Argentina than Ann was able to be in England, and indeed owned a great many cows though not, I fear, Dexters.

For other vacations I stayed with my guardian, Judith Thornton. College required me (as being under 21) to have a guardian, and my parents had decided this should be someone other than my aunt, so that there were two people to consult in case of any emergency. Their choice fell upon Judith St John Thornton, the English wife of an Anglo-Argentine friend of theirs. Judith had returned to England in order to make a home for their three sons during their English education. For this purpose she had bought a house in Forest Row, not very far from where I live now. The house was called Green Path and was large, with a sizeable garden, including lawns, a shrubbery, vegetables, and other things. All this was something of a revelation to me. For instance, there was a cage full of raspberries and I was supposed to pick these, and allowed to eat as many as I liked while I did so! Moreover, it was the first time in my life that somebody brought me a cup of tea in bed, which struck me as a curious custom of the natives, but I quite soon got used to it!

The first spring vacation, 1949, Judith was taking her eldest son Edward and his best schoolfriend to Florence, and she suggested I should join the party. We spent about ten days there, including my nineteenth birthday, for which she gave me a coral necklace. It was the best possible time to visit Florence. The war was over, the Ponte Vecchio had avoided destruction, and there were not yet the busloads of tourists who now invade the place. We lived at a *pensione* on the Arno itself, and did most things on foot. That was my first exposure in real life, as distinct from reproductions, to Botticelli and to a number of other painters, also to the beautiful churches of Florence. My own favourite remains Santa Maria Novella.

We also went up to Fiesole, to the splendid Roman amphitheatre, and after looking at this, we sat on the terrace of a restaurant a little downhill from there and had *zabaglione,* a delicious dish of egg and sweet wine, which Judith said she'd had there as a young girl and it still tasted just as good! That was a very happy visit.

Other friends in Oxford

Judith Thornton did one other thing for me. She introduced me to a childless couple called Baden-Powell who lived near Oxford, up on Boar's Hill. I think she had been a college friend of Jane Baden-Powell. I found out soon enough that they were embarrassed by their connection with the founder of the Boy Scouts: they were academics and this was not to be mentioned! But they were exceedingly kind and used to ask me to their grown-up dinner parties, where I was always the youngest person present. They had an interesting convention, very suitable for the period, whereby women wore evening dress for these parties and the men didn't have to bother. As all women like getting into evening dress and very few men do, this worked very well.

It was there, I think at the first dinner party, that I met two very interesting people. One was Father Victor White, a Dominican from Blackfriars, whose professional expertise was as a Jungian psychologist. The other was no less than Nevill Coghill. I wish I had followed this up, because I could have been, if only as a member of the crowd, in the wonderful rendering of Shakespeare's *Tempest* that he produced later in Worcester College. Instead of which, my playacting was with the rather humbler St Catherine's (the old St Catherine's, not the handsome new one) production of T. S. Eliot's *The Family Reunion*, for which I was chosen because of my deep voice. The man who directed us wanted the chorus of Aunts and Uncles to be an operatic one; and I was supposed to be the contralto.

A powerful part of my first impressions of Oxford was the sheer age of the buildings. They had not then been restored, as most of them now have been. I remember particularly the peeling wall in Peckwater Quad in Christ Church. Then there were the time-battered heads of the Caesars on Broad Street in front of the Bodleian.

Across the way from them, I had, of course, an account at Blackwells; and I kept looking up at where the Duke had lived in *Zuleika Dobson*. I had also read *Brideshead Revisited* and, of course, *Gaudy Night,* so I had my pre-conceived ideas as to what should happen in Oxford. And a lot of other people had these ideas, especially from *Brideshead* and *Zuleika*. The young men in particular tried very hard to live up to this kind of Oxford – which post-war, with clothes rationing and so on – was a little difficult. The really sensational figure, at the time, was one Milo Cripps, a nephew of Sir Stafford Cripps but very different in attitude. Milo actually attempted, during the 1949 summer term, to stage a "Zuleika Dobson" episode; but it was not a success. I forget who was to act Zuleika; but I do remember very few young men were, in those clothes-rationed days, prepared to jump fully dressed into the river.

Now, I had been well provided with clothes from home. I even had the necessary evening dress – essentially a long black skirt with several different tops, so I could go out to the Baden-Powells and, later, elsewhere. Then, I had that fur coat – something not seen as particularly exotic in Buenos Aires. I also had an Argentine poncho, for wear in coolish weather, before it was fur coat time; I heard later that I was known throughout Oxford as "the blanket woman". On the other hand, nothing in my wardrobe was "new look": that fashion hadn't yet arrived in Buenos Aires when we left in 1948, so when it really hit Oxford I had to spend my coupons on longer skirts for daytime – trousers were not yet permissible wear with an academic gown.

And I did feel the need to be fashionable! Suddenly, I seemed to have a great many social engagements. Back in Buenos Aires, I had met a young Englishman, there on some sort of journalistic fellowship. An article he wrote for the *News Chronicle* had brought him a sheaf of requests for pen-friends; he had passed on to me, as "the most civilised-sounding", a letter from one Frank Fenton, interested in Classics and so reading Greats at Oxford, who wanted a pen-friend in Argentina. I had written to this Frank that I would be delighted to correspond with him, but was perhaps not exactly what he was after, since I was coming to England any day now and would be joining him at Oxford.

By Hilary 1948 he was in his second year of what I soon learned was a four-year course. I very soon went to see him at his rooms in Magdalen, where he gave me tea and then walked me back to LMH. Over the months I began to find that this friendly and welcoming Frank Fenton was a very curious creature indeed. He disapproved of so many things and people – foreigners, Jews, Roman Catholics and anyone who read an Arts subject (other than Greats, of course). At the same time I noticed that all his friends fell into one or more of these categories; though I think I was the only one who fell into all! It was as if Frank could only like people he disapproved of.... He was also what would nowadays be known as "gay" and in those days "queer" – and certainly he was queer in every other way.

Frank eventually introduced me to his friend Denis Paul of New College, who was to become very important in my life. This was a tall blonde good-looking lad, a little older than the rest of us because of war service – though in his case that service had not been in the armed forces but (since he was a pacifist) with Quaker stretcher-bearers in Germany. However, this counted in the same way towards a place in Oxford afterwards. In addition to his good looks, Denis was also rather vain: he thought a lot about his clothes – and very good they were; moreover, he fancied himself, with some reason, as a cook (a skill he had learnt while with the Quakers). His father was the caretaker of a building in the City of London; but Denis himself was clearly going up in the social world.

At some point quite early in our relationship, Denis decided to become a Roman Catholic. Catholicism was at that time very fashionable among intellectuals; this is a fashion that, like others, goes in swings of the pendulum but, just at that time, Oxford was full of converts and Denis became one of them. Like many converts (but not my parents) he became very exaggerated and fanatical – *plus catholique que le Pape!*

He also had a strong relationship with Germany. He had enjoyed his time there, had made friends, was well-read in Thomas Mann and other modern classics. He both spoke and wrote good German. And I – in love with him – thought that, with his elegance, his Catholicism and his knowledge of languages (he also had fairly decent French), this was the kind of suitor to win the approval of my parents. Little did I know!

Denis Paul, his friend Michael Dummett, and for that matter Frank Fenton were all, like many of their circle, studying philosophy at some level or other. Frank was embarked upon a Greats degree; both the others were reading PPE, but concentrating on its philosophy component. Denis was lucky enough to have had Isaiah Berlin as a tutor, Sir Isaiah also being based in New College at the time.

As "philosophers", obviously these young men liked to talk philosophy. The intellectual fashion at that time was logical positivism – a fashion that has probably just passed its apogee, but was still very much there. The problem was that, aside from their logical positivism, they were all (except Frank Fenton) Catholic converts. How to reconcile the two? They stayed out of what was known as the Socratic Society, dominated by C.S. Lewis, as being entirely too pedestrian; instead, they concentrated on another university society, the Aquinas, which had very little to do with Thomism but did discuss religio-philosophical matters. This society was quite small, and very intense. Basically, Aquinas members read papers to each other. One of our speakers was Iris Murdoch, then still known simply as a philosophy don. There was supposed to be a new chairperson each term, so eventually we ran out of suitable people to chair, and one term I had to do it! I knew as much about philosophy as I did about classical Greek; but chairing requires neither opinions nor knowledge – you just let the others get on with it, keeping order if necessary.

At one point however, during my second academic year, I did feel I ought to enlarge my knowledge of philosophy. I said so to my moral tutor Katie Lea, and she got me tutorials with a younger don in what was supposed to be philosophy but was rather concentrated on the Cambridge Platonists. They were a nice well-intentioned lot of people, in the 17th or 18th century – I don't quite recall – but their approach did not prove much use for reconciling logical positivism with Christianity.

Wittgenstein was an overshadowing presence in the philosophical background rather than anything else, an intellectual grandfather so to speak – obviously much revered, but not really discussed. And during my time, as far as I know, he never came to Oxford to speak.

Neglected studies

I should say something about all that work I didn't do, because I was always going out. My father had not endeared himself to me by saying to the Vice Principal (also my moral tutor), Miss Lea, "It is impossible to overwork Eva." Miss Lea was too polite to try, but in any case I was not overworked. Once a week, of course, there would be an essay crisis and, like everyone else, I would pin a notice to my door saying "Essay crisis, please keep out." One friend of mine was nicer than that and said on her notice "I love you! At *any* other time I would be glad to see you, but just at the moment I have an essay crisis."

During my first year at university, there was to be an exam at the end of the second term; but you had another chance at the end of the third term. My main problem with this vital exam was not with literature but with the two additional subjects – Latin and Anglo-Saxon.

My father had tried to have me taught Latin at school, but at the time I had not been very interested and had not absorbed much beyond *mensa, mensam*. Not unnaturally, for a degree in English literature, you were supposed to be quite well acquainted with books IV and VI of the Aeneid, in other words, the story of Dido and Aeneas and also Aeneas's passage through the underworld. I had considerable trouble with these – I managed, but only just. I suspect it's one of those cases where my answers to the English literature papers were good enough to save me.

My other problem was with Anglo-Saxon, "Old English". At the time, I was not as interested as I have since become in the origin of words, but we did have to tackle quite a bit of *Beowulf*, and of course learn the very different grammar of Old English. It actually has a more apparent grammar than modern English, rather like German, to which of course it is related. It is indeed an early form of English, with no Norman influence. By the time you get to Chaucer, and Middle English, the Norman influence has come, which makes it all much easier.

We, however, had to face *Beowulf* first. My friend Betty Marcus and I invented a myth, whereby it had in fact been written by Professor Tolkien and if there were textual cruxes, it was because Priscilla and her immediately elder brother Christopher had torn up the manuscript in the nursery! (We didn't tell Priscilla.) It starts, I still remember, with *Hu waer Gardena* and then goes on. It did introduce me to a new form of poetry, operating not by rhyme or what we would call scansion, but entirely by alliteration

And beyond *Beowulf*, there was the *Anglo-Saxon Chronicle;* and all sorts of other things. Priscilla Tolkien says she caught me one day in the library, apparently making very odd faces; what I was trying to do was to pronounce some of the stuff. At a later stage, she and I used to go to her father's lectures, which were not of course on anything as *passé* as *Beowulf*. By now, he was into Old Norse, and he recited to us the Lord's Prayer in that language, which was a little difficult to follow, because he had just had a new set of false teeth fitted. So we didn't follow it terribly well, but I knew, if I went with Priscilla and the two of us sat on the front bench and were visible, her father would ask us to his rooms in Merton afterwards and give us sherry, so we persevered.

Despite all this, I did manage to pass those first year exams, in fact the first time I took them, at the end of the second term, which left me the summer to get on with more frivolous activities, like falling in love.

The Principal at LMH in my day was one Miss Sutherland, later Dame Lucy Sutherland. She had been, I believe, a civil servant most of her life. I did not find her an attractive personality; she may have been only shy, but she came across as cold and difficult. She was also, I think, in accordance with the college's "ladylike" tradition, something of a snob. This meant that foreign scholars among the undergraduates, particularly if they had parents of distinction, would sometimes get invited to her parties. I was, for my sins, one of them.

The Vice Principal on the other hand, Miss Kathleen Lea, was utterly delightful and I was very lucky to have her as my moral tutor. All of us called her to ourselves, and to each other, "Katie", a most affectionate nickname. I suspect I was a disappointment to Katie, because she had hoped (though of course too kind ever to say so) for better things than I actually produced. Thus for instance, in my first summer she made me go in for an essay competition on a literary theme, and suggested that I take for my subject Sir Phillip Sidney's *Arcadia*. I did actually read through the whole thing. I had no idea, then or later, how one did research; so I did nothing to find out when Sidney wrote it and in what circumstances. I did do, as far as I remember, quite a detailed analysis of its structure; I did not get the prize.

Katie was so nice, one didn't want to hurt her feelings. Sometime, quite early on, I think, during that first year, I thought that I would be better off reading History rather than English Literature and Language, and this was not only because of my difficulty with Anglo-Saxon: I genuinely had rather more interest in history. But this would have meant telling Katie and having to leave her, and I never quite worked up the nerve for this.

I had other tutors as well. At one point I was sent to Mrs Ing, one of the few married dons at LMH, who therefore did not live in college. Mrs Ing's teaching style was very different from Katie's, rather sharper. She would listen to your essay, she would sometimes say "Good", and other times "Interesting". We always waited for the time when she would say "Uninteresting", though she never actually did. Having listened to your essay, she seemed in fact no longer interested in what you had said, and would speak about the books she had asked you to read. I learned a great deal from Mrs Ing. Among other things she introduced me to the writings of that wonderful man, Thomas Love Peacock, who wrote funny novels about his Romantic contemporaries, particularly *Nightmare Abbey*. This is the kind of thing I might well not have found out for myself.

I was also sent, quaking in my boots, to Lord David Cecil, who was at New College at the time; I remember asking Katie how did one address him, did one say "My lord", or what? – and she said I should just call him "Sir", so I did. I remember his tutorials as interesting, but not outrageously so. I also remember an argument about whether some Shakespeare play, probably *King Lear*, was "cosmic", and that I thought it wasn't. Because to me the cosmos meant the outer stars and they didn't seem to come into it.

The best of my outside tutors was Hugo Dyson of Merton. He, too, had his own style of teaching. He taught four of us in any given term, and decreed: "Two of you should come at 10 o'clock, the other two can come at 11. Anybody who's still holding the fort at 12 will get sherry." This made him a very popular tutor. He was also a very good one; and a truly magnificent lecturer. I didn't go to many lectures, but I always went to Dyson's. I quote: "Hamlet – was a man – who thought he had a mother – and found he had an *aunt!*" He also said things like "And there is that man Tolkien [who was also at Merton], the most gifted language scholar we have, the sort of man who thinks up new languages before he goes to sleep. And what does the man do in his spare time? – write *fairy stories!*" I also remember in my very last term – I was still going to Dyson's lectures because I couldn't resist them and I would sit right up front – that he came up to me and said "Eva, haven't you got Schools this term? You ought to be doing serious revision, not coming to frivolous things like my lectures." I said a girl needed a little fun! Hugo Dyson remains a very happy memory. I have found out since that he was bipolar and had some very, very difficult depressed times.

More friends

My mother's insistence, back in Buenos Aires, that I apply for a scholarship at "ladylike" LMH rather than the "more intellectual" Somerville had, from my point of view, been a mistake. I would have fitted in rather better in Somerville, and might have got to know better people like Shirley Catlin, later to become Shirley Williams, now Baroness Williams; Val Richardson daughter of Naomi of that ilk, and the beautiful, *really* beautiful, Barbara Belloc, granddaughter of Hilaire, of *that* ilk. Bar was so beautiful and had such a social life that she went to *nine* Commem Balls and (not very surprisingly) twice failed her first-year exam and had to leave. But this was not a very serious problem – Bar was hardly the Somerville intellectual type! She married one of her many suitors, a young man who had some kind of administrative job at the University, so she continued to live in Oxford. My boyfriend Denis Paul and I were invited to their London wedding; we were announced, I remember, as Mr Krapf and Miss Paul! Who was *not* present was Hilaire Belloc, who wrote like an angel but was not actually a very nice man. And his granddaughter, scandal of scandals, was marrying an Anglican, *outside* the Roman Catholic Church; so, no Hilaire Belloc!

I did have two quite close friends in my own college. I've already mentioned Priscilla Tolkien. She'd got into trouble, that first Michaelmas Term, for having her father and an old family friend (male) in her room after hours, even though chaperoned by her mother. Priscilla was, and remains, a very affectionate person. She was extremely strictly kept by her father; she was not, for instance, allowed to go to London by herself.

There was also my other friend, Betty Marcus – and a greater contrast with Priscilla, or "Prisca" as we called her, cannot be imagined. Betty was the daughter of an East End Jewish tailor; her father, whom I later met and enormously liked, was *exactly* the wise little tailor of Jewish folklore. When Betty had a Commem Ball her father would come up, bringing her evening dress (made by him) and iron it in our pantry as only he knew how; he was not in the least ashamed of what he was.

Betty, reading English like the rest of us, had a beautiful speaking voice, and was in general quite talented for the drama. When we put on *The Family Reunion* she got the part of Agatha, and I remember her saying emphatically that she was "a Head of a women's College *trying not to dislike women*", which she did extremely well. She was not quite so good at moving around the stage, but the voice and the diction were superb. At some point, and I think it was early in the first summer, Priscilla and Betty, plus another friend Alice Hodgkinson, from a northern working-class background, all went up north ourselves. We stayed in a cottage near the Jesuit public school Stonyhurst, in Lancashire, where old Professor Tolkien had connections. During our stay, we visited the school, which I found fairly terrifying; the portraits of distinguished old boys were all of Generals or Cardinals. (I didn't at the time realise that Army and Church were the only careers open to Roman Catholics since the Reformation.)

But mostly we stayed at the cottage; its owner took our ration cards, as hostesses did at that time, and fed us. I best remember the breakfasts, but we also got supper, and a picnic to take with us on our long walks. That was when I discovered that cooking in the North of England was infinitely better than in the South, at least in those days. When I think not only about LMH, but about the Toxova Hotel of my childhood and how dreadful the food was, I begin to realise that our Stonyhurst landlady was able to do quite miraculous things with our rations (she may have got the odd extra egg from some neighbouring farmer, even perhaps a little bit of bacon, but not a lot).

In that first summer vacation, Denis got himself and me involved in a course that was taking place in Germany, in the south near Freiburg im Breisgau, at a place called Schauinsland, which means "look into the country". It had, I think, been built as a Hitler Youth ski lodge, at any rate there was lots of dormitory space for everyone. The course we joined was supposed to bring German and English students together to try and find some way of conversing with each other. It was run by a remarkable woman called Ann Dreydel, from Oxford, together with a Jesuit, Father Tom Corbishley.

With hindsight, the most remarkable thing from my point of view was the presence of one Donald Nicholl, who acted as one of our tutors. Donald was at the time a lecturer at the newly-established University College of N. Staffordshire (later the University of Keele). He was another Northerner, and another convert – in his case a totally unfanatical one. At the same time he seemed to radiate goodness in a quiet way, which struck many people at the time; many years later, my husband, Mick Gillies, commented on it after spending time with him. Donald was also the tallest man I have ever met – you couldn't ever not find him, because he was always a head-and-a-half above anyone else. He had been a miner's son, had gone to a decent grammar school, where apparently the teachers fought over him and the history master won, so his subject was history. He had then served in the war, in India; he was enormously gifted for languages and had picked up a couple of Indian ones. He also had good German, which was one reason for his presence. I once asked him, years later, how he had come by his German and he said "Well, we were a very political family, so in the 'thirties we read Hitler's *Mein Kampf* in translation, and I wanted to know what it was like in the original."

Now Denis felt he had to leave after a while, I have forgotten why. I found myself lost without him and went on to join him. We spent some time with my paternal grandmother, *Oma* Ada in Munich, and some further time with a young friend of Denis's, Gita, a German girl whom he had known in his pacifist work days, wandering through the Moselle Valley. I need hardly say that Denis was also a wine snob, and Moselle as far as he was concerned was *the* stuff. So we three went all the way up the Moselle Valley, at which point we ran out of money. There was just enough to send Gita back to her family. As for Denis and me, we began walking, sleeping in barns and the like; which I thought absolutely wonderful – this was the kind of life I'd like to live! My parents, however, disapproved; they felt it would give rise to scandal; and indeed, years later Michael Dummett told me that everybody was quite convinced we were having an affair – but in fact it was all exceedingly chaste. (One thing about this journey, though, my father *did* understand: I later found he had said to my mother "She's got to come to terms with Germany somehow".)

Nevertheless, it was becoming increasingly apparent that my parents did not approve of Denis. It was not only the pacifism and the Germanophilia; they also disliked, as I came to do, the puritanical fanaticism of his religious attitudes. The break, though painful for both of us, eventually came during our second summer vacation in 1950.

But what was I to do after my Finals?

A visit to what was, in 1951, still the separate O.U. *Women's* Appointments advisory service had only produced the advice that I should take a shorthand and typing qualification, which did not appeal. And my degree, when it came, was only what was then still called a "Good Second" – certainly inadequate for an academic career. And for just about any other job I might have liked, my lack of UK nationality was a very serious drawback: any prospective employer would have to swear that he or she could find no British candidate as well suited. So, inevitably, back to Buenos Aires.

Chapter 2

Return to Buenos Aires, 1951

Arrival Geneva, 1952

In Argentina too, however, a Second Class Honours in English Literature and Language had made me totally unemployable. I could, of course, have given English lessons, but that was not what, at twenty-one, I wanted to do.

The government was still Peronist, and would not have employed me in any case, even had I sought such employment. The head of the British Council, Arthur Montague, a friend of my father's, would have loved to employ me, but the Council had, as usual, no money. Arthur did what he could; he gave a luncheon party, at which I met some of the Argentine writers of the period. He also got me the chance to give four lectures at an institution then known as the Argentine Institute for British Culture, the subject to be chosen by myself.

I had then, and still have, a great interest in William Blake. I decided that I could not possibly cope with the Prophetic Books, but might be able to offer something on the *Songs of Innocence and of Experience.* After duly preparing four lectures, I was introduced to my rather small audience (consisting of some of the plainer girls I had known at school, a Yugoslav nun to whom I was for some reason teaching Anglo-Saxon, the husband of my friend Margaret Frers and, at a later stage, a woman called Eleanor Salmon, who was of my parents' generation, though not a close friend) more or less as follows:-

"Ladies and Gentlemen, some of you may remember that last winter Mr Jorge Luis Borges lectured to us on William Blake. This year Miss Eva Krapf is going to go into rather more detail about a particular aspect of that poet's work."

Now, I knew Jorge Luis Borges slightly and was aware of his reputation, even at that time, as an outstanding writer and lecturer – and wished the floor would swallow me, which it didn't.

I delivered my lectures as best I could. After the last one, Eleanor Salmon, a beautiful woman I suppose in her fifties, came up to me afterwards and said "Tell me, are you Interested in Art?" and I said "Well, er yes," and she said "And you do believe, don't you, in International Understanding?" and I said "Yes, of course." "And don't you think Art could further International Understanding?" And hazily I said "Yes, why not?" "Well, how would you like to go to Geneva and defend this thesis before the United Nations?"

I was somewhat dazzled. The real facts of the matter were that Eleanor Salmon, along with some half-dozen of other well-intentioned ladies, were all members of something called the *Fundación Ana María Berry Para el Estudio de las Naciones*

Unidas (the Ana María Berry Foundation for the Study of the United Nations) – named after the author of the book, *Art for Children*, that I had been given by my parents as a child. They could not call themselves anything but a "Foundation for the Study of...", because Perón disapproved of the United Nations, so you could not have a United Nations Association – it would have been "anti-nationalist". There was just this group of half-a-dozen or so ladies; and that particular year, 1952, none of their husbands wanted to pay for them to travel to Europe. Thus, the choice fell upon me, for I *was* travelling to Europe, essentially because I could not find a satisfactory job in Buenos Aires. My father had said he would pay for my trip and would, in addition, give me the sum of £100, which had to last me three months; which in 1952, if you were very, very careful, it could just have done. If, at the end of three months, I presented him with accounts, I could have another hundred quid, but at the end of six months I would have to come back, because he couldn't keep me in Europe for ever and ever. So I had to find myself a job before six months were out!

So I *was* going to Europe. I intended to spend some time with my maternal grandmother, *Oma* Lilli, who was now living in Switzerland again; she spent her summers in Montreux, so I would be quite near Geneva. So it was all quite convenient.

Introduction to a portable skill

By the time I first arrived in Geneva at twenty-two, I was, heaven help me, not a mere delegate, but the actual head of a delegation; in other words the ladies of the *Fundación Ana María Berry* had found two more young women who were travelling to Europe that year. (I later found out that other delegates at the Conference had nicknamed us "the Argenteenagers"!)

The annual Conference of WFUNA – the World Federation of United Nations Associations – was meeting in the building of the International Labour Office. I enjoyed all this very much, and thought it would be lovely to have a job in Geneva. Then, at one of the evening receptions, I met, for the first time in my life, a black African.

He was a Sierra Leonean, by name Solomon Pratt, who in fact worked at the ILO. He must have been good at whatever he did because (Sierra Leone not being yet independent) he was part of the British geographical contingent. In any case he looked very splendid in his blue and white robes, and the following conversation took place:

"I understand – I have heard – that you would be interested in a job in Geneva?"

"Yes, I would."

"And I hear also that you have four European languages at your command? And I have heard also that you are an Oxford graduate, is that true?"

"Yes, that is also true."

"What was your subject?"

"English Literature and Language."

"Well," said Solomon, "I work at the International Labour Office here" (he had in fact taken a few days out of his annual holiday to represent his country at this Conference). "You realise, of course, that we can't offer you a job in English Literature. But if you are prepared to take another job, why don't you come to my office tomorrow morning, before the meetings start, and we'll see what we can do."

So, the following morning at nine I was in his office and he dictated to a typist, and made me sign, a letter brilliant in its simplicity, which I would never have had the nerve to compose.

"To the Chief of Personnel:
Dear Sir
I am 22 years old, a recent Oxford Honours Graduate and I speak, read and write fluent English, French, Spanish and German. Can you offer me a job?
Yours faithfully..."

Solomon got this typed, made me sign it, and then carried it off in his own hands and placed it on the desk of the Chief of Personnel, thus bypassing all the personal assistants and secretaries whose business it is to protect a chief of personnel from just such demands. Three weeks later the ILO did offer me a three-month job! It was to do research in vocational training, not something I knew anything about. They were quite up front about it, telling me at once that this was a supernumerary job and that it wouldn't last forever. It did in fact last for five and a half months, which was decent of them; and while I was there I received my first, indeed my only, training in simultaneous interpreting.

I don't know what actually goes on at interpreting schools, since I never went to one. But what the ILO did for their younger polyglot staff was to put each of us in an interpreting booth, have somebody read us a speech (not too fast) for us to translate, and somebody else, an experienced interpreter, listen and offer constructive criticism, like "You did all right, but you got a little lost at the point where such and such." It still seems to me an excellent way to teach interpreting, indeed I can think of no other.

When my contract with the ILO came to an end, I started going around Geneva telling people I was a simultaneous interpreter. The first question was always: "What interpreting school did you go to?"

To which the answer was "I never went to one."

The second question was "Ah, yes, and what experience have you got?"

"Well, I did do the ILO Staff Union one evening, after work, when the normal interpreters were off."

"Ah, thank you! Don't ring us, we'll ring you."

And of course I filled in all the forms there were to fill at every one of the international organisations.

Meanwhile, in that same year of 1953, my family moved from Buenos Aires to Geneva! My father didn't really like Perón any better than he had liked European dictators; though, as he occasionally pointed out, in Argentina one was less likely to be persecuted – not only because the dictatorship lacked Germanic efficiency, but because people were more interested in each other than in politics. He would instance the attitude of the top male nurse at his own Government psychiatric ward: the nurse was a good Peronist, yet my father's ward was the only one in that hospital without a portrait of Our Dear Leader hanging on the wall – not because my father had refused it, but because the nurse had not wished to embarrass him, and had therefore dissuaded the distributor of portraits from presenting it to him.

However, my father, then already Professor of Psychiatry at Buenos Aires University, had noticed that the young doctors he taught seemed peculiarly unlikely to get decent jobs. What with one thing and another, it seemed best to move to Geneva, where he already had a daughter, and which was, moreover, the seat of the World Health Organisation. So over they came – he and my mother, with 17-year-old Trixie and Tommy aged nine, and took a furnished flat.

My father then spent the next two years or so writing the first volume of what was to be his psychiatry textbook, while he waited for the job he wanted to become vacant. When it eventually did so, he became head of WHO's Mental Health Department (possibly assisted by the UN's "rules of geographical distribution", which decreed that not all plum jobs should go to Europeans or North Americans: he having long since acquired Argentine nationality, WHO – a UN Specialised Agency and therefore bound by these rules – was, so to speak, getting a good pre-Hitler-German-trained psychiatrist for the price of an Argentine!)

The family then moved to more permanent accommodation, and my father stayed in that WHO job till his dying day, or very nearly. He valued it for many reasons: one was, that anything he now said about mental health was bound to be noticed by the world at large! And he had a few unfashionable things he felt needed saying. He was, for instance, against the idea (I'm afraid still in vogue) that in order to be mentally healthy you had to be cheerful, to "feel good". No! – you did not always have to feel good: often enough, as in bereavement, or in certain political circumstances, the healthy thing was to feel bad. "And now," he said to me, "I can actually say this kind of thing and people will listen!"

He also enjoyed the chance to travel, forging links with related disciplines and forming links of friendship, for instance with a Nigerian psychiatrist interested in "native healers". Every so often, he would convene a conference of some kind, and could ask whom he wished – such as, for instance Margaret Mead, whose work he had read, so long ago, in Buenos Aires.

The rest of the family adjusted as best they could to this new situation. My mother was not best pleased that she could no longer be her husband's indispensable secretary, since WHO provided their own; she responded, rather admirably, by asking these young ladies to "a good meal in a family home" and befriending them. Trixie, who had not wanted to come to Geneva at all but who had, unlike me, learnt typing and shorthand in four languages, soon found a job with Rolex the watchmakers; and, when she resigned from this (because annual holidays were too strictly regulated) got a rather better one, as secretary to the boss of a World Touring Organisation, which offered her plenty of interesting travel of her own. Tommy was sent to the Geneva International School.

As for me, I retained my own small furnished flat, and thus my independence. I wasn't at all sure I wanted this: I remember feeling rather excluded. But I was certainly not going to ask to be received back into the bosom of the family!

Meanwhile on the interpreting front, I decided that the one thing I could really do for myself, having already filled in all those forms, was to take myself once a week to the old Palais des Nations, to the Journalists' Bar – frequented by all sorts of people other than journalists – and order a coffee. I would make it last for as long as possible while I read a fairly highbrow paper – *The Times* or *The Guardian* or *Le Monde* – to make it quite clear that I was *not* after a job in the typing pool. On one occasion, when I could not make the cold coffee last any longer, I was just leaving, when there passed by the Chief Interpreter of the United Nations Geneva, a Frenchman whose name was Confino.

"Ah Mademoiselle Krapf, are you free at the moment?" Free? I was down to my last 50 francs.

"Yes, Monsieur Confino, I am."

"Right, follow me. You do English and Spanish don't you?" I followed him down some rather Kafkaesque underground corridors and in the middle he stopped and said "You have work for three weeks", which, as far as I was concerned, was the end of the horizon. "But," he said, "I think I'd better tell you now that during these three weeks your boss is going to be a Jesuit."

"Monsieur Confino, don't worry about it, I am quite used to them!" said I. Thinking back, I believe Confino was probably a Jew, and a little scared of Jesuits.

I was taken to a small office where the tallest and handsomest priest you ever saw in your life shook my hand, looked deep into my eyes and said: "Ah, Mademoiselle, I have always believed in Divine Providence."

"So have I, Father!"

I was hired.

I have to say my financial situation was not quite as desperate as I have made it sound: I could have turned to my parents, but I was trying to dodge that. Instead I rang up: "Mummy, mummy, I've got a job! – and I'm in love with my boss – but it's quite all right, he's a Jesuit!"

Father De Breuvery was not only a great charmer, but a very remarkable man in his own right. An economist by training, he had been Rector of the Catholic University in Shanghai where he absorbed much about Chinese language and culture. When the Communists came, they had their troubles getting rid of him because he was too popular among the students, but in the end they did manage it peacefully enough. He fetched up in Japan, where the UN in its Far Eastern branch (ECAFE) got hold of him. He was now an International Civil Servant like any other, based in New York. He had only come to Geneva for this little meeting, which consisted essentially of English-speaking engineers, with one Chilean delegate who had no English (and was the reason for my presence). The discussion was about the remaining stocks of iron ore in the world.

This little committee, perhaps eight or so in all, would have their luncheon every day at the Delegates' Restaurant on the top floor of the Palais, a beautiful place with a wonderful view (on the right sort of day) of Mont Blanc, and very good food – and of course very expensive. However, one has one's pride, and the first time I did try to hunt in my handbag for such money as I had. Father De Breuvery said "Put that back, put it *back* I tell you! Don't argue, you're not here to argue. You're here to interpret!" In other words he saw to it that I had a really decent lunch on the house every day. He also saw to it that during those three weeks I was presented, by him, to all the important people in the interpreting world in the Palais des Nations in Geneva. And I got a very good write-up signed, not by him of course, but by the President of the little committee.

We remained on very friendly terms, though I have only seen him once since. I knew he had gone to Africa. Years later, when my husband Hasan Askari and I were living in Nigeria, I took on an interpreting job, on something or other medical, in the country then known as Dahomey – but whether it was in Cotonou or Porto-Novo had not been made clear in my contract. (Porto-Novo is the one that is *not* a port, Cotonou is.) So Hasan drove me first to Porto-Novo but nobody there seemed to know about this medical conference. So we went on to Cotonou, and at the Beach Hotel were told yes, well, there *was* an international conference and that gentleman over *there* seemed to know about it.

The gentleman over there was Father De Breuvery! He and I were at once locked in a warm embrace. He was indeed there with an international conference too, but his was on, as far as I remember, hydrology; he had once had a part trying to "rationalise" the River MeKong in Asia. He directed us back to Porto-Novo where I did find my conference in the end.

The government of Dahomey, very sensibly, combined both conferences in a single official dinner, at which Father De Breuvery and I managed to sit next to each other. He said to me, among other things, "You know, that Muslim husband of yours, he must have thought it a little odd to find you embracing a priest, didn't he?" I said Hasan was by this time quite used to me. I found out many years later that a dear friend of mine nowadays, an Indian, Jain by origin, had also had a United Nations career, much of it in New York. Who was his best friend there? One Father De Breuvery, naturally.

So that little iron ore committee was the real beginning of free-lance interpreting for me. I was then told that outside the Palais des Nations, I *must* see Mademoiselle Ginsberg. So I did go and see this lady and was, I suppose, interviewed.

Who was Mademoiselle Ginsberg? Well, I had seen her interpreting, with much flair and drama, at a committee during that first WFUNA conference. She was by origin Polish/Jewish, and had been a librarian for the League of Nations. She had managed to get away to America before the Second World War, together with her mother.

The Ginsbergs had been wealthy people in Lodz, and Marie's mother had been in the habit of having a hairdresser come every day to the house and do her hair while she read the newspaper. On one occasion the normal hairdresser was not well, so they sent a young apprentice; Madame Ginsberg read her newspaper, and when she looked up into the mirror, found herself transformed.

"What is your name, young man?"

"Antoine, Madam."

"Well Antoine, you seem to me worth training. I am now going to send you to Paris for just that."

When mother and daughter arrived in New York, they hadn't got many pennies to bless themselves with, but a good impression was felt to be important, so they spent their first night or two at the Ritz. The morning after their arrival there was the most enormous vestibuleful of flowers beside their room with the card of Antoine – by now the greatest hairdresser in New York – who made it his business to know who was arriving at the Ritz, and recognised the name of his generous patroness. He had sent them all these flowers, and now engaged mother and daughter to ghost-write his autobiography, which kept them going for quite a while.

Eventually, after the war, Marie bought some simultaneous-interpreting equipment and created a company which she called Simulta. She also got herself named as the American representative in Geneva of I forget which feminist organisation, because it was then (and perhaps still is) the law of the United States that if you are a naturalised citizen, you have to continue living there, or at least must not return to the country of your previous nationality – I think Marie had acquired Swiss nationality. But as she was representing Whatever-it-Was, and as her address in Geneva was "only" the European office of Simulta, which had a nominal office in New York, that was all right.

So now I was interviewed by her, largely I think about my politics and those of my parents; after which Marie would employ me once in a while. She operated from a paper-strewn office in her small flat, which she shared with another Polish lady, whom I never met. Marie said "The one thing we have in common is that we both like lemon tea at three in the morning." She herself wore out two or three secretaries a year, not because she treated them badly, but because, as she once put it: *Je ne travaille bien que dans la pagaille* – "I can only work well in a real shambles".

INTERLUDE 1

On Interpreting, and Interpreters

Interpreting – the "portable skill" with which I earned my living over the next few years – is not the same thing as translation. Both require a good knowledge of languages; but while translation deals with written documents, interpreting is purely oral, and tends to happen mainly at conferences; which is why our trade union is called the International Association of *Conference* Interpreters. The two professions do appeal to two very different personalities: a translator is somebody who has to get things *exactly* right, sometimes taking quite a long time to do so. An interpreter has to produce his or her oral version *fast*; must therefore be rather quick on the uptake, and not too fussy about getting things *totally* accurate. It also helps to be a bit of a show-off! I am, by temperament, very much an interpreter. I can and do translate when required, but don't enjoy it as much.

Something that may have helped me be a good interpreter is that, in my earliest primary school days, I often had to give oral presentations in class. When we first learned to read, we would be taught to stand up in front of the class, hold the book in the left hand, and at the end of each sentence, at each full stop, raise our eyes to the audience. We were also expected to recite poetry. I had a good memory and learnt it very easily, and would happily get up and recite for the (very small) class. I remember at one stage I learnt the entire Argentine National Anthem (only a small piece of which is ever sung the whole thing is nine long stanzas). I was supposed to get up and recite the lot, but unfortunately I got the hiccups – so I went "*Libertad*-hic, *Libertad*-hic; *Libertad*-hic!" whereupon the class collapsed in laughter.

Interpreting: Simultaneous

The kind of conference interpreting I had been taught at the ILO is the type known as "simultaneous", which, with its microphones and earphones, is quite dazzling to people who know nothing about it. It is in fact a parrot's trick: you can either do it, or you can't, like wiggling your ears. I can't wiggle my ears, but I can do simultaneous interpretation. If you are born with the gift (and have the languages), it's not in fact difficult.

I should explain a little about the basic technique. For a start, you wear earphones, through which you hear the delegate's voice. You're sitting in a booth – usually two of you. Union rules say that there should be two at all times; but of course, if you know each other well, quite often whoever's taking a rest, goes out and has a cup of coffee and a fag, or whatever. I once did a long International Telecommunications (ITU) conference with Ángel Sifre. He and I trusted each other and if I wanted to spend the afternoon at the hairdresser's I could, and if he wanted a morning off, he could have it. But, by and large, there are supposed to be two of you. You have either one or two microphones; if you have one, you have to pass it to each other, and all this is connected in some way, so that the delegates, if they have their earphones on, hear you and not the speaker, just as you hear them when they use the mike. Sometimes interpreters have to interpret from each other: I, for instance, have no Russian, so if I am interpreting into Spanish at a meeting where Russian is spoken, I would first find out who is in the French and English booths. If both also speak Russian, I will take it from either. If only one of them does, then that one person is absolutely vital – he or she is the "pivot", and we all take it from the pivot. But this is less satisfactory than interpretation direct from the speaker.

Getting the hang of things, however, wasn't at first very easy. My main selling point as a fledgling interpreter was that I was then one of the few people, perhaps even the only one, who could interpret direct from German into Spanish, though not the other way round. So I was made to do that, and very hard work it was! I learned eventually that if I kept up with the newspapers I *could* guess the verb at the end of the sentence, but if it was science, I had no way of guessing whether that verb was not preceded by a nasty little *nicht*, in other words, whether the patient had or had not recovered, or whether the experiment had or had not proved whatever it was. So, even at a later stage when I was doing it mostly into English, I tended to say "Such and such a thing; this is what does *not* happen", or rather "the opposite is the case!" I remember an English colleague, who did English, French – and German. Nancy was a very good interpreter indeed: she was capable of following what the delegate was saying a whole sentence behind, and remembering it. So she always got it right, and then only had to hurry the last sentence a bit.

Most English-speaking delegates were very good about such problems; I was lucky enough not to have to sit in the French booth. French delegates are said – and I believe it – to be exceedingly fussy about what they themselves call *l'imparfait du subjonctif*, the past imperfect tense of the subjunctive mood. They complain if the interpreter gets the syntax even slightly wrong.

At any meeting, you do as an interpreter have to remember to turn the mike on when a delegate is speaking, and off when you're making rude remarks about him, or another! Though occasionally, if you've come to know delegates fairly well, it's possible to have a joke with them – as when, during that interminable ITU conference, I used to start off each morning, in Spanish: *LRX y LR1, Radio El Mundo de Buenos Aires* – a long-ago radio-station signal which made the Argentine delegation look up at my booth and grin. The same delegates once complained to me about one of our newer colleagues, whom I had listened to and found to do quite nicely – what they didn't like was that she spoke in a dull monotone. Even simultaneous interpreting continues to be very much a living thing.

Simultaneous is far, however, from engaging all your mental faculties. I remember when I was sitting with Ángel towards the end of a working day, we used to do the *Herald Tribune* crossword together – in theory, the one of us that was "resting" would do it, but sometimes whoever was speaking had a bright idea and pencilled it in. But that was the ITU conference which had gone on forever and we both knew the stuff by heart.

At one point – several points – there would be among interpreters a sort of humorous panic – all translation would shortly be done by computers, we'd all be out of a job! A witty colleague once said this would never happen, because when the delegate says "I can" the computer will undoubtedly say "*Je peux*" but the speaker might have meant "*Moi, boîte de conserve*". There used also to be a lot of jokes about things being translated and then translated back by machines. For instance, what does "invisible idiot" mean? "Out of sight, out of mind!" And there were others of the same sort. But that total computer takeover has not yet happened: I have several former colleagues still interpreting, and seem to be doing it in much the same way as ever. And I myself wasn't much worse when I first interpreted than I was the last time I ever did so. It *is* a natural talent, and some people have it and some haven't.

My friend Kenneth Syers, on the other hand, was by temperament a translator. I first met him behind the booths at some conference – the one and only time he tried interpreting. What he was like at it I don't know, since I didn't listen to him. But he hated doing it, and decided then and there not to do it again, but to continue making his living by doing scientific translations. He knew several Eastern European languages, and at that time science was beginning to come in from the Soviet Union. Kenneth was the sort of person who didn't in the slightest mind reading a couple of books and ringing up a couple of scientific friends to make sure he'd got it right. He worked from home, slowly but exceedingly well, and was able to charge a good deal for his work, unlike the poor little Russian refugees who in those days did non-scientific translation. In those pre-computer days, Kenneth would dictate his stuff, complete with punctuation – I've heard him do it – and then send the resulting tapes off to various typists in the outer suburbs of London, who would then send back the completed typescripts.

Once, I arrived at his flat when he was still working. He emerged from his study quite excited: "Can you help? I'm doing something from French. How would you put Such-and-Such in English?" I suggested something. "No, that's not quite right in this context because ..." I made several other suggestions; after about the fourth I got bored and said "Kenneth, for heaven's sake, I've given you four perfectly decent translations – surely you can use one of them?" and he looked at me with the utmost contempt and said "*Interpreter!*"

Simultaneous interpreting has, incidentally, very little to do with brains or thought most of the time. I have had some very intelligent colleagues, and also some dull ones; but if they had the gift they had it. Simultaneous, so dazzling to the uninitiated, is in fact easy: anyone who has the languages can say "Mr Chairman, Ladies and Gentlemen," and go on from there. Every so often, however, there's a hitch – not usually about technical terms (you can mug those up in advance); but if someone uses a proverb, you have to find the equivalent in another language, and do it *fast.* There was a famous story (I didn't in fact witness this myself), about an ILO Annual Conference, at which the chief Soviet delegate, replying to his American counterpart, had – as Russians are apt to do – used some proverbial expression, and whoever was in the English booth said "I can't help feeling, Mr Chairman, that there's a nigger in the woodpile somewhere." It hadn't occurred to anyone that the head of the American Government delegation had what today would be called African-American forebears: he was light-skinned, and his hair not particularly kinky. But he *did* have this family background and, feeling himself personally insulted, indignantly said so. The poor Russian had no idea what he had said that was personally insulting – he had meant to disagree, but quite politely.

Interpreting: Consecutive

The really difficult form of interpreting is the consecutive kind, which of course goes back to the League of Nations days before the technology for simultaneous interpretation had been invented. In this context, your delegate makes a speech (or, if you are lucky, part of a speech). You can take notes; I am told it is fatal to do so in shorthand – fortunately I never managed to learn it – for, if you do, you will then have to read out your English shorthand notes in Spanish or French. So you invent your own system of note-taking and abbreviation – for instance, for countries, I use what is on car bumpers – CH for Switzerland and so on.

Kenneth, with his love of translation, had also in his day done a good deal of adult education. Our friendship matured during the period when I was thinking of maybe returning to university, but was not sure that I wasn't, in my late twenties, a bit too old for it, too set in my mental ways; so Kenneth gave me a test. He said "All right, you tell me you can do consecutive interpreting. Don't bother to change the language; but I am going to read you an article and you can give me a summary afterwards." So he read me an article, I think it was about science fiction (of which he was rather fond) and then stopped. I rendered what he had said, in the original English, and he said "Right, show me your notes," so I showed him my notes, and he said "Well I don't understand a word of these scribbles but you clearly do. So that's quite all right, you can go back to university."

If you're having to do *consecutive* interpretation, you really do have to know what it's about, as I found out over the years. And thank heavens I did, because of the nine months I spent in Vietnam, where they had no equipment for simultaneous; it was all consecutive, as between English and French. The worst is when some delegates think they know the language. Somebody said in French, one of the Poles I think, "*Monsieur le Président, je me demande si...*" which I translated, I still think quite accurately, as "Mr. Chairman, I wonder whether.." and he said, "No, no, no, *not* 'I wonder' (in a heavy accent), '*I ask myself*'....")

There is also the problem of how far you should reproduce the emotions your delegate may display. I once had to do a speech by a Latin American who had known Woodrow Wilson, on some kind of anniversary of Wilson's death. He went (genuinely I think) very emotional, and said that *nobody* who had lived at that time could help but remember the idealism etc, etc, of Woodrow Wilson. At one point he broke down, and had to sit down. I had to get up and do it after him. Well, there are two ways of doing this. Either you do it cold, and say "At this point the delegate interrupted himself", or you can do what I did, which was to do a Marie Ginsberg, speaking as dramatically as possible and say at the end "Gentlemen; I *cannot* continue!" and sit down again.

At one point, in some discussion between the wars, the English – or British – delegate had adorned his speech with quite a long quotation from Hamlet's monologue "To be, nor not to be, that is the question." The French delegates, ever anxious to detect errors in interpretation, promptly put on their earphones to see what on earth the interpreter was going to make of that. The interpreter happened to be a personal friend of André Gide, who was at the time translating Hamlet into French. He also, having spent the previous night with Gide, happened to have a good memory, and remembered what Gide had said about how he had turned the famous monologue into French; so he quite simply recited Gide's *Hamlet.* I don't know whether this story's true, but it has gone down the generations of interpreters.

There is also another story from League of Nations days, in which the French-speaking chairman said: "Gentlemen, having begun to consider all these very important matters, I feel the time may have come when we need a certain amount of reflection, perhaps even relaxation, before we continue to discuss these grave problems" – he said all this in French, which was interpreted into English as: "The Chairman says it's time for lunch."

I sometimes found myself interpreting at psycho-analytical conferences, where occasionally my father was present. At one of these (though he was not actually there) I committed the worst crime known to a simultaneous interpreter. For once in my life I'd done my homework, because I knew a lot of people were going to be there whom I knew and so did my parents, and I didn't want to make a fool of myself. So I had read up on the subject and asked a few questions and so on.

When I got there, one of those present was Ángel Garma, the anti-Franco refugee who had done my father's "didactic analysis" back in the 1940s. Ángel had spent some time in Paris before he went to Argentina. He had that characteristic of many Spaniards, at least in the old days: he *could not* speak foreign languages. (Spaniards seldom could, they were much, much worse than the English who only *think* they are bad.) He had a go at one point – speaking something that may or may not have been an attempt at French. My French-language colleagues came to me (I was in the Spanish booth) and said "Look Eva, you know this man, don't you? Do you think you could possibly ask him to speak Spanish and then you could run into the English booth and do him from Spanish into English, and we'd take it from you?" In other words, I was to be "pivot" in the English booth, for the benefit of my non-Spanish-speaking colleagues.

I went to Garma and I explained, very politely and tactfully, "Look Ángel, it is easier for us if people speak their own native language; we are equipped to deal with it. "*Si, si, si, claro....*" So came the great event of that week – a symposium on what was at the time an almost unmentionable subject: *Homosexuality*. (This all happened a long time ago – the late 'fifties I think.)

So when Ángel Garma rises to speak, I rush into the English booth. He is saying (in Spanish) that in all the countries in which he has worked as a psychoanalyst, it has always been the case that homosexuals do such and such, or avoid so and so, I can't remember – and I, somewhat out of breath, say in English: "and in all the countries in which I have ever worked as a homosexual..." Of course, the house came down! Poor old Garma didn't know what on earth he'd said that was so funny, and just went on saying "*Si, si, si...*" and so on, and my colleague was killing himself in his corner of the booth. I had the decency to say that the Freudian slip had not been the speaker's but the interpreter's, which got me another laugh.

But at the end of that session, I thought, *Now, this is a family friend, he's done my father's didactic analysis, he's done my mother, he even did me for a few months. I cannot let him hear this from other people, I must go and apologise in person.*

Have you every tried to apologise for a Freudian slip to a very nice, but somewhat blinkered Freudian psychoanalyst? He *was* very polite about it – "*No importa, Eva*", but I'm sure that if he ever thought about me, to his dying day he must have thought I had something against him, or else maybe really think he was a homosexual, and he was – well a bit of an exhibitionist about his heterosexuality. Legend had it that he had a mirror on the ceiling of his bedroom. I've never been to his bedroom, so I don't actually know.

But for the rest of that Congress, at receptions, I was the most popular creature imaginable; Garma was a rather senior psychoanalyst – and he and various other people (it was felt by the younger ones) were hogging the show. So people would come up to me at drinks parties and say "Was it you who said that *wonderful* thing about homosexuals?"

Years later, in London, I told this story, which I have always considered funny, to one of my younger colleagues, who looked at me in wonder and said, "You know, you must be quite popular in the profession, because I have heard of this story before, but not about you!" So I said "Well, I can assure you that it was I that did it!"

Interpreters

In the 1950s, we interpreters were a distinctly odd bunch. The era was only just beginning when interpreting was regarded as a suitable job for young ladies of good family who had been to interpreting school. (After all, at that stage, the people who taught at interpreting schools had never been to one either!) Our lot were partly interpreters from "before-before" (meaning before the Second World War); and then there were Russian refugees and anti-Franco refugees, as well as various young men from Latin American countries who, while not quite refugees, found it pleasanter to live abroad rather than under their several dictatorships. A fair sprinkling of homosexuals, Jews of all nations, and quite a number of assorted eccentrics – a motley crew. Between ourselves we spoke to each other in the old diplomatic language, French, and we referred to our trade as *la profession*, rather as diplomats used to talk about *la carrière* (and Catholics about "the Church", and Communists about "the Party", as if there were no other.)

So in *la profession* there were all these varieties of people. But all of us did have much the same problems about who was paid how much by whom; so, at about this time, a trade union was formed. Of course it was not called a union, we were after all *la profession!* – it is still, I believe, called the International Association of Conference Interpreters. The French initials – because, naturally, it was known by its French initials – were AIIC, pronounced "AYIC"; and I was actually *asked* to join it, which I gladly did. (At a later stage, you had to have so-and-so many days' working experience to be even *considered* for AIIC.) Members appeared, naturally, in the Handbook, so that potential employers could choose whether your particular language combination suited them.

Languages were divided, in the AIIC classification, into A, B, and C. "A" was your own language, or one you spoke as your own; "B" a language you spoke really quite well and could interpret into at need, but would sooner not; and "C" a language you professed merely to understand. I was fortunate in having two A languages, English and Spanish. My French was B; my German, in which I had never had a lesson, C. On that, I managed quite well. Of course problems varied as you switched from one language to another. It is easier to interpret from Spanish and French into English than the other way round, for example, simply because those Latin languages have longer words. I have quite often been told later in life that I speak very fast, and I think to some extent this is what interpreters themselves recognise as a *déformation professionelle*, an effect that comes from long practice at the job itself.

There were a very few interpreters who had only two languages, usually both A. Some of the older ones, from League of Nations days, had simply English and French. For more recent interpreters, if you were going to have only two languages, one of them had to be Russian. We did not yet have any Soviet colleagues – this happened only later; so these bilinguals were all refugees. I have been told that in the Russian booth, it was a matter of etiquette of some importance that Prince or Princess So-and-So took the microphone before people who were mere Counts or Countesses. Commoners, never mind Jews, were naturally at the bottom end of the hierarchy. This was not so in the Spanish booth.

There were, at the time, two actual dynasties of interpreters, both of Eastern European origin. The more important and older one was that of the Rabinovitches, one brother and two sisters. The brother was Chief Interpreter at the United Nations in New York, no less. The sisters, who both operated under their married names, Lydia Kerr and Nina Himly, lived in Geneva. Although the ILO didn't officially have such a position, Lydia was pretty near to being its Chief Interpreter. She was often known as the Grand Duchess, because of the way she bore herself, and her imposing silver-grey hair.

Lydia was always exceedingly good to me. She did not think of herself primarily as an interpreter, or as an International Civil Servant, but as a poet, which indeed she was. She had several published volumes of really rather good, though minor, poetry. I began to visit Lydia quite frequently at her house, which was not very far from mine. Soon after I began these visits, she asked me to address her as *tu*; this I found extremely difficult, because I revered her so deeply; but if Lydia wanted it, Lydia should have it and so we were on *tu* terms thereafter. Her sister Nina, the madcap of the family, I found much easier to call *tu;* she was one of the people to whom Father De Breuvery had got me introduced, when he took charge of my career, all those years earlier, at the United Nations.

The younger dynasty of interpreters, the Seleskovitches, came, I believe, from Serbia. There was a brother and sister, Zoran and Danitsa. Zoran was married to a Frenchwoman whom I never met, but who was also a Seleskovitch, even if only by marriage. They were all very good and they rather dominated their generation, as the Rabinovitches did the older one.

AIIC, in its real capacity as a union, got us what were at that time very good rates, $25 a day plus travel and *per diem* expenses. However, this did not make us rich, because nobody, but *nobody*, among freelance interpreters got work all the year round. You were lucky if you got 200 days! Most of us, approximately successful, managed between 100 and 200, depending a bit on which year it was. One colleague of mine, who disliked interpreting very much (as many of us did) once said to me: "You know why we are in this beastly profession? Because it gives us the illusion of being rich and the illusion of being free!" True enough: we *did* have the illusion of being free, because we ran around so much; but it wasn't usually travel as one would like it. I remember rushing from one European capital city to another in the summer, and in each of these cities I would get to know the hotel I was staying at, the conference venue, wherever it was they held evening receptions – and the airport of course! If I was lucky and had an afternoon off, I might also have got to know *one* of the museums or picture galleries. This is *not* how one wishes to travel; but the next day I would already have to be in Helsinki or somewhere; and so it went. One could not afford to refuse jobs: the summer conference season was short.

I have spoken already about the incapacity of the older generation of Spaniards to speak foreign languages. They were well-read people, and could understand *all* the jokes in the Paris satirical weekly, *Le Canard Enchaîné*; but French pronunciation defeated them.

There were exceptions, such as Ángel Sifre y Fernández de Córdoba (whom I have already mentioned). Through his second surname (his mother's surname, as is usual in Spanish-speaking countries), Ángel was in fact a Grandee of Spain; and he came across very much as that. He was extremely good looking, with the most delightful manners imaginable. I am told that he once said of me, "Eva is a gentleman," and I took this as the greatest possible compliment in his power to pay me. He lived in a beautiful, exquisitely appointed little flat in Geneva's "old town" and had, of course, a manservant. He once confessed to me that in an ideal world he would have liked to have had dwarf servants, such as the Infantas of Spain are portrayed as having in some of Velasquez' portraits, but his was just a manservant, who kept the place exquisite.

Ángel was a great friend of Lydia Kerr's, with whom he shared a taste for poetry, and also a friend of her son Sebastian. (I know, or guess, that Lydia rather coveted me as a daughter-in-law and sent me out with Sebastian a couple of times. We were perfectly amiable to each other but it never came to anything whatsoever.) Ángel and Lydia, though, had a number of shared certain tastes; but once he said to me:

"You know, Lydia has no taste whatsoever."

"Oh," said I, "what can you mean by that?"

"Well, I mean *no* taste, which is much better than having bad taste."

"What can you mean, Ángel?"

"I mean that sometimes she is quite beautifully dressed and at other times dowdy. If she had bad taste she would always try to be beautifully dressed and get it wrong. As it is, she gets it right quite a bit of the time, by accident."

Ángel was very hospitable: I was often invited to a meal or a drink at his beautiful flat. I had by this time a rather nice one-room flat of my own. The one room was very large; it was the attic of an oldish house and therefore had a great many corners and nooks; I enjoyed furnishing it. I remember some good advice Ángel gave me: "Now, you are not a tidy woman and you never will be. What you need to do is get yourself quite a large table, preferably round, cover it with a large plain tablecloth, and on that you will put a vase of flowers, a bowl of fruit, and some magazines – and then when you return from downtown and dump all your shopping on the table, it will just look like part of the decoration."

I took this very good advice, and have followed it ever since.

At that time, however, I felt I should invite Ángel to lunch. I was very, very careful to remove all the bits and bobs off that table, and to lay the table and to arrange a meal I knew I could deal with – and what did I do, but forget the forks? Ángel of course said oh, it didn't matter in the slightest, but I felt it for quite a while afterwards.

Ángel also made friends, as did some of his companions, with somebody new in the profession, one Eugenia Wolfowicz; quite famous nowadays but in another capacity. Eugenia Wolfowicz, who will not allow herself to be called anything else and it always has to be pronounced *as in Spanish*, is a compatriot of mine from Argentina, rather younger than I, and had to leave Argentina (I think) for political reasons. She took herself off to the United States where she got a job as a maid and learned English while doing so; and saved enough money to get herself to France. There, she managed to get herself an extremely junior maid-type job at UNESCO in Paris; sought permission – which she was granted – to use any empty booths in UNESCO conference rooms to speak into a disconnected microphone – to practise interpreting; and turned out to be another born interpreter! One fine day, the inevitable happened: somebody fell ill or fainted or whatever; Eugenia had to fill in and did so very creditably. I first met her at that interminable ITU Conference where Ángel and I worked together in the booth. Sometimes, however, I worked with Eugenia; my boyfriend of the period told me that there was a new young interpreter, very shy, so that I should be nice to her. So I was nice to her and have tried to be ever since.

Eugenia was, and is, rather pretty, but physically tiny. A few years after all this, by which time I think she was already living in Italy, she decided that what she really wanted to do in life was sculpt: she has done so ever since, very successfully, though she does grumble: Eugenia was always one for dense gloom. She grumbles, she complains, nothing is ever good enough; however she is in fact a highly talented sculptor and is recognised as such. Both the city of Paris and that of Florence have bought sculptures from her, which doesn't, after all, happen to everybody.

She now lives near Carrara, where Michelangelo used to get his marble, because – while she can and does, herself, live off the smell of an old oil rag (as another old friend used to say) – she does have very expensive tastes in marble, which has to be the absolute best. So she lives near Carrara in some kind of broken-down shelter; but does also have a flat in Paris which she herself reconstructed out of a bicycle shed and which she lets out when she can. I have in my Hamsey garden a sculpture of Eugenia's, which I chose myself; I wish now I had chosen one of her tombstone-like efforts in Carrara marble but I didn't quite see what that would be doing in my garden. At one point I had asked Eugenia, who of course is always broke, whether I could help in any way and she said "Well yes, as a matter of fact you can! You could buy a sculpture from me; I would love to give you one but I really can't afford to – but if you come to my place you can choose one." So I could and did; I chose one which she calls *Partenza*, departure, depicting a bird on the point of flight, and that is what sits in the middle of my garden. Eugenia herself brought it here – quite how she lifts those heavy weights I have no idea; she is obviously less frail than she looks.

Ángel befriended her, as did his mates. They kept trying to find her some kind of permanent lover but as far as I know it didn't work; Eugenia, so eloquent on the subject of all her economic and professional misfortunes, is less so on her private life.

There were also interpreters based outside Geneva, largely in Paris of course; in England there was something called the Linguists' Club which, among its many other activities, dealt with any interpreting that had to be done in or from England. Its founder and president was one Teddy Pilley, another man who was kind to Eugenia, though he did insist on calling her Genia (pronounced "Jenya"), which she didn't like.

However, Teddy Pilley himself was not born Teddy Pilley, but Tadeusz Pilekowski. Like so many other people I seem to know, Teddy was by origin a Polish Jew. But he had lived in England a long time and spoke English, as they say, like a native, as well as several other languages. He had a Dutch wife and it was said of him, that he once fell ill in some French-speaking country and was unconscious for a while. When he recovered consciousness, he addressed the nurse in French, his wife in Dutch and a concerned colleague in English, all in the first few sentences. I'm prepared to believe it.

Teddy was an extremely good interpreter, as well as a kindly man. It was always rather fun to go anywhere with him, a bit like taking a small dog for a walk (except that you were usually in his car) because he could not resist going into any highway or byway in order to see some church, some lake, some mountain he had heard of. So, in fact, one learned quite a lot, even if one was then somewhat late for whatever reception Teddy was going to. It is also said of him, that once in Vienna, he got himself into a reception to which interpreters had *not* been asked (which of course interpreters resent), with two of his female colleagues (one on each arm) and merely said at the door, very grandly: "*Ich bin Pilley!*" – I am Pilley – whereupon they let him in. He was not an impressive looking man, being small, bald, and plump, but he *was* Pilley. In England, most of the time he rushed around on a motorcycle, and it used to be said also that all his stories (and he had many) started with: "There I was on my motorcycle –" and ended with "and do you know, he was a member of the Linguists' Club!"

I continued working, of course, for the ILO as a free-lance and, through the agency of Nina Himly and others, also for various UN organisations, most of which were based in Geneva. And after that four-month ITU meeting at which Ángel Sifre and I did so many crossword puzzles, I was really quite flush. But the ILO, and other Geneva-based organisations, held shorter annual conferences.

These big meetings used to take place (and still do) in the Palais des Nations, originally built for the League of Nations – a huge one-storey building in its own park. During ILO Conferences, I quite frequently worked for a particular committee that met in something known as Room XV. Now Room XV was many miles of corridor from anywhere else: you had to walk quite a long way to get there. (Interpreters need to be punctual: delegates can be allowed to arrive late, but no meeting can start without interpreters.) However, in Room XV, only two people were always there on time, indeed a little before: one Mrs Calmann, and one Miss Krapf (myself). Mrs Calmann was considerably older than I. We both would take along detective stories to read while we waited. It quite soon came to the stage of exchanging detective stories, and *that* was the beginning of *that* beautiful friendship.

Lia Calmann had been born the daughter of wealthy, cultivated Russian Jews, somewhere in the west of the country. Her father was a grain merchant, successful enough to be allowed to go to both Moscow *and* St. Petersburg, which was by no means the case for all Russian Jews. I know they were not particularly observant; her mother did keep a *kosher* household, but that was only because she would not wish to have to refuse hospitality to any fellow Jew.

Lia once told me that as a young girl, she had, on the streets of Moscow, actually sold a Red Cross lottery ticket to Rasputin his very self; and that she had been present at the performance of *Boris Godunov* at which Chaliapin announced Rasputin's death and everybody cheered. She had been brought up, as such people were, to speak French, German, and English in addition to her native Russian. I think her father died before the Revolution; at any rate when it took place, she, her mother and her sister reached the Crimea only to be imprisoned; when the Germans arrived they were released. With her fluent German, Lia had the good luck to be offered a job as personal assistant to a key German officer. She did very good work: he trusted her to draft his letters and would sign anything she passed on to him. One morning she said: "Well, Comrade Commissar, the time has now come to take my leave, because you have just signed the exit visas for my mother, my sister and myself." He, being a decent man, did not stand in their way; and so they all left: – where to? Well the obvious place for Jews at that time, Berlin! – at that time the capital of the world for that kind of enlightened Jewry, and where, naturally enough, they had relatives.

In Berlin Lia trained as an architect, spent some time with the Bauhaus people, and married some cousin of hers. The marriage eventually collapsed, in the politest possible way. Lia opened a small antiquities shop (rather more her thing really than modern architecture); she was still there at the time of the explosion of anti-Jewish violence that became known as *Kristallnacht*. The following morning she was visited by two of her customers – aristrocratic Prussian ladies – who said: "Mrs Calmann, we are not actually intending to buy anything today, but we thought that on a morning such as this, we *should* pay you a visit" – which Lia remembered all her life.

Soon after that she left Berlin, and spent some time in Persia, as it then was. I don't quite know what her life was like there; but she eventually moved on to what was then still British India, where she made friends with an Englishwoman; the two ladies started a firm of interior decorators which, since the Englishwoman was the mistress of some Maharajah or other, got them a great many jobs in the palaces of a great many rajahs. This lasted a few years, but then Lia and the Englishwoman no longer got on so well, so Lia moved on to what had just become Israel. There in Israel she started a love affair, not this time with a cousin, but with a distant older relative, some vague kind of uncle. I can't remember whether I ever dared tease Lia about her exaggerated Jewish family sense, but at any rate, this relative was the love of her life. He had been quite high up among the founders of Israel, and was still prominent there.

Lia, however, didn't like Israel – too regimented, too rule-bound, and then it didn't help that somebody stole her jewels. So she moved again, with some help from a senior British civil servant, this time to London.

She was by now fifty or so and had her living to earn, so she worked as a salesgirl in Peter Jones; and her feet were *killing* her. At this point, some sensible person said: "Look my dear, you are a native Russian speaker, you are quite equally good at German, you have very decent English and French, your place is in an interpreting booth!" Such was the beginning of Lia's interpreting career. She was indeed extremely good – "A" in German and Russian, "B" in English and French. She was also the most cultivated person I have ever known: she knew everything – had read everything, she knew all the music, all the paintings. She did a great deal towards my education.

I missed my chance of meeting her "uncle" who remained in Israel (they never did marry). She once invited me to somewhere in Scandinavia, with "my old gentleman", as she called him by then; for some reason I couldn't or didn't, and I've always been rather sorry I never met him.

I continued to see a great deal of Lia in the late 1960s, after I had returned to Oxford for graduate studies, carried out field research in West Africa, and was living in London with a teaching job at the School of Oriental and African Studies (SOAS). I remember one party I held, at which she was present, and so was my friend Kenneth Syers. Kenneth, an English left-wing intellectual, had the tendency, common enough among such people, to run down his country as "bourgeois" and "colonialist" and all the rest of it. And Lia said very calmly: "Well you know, I have had five nationalities, of which British is only the last; but I do have to say, I prefer it to all the others." Kenneth, who – left-wing intellectual or not – was a gentleman, said: "Sorry. You know what you're talking about, and I don't", and shut up.

At an even later stage, after my marriage to Mick Gillies, I decided that since I was no longer be going travelling with Lia, I had best introduce her to June Stephenson, my staunch friend from those days as a graduate student in Oxford. I never did a better thing! Lia, who knew everything, did not however, know how to drive. June on the other hand is an extremely good driver and map-reader. So they went travelling together, and Lia introduced June to Renaissance art, on which she is now very knowledgeable.

In London, Lia had a very nice little flat in St John's Wood. I remember a wonderful engraving of a plant in her small entrance; she said "Well, that's the form in which I like to take pot." I also admired the carpet in the entrance hall. She said "Yes, quite nice; won't last very long; but then, it doesn't need to."

Very shortly after that she had a stroke, and was no longer able to speak, though she still could reason. She was looked after by a niece, who would make a list of things, like facewash, water, food, comb, etc, and put it in front of Lia and point, and Lia would get very cross if the unfortunate niece didn't get it right the first time or even the second; but this stage did not last very long. I went to visit her several times. Oddly and mercifully, she still enjoyed her food, so that I could take Lia something nice to eat. She always had enjoyed her food. I remember, during our interpreting years, going with her to restaurants: "Your car, my dinner", she would say, and so we would go to these restaurants, where quite often two lone women would not be given a very good table. Lia, of course, did the ordering in her impressive way, and after that, we were treated quite differently. We ordered the kind of food that women seldom did in those days, and Lia encouraged my own inherent tendency to over-tip, because she said most women under-tipped, and this gave us a bad reputation.

Lia eventually died, at a ripe old age, in London, in the 1970s. She had been suffering for some time from leukaemia, and at one stage decided that she was having to go to hospital so often that the quality of life was no longer worth it and she would renounce further hospital treatment. She did not do so until she had invited all her closer friends, including me, to tell them what she had done, and what she was proposing to do, and to bid us farewell. The thing that she said to me is “remember me”. Which I do.

PART THREE
GENEVA-HANOI-GENEVA

Chapter 1
Hanoi: The Armistice Commission

In the early 1950s when I was beginning to live as a free-lance interpreter, those of us who took an interest in international affairs were obsessed with the French war in Indochina, culminating in the sustained battle campaign against the French at Dien Bien Phu. Half a generation later, it is not surprising we were all obsessed again with the war against French colonial rule in Algeria, as well as with the American Vietnam War.

The *guerre d'Indochine* formally came to an end in 1954, shortly after Dien Bien Phu, at an international conference which took place in Geneva. It was held in the Palais des Nations, though not under the aegis of the United Nations. Two sponsors remained in the background, the United States and Russia. China was a participant, as (naturally) was France. And of course, for security reasons, no person *not* involved in the conference could be allowed into the Palais.

I was quite determined to get into the Palais; so I got Jaime Potenze, whom I had known from his involvement in my father's magazine *Orden Cristiano* back in Buenos Aires, to send me a journalist's ticket on behalf of that publication. This did get me into the Palais, but not much more than that – I can boast only that I have seen the top of Chou En-lai's head and also that of Georges Bidault; but then I became rather more casual about it. Indeed, when the Geneva Conference *did* end with the Geneva Agreement at last hammered out, I was not in Geneva at all, but in Zürich, at work, and heard about it on the hotel radio.

The Agreement had divided Vietnam into two parts, North and South. North Vietnam was Communist; South Vietnam was not. Its President, probably American-inspired – certainly French-inspired – was one Ngo Dinh Diem. The North was presided over by Ho Chi Minh, known to the locals as Uncle Ho. Ho Chi Minh had been a freedom fighter, *the* left-wing freedom fighter, though not originally Communist. He had been a photographer in Paris, was a highly educated man, and was now in charge of the North, which henceforth, was sometimes known in Europe and elsewhere as Vietminh rather than Vietnam. Vietminh was in fact the word used locally for the People's Army of North Vietnam.

The next thing I knew, they were trying to recruit interpreters and translators for the Armistice Commission (officially, the Intergovernmental Commission for Supervision and Control of the Armistice in Indochina, or ICSC). This Armistice Commission was well chosen, much better than the previous Korean one: it had India, as a neutral country, in the chair; representing the Eastern side, it had Poland, and on the Western side, Canada – two countries each solidly embedded in its own side, but neither of them fanatically so.

The Commission now wanted interpreters who would also act as translators, not from Vietnamese, but as between English and French. Back in Geneva, I promptly presented my candidature; this meant going to the Indian Consulate to be interviewed. I was asked *why* did I want to go to Vietnam. "Well, out of interest." "Yes, but – professional interest, political interest, or just a sense of adventure?" "All three," said I. "Well yes, but which predominates?" – and I thought, what the hell, let them have it. And, aloud, "A sense of adventure!"

I got the job, for nine months.

People were very odd about this. My parents, by now well established in Geneva, could quite see my wanting to do this; my interpreting colleagues, however, mostly said "You are absolutely mad – this is professional suicide. Away for *nine months*, maybe more! Everybody will forget you even exist." The other mantra was "That's no place for white women, they don't even have proper loos." I think what they actually meant was rape, but what they talked about was "proper loos".

I went to see my patron and occasional employer, Marie Ginsberg, and even she began by saying some of the same things. But when I said "Marie! I am 24 years old. If I don't go to Indochina now, just when do you suggest I go?" she answered "As a matter of fact, you are quite right. At your age I would do the same." So off I went.

I stopped over in Bombay for reasons to do with Air India flights. But I lost my passport there, and had to recover it in Calcutta. Air India were very good – they put me up in a rather grand hotel in Calcutta and detailed a pleasant young man to show me around. The airline flew me the passport and then flew me on, leaving me at last at Saigon airport. Somebody from the Commission did apparently come to meet me there, but they were expecting a man, so we missed one another. I was rescued by a French businessman, who took me into the city, where I did find the room reserved for me at the largest hotel there.

Saigon was in South Vietnam and I was due to go to Hanoi in North Vietnam, so I had to spend a night in Saigon. My Frenchman, who took me out to dinner, said one very illuminating thing: "As you can see, we've lost Indochina. We deserve to; and I'll tell you why. The British, when they had India, used to send their very best civil servants there, the ones that were too good for the Civil Service in England. We sent our secondraters, who were placed over Vietnamese whose bootlaces they were not fit to untie. No private firm could have been so stupid, but our government was."

The following day I went to Hanoi on a DC3, which flew low over Angkor for our benefit. I also had it explained to me on the plane what all those funny insignia on the arms and shoulders of military men were; I'd never known before how to distinguish a colonel from a second lieutenant, except by age.

The Commission's northern headquarters were in Hanoi, then the capital of North Vietnam, and now once again the capital of Vietnam as a whole. It had indeed been originally designed by the French as the capital of their whole colony of Vietnam. The French have always been extremely good in designing capitals for their colonies; Hanoi is no exception. It has a beautiful situation, around a small lake with a couple of islands; on the larger island there is a small Buddhist temple, and a graceful little red bridge connects both islands with the lake-shore. But even aside from that, Hanoi was, and remains, a very well planned city with wide avenues, trees, a substantial Cathedral, an even more substantial Opera House, and all sorts of other commodities – including a large and handsome hotel, the Métropole, where the Commission (or the senior part of it) were quartered. The Métropole Hotel still exists; nowadays it is the sort of place where even I, a well-to-do woman, can't afford to stay! But I was delighted, when I returned to Vietnam many years later, to find it had escaped being pulled down and replaced by something else "more modern".

Arriving back then in October, 1954, I found it was the best part of the year just before the rains, cool and pleasant. When the rains come, local French-speakers talk about the *crâchin,* a word meaning "spit" or "spitting", and this is more or less what the rain is like – an almost continuous drizzle. But before this, I had witnessed the very peaceable celebrations of the country's Independence. A civilian crowd had gathered around the lake for a rather wonderful display of fireworks. I think I was the only person from the Commission actually to witness these fireworks, and the *ooh! ahh!* cries of admiration from the local people around me; I found that, on my right side, a small hand had been slipped into my own. It was that of a Vietnamese woman, who obviously felt the need to touch another human being at this great moment in her life. I remember the occasion very well, and the quite peaceable joy of it.

One of the charms of Hanoi was the dress of the women. They all wore the traditional costume – a pair of loose long trousers, rather like pyjama trousers, topped by a long *cheong sam* which, however, on each side was split to the waist; at the top it ended in a tall high collar. You could tell the social class of the wearer by the colour of the trousers: working class women wore them black, and ladies, such as my later friend Quy, wore white, because of course ladies could afford to get their trousers changed and washed more frequently.

I became very fond of the little lake. But then, I liked Hanoi in general and not only the town. The vegetation got me, in particular the bougainvillea spilling over every wall it could; that reminded me of Argentina, of San Miguel, of home. It did get very warm in summer, and I was also thrilled by this. It brought a realisation that living in Geneva, fairly far north in the heart of Europe, was all very well in its way, but there was a side of me that yearned for being back into the tropics, or at least the subtropics.

The Commission, as I have said, consisted of three nations: Canada, India and Poland, with India in the chair. It had another centre in the southern capital Saigon, which I never had much to do with; but the major centre was in Hanoi. Each of the three nations had both civilian and military staff there. In the case of the Indians, the senior military officer was one General Djarghalkar; I have forgotten the name of the civilian Chairman, possibly because I disliked him. India was supposed to be the neutral Chair of the Commission. It didn't, in real life, work out quite that way. Quite simply, all the Indian military officers were pro-Western, and all the civilians were, understandably enough, on the side of those who had fought the colonial French – ie. the Vietminh, and also of their Polish supporters. In my capacity as a translator, my immediate boss at work was an Indian civilian, who I think disliked me about as much as I disliked him. The Canadians had a very nice civilian head and also a military head, one General McGill.

The Poles had a Colonel, clearly of working class origin – he used to address us women in general, rather endearingly, as "Madamska", little Madame. I don't believe he would have used this when talking to the civilian head of the Polish Delegation, one Madame Czechanovska. Her accommodation at the Métropole Hotel was not far from mine, so that I used to hear her playing Chopin, passionately and execrably, far into the night. She had suffered considerably under the Germans and this showed on her face: she had clearly been very beautiful once, but now had a ruined doll's face. I remember being told, about some Frenchman who needed to go to the non-Communist South, that *she* needed to know whether he had collaborated with the Germans during their occupation of France. When he was able to show to her satisfaction that he hadn't, she had said, quite publicly, "I am glad about that; otherwise I would have found it difficult in allowing him to leave."

One of the things I had to learn rather fast (I had already started on the plane from Saigon) was the distinction between various military ranks – who was a major, who a colonel, who a mere captain in the three forces. The Indians and the Canadians, both members of the Commonwealth, had the same insignia; those of the Poles were slightly different. At the Métropole where we were quartered, we all ate together in the dining room, sitting with whomsoever we wished – in my case, usually Indian or Canadian officers.

Work took place in what had been the Hanoi Chamber of Commerce, situated very near the little lake. Office hours were on the Indian pattern, suited to tropical conditions. We started early, at 7.30 or 8, and worked through until 2 pm. That was the end of the working day, and the rest of our time was free. Meetings, at which I had to interpret, took place on the ground floor of the building. I would sit facing the Indian chairman, who had on each side the Polish and Canadian representatives and, where appropriate, the Vietminh and French delegations, present to discuss some disagreement about implementing the provisions of the Agreement.

Upstairs, in a large room, written translations took place. "Low grade" or junior translators (that is, locally recruited Vietnamese who were paid much less than we were) translated letters written by the People's Army of Vietnam (PAVN) from Vietnamese into French. We senior translators rendered both these translations and the original letters sent by the French delegation into English, for the benefit of the Indian chairman and some of his colleagues. Among the junior translators I soon made friends with a young woman called Quy. Her full name was Nguyen Thi Quy.

The letters I had to translate all started out with the polite French opening for official correspondence – "of our highest consideration" or some similar formula. They then put their case on whatever the topic of the moment was and then ended, again with conventional politeness, "We avail ourselves of this opportunity to express to the Chairman of the Commission and its members our most distinguished consideration." Which is rather a long thing to translate. I had a highly intelligent and very pleasant young Indian male typist, and after awhile I would shorten this to "love and kisses", which became "L&K". My typist, highly amused by "L&K", would then put in the appropriate phrase.

But the very first time I gave a few pages of translated stuff, which I did longhand, to this typist, he sort of half shook his head and I thought: *Oh dear, he doesn't like working for a woman. Perhaps he particularly doesn't like working for a white woman. Now what?* My friend Mac, the Anglo Indian doctor, saved me from cross-cultural distress, by telling me that this was the Indian gesture indicating "yes". I have since found that, at one particular latitude, that of Istanbul, the line between nodding for "yes" and waving one's head sideways to mean the same thing, passes neatly between Greece and Turkey. I don't know what happens further north or further south.

At that early stage, and indeed during most of my stay in Hanoi, I was the only person on the linguistic staff able to take on the task of interpreting. The interpreting was invariably consecutive. The Viet military officers spoke good French for ordinary purposes; however, their main speakers didn't actually use it in the conference setting, for reasons of prestige. They would present their case in Vietnamese; their own interpreter would put it into French; I would put this into English for the benefit of the non-French speakers on the Commission, who would answer in English. I would then put this into French. The French representative would answer in French; I would put this back into English, and so it went. This used to take pretty much all day when there were meetings: there were a good many details in the Agreement on which Vietminh and French took different views.

The Geneva Agreement, on which the Commission's work was supposed to be based, had been reached during the brief French premiership of Pierre Mendès-France. Mendès-France, when he came to power, let it be known that he undertook to end the disastrous war in Vietnam within a month; if he didn't do so, he would resign at once. My father remarked at the time that this was very clever of Mendès-France: he was not only sending a signal to his own electorate, but also to the Vietnamese (the Vietminh side) telling them, "For the next month you have me to deal with, and it is in my interest that we reach agreement within that time, but *après moi le deluge.*" In other words, "After I'm gone, I can't tell you who you'll be negotiating with, but they will almost certainly be more right wing, and thus much less anxious to reach agreement."

Mendès-France won his bet, but only by a mild form of cheating. Agreement was reached between two and three in the morning of the day *following* the expiry of his month. It bore the marks of this. It had been reached in French; and the translation into English also bore the marks of great haste. It was quite badly drafted, especially in the detail; this was to cause a great many problems. One provision was, that, since the agreement had been reached in the middle of a national war, Southerners (South Vietnamese) who were in the North should be returned to the South; and Northerners who were in the South should be returned to the North; and thereby trouble lay. I have forgotten the details, but I do remember these provisions were not very clearly expressed. The Commission, which had a certain number of fixed teams in various places in both the South and the North, also had mobile teams, always consisting of military personnel (one Canadian, one Indian, one Pole), who had to go and expedite this exchange of people between the two halves of the country, or one might almost already say the two countries; this did not always work out.

I don't have much substantive recall as to the contents of the meetings. But they were all about this exchange of people, about where a mobile team was going next, how it had been received, possible disagreements between its members and so on. And of course in each case, the Vietminh (officially The People's Army of Viet Nam) would say one thing, the French would say the opposite. It is curious how many countries in very different parts of the world have a north/south split. Italy, Germany, Ireland, Argentina; even the Church of England has two archbishops, northern York actually preceding southern Canterbury as Primate of all England!

The Vietminh general, Giap, had, I am fairly certain, been responsible for the French débacle at Dien Bien Phu. (I knew a little about General Giap: he had been the maths teacher of my office friend Quy, at her secondary school.) Now it was all over, Giap and the French general De Beaufort exchanged polite nothings, as between generals whose countries had agreed an armistice. At one point – I think I was actually sitting between them – De Beaufort said "Really, General, I must say, though I come from the other side, I greatly admire your military strategy and tactics; and I do know that you weren't a career officer by profession. Where do you get all this knowledge from?" and Giap said "Oh, I have an absolutely wonderful manual, I'll show it to you." The wonderful manual turned out to be the French Military Service Manual for

Privates, which Giap said (no doubt a little cruelly) "contained enough information to enable you to plan a campaign very successfully."

In addition to the staff of the Commission was the Indian Consul, a Mr Sen. Being an Indian nationalist, during the Second World War he had joined the Indian National Party, who had carried their opposition to the British colonial power so far as to assist the Japanese. In this, I think Mr Sen had acted according to his convictions; but General Djarghalkar, who as a loyal Army officer had spent much of the war very uncomfortably in a Japanese prisoner-cage, had made it quite clear he never wanted to be in the same room with the Consul.

Also in accordance with his Indian-nationalist convictions, Mr Sen had given his very beautiful daughter a Muslim name, Riziya. Riziya did act as a delicate link between the various national delegations in Hanoi. She had a gorgeous wardrobe of saris, and used to invite all of us women to try them on at her father's flat. Of course neither Polish ladies, nor Canadian ladies, nor indeed I myself could resist! We all went and tried on Riziya's saris and giggled at each other; it was all very friendly. She gave me a few cooking lessons too, which I have forgotten now, but at the time I did learn how to make *pakoras* and a few other Indian delicacies.

As for the Indian General, one saw him sometimes in uniform, but in his leisure time in civvies. General Djarghalkar was the first instance I have come across – and I have come across only one other – of what was essentially a brown-skinned English gentleman. He was accompanied by a spaniel, he smoked a pipe, he walked around in a blazer. He even had an English wife; but I think had married out of his class, somebody like the landlady's daughter – he was the sort of man who actually *marries* the landlady's daughter. And throughout the war he had remained utterly loyal to what was then still the British Empire.

The colleague I remember best is Olga Afanacieva. French, born in Paris as the daughter of Russian refugees, she was there as a translator, not an interpreter. I don't know whether the Poles regarded Olga as a spy, quite possibly they did; she found herself more drawn to her fellow Slavs than to anyone else, and spent a lot of time with them. We got on very well, except that I think my command of English gave her what used to be called a complex: she would never speak it in my presence. (Her company vastly improved my French over the nine months we spent together.)

There were also, partly because of Riziya's sari parties, a few Poles with whom I got to be on friendly terms. One was an austerely beautiful woman called Beata Babad who was I think quite high up, though not as high as the dreaded Madame Czechanowska. Beata was much friendlier and more civilised. She was Jewish, and how she had survived, I do not know: she still wore her number tattooed on her wrist; as did the Polish legal adviser, Manelli. And then there was (non-Jewish) Lucina Stanicka. All these I was to meet again many years later in Warsaw.

I was never on very close terms with any of the Vietnamese delegation, though one Vietnamese Captain, in the first few weeks, used to take me out to a small theatre where they showed patriotic, anti-French, plays. That theatre still exists; I have been there since then, to see water-puppet shows.

The seniormost French officer was General de Beaufort, a pleasant man though somewhat limited in his outlook. He didn't have very much conversation with me, but he once put it to me politely, meaning it clearly as a compliment, that I was no doubt an officer's daughter. He had a very ladylike secretary, Solange.

The work in Hanoi was fairly continuous, there were few breaks. But I did once get off with Solange and two of the French junior officers (semi-legally in my case because I wasn't supposed to take holidays) to visit Angkor Wat. We stayed in Siem Reap, the nearest village, probably a town now.

Angkor Wat is one of the most magnificent ruins in the world, rivalling the pyramids of Egypt, the temples of Athens and anything else you care to mention; it was built by the kings of Cambodia around the 12th century. It had been swallowed by the jungle and rediscovered by the French when they had control of Cambodia; their archaeologists went to work and did so very effectively. I walked right up the narrow stairs to the top of Angkor Wat itself, the temple, and there is also the palace, called Angkor Thom. We spent two or three days visiting all this, and saw many of the local people who were holding some kind of festival. I am very grateful that I did so then, before the tourist invasions. It is one of the great sights of the world.

This trip was a welcome change from Hanoi; both the work, and the somewhat intense social and emotional life I led there.

Chapter 2

Hanoi: Social Life, Encounters, and Farewells

My social life was mostly with the Canadians. (I suspect my parents had rather hoped that I might find myself a nice Canadian husband; and there was indeed one Canadian captain who actually proposed to me on very short acquaintance, but I politely declined.)

Fairly early on, however, I did fall in love with another Canadian – at that stage a Wing-Commander, Jack. I had not realised that his occupation was not military: he was their top legal adviser. I was not aware of this, only of Jack as a very attractive man. He was, I think, fifteen years older than I, and married, but the wife was far away in Canada. And then, a couple of days before Christmas, Jack was summoned by General McGill and told to steer clear of me – partly because he was a married man; but mainly because I was quite obviously a spy.

Looking back, I can see why he thought that way. I mean, there I was, saying I was Argentine; I didn't look like a Canadian's idea of a South American – I happen to be fair skinned and green eyed. I also went around saying that I found living here very agreeable, and that I had come to Hanoi of my own free will. Now, *nobody* did that – a place without cinemas or the smallest ice-cream parlour. I had clearly been *sent* – and then had made a beeline for their senior legal adviser. I was *obviously* a spy!

At the time I didn't know any of this. Jack just told me that he'd been instructed to steer clear of me. I went to see Vincent Anthony Gordon; it was Christmas Eve, and I said "Anthony, please get me completely drunk tonight," which he did. I can't remember much about Christmas Day.

But on Boxing Day, or maybe the day after, Jack decided he thought rather more of me than he did of his military honour, and told me the truth.

I was rather distressed, especially as there was absolutely no way I could prove my case. I did of course have an Argentine passport; but the nearest Argentine Consulate was probably in Delhi, and here I was, sitting in Hanoi. So Jack and I continued to see each other, but rather more privately; it turned out to be extremely convenient that his hotel room was number 239, when mine was 237; they even had a communicating door! The French are said to understand these things....

Quite how much other people suspected, I don't know. One person who certainly knew was the delightful Anglo Indian surgeon Eric MacFarlane, usually just called Mac. Jack kept pressing various remedies upon me, vitamin pills and salt pills and so on. Mac said to me privately, "You could put a bit more salt in your food, but don't bother with the pills." I forget what he said about the vitamin pills, but in any case he was and remained our good friend and we would occasionally have drinking sessions *à trois*, usually in Jack's room. I did notice that both Canadians and Poles worried continually about their health in Hanoi; the Indians were very much more relaxed, as indeed were the few remaining French.

Jack came from what was clearly a somewhat puritanical, certainly teetotal, background in central Canada, as a result of which he drank far too much. So did I at that time; but I used to get rid of my hangover, which was never very great, by running around the little lake in the mornings, at least until the rains started.

I also went once with Jack on a weekend to the capital of Cambodia, Phnom Penh – in those days a peaceful, rather provincial place where we did nothing much but go dancing in the evening, and which I have thought of often since the terrible wars and massacres in Cambodia. At that time there still was a King of Cambodia, supported by China; he seems to have been rather a good King (as well as having a fondness for jazz quartets). It is a pity Cambodia lost him; it would have done much better with him still in place.

Mac told me, at one point in our acquaintance, that he was the only member of his family who, at the time of Indian Independence, had opted to remain Indian, rather than return to Britain and take British nationality. He had decided against that, notwithstanding his occasional rude comments about the Indian Government. However, it wasn't all easy. He once pressed a novel into my hand: John Masters' *Bhowani Junction,* about the life of Anglo-Indians. Mac said "Read that, and you will find out a little about what it's like." He it was who told me about the past political gulf as between the Indian Consul and General Djarghalkar.

Mac had been sent to Vietnam as a kind of punishment station; he was in fact one of the top surgeons in the Indian army. I don't know what he'd done to queer his pitch; but he was apt to make politically incorrect jokes, like the time he had been given a very small salary supplement because of some work he'd done, and sent it back with a note saying he didn't really need this, so it could be donated it to the next three-and-a-half year plan. This was the kind of thing the Indian government didn't like.

Mac was fascinating to look at. Quite handsome, a little on the short side, he had ginger hair, skin light enough to show his freckles and deep brown, Indian eyes. The French nun still in charge of the remaining hospital in Hanoi, told me privately that she had never in her professional life met a surgeon as deft and delicate as he was.

I have already said that one of my earliest friends outside the Hotel Métropole was a young woman working as a junior translator at the Commission, Nguyen Thi Quy. (The Vietnamese, like the Chinese, have their surnames at the beginning. Nguyen was a very common surname in Vietnam, meaning "King".) Quy was a little older than I, and a rather sad young woman because she had lost her love at some point in the wars. She was a qualified pharmacist, spoke splendid French and was in herself a most delightful person.

I remember, just before that 1954 Christmas, finding on my desk two beautifully hand-embroidered lace handkerchiefs (embroidery is one of the Vietnamese skills); together with a little note: "I am an emissary from *Père Nöel* – do not try to identify me." Of course, I knew who the emissary was, and when Quy next appeared on the horizon, I said "If by any chance you should meet *le Père Nöel,* whom we call Father Christmas, do say that I render many, many thanks for these lovely things." "*I* don't know any Father Christmas," she replied. "I'm a Buddhist!"

It was a pity that the South of the country had been much evangelised and was therefore largely Catholic, while the North was still almost entirely Buddhist and would have more easily lived under a Communist regime. Quy wanted very badly to get to the South, where she had a brother in the banking business; but, of course, she was by birth a Northerner. She was not comfortable with the regime, and I think had personal troubles of her own. What with the difficulties of the North/South repatriation policy, it was not going to be simple to get her across the border.

I looked around for possible help and decided on Jerry Menon, an Indian Officer, a nephew of the famous left-wing politician Krishna Menon, but exceedingly unlike him. Jerry had been converted to Catholicism of a singularly old fashioned kind. He was a kindly man, not very bright, and I thought I could enlist his help to get Quy to the South. So I said to her, "I am going to take you to the Hotel Métropole and you will meet a man called Colonel Menon, who will probably help you out; only for heaven's sake, if he asks you, say you're a Catholic!"

I smuggled Quy into the hotel (despite the curfew applied to the Vietnamese), and we went to Jerry Menon's room. Arrangements were made, how she was going to leave through Hai Phong, a city still in Commission hands though about to be devolved to the North fairly soon. Then Jerry said to her compassionately "You are a Catholic aren't you, child?" Quy was, and has remained, extremely bad at lying. She just looked blank, and Jerry Menon said "Oh, and you're even scared to tell *me,* but look ..." and he produced an image of Our Lady, and Quy looked at it, as I might have looked at an image of Kwan Yin the Spirit of Mercy, and said "*C'est la Vierge Marie, n'est pas?*" And, thank heavens, it was indeed the *Vierge Marie* and not some other female saint, so Jerry was satisfied, and duly helped Quy out. Quy rejoined her brother and sister-in-law in Saigon; I saw her again on my way out. She had got herself a job translating for the Americans, who by this time were very much present in Saigon. She said to me "You know, in my office, I am the only person who is anti-Communist, everybody else is on the side of the North; I am not, because I've lived there, but of course I can't peach on the others."

Quy and I exchanged Christmas cards for some years and then lost each other's addresses. In the end I sent her a postcard to the last address I had and was a little surprised when a while later there arrived a letter from a Mrs Peter Stanley from Australia!

She had got herself some kind of a scholarship to go to America, had there met an Australian, who had fallen love with her, had actually gone to Saigon to ask her brother for her hand and they had got married and lived in Australia. I was a little puzzled by this – it was not my idea of Australians! But eventually I found out that Peter Stanley was a Central European refugee who had acquired Australian nationality and would, of course, have had a lot of fellow feeling with Quy. They had two sons. Peter Stanley died and so did the elder son sometime later; Quy still lives with her younger son somewhere outside Sydney; over the years she has made herself extremely useful to the Australian government by interpreting for people who had arrived as refugees from Vietnam.

Another friend I made early on in Hanoi was a Frenchman, *Commandant* Fiamma. There must have been some Italian origin there, but he came from Algiers. He was in command of Hanoi airport, due shortly to be handed over to the Viets. He took a shine to me and used to ask me out to dinner in one of the two restaurants still open. He taught me how to eat with chopsticks, and we used to tease each other flirtatiously about the colour of our eyes. "*Vous avez des yeux noisette*" – you have walnut coloured eyes. "*Mais pas si noisette que les vôtres!*" – but not as *noisette* as yours, and so on.

Commandant Fiamma had very nice manners, and he was the one Frenchman who I was prepared to introduce to Quy in the certainty that he would address her as Mademoiselle and *vous*, and not treat her as a lower form of life. One of my less desirable senior translator colleagues at the Commission, a refugee Pole with a French passport, said the one thing he really liked here in Vietnam, was that one could once again call the servants *tu*, rather than *vous*. This was also the attitude taken by a number of Europeans there – Commandant Fiamma was the exception. He would also occasionally ask me to his *popote*, which was French military slang for "Mess" at the airport, and we would eat whatever the *popote* offered that day – usually quite good. Sometimes, his juniors there would say rude things about the Viets. Commandant Fiamma always interposed: "No chaps, you've got to remember it *is* their country and no, we will *not* take all the light bulbs out when we leave."

I grew fond of *Commandant* Fiamma. He told me how dreadfully he was going to miss Hanoi when he left: "I am in love with that little red bridge, as one might be in love with a woman." I missed him when he went.

Among the French people still in Hanoi, there was also the manager of the Métropole Hotel. He was known as Pilou, and was clearly somebody who had always found a way to make money out of any situation. His wife Lucienne had been a nightclub singer, and rather charmingly sang French popular songs; and there was also an adolescent girl, not related to either, but a friend of Lucienne's, called Miki. Miki was adored by all the Canadians, who saw her as a cross between a little sister and an unattainable girlfriend.

On one occasion, however, I was in town with Quy when we ran into Lucienne and Miki, who embraced me warmly, and insisted we *must* see each other soon, and I must learn to play bridge! We then parted, and Quy said disapprovingly: "Those are not the kind of women you should be going around with, Eva." Quy was acting as my elder sister; in her view, Miki and Lucienne were *vulgar*.

There was also a French doctor, whose name I can't remember, who had elected to stay in Vietnam at the time of the Agreement, when most of his countrymen had gone home. He had friends in Hanoi, mostly in the Chinese community. He liked it there, and told me he was there quite legally: he still had medical work to do and every so often would go home to France on holiday. And he took me to dinner, to a Chinese household where there was a large and delicious Chinese meal. There was no rice, and soup only towards the end of the meal. It was a feast – only the poor ate rice, to fill up their tums. We had all sorts of delicacies and didn't need the rice. But in case there was a bit of space still left to fill up, there was the soup.

It was all delicious and, after that, on the point of taking me home to the Métropole, the doctor said: "White men who live in the tropics either take to drink or they take to opium. I decided it was better for me to smoke opium. Better for the liver and everything. I have a bit of a hard time every time I go back to France, because I refuse to get involved in the black market in drugs. There is one, but it's too complicated and too compromising. So every time I go back I have a bit of a hard time, but not too bad. Now, would *you* like to try it? – because I could, just now, go and fetch the man who prepares my pipes for me and we could go back to my place and you could smoke a few pipes. Then, after I've taken him home, I'll take you back to the hotel." And I said: "Doctor, when I was a young thing – " (I was only 24 at the time) "my father, also a doctor, told me that if ever I intended to do this kind of thing, I should do so under medical supervision. Since you *are* medical supervision, let's!"

So we fetched the local Chinese man who mixed his opium pipes, and then went to his small flat, not very far from the Métropole Hotel. I was told to lie down on the floor with a hard pillow under my neck, to keep my head up, and as this was my first time, not to smoke more than six pipes. A pipe contains very little, you just draw in once or twice and that's it. The doctor said: "You will not have the whole of your past life passing in front of your eyes – that's a myth – but you might have some quite interesting visions or dreams. I'll just take this chap back home, then I'll come back for you." So off he went, and after a bit I thought: Well, I feel quite all right really, I feel as if I'd had a sherry or two but no worse than that. I wonder what books he has? Indeed I got up and started looking at his bookshelves, as I always tend to do in other people's houses. Eventually my host returned and said he was glad I seemed to be so well, and only then did I notice that he genuinely had the tiny pupils that opium smokers are supposed to have. I did sleep very well that night in my room at the Métropole, and had beautiful dreams. I've never smoked opium again.

Another Frenchman remaining in Hanoi was a captain, somewhat oddly not part of the French military mission, but who lived at the Métropole. Perhaps he really *was* a spy? He was extremely fat, and nicknamed Babar, after the elephant. His room was not far from mine, a bit beyond Madame Czechanowska's. Babar used to invite me over every so often, to listen to music. He had a complete set of *Porgy & Bess*, at the time still quite new; I greatly enjoyed listening to those records with him. We occasionally talked a bit of politics, and what was interesting was that his only views on any *political* subject, consisted of loyalty to General de Gaulle. De Gaulle was a great man, De Gaulle had been right, De Gaulle would return and would continue to be right. So Babar himself turned out to be right.

For Shrove Tuesday, the Canadian delegation decided to give a Carnival party. People had all sorts of ideas for this. I remember a girl who dressed up wittily, though I've forgotten how, as a Diplomatic Bag. I also remember that General McGill's entourage dressed as American Indians, and kept running around the place saying that they'd just concluded a very, very important pipe-smoking pact with big Asian/Indian tribe – a bit puzzling to those Indians present. Olga, on the other hand, expressed her true self by going as a Russian peasant. And I, well, I thought I had an idea! I got a Canadian colonel with a sense of humour to give me several large envelopes and rolls of paper, sealed, and stamped all over the place with "Secret", "Top Secret", and "Confidential". I also got the youngest member of the British Consulate to buy me a toy pistol. I remember his coming and standing, like somebody in a spoof spy film, in the corridor outside my room, and sending a message in German: "*Bewaffnung gefunden*" – weaponry found! I got hold of a black cloak from somewhere. I let my nails grow long and painted them the darkest red I could find, I wore long earrings and appropriate make-up. Certainly I had a long exotic cigarette holder and thus I appeared at the Canadian party. "Eva," said somebody; "Mata Hari?" "Oh, no!" said I, "Just any old spy." Which did at least make the point, that I knew what some people thought.

Not long after that came my twenty-fifth birthday, so I thought *I'd* give a party. By this time, the weather was warm, so I decided to hold this at the former French Athletic Club, now given over to the Commission. I had invaluable help from Babar, who made some wonderful drink using rum, lemon or lime and crushed ice. I left Babar at the bar while the rest of us partied around. After a while we all started throwing each other into the pool and had an absolutely lovely time.

Mine was the first Athletic Club party, but there were others; most notably, the celebration of Canada Day on 1st July. I remember shaking General McGill's hand, and exchanging icy greetings...

Not long after that, my contract with the Commission came to an end, and it was time to set out for Geneva. In the vehicle taking me to the airport, a young Canadian officer said, innocently facetious –

"Well Eva, I suppose you're sorry to leave Hanoi?"

"Yes, Jim. *Very* sorry."

Journey "home"

Over my nine months' stay in Hanoi I had saved quite a bit of money: I was quite well paid, and at the hotel I spent little. I needed only to buy the odd drink for other people, flowers for my room and one or two other things, and for this purpose my parents would send me, I think once a month, a twenty dollar bill nicely wrapped up in carbon paper and popped into an envelope. I soon learned that the thing to do was to pass this on to my South Indian typist (the same one who enjoyed "L&K"), who knew all about how to get the best (though not the most legal) rates of exchange. He would change it first into South Vietnamese money, then into North Vietnamese money: I did rather nicely out of this, and I expect he did too.

So I had quite a lot of "real" money saved up, and thought I would like to see more of the East; so I organised a trip, starting with Japan. This I did on my way out, from Saigon, through a travel agency, where they assumed (understandably enough) that I was not English-speaking and thus booked me on a French-speaking tour. In those days there were not many French speaking visitors to Japan, so my supposedly "group" tour consisted exclusively of me – and I had, at each place in Japan, a guide supposedly speaking French. The first day, it was a middle-aged man who had at one time been the secretary, or possibly even the president, of the Japanese Spiritualist Association; he did in fact speak quite good French. Later I got a young lady who must in fact have lied to get the job, so I taught her a little French. I still remember our visit to Kyoto – a beautiful place, but before touring the sites we were going to have lunch at the local hotel. My guide had remembered to tell me to bring a bathing suit; I had done so, and she then rang for a maid. When the maid came, I noticed with interest that when she bowed to my young lady, the latter bowed back – a less steep bow but acknowledging the maid's presence in a similar way. Then came "Honourable lady needs honourable bathroom for changing"; and I did have a little swim, before gazing around wondrous Kyoto. Also in Kyoto there lived the brother of some people I vaguely knew through my great-uncle's firm in Buenos Aires – an antique dealer with a Japanese partner. The two of them took me out to dinner at a restaurant where you duly had to take your shoes off. It consisted of a series of small rooms, and we were served Japanese food, most of it delectable, except for some kind of thick white pasty substance relieved only by a few black beans. We were greeted by the hostess, who I do hope really *didn't* understand English, for my host said in his most amiable tones "Madam, this is the most *disgusting* stuff I have ever eaten in my life."

After Japan I spent a few days in Hong Kong, and then I went to Bangkok. Here there was an Asian conference of the same World Federation of UN Associations (WFUNA) through which I had first entered international life in Geneva, so I spent some time working for them, and had a final meeting with Jack. We stayed at an hotel which had been recommended to me – I believe it exists to this day, but then it was still run by a colleague (or maybe a relative) of my godmother's husband. She had been a photographer on the Allied side during the North African campaign in the Second World War, and was now running this beautiful hotel in Bangkok on the river. I insisted we stay in the old part, introducing Jack to the very un-Canadian idea of taking a shower by scooping up water from a tall jar and pouring it over yourself. After a few days of this, and of travelling by boat along the canals of Bangkok, we bade one another a sad farewell, and I went on to India.

There I first spent some time in Delhi. I had met through WFUNA an Indian journalist, Raj Chawla, who first lent me her flat and later had me back as her guest. Raj came from a Sikh family; her two brothers, both doctors, had known my young uncle (my father's brother Rolf) when he was there buying jute for the family firm. They very kindly took me round Delhi and showed me the wonderful astronomical observatories and a number of other things.

Then I flew to Kashmir, and spent a few days there. I had been advised by Raj not to stay in a houseboat (as they tended to vary a lot) so I stayed at some kind of hotel. I visited the Shalimar gardens and went up to the hills on a pony, which was lovely. Only, when I needed to leave Kashmir again, the weather had broken and planes were not flying. I dare say if I had been Indian I would have taken this in my stride and just stayed there. As it was I felt I really did have to get back to Delhi, and asked about other means of transport. There was a bus that took you as far as Amritsar; after that you had to take the train.

The long coach was skilfully driven down a steep, narrow mountain road with many hairpin bends. I found myself sitting beside a diminutive American missionary lady and her son, who had been having their holiday in Kashmir. They had lived in India a long time and knew their stuff. Under her guardianship, I actually ate things from stalls in the street when the bus stopped, and very nice they were, and I did *not* fall ill from them. When we had to spend the night at a *dak* bungalow, on portable bedding which (of course) I hadn't got, the son very kindly provided me with some of his and slept on the remainder outside on the veranda, to guard his mother and me from all harm.

Next day I took a train back to Delhi. I travelled second class, which was also patronised by NCOs of the Indian army. They spoke quite a bit of English, of a somewhat Kiplingesque sort. They asked me where I had come from. In those days I always said Switzerland, Argentina being too complicated to explain; and if I had said South America they would have thought I had come from the South of the USA. So I would say "Switzerland" which does mean cuckoo clocks and chocolate to most people. One of the NCOs said, "You have much pluck to come so far by yourself."

All of them were perfectly sweet. Did I want the window open, did I want the window closed, would I like a cup of tea, would I like a glass of water? One of them was a Sikh and before we all went to sleep he put a hairnet around his beard and when I said "Aah, you're putting your beard to bed," this was regarded as a major witticism; they absolutely loved it. And thus I got back to Delhi. And it was there, at Raj's flat, that I read in one of her English-language newspapers about the military coup which had removed Perón from the Presidency of Argentina! I was thrilled.

On my way out, I spent a little time near Bombay with Mac's family. His wife and sons were then living at some kind of military cantonment. Only after that did I return to Geneva. Just about this time, the ILO, where I had worked before, was running a competition to recruit translators. Thinking *after all this gadding about the world it is about time I settled down*, I went in for this competition; they offered me a place as a translator, which I accepted.

Chapter 3
Return to Hanoi

It was nearly four decades before I was able to visit Vietnam again: in the 1990s, when I had already long been married to Mick Gillies, and we were living in the Sussex village of Hamsey. Mick, an entomologist, had an endearing habit of picking up interesting foreigners at entomologists' or other biologists' meetings in London; it was to this I owed the chance to see Hanoi once more, a trip which I had never dared hope for, and which was to mean so much to me.

Mick had asked a young Vietnamese scientist to come to lunch in Hamsey one Saturday. The man arrived with a small suitcase. I thought, *O Lord. He clearly expects to stay the night and I haven't got a bed made up – oh well, I'll deal with that later.* But, as the day wore on, it became clear that the suitcase contained nothing but gifts for us, starting out with a little wood carving of a Buddhist monk. Later, more and more presents gradually emerged, including an exquisite black and white embroidered kimono-type dressing-gown which he said his wife had asked him to give to the lady who most hospitably received him abroad.

Finally emboldened, I confessed to my own Vietnamese past. I wasn't quite sure how he would take this; in fact he was delighted. As he was a few years younger than I, we quickly established that, when I was in my 'twenties, he had been a schoolboy. He told me where his school had been, I told him where the Commission's offices had been – clearly, we had many times crossed one another in the street.

Later, he had become involved in the Vietminh resistance movement against the French (I have always thought it interesting that French-speaking Vietnamese used the same term the metropolitan French had used for their efforts against German occupation during the Second World War). The Vietnamese Resistance did, however, have "universities" out in the bush; he had attended one of these and eventually become a biologist. He was now working for a Ph.D. in Germany.

"Look," he said, "you really must go back to Hanoi. I'm not there at the moment, but my wife is, and my daughter, and my colleagues, and they'd all be so delighted to see you... you really *must*!" We took his advice, and it was thus I got the fresh perspective on Hanoi that meant so much to me.

Wife and daughter awaited us at the airport, both dressed in European clothes, extremely elegant as all Vietnamese women invariably are. They took us to a delightful small hotel, known as the Phoenix 2 – because the same lady proprietor already owned the Phoenix 1. I never found out her name, as she spoke no European languages; I think she must have been a war widow, dating back to the time when no foreign languages were taught. *Madame* was clearly a woman of the utmost respectability; she looked about twenty-three, but can't have been, because there were two children, one in his early teens and one slightly younger.

We were not the only non-Asians staying at the Phoenix 2; a couple of young American businessmen also lodged there and were perhaps even more impressed by both *Madame* and the hotel she ran. For run it she did. Unable to communicate with her guests in words, she did so through the very able young woman behind the small reception desk, who also served, efficiently, as telephonist, barmaid and no doubt a number of other things. It was she who transmitted *Madame*'s authoritative advice to us: Woe betide me if, in weather she considered inclement, I wanted to venture out without my cardigan. Woe betide Mick if he had his shoes shined by a shoe-shine boy not under her protection. Or either of us if we tried to take a *cyclopousse* not specially called for us! We were her guests, and she clearly felt responsible for us.

The hotel, converted from a private house, was on three floors, the top one devoted to a coffee-shop, which also served excellent small meals; but on top of *that*, and visible from it, was a small Buddhist shrine, exquisitely neat and always decked with fresh flowers, for *Madame*'s private devotions.

International Women's Day, always a big thing in socialist countries, happened to occur during our stay there. The girl at the desk rang us up in the morning to ask whether we'd be staying in our room for the next half-hour; we said we would – and within that half- hour a large bunch of flowers arrived for me, wishing me Happy Woman's Day! We found out a little later that by local custom every man had to give flowers on that day to his mother, sister, wife – I'm not sure about daughters – and clearly *Madame* and her staff knew that my ignorant husband would not offer them to me!

We explored Hanoi largely on our own, and mostly on foot: the centre of town is not very large. Already in the car on our way to the hotel I had been amazed at how unchanged things seemed to be.

Western propaganda had been that the Americans had bombed Hanoi to blazes in the early 1970s. This is untrue. They may have bombed – probably did bomb – some industrial suburbs, but the centre of Hanoi was untouched. There had been a fire, well after the war, in the big market, and the flower stall that used to be at one corner of the little lake was now occupied instead by some park plantings, but there were plenty of flower merchants around. In fact, the main difference from the Hanoi I had known was the number of street merchants. The architecture, which had always been pleasant, was exactly the same. A few of the older houses had fallen down and had been replaced by more or less identical ones, two or three storeys high with balconies, often flowers on these. Also there were still, at that time, a great many bicycles. Some of them were in fact light motorcycles, motorised bikes.

Many, perhaps most, were ridden by women; and these women at first sight looked exactly like the beautiful women cyclists I remembered. It took me a while to realise that they were no longer wearing (at least not the younger ones) the handsome Vietnamese costume of long wide trousers and a longish *cheong sam*; their wide hats were no longer the traditional Chinese ones (now only worn by peasants), but large European-type hats (often much decorated with fruit and flowers) – but the outline was the same. And of course these ladies were wearing trousers as their mothers and grandmothers had done before them, and did not therefore look like Japanese ladies *trying* to wear trousers; and they were one and all beautiful, as Vietnamese women always are. Mick used to say, staring after a girl, "In England, anywhere in Europe, she'd stop the traffic, here she's just one more pretty girl!"

The women were still beautiful and elegant, the city still charming and marvellously clean, the food still the best in the world. And a couple of savvy countries, such as the Swiss, seemed to have consulates there. Mick and I said to each other "I wonder whether this is not going to be the capital of Vietnam again." It became so shortly afterwards.

I never learned Vietnamese, beyond *Ho Chu Tich Muon Nam*, which means "May Uncle Ho live long", referring to Ho Chi Minh, and one or two other things like that. The main reason is that it's a tone language. Now I once heard my father say about me to a younger colleague that in my cradle I had hummed perfectly in tune, but that when I learned to speak (which I did very young) my musical ear seemed to disappear. I have since been told, by my niece's guitar teacher, that this is not quite true, that I can sing a well-known nursery song perfectly in tune; what is bad is my musical memory. Probably initially bad, and certainly, she said, quite untrained. She advised me to train my musical memory, which I have since tried to do, but it does mean that I have always been very bad at tonal languages.

Nor did I, alas, pick up any Vietnamese cooking. They are so much better at it than we are. It is the best food in the world, bar none: the French and Chinese can do whatever they like, Vietnamese remains the best. Moreover you can find it all over the shop, or indeed outside the shop. You can buy anything from any street stall and it will be delicious.

And now at last, I could cross that Little Red Bridge again and pay my respects at that small Buddhist temple! And we went to the theatre, to watch a fascinating play based on Vietnamese mythical history performed by water-puppets – a traditional art which had been impossible during the two anti-colonial wars. We tried restaurants too; and once, greatly daring, had tea at the now rejuvenated Hotel Métropole. The waitresses wore traditional Vietnamese costume – and how much more elegant they looked than the touroids! We were surrounded by people who treat their overfed bodies as display areas for bad t-shirt jokes. I felt ashamed of my own culture.

Mick and I had been allocated a guide – not a professional one, but a junior member of the Hanoi University Biological Faculty, a young woman called Tran. For expeditions outside Hanoi, Tran got us a car to hire, which broke down only occasionally and not for very long; so we saw landscapes quite other than the eternal rice fields, were paddled to remote shrines along waterways studded with small but curiously impressive rocks, and were able to sail across vast Halong Bay to the island caves, full of mysterious stalactites and stalagmites not yet trivialised by artificial light for the benefit of tourists.

Tran, meanwhile, made good use of her time with us by asking Mick to help her fill in a form, which she wanted to send in to get a place at something called the Technical University of Brussels, which was I suppose the West's answer to the Lumumba University in Moscow. It was for people from non-European countries, who were initially taught French, and then advanced in their respective fields of study. Tran was trying to get into this. But before we found out whether she had done so, the time came – all too soon – when I was once again very sad to leave Hanoi.

Tran did make it to Brussels and naturally, once there, she came to visit, just like her Vietnamese senior colleague, with a suitcase full of presents – in her case mainly food. Tran took over the kitchen for the 48 hours of her stay, and fed us magnificently. Clearly, she didn't quite trust my cooking.

Chapter 4

Home-base Geneva

Professional and Personal Life, 1955-60

A regular office job

Taking a nine-to-five job at the International Labour Office (or anywhere else) was, at this stage of my life, a big mistake. I had been seeing the world; I had touched the fringes of greatness – shaken, once, the hand of Ho Chi Minh and, at that WFUNA meeting in Bangkok, that of Eleanor Roosevelt; by gate-crashing a Canadian party in Hanoi, spent an evening in the same room as Graham Greene, researching for his novel *The Quiet American*. Now in my late twenties, I was no longer (if I ever had been) well adapted to regular hours of work at a regular pace. I was used to working by fits and starts, intensely at some point, with a rest afterwards. Office work at the ILO was not like that.

A further mistake was, that given my choice between general translation and specific duties for the Legislative Series, I chose the latter because it sounded more interesting.

It wasn't.

Work at the Legislative Series consisted partly of translating labour laws, and partly of reviewing all new legislation passed anywhere in the world on labour matters. The translating bit was all right; the reviewing was extraordinarily boring. I had to review labour legislation in Spanish language countries. One was Paraguay, where ever since the 19th century Paraguayan War, there seem to have been only two sorts of legislation, both decrees rather than laws. One is to enable a member of the Paraguayan Armed Forces to go to Buenos Aires for further training; the other, to permit some poor widow to import (also from Buenos Aires) a sewing machine. I soon got bored with this, as well as with the regular hours demanded of me; these included a very long lunch hour, for those of the (male) French-speaking staff to go home to a solid lunch with their wives. Nor was this two-hour break any use for shopping, because all the shops in Geneva also closed between twelve and two.

Mexico

However, while I was working with the ILO, I did get one or two interesting trips. One was to interpret at a large conference that took place in Havana.

This was in pre-Castro days; it was still Batista's Havana. My memory is of huge nightclubs and tourist beaches, and also of a bar we visited, which had been used by Hemingway when he lived there. One of our senior interpreters, who was also the Chief of Protocol of the ILO, had translated Hemingway into Spanish; Nico Dorantes knew his way about, and he used to take us to this bar and order the drinks: all of them rum-based, all absolutely delicious!

At one stage, one of the American delegates took me out to lunch. I was allowed to choose the restaurant, so I chose one which I'd heard praised by Nico. I asked my host to let me do the ordering; we had a very fine lobster dish, rum-based drinks, and afterwards a rum liqueur. My American host said this was the best meal he'd eaten since he'd arrived in Havana: he'd been following what the American Embassy had told him – always to eat at certain restaurants and always to ask for steak. I pointed out to him that it tended to be a mistake to follow one's own embassy's advice.

From Havana I went on to Mexico, at the suggestion of the Mexican delegate, Fernando Yllanes Ramos. Fernando, a lawyer, represented the employers' interests in Cuba. He was an open-minded man, with connections everywhere, and he said he thought he could organise me quite an interesting time in Mexico. His family being away on holiday, he was free in the evenings, and would take me out to all sorts of places and also to the markets to listen to music – particularly to what is called Mariachi music. He pointed out to me that Mariachi (the Mexican word) was derived from French *mariage*, marriage, wedding. This music had originally been played in the days of Maximilian and Carlotta at French weddings.

Then at one stage Fernando said: "There's something I would very much like to invite you to, only I can't go with you I'm afraid, I haven't got the time." He had got me a return ticket and two nights in a hotel in Oaxaca, which is quite a different part of Mexico, and was the home of the Olmec Indians, the pre-Aztecs, whom I still think a whole lot more interesting. They had built their own monuments near Oaxaca. I saw the Olmec ruins, and then returned to Mexico City and eventually Geneva.

I'm still grateful to Fernando for that Olmec trip. I know he was a rich man, but his was a very imaginative form of generosity. And I am particularly grateful to him for not having tried to make me go to any of those beaches on the other side of Mexico, on the Pacific, which were then already becoming fashionable. No, for me it was Mariachi music and Oaxaca.

Back to free-lance

A little after this, my private life was becoming so complicated, due to my inability to make up my mind between two different men, that I decided to ask my father – with whom (because of my irregular behaviour) I was not at the time on very good terms – to recommend me to a psychoanalyst colleague of his; which he did. Dr Gressot was Swiss and worked in Geneva, not far from my little flat. He was married, I found later, to a woman who had been a heroine of the French

Resistance in the Haute Savoie. She was extremely beautiful; her photograph was on his desk, and I found this reassuring.

Dr Gressot was very good indeed at his profession. I was a little worried at first as to whether I could describe the state of my soul in French. He said my French was quite good enough and that, anyway, it would be quite interesting to know what things were, for me, the most difficult to talk about in a foreign language.

The first fruits of my psychoanalysis, however, had nothing to do with my complicated private life. During the first few months, I discovered that I felt about my ILO job very much as I had about my convent school all those years ago. But, said I to myself one sunny morning, I am no longer thirteen or fourteen years old, I am twenty-seven: I can get out! And before I could change my mind, that very morning I presented my resignation.

This resulted in a bit of a quandary for the ILO authorities, for I was still in fact on probationary contract; in other words they weren't quite sure about me either. I was in my second year of conditional employment, and they had never, in the entire history of the Office, had someone resign while still on probation. However, we reached an agreement, whereby they and I would give each other a month's notice (ie., I would stay another month and then leave). During most of that month, there was a procession of my ILO colleagues through my office, partly to congratulate me, and partly to express their envy – "Ah, if only I didn't have a wife and children to keep!"

While I was still an international civil servant at the ILO, oddly enough one of the people I did get on with was the Director General, an American called David Morse, who I think had been one of Roosevelt's bright boys. I don't quite know how this started, though I do remember he once gave me a lift in his car to the Palais des Nations building. He was grumbling, essentially to himself but aloud, about how awful his life was and how regimented; "I'm not even a man any more, I'm a machine!" I, equally tired and bored, just said "Shucks!" Whereupon he looked at me with a grin, and liked me ever afterwards. In fact, he invited me on one occasion to his own private office and showed me all sorts of very peculiar objects he had been given by various national delegations. What particularly bothered him was a small hanging, with his own portrait on it, given him by what was perhaps already Iran or perhaps still Persia; he was absolutely certain that this had been made by child labour, but he couldn't, of course, prove it; and moreover, what did one do about a carpet with one's face on it? I said: "Mr Morse, I think what you do, is you take it off the wall and put it on the floor and then all your enemies can trample on it!" – and this went down rather well.

At a later stage, when I was again a freelance, but working again for the ILO, I went up, as I usually did, to the staff restaurant for luncheon and found most tables occupied. Poor old David Morse was sitting by himself at a table, because nobody wanted to appear to curry favour by sitting near him. I thought: *"Well thank heavens, I don't have to care any more, I'm a freelance; he can do me neither good nor harm. I am going to join the poor man."* So I did and we had a pleasant conversation with no particular consequences.

There were, of course, also a number of assistant directors at the ILO. One I remember with some clarity was a Peruvian, Alvarado – a little fat man, who had, in a big way, the Latin American obsession about chasing every girl in sight. He was infamous for it. However, I found I could escape his attentions by mentioning my family every few minutes, especially my parents, then already living in Geneva. Because, of course, Latin Americans of his sort always believe European girls to be of easy and accessible virtue, but not their own women, who are sacred. I used to have the same experience with some Latin American delegates, though others assumed I was a native Spanish speaker and therefore a kind of sister – so, while it was quite all right to borrow money from me or ask me for stamps, it was *not* all right to make a pass at me. (Of course I used to compare notes with other girls, didn't we all?)

The month of notice past, I left the ILO. Before then, I had informed my former employer and patroness, Marie Ginsberg, of my decision. Marie said "Oh, *good!* Come and have a drink tomorrow evening." I found she had got together a number of our freelance colleagues, to whom she presented me: "Here is Mademoiselle Krapf, who is one of us again!"

I was immediately surrounded by colleagues, saying: "Why didn't you tell me before?" and "Have you got a job for next month?" "No, no, no, *I* want her next month!" – and so it went on, and I suddenly found that, having been – before my long interludes, first in Hanoi and then in the ILO – a beginner, I was now an old hand, and accepted as such by all.

Travels of a free-lance: Poland

I still sometimes have the impression that any Jews that *did* survive the Polish Holocaust, I seem to have met at some point or other! A very important one to me was Irena Dobosz, always known as Bella. Bella and I met in an interpreting booth at a conference on which we were both working in Warsaw, on Agricultural Statistics. Several of us Westerners had an interest in going there; we had been hired (largely for that reason) by the Food & Agricultural Organisation's Chief Interpreter. I had, of course, no Polish and no Russian. One of my colleagues, Stéfan Priacel, was originally Polish, the other, Zoran Seleskovitch, had Russian; the Poles provided their own interpreters to deal with the Eastern languages. So Bella was with me in the English booth, interpreting into English from Russian and Polish, I doing so from French.

I soon noticed that doing things from French was quite important in Warsaw. If I needed to ask my way in the street, I would have to start out in French, which was then, in the 1950s, still the language of civilisation to any Pole: if Warsaw was the capital of Poland, Paris was still the capital of Warsaw. So if you spoke French – which very few people from the plebs (if any) understood – they would at once classify you as a civilised being. You then went on to reinforce this impression, by asking the question again in English, with which they were quite likely not to understand either, and only after that, did you go into German, much more readily comprehensible, since they had been occupied by the Germans – but you had by then made your point: you were *not* German.

It also helped to be a woman. I found out much more, at least about middle-class life in Warsaw, than my colleagues, despite their East European languages and their political sophistication. There was, for instance, the hairdresser that Bella sent me to. She said he was the best in Warsaw, though he did work in a State hairdressing parlour. He owned his equipment, such as combs and rollers, but was paid a salary by the State for his work; and he said firmly (in English): "*Madame*, you need a permanent wave." I said, I didn't see that I did. "*Madame*, at present your hairstyle is suitable only for playing golf! You do not, I imagine, spend your life playing golf? I assure you, you *do* need a permanent wave." As I was still demurring, he went on to say: "Look, it's exactly the same to me, I get paid a salary by the Government, which will be same whatever I do. But if I'm saying this, it is because, as a professional, I believe it." At this I capitulated. I have to say he gave me a superb permanent wave. Even my Geneva hairdresser couldn't fault it when I got back there.

While I was about it, I thought I'd have my nails done. Now, how to find a language in common with the manicurist? She had no French, no English, no German; how could I say: "I don't want this colour of polish, I want that one." Simple! Her little daughter was learning Italian in school, so on the basis of my saying: "*questo rosso*" for "*this* red", we got on fine. So, between her conversation and that of the splendid and seigneurial hairdresser, I learned a bit about life in Warsaw not open to my male colleagues.

I also met again, Lucina Stanicka whom I had known in Vietnam. My friend Olga Afanacieva, the French translator of Russian descent, had asked me to bring Lucina a present from her; I think I had brought her some French undies. Olga also said to tell Lucina that she had not been writing to her because she didn't want to get a friend into trouble with the Polish authorities.

Lucina, delighted to see me, invited me to have supper with her mother and immediately afterwards said: "How's Olga? You know, I often think of her, but I've never written to her, because I know she lives in New York and I didn't want to get her into trouble with the American authorities."

Beata Babad was also in town, and she and Manelli (who in Hanoi had been the Polish legal adviser) invited me to luncheon at the Journalists' Club in Warsaw. A splendid place, where we lunched on the terrace. There was a fountain in the garden, water issuing from the bill of a sculptured duck, and Manelli said: "Do you know what that is?" A duck isn't it? "Yes. The journalistic duck!" After which the famous French satirical paper *Le Canard Enchaîné* (The Chained Duck) had been named. In French slang, a *canard* is originally a rumour, and at one point satirical papers in France had been censored.

We had a number of days off from the Agricultural Statistics meeting in Warsaw. I spent some of the time with Bella, who was just moving into a new flat. "It's smaller than the old one," she said, "but the old one's a bit too near the place where my parents got killed." (They had died in the Holocaust.) Bella, married to a composer, had been away with her husband in Georgia at the time. Her new flat was still at the stage where it needed shelves putting up and other such things, so workmen would come. When they arrived, the procedure was quite interesting. They would start out by kissing Bella's hand. They were then formally presented to me, and kissed mine. They were then offered a cigarette, and only after that did they start work. One of them explained to me that one of the great achievements of People's Socialism had been that nowadays, anybody could kiss a lady's hand. It used to be that only the bourgeois could! On one of my forays near the University, a very shabbily dressed male student crossed the street to talk to two just as shabbily dressed women students, but before starting the conversation he did the proper thing and kissed their hands. Bella also told me that, while everybody was officially Comrade, everybody also still knew who was or was not a Count, and if somebody was an aristocrat he was addressed by his title.

She also said: "Look, while we've got these free days, you really ought to go and see Krakow, it is the most wonderful place." "Oh – and how do I get to Krakow?" "By train! At this time of year you wouldn't find a hotel room there anyway, because they're having a commercial exhibition and all the hotel rooms will be full. In any case, it's better that you travel by train, because then nobody wants to look at your papers. So you take the early train and you arrive in the morning and spend the day in Krakow and return by night train."

Bella had informed me that while they didn't officially give you morning tea on the train, you could make an arrangement with the guard whereby he would. So I did make such an arrangement, and duly got it. We were just about to arrive in Krakow when I also wanted a cigarette, and asked in all the languages I knew for a light. Sure enough, I got a polite answer, in English, from a good-looking young man, who asked me what I was doing there. I explained and asked him the same question. He said oh well, he was an actor in Krakow; he had just been to Warsaw for a competition.

(I found out later, from Bella of course, that he had won it; but that he didn't say.) Then, he said: "So you want to see Krakow in a day? I'll tell you what, I'll try and get them to excuse me from my rehearsal and then I shall show you round. Meanwhile you had better sit down at the station restaurant and have some breakfast."

Poles went in for late morning breakfast in a big way: ham, eggs and the like; they also went in for an early supper – lunch was not much thought of. So my young man installed me at the station restaurant, went off to his theatre, cried off from his rehearsal, and came and collected me. He then took me round Krakow, which obviously he knew very well. We went to the cathedral, climbed up to the top of the tower and enjoyed the view, then we went to the castle and there he mimicked for me, as only an actor could have done, all the various activities that had taken place there, such as jousts and the like. Then he looked at his watch, and said: "Well now I really *do* have to go to the theatre for the play. What would you like to do?" I said I would like to see this play. "Right," he said.

His theatre was called the Rhapsodic, which had in its day been anti-Nazi and was now anti-Communist, but in a very discreet way. They specialised in dramatised versions of the great epic poems of Europe, *Eugene Onegin* and things of that of nature. On that particular night it was the *Odyssey*: at least I knew the plot. They started out with Odysseus struggling in the waves. They had a very fine cast of actors, and one of the wonderful things was that all of them were dressed in the exact colours of Greek vases. In other words, redheaded Menelaus had a red beard and red hair and his garments were black and white, any old person had white hair and garments of ruddy and black and so on. My young man was Hermes. They all did it beautifully, because in addition to the costumes, they had been trained to put themselves into the position of figures on Greek vases.

During the interval, I had a conversation in German with the couple sitting next to me. As usual, they asked me where I came from and what I was doing here, so I told them about Agricultural Statistics. "Huh! In this country you will learn how to do Agricultural Statistics all wrong," said they. Then, at the end of the play, I became a regular Stage Door Jenny, collecting my young man from the back of the theatre. It occurred to me later that this had to be the very theatre where the man who later became the Pope John Paul II was, in his youth, an actor and playwright. This was when it had been an anti-Nazi theatre. I have long thought it had to be the same, because he was from Krakow and there can't have been that many not-very-official theatres in Krakow, but I have since had it confirmed.

My train didn't leave until about 11 pm, so my new friend took me to a nightclub. At any rate a place, open at night, which contained two things perhaps frowned on by the authorities: abstract art and red wine. Neither was very good, but they mattered. In the end, after the red wine and the abstract pictures, he took me to the station, and settled me in my First Class compartment. He sat down beside me and began to talk about his theatre and also about the future of Polish poetry. I said: "Look, shouldn't you be getting off, this train's about to leave?" "No, no," he replied, "Plenty of time!" Then the whistle blew. He kissed my hand, and in an athletic leap landed on his feet on the platform, whence he waved me goodbye. I never saw him again. I wrote to him; at some point I think he sent me some pictures of Krakow, and I thanked him for these.

Berlin

One of my most interesting journeys as a freelance was to Berlin. The conference was of course in West Berlin, and so was my hotel. But those were the days before the Berlin Wall, and it was perfectly possible to move between the two zones.

The first evening I went to a theatre that had been recommended to me, in West Berlin, where they showed one of Samuel Beckett's plays in translation, *Endgame,* the one about an old man and an old woman, each ensconced in Rubbish Bins on different sides of the stage. I found it a bit depressing and on my way out, as I was putting on my coat, I trod on the foot of the person behind me, and turned round to apologise. This was, as good luck would have it, a charming young man, who agreed with me about the play, and then said he must show me some other things in Berlin.

He took me, first of all, to what the Germans call a literary cabaret, a satirical performance art that Hitler had sat upon, which was now being revived; indeed it had never died in Zürich. It tends to be highly political, and is presented in short sketches. In this particular case, they had printed on the programme: "Working as we do in West Berlin, there is really no need for us to do sketches representing our attitudes to communism. So we're not going to bother with that, we shall concentrate on satirising our own society." Which they did very well.

My guide also suggested that I went to East Berlin, to Brecht's own *Berliner Ensemble*; so I did, on an evening when they were doing *The Good Woman of Setzuan*. I was wearing trousers, because I was off work and it was a cool evening; the porter at the theatre, when I handed in my ticket, read me the riot act about this. What did I mean by coming to the theatre dressed like that? This was what the capitalists always said happened in East Germany. "They think we don't know how to dress or how to behave, and it's not us, it's you lot – tourists, etc." It took quite some time. I did the best I could with a fake Argentine accent: "Oh, I am only a poor little Argentine student, I have no other clothes and I do so want to see Brecht!" By the time I had melted his heart, the play had started; Madame Weigel, Brecht's companion, quite rightly never allowed anybody to enter the theatre during an act. So I was sitting there disconsolate, when yet another nice young man came by and saw my tears. I explained, and he said: "You really do want to see this don't you? Follow me." He was one of the electricians working backstage, and he settled me very near the stage from where he did the lighting! I got a very good view of *The Good Woman of Setzuan,* admired it mightily and then returned to West Berlin, and my hotel.

Delhi

Another interesting journey as a free-lance took place in 1958. I was to go to Delhi to interpret for a rather lengthy International Youth Conference. I had been advised to stay at a sports club, a bit outside Delhi but within view of the old walls and fortifications, on the grounds that it was both cheap and comfortable.

The conference was dull, except when a few delegates spoke – ridiculously, we interpreters thought – of several African colonies quite soon becoming independent. The rest was boring. However, there was somebody I actually wanted to meet, a novelist, whom I knew from the titles of her books as R. P. Jhabvala. I asked around among my Indian friends – I was still in touch with Raj Chawla's family – and was told: "Ah, well, yes, no, she *never* goes out. You can never see her, she's never available anywhere. Husband's an architect." And then one Saturday or Sunday when the conference was not on, greatly daring, I looked up Jhabvala in the telephone book. There was only one there: Architect. So I rang up the number and got a very pleasant Anglo-Indian woman's voice, who identified herself as Mrs Jhabvala, and to whom I said how much I admired her novels; I was in Delhi for a short time, and would very, very much like to meet her. Her daughters have since told me they don't know what came over Mum, who *did* normally refuse to meet anyone; on this occasion, however, she invited me to come over for a cup of tea that very afternoon.

The novels I had so admired read very much as if they were written by an Indian Jane Austen. They had that kind of plot, ending usually in a happy wedding; and that kind of very accurate social observation. Beautifully written, very elegant, very soft-voiced. I was expecting a highly educated Indian writer; but when my taxi arrived at a smallish but modern house in Old Delhi and a servant opened the door, there rose from the sofa a girl exactly as Indian as I am (wearing, however, a sari) who introduced herself as Ruth Prawer Jhabvala.

Ruth is of Polish-Jewish origin, though herself born in Germany. Having come to England as a small girl with her refugee family, she had attended London University and had there met "Jhab", her architect husband. We got on extremely well that afternoon, and agreed we must meet again.

A couple of nights later I had a slight misadventure, not to me very serious, at the club where I was staying. The night porter, to whom I had said goodnight before retiring, later appeared at my door. He knocked, I opened, and there he was in his pyjamas, a wide smile on his face and intentions fairly obvious. I said

"No, no thank you," closed the door and had no more trouble out of him. I told this as an amusing story to Ruth when I saw her. She, however, was horrified, and told me I could not go on staying there. "Probably all you did was smile when you said goodnight, but he would have taken that for an invitation. You move all your belongings here – now!"

So I moved *chez* Jhabvala, where I got a bit of flat roof to myself. This was August, very hot and humid; everybody who possibly could, slept out of doors. In our case, on the flat roof of the house, or rather roofs: there was a bigger one for the family, Ruth and Jhab and their three little daughters, and a smaller one for guests, which I occupied. In the morning Jhab would poke his head round and say "Time for morning tea" and I would join the others, and contemplate around us all the neighbours who didn't have anything as luxurious as a flat roof, but would be having tea in their respective patios. I enjoyed staying there very much, the more so as I was amused at Ruth's total incompetence on the practical affairs of life. At one point I think she invited somebody else to dinner (I can't quite remember who) but the cat had eaten the dinner! When Jhab came home from work, he said: "Don't worry darling, there will be a nice chicken flying out right now from the Moti Mahal Restaurant, in time for supper..." And a nice tasty chicken flew out from the Moti Mahal and we all had supper.

Jhab is of Parsee origin. I do like Parsees – followers of the Zoroastrian religion, found across India but still treasuring links with the ancient Persian empire. Every one I've ever met has been intelligent and articulate. They were blamed, and I believe still are, by their fellow Indians for having been far too friendly with the Brits and the West. This was not, however, the case with Jhab's father, who had been involved in Congress in pre-Independence days. So much so, in fact, that at one point the colonial authorities had deputed a man to follow him wherever he went. Mr Jhabvala senior very soon realised that he was being followed; he turned to the man and said: "Look my friend, I know you're being paid to follow me. I don't know what you're being paid" – it was a rupee a day – "but I'll tell you what, I'll double it, if you'll carry my briefcase." So henceforth the peon continued to follow him, but now carrying his briefcase, which made the Occupying Power look ridiculous in a totally non-violent manner.

The conference over, Ruth and Jhab wanted me to stay a little longer, especially since the following week their household had been invited to a wedding, and they thought I would be interested in an Indian wedding. "And," said Ruth "we're invited by the boy's side, which means we'll get enough to eat. The girl's side never does." However, there was somebody else getting married that summer and it happened to by my sister, so regretfully, I had to say no and return to Switzerland for her wedding.

Trixie's wedding

My sister, by dint of considerable perseverance, was marring her girlhood sweetheart, Bernard Ingham, more generally known as Bernie. The wedding was due to take place in Switzerland in a town which has two names, Murat and Murten, because it is precisely on the linguistic frontier. Also, it has hotels enough to put up the guests, not a very large party; there were, perhaps, some thirty of us, including Aunt Lisa from Buenos Aires, with whom Trixie had been staying during Bernie's courtship. My old friend Iris came, and various other people; the wedding was celebrated in the small local Catholic church.

But before the church wedding, there had to be, according to Swiss law, a civil ceremony in the town office, which we also all attended – bride and groom already in wedding costume. Here, they were officially married to each other, and the civil servant in charge wished them good luck, despite what he called *die unvermeidlichen Unannehmlichkeiten der Ehe* – "the inevitable inconveniences of marriage".

Then came the church ceremony, and after that a pleasant luncheon. Then, another very Swiss thing: the bridal couple sitting up on the front seats of a small bus garlanded with flowers and ribbons, with the rest of us behind them. We went for a ride around the nearby countryside, including utterly delightful Gruyère – a tiny old town perched on a hill, where the cheese of that name should properly come from. My father had always wanted a house there, but my mother demurred: where was she supposed to get servants? But on this occasion, we stopped for tea there; and I still have a photograph of my sister in full bridal finery, making friends with a hillside goat.

After a Portuguese honeymoon, Trixie and Bernie settled down in Buenos Aires.

The idea of anthropology

When Geneva got too boring and no exotic travel was on offer, I occasionally went to Zürich, as others to Paris, for the good of my soul. Zürich is more than just banks. It is rather an intellectual town, with a great many bookshops, a good theatre (for serious plays), quite a number of good literary cabarets and any number of art galleries and other events, never mind the music. This, my father used to explain to me, was because it was a city of patricians – he was something of an élitist – a city run by its first families.

Not long after Trixie's and Bernie's wedding, I was attracted there by a huge exhibition of pre-Columbian Mexican art. Magnificent artefacts were shown from the most diverse collections, including the British Museum and, of course, the National Museum in Mexico itself, where I had, a few years before, first become fascinated by Mexican pre-Columbian art. The large catalogue informed me that the exhibition had been jointly organised by the government of Mexico and something called the Swiss Society of Americanists with headquarters in, of all places, Geneva. So, as soon as I was back, I joined it, went to a couple of interesting lectures, and found that an International Congress of Americanists would be held in the summer of 1959 in Vienna, under the chairmanship of one Professor Heine-Geldern.

I wrote to Professor Heine-Geldern, offering the Congress my services as an interpreter free of charge. (This, AIIC regulations allowed me to do: no undercutting, ever – but one was allowed to make a present of one's skills to a good cause; Marie Ginsberg occasionally did so for feminist or democratic-socialist meetings.) Heine-Geldern wrote back to thank me, saying he looked forward to meeting me in Vienna. I can't remember whether he ever did: once there, I realised these Americanists (archaeologists, geographers, ethno-botanists, anthropologists) all spoke several of each other's languages and actually had no need for an interpreter!

I listened to such lectures as looked most accessible, and soon decided archaeology sounded a far more worth-while occupation than all this repetitious conference interpreting. At this point, I began to keep a look-out for anybody there who might give me some idea of how one became an archaeologist; and, a day or two later, scraped acquaintance with a youngish German archaeologist, Professor Thomas Barthel, who asked me out to lunch. During the meal, he convinced me that – unless I felt a *very* strong vocation towards archaeology – I would, as a woman, be better off as an anthropologist. An archaeology qualification, he explained, risked landing me in some museum for life; whereas, since half of any tribal population was female and often somewhat segregated, women anthropologists were in great demand. He added that ancient artefacts would long remain to be dug up, but tribal customs were already disappearing fast, so anthropology was the more urgent avenue of research.

As always, other things got in the way of my making immediate use of Tom Barthel's suggestions as to where to study anthropology; but the option of taking it up remained at the back of my mind for later use.

Buenos Aires via Brazil

At the beginning of 1960, I undertook a trip to Buenos Aires to visit Trixie and Bernie; I travelled by sea, on a ship belonging I believe to the Vatican. We called, among other places, at Santos, the port of São Paulo, the most important industrial city of Brazil. And since Trixie could not receive me immediately, being away on summer holidays with her new in-laws, this provided an unexpected opportunity. A person who could receive me, and wanted to, was an old friend from my undergraduate days, the American Herb Cahn. Herb had since married his French girlfriend Monique, and gone to Brazil to make money. Even back in Oxford in 1951, he told me he was thinking, now he had finished his university education, of going to South America; did I know anyone who might give him a job there? "Well yes, as a matter of fact," said I. "You've come to the right address. My great-uncle runs a firm called Bunge & Born." Oh no!" he said "Not that. Anything else, not that!"

I only found out later what the trouble was; my Uncle Alfred, who had bought out cousin Conrad and various other people from under the Nazis at a time when this was still possible, had, however, refused to buy out people unrelated to him, such as his employee Mr Cahn senior, and Herb had therefore a great hatred for the entire Hirsch clan.

Herb told me later it had been rather a shock to him to find out that I, who had been his good friend, was on my mother's side a member of that loathed clan. At the time, he just asked whether I could think of anyone else, perhaps in Brazil? I then remembered that when we had gone to Europe in 1948, we had stopped in São Paulo and there had been an architect, some friend of my parents, who had come down and had taken us out to lunch.

So I said: "Yes, I do in fact know somebody, not very well, in São Paulo." I gave him the name, and I may even have had an address. Now, in 1960, Herb told me that when he went to meet this Brazilian architect and mentioned my name, he could tell the Brazilian couldn't for the life of him remember who I was, but thought I might very well be the wife, or the mistress, of somebody important; and anyway why not try out this hopeful American? Herb said he was a draftsman; so he was given a job as a draftsman, and at the end of the first month his employer said: "Mr Cahn, if you were able to persuade us that you were a draftsman, you are clearly able to persuade anybody of anything. You are now a salesman." This enabled Herb to marry his Monique. Her mother, a French anti-Semite, objected; and Herb now told me that, all those years ago, in the 1950s, the lady's parish priest had said to her: "*Madame*, I am sorry to have to inform you that our Lord Jesus Christ was not a Catholic. He was not a Protestant either, he was, *Madame*, a Jew. You have no absolutely no reason to object to a Jewish son-in-law, the more so since he seems willing for the children to be brought up as Catholics."

Pretty good for a parish priest at that time! Nowadays such a reply would be quite normal.

At any rate, by 1960 Herb and Monique were living in São Paulo, on its outskirts, in a pleasant leafy suburb. Monique was in fact at a clinic having their third child, and Herb had received permission to stay with her. So, he said, would I mind very much having the house for myself for the first night or two? He assured me it was perfectly safe, which it was. I still remember the sheer bliss before I went to sleep that first night, breathing in the tropical scents and seeing through the window the bougainvillea, climbing up the wall. Bougainvillea, which I had last seen in Hanoi, and before that at home in San Miguel. I was glad to be able to have this silent ecstasy without needing to make conversation.

Later on, when Herb got back home he said, "We do have some relatives of yours around here. No, not Hirsches – other relatives." These were a young couple, he a brother of Uruguayan Sarita, whom my mother's cousin Rodolfo had married – Juan Carlos, also known as Jean-Charles. And he was married to Suzanne, with whom I'm still in touch. We got on very well, and when Herb was away at work I spent most of my time with them, and she it was who asked me: "Eva Krapf – you must be related to that Trixie Krapf who got married in Switzerland?" "Yes, indeed, I am her sister!" "Ooh! Tell me about it. We heard it was the most wonderful wedding, in a chateau in Switzerland and that three hundred people went over, all their travel paid by Bunge & Born." So I said: "Well a zero has been added, it was more like thirty than three hundred – and while my Great Aunt Lisa went over, I don't know that anybody else from B & B did."

After which eventually I did join Trixie and company in Buenos Aires, where there was, among others, my beloved cousin Herbert Hirsch. His father *had* been brought up by Uncle Alfred, and Herbert and Herb must never be in the same room together because they could not stand each other, and not only for the obvious historical reason, but also for different temperaments. Herbert, much though I loved him, had become a rather pompous sort of snob, especially about the glories of the name Hirsch.

INTERLUDE 2

On Language: Pidgins, Creoles, Dialects

Languages and language

During my childhood in the 1930s, my father told my Swiss Nanny, who always spoke to me in the correct *Hochdeutsch* she had learnt at school, that he wouldn't mind in the slightest if I grew up to speak German with a Swiss accent; he was at the time strenuously rejecting his own German background. It was no doubt for the same reason that I never had a German lesson, and am thus living proof that one's mother tongue is not necessarily the language one speaks best. Early in my interpreting days, I had my troubles convincing the UN and even the interpreters' union, AIIC, that both my Spanish and my English were "quasi-native" and far better than my German.

Spanish and English I acquired too young (between the ages of three and five) to remember much about the learning process; the only one I really remember *learning* was French, for which Mademoiselle Jacquard put me through all the irregular verbs and many of the *Fables de La Fontaine*. I was fortunate in that Mademoiselle (though herself Swiss, not French) came from Neuchatel, where they pride themselves, with some reason, on not speaking with "that horrible Geneva accent"! For, as every Briton knows, accent as well as dialect often serves as a mark of social stratification.

This was doubly fortunate since, having no gift for mimicry, I speak those languages I do know exactly as I was taught them; thus, my Spanish is recognisably "River Plate", i.e. with the Italian accent we owe to our immigrants, which has come in very useful whenever I've been in Italy. Three Romance languages are spoken in Spain: Castillian, Catalan and Galician, and of course Portuguese is also very similar. However, I've learned the hard way that, for political/historical reasons, I must never, when in Portugal, try to make myself understood by speaking Castillian Spanish!

Essentially, though, all forms of Spanish are – as with English – perfectly understandable to speakers of other varieties of the language. Oddly, I grew up in Buenos Aires to hear Spanish as spoken in Spain not as posh or lah-di-dah (as people on the US eastern seaboard often hear the various accents of England) but as lower-class comical, the equivalent of Cockney. This too is due to a history of immigration: Spanish immigrants into Argentina came from the poorest and most illiterate parts of the Iberian peninsula. "Ramona", a cartoon character in the newspapers of my childhood, made people laugh as "everyone's Spanish maidservant"; I was grown up before I ever heard Peninsular Spanish spoken by an educated person. Fortunately for me, my own instantly recognisable River Plate Spanish enjoys, among other speakers of the language, a certain showbiz glamour – it is that of the tango singer Carlos Gardel, about whose exact birthplace the two River Plate countries, Argentina and Uruguay, are still arguing.

Having once heard my father explain to one of his students that, when I first learned to speak (which I did early and well), I immediately became tone deaf, I believe that this accounts for the inability I encountered, in later life, ever to master tone languages such as Vietnamese or Yoruba. But then, I am not somebody who just picks up new languages; I have met two or three such people, and know they are rare. So, whatever monoglots tend to say, I don't believe myself to have "a talent for languages", only a feeling for *language* as such, the same *Sprachgefühl* which enables me, to this day, to get the grammar right in the German I was never formally taught. Years later, in Geneva, on the lakeside beach – by this time I was studying anthropology – I had the privilege of seeing a small boy who had been left in charge of a smaller child. The younger child was sitting up, it couldn't yet speak; and the little boy, very gently, was moving the child's head from side to side with his fingers, and going *Non, non, non, non, non* – so I have actually witnessed the cultural indoctrination of the mute sign for "No". If I had stuck around, he would have moved the child's head up and down with his fingers and gone *Oui, oui, oui, oui, oui.* I was reminded of the time in Hanoi, when I had been so puzzled by my Indian typist's "yes" gesture.

I spoke, as I still do, my parents' educated pre-Hitler German. But Michi Jakob, born under Nazism in East Germany and later schooled under Communism, had a totally different vocabulary for abstract nouns. She and her family had managed, through the conference circuits, to get out of East Germany and had spent some time with us at Hamsey in the early 1980s (as I describe in Part Six). The Nazis had exiled as many non-Germanic words as possible, and the Communists had not, it seemed, welcomed such nouns back again, though no doubt they had introduced some new Marxist ones. Now, during my interpreting years I had learnt to understand *Fernsprecher* as *Telefon* (television is still known in German as *Fernsehen*). Scientific congresses had also taught me to recognise *Sauerstoff* as "oxygen" and even *Stickstoff* as "nitrogen". Michi and I had no need to talk chemistry to one another; but every time our conversation attempted a higher level of abstraction than the menu for lunch, we were both of us stuck for words! And nowhere, at home or elsewhere, could I find a dictionary that would translate "Nazi-language" into the sort of German I knew. I had been puzzled, too, by the surname Jakob, which I had guessed, correctly, to be Jewish; I then found out that Michi's husband Udo bore his mother's surname, and had no idea who his father had been – presumably a decent German who had concealed his Jewish partner (as well as their child) for their own protection.

The emergence of a modern nation has often involved the standardisation of its core language, in many cases through the provision or translation of sacred texts. For example, in England the King James Version, and among German-speakers Luther's translation of the Bible, provided models for the development of official national languages. The Florentine Dante Alighieri's *Divine Comedy* fulfilled the same function among the many dialects of the Italian peninsula. In Muslim countries, the Holy Koran played a similar part; but spoken Arabic differs, I believe, far more within that linguistic community than English, German or Spanish within theirs. France, however, with no sacred text to serve as model, had to rely exclusively on political centralisation, governmental decree and the perceived superiority of the Île-de-France form of speech.

"Dialekt"

The situation was different in the German-speaking cantons of Switzerland. These would never have tolerated a strong central government – Bernese are, even now, seen as rather slow-witted people – but they too needed an official language for legislation and the like. For such purposes they also used Luther's "High German", *Hochdeutsch*; but they took a totally different attitude to regional variants.

In my later years, following my marriage to Mick Gillies, I went to stay with his charming Swiss stepmother-in-law, Didy, now a widow living with her sisters in the family house near Lucerne. She greeted me at the door and, immediately after the first hug, asked in her native *Luzernerdütsch* "We *can* talk Dialekt to you, can't we?" To which I, fondly remembering my Swiss Nanny, replied "Of course you can, just as long as you don't expect me to answer in Dialekt! But I'll almost certainly understand everything you say." Huge sigh of relief: I had now really become part of the family. My understanding of *Schwyzerdütsch* went back a long way: as a seven-year-old in Zürich, I had been taken to a (pre-Disney) *Snow White and the Seven Dwarfs* in which Snow White, the Prince and indeed her evil stepmother all spoke "proper" German, but the dwarfs the homelier Dialekt.

Didy had used Dialekt in a way both accurate and perfectly respectful, clearly not regarding it as inferior to the *Hochdeutsch,* "high German", that all Swiss children from the German-speaking cantons learn at primary school, and which is used on any formal or official occasion. The Swiss cantons have only slowly and often reluctantly, bit by bit over many centuries, joined forces with one another, not becoming a real nation-state until late in the 19th century. The French-speaking cantons, among the last to arrive (only just before the few valleys where Romantsch is still spoken), seem to me to display differences of pronunciation that have not yet developed into genuine dialects; but each of the old German-speaking cantons takes a pride in its own brand of *Schwyzerdütsch,* and its people continue to speak it, and indeed to write it.

While still living in Geneva, I had known a local German-Swiss couple. He had done his military service (still compulsory for all Swiss males) as an officer, which implied, for the rest of his service life, quite a long annual absence from home on military duties; during this period, he and his wife always corresponded in *Schwyzerdütsch*. I have also seen a couple of books of poems in Dialekt, which I only understand if I read the texts aloud to myself: the spelling defeats me.

Linguists and polyglots, pidgins and patois

My trips to Africa opened up further aspects of the manners and politics of language. In Lagos in 1962, a colleague and I once consecutively interpreted the proceedings of a meeting of what are, I believe, properly called linguists. I take this term to mean, not people speaking several languages as my colleague and I did – we were, correctly, "polyglots" – but scholars in the discipline of linguistics. (These are nowadays sometimes called linguisticians, which makes me wince.)

This particular set of linguists certainly needed polyglot interpreters! None were black Africans; about half were French speakers, the other half English speakers – and all, at least officially, spoke only their own language. They were meeting to discuss desirable language policies for the then newly independent African countries – basically, at what educational level a (non-native) world language should become the teaching medium. My colleague and I, recalling our own backgrounds, were amused at the great discovery announced by one delegate – namely that a child growing up with a French-speaking father and a Wolof-speaking mother would speak French to his father, Wolof to his mother, and thus gain a good understanding of both languages. What, I wondered, would these determinedly monoglot linguists have made of my own childhood experience, as the daughter of two parents who habitually addressed one another in more than one language (though anything supposedly secret from me was always in one I hadn't learnt yet!)

Of more serious interest was the difference, between the two groups of delegates, in their attitude to what the English-speakers referred to as *pidgins* and *creoles*. For the French-speakers, there were no such modes of speech: people either spoke French or didn't. Anything else was *patois,* and not worth bothering about.

The English-speakers, on the other hand, attempted greater accuracy. They defined pidgin (said to be derived from "business") as a language spoken, mostly for trade purposes, between a technologically more advanced and a less advanced society; with a vocabulary largely from the former, and a grammar derived from the latter. A "creole" (from one of several New World terms meaning "native-born") was a former pidgin which had, in the next generation, become some people's childhood language or "mother tongue", potentially the sole language of a community, as a pidgin never was – a distinction I have found very useful.

"Pidgin" may be a loaded word, but *patois* is very much more so. That beacon of the 18th century Enlightenment, Diderot's *Encyclopédie*, already defines it as "corrupt language as spoken in almost all the provinces", and adds "Language proper is spoken only in the capital." This attitude itself goes all the way back to the Renaissance, to the reign of King Francis I (Henry VIII's contemporary) when the Decree of Villers-Cotterêts made Parisian French the official language of all legal documents.

In France the creation of the standard national language implied actually *forbidding* the written use of the *langue d'oc* (more often called *occitan*), the southern version of the language. It was contrasted to the mainstream *langue d'oil* on the basis of their different terms for "yes" (the latter leading to the modern *oui*). The *langue d'oc* has, however, survived in speech, and indeed experienced a literary revival in the 19th century, when dialects of *Provençal* became fashionable. The same centralising attitude must also have inspired educational policy in French African colonies, *France d'Outre-mer* or Overseas France as they were known, where local people either got no education at all or one equal to the best available in the metropolis – which accounts for a major French-language poet like Léopold Sédar Senghor, the first president of independent Senegal.

Contrasting with these historically-based, carefully planned French policies on education in their African colonies, the British had no governmental policies at all in the matter: the metropolitan authorities were more concerned to save money. Education in the British colonies was initially brought by Christian missionaries, whose primary schools operated in whatever was seen as the most widespread local African language, English being postponed until secondary education. But here too, any widespread language was a cluster of different dialects: how to choose the "correct" form of speech most suitable as a vehicle of primary education?

For the very widespread Yoruba linguistic community in Nigeria, the choice was in fact easy: here, the Bible had been translated into the Oyo version of the language by a native of that kingdom, one Bishop Samuel Ajayi Crowther who, rescued from a Portuguese slave ship near the beginning of the 19th century, had been educated in England by the Church Missionary Society (CMS). In baptism, he had taken the names of the CMS leader who had been his godfather. Eventually, having been ordained an Anglican priest, he returned to Nigeria as a missionary, and key player in the standardisation of written Yoruba generally.

INTERLUDE 3

Photography

1. EVA AS A SCHOOLGIRL, EARLY 1940S.

2. KRAPF FAMILY GROUP, BUENOS AIRES:
EVA BETWEEN HER PARENTS, WITH SISTER TRIXIE AND YOUNG TOMMY, MID-1950S.

3. EVA IN NIGERIAN DRESS, KABBA (STUDIO PORTRAIT, c.1965)

4. A WEDDING PORTRAIT:
EVA AND HASAN ASKARI, FLANKED BY HER PARENTS, GENEVA 1961

5. A GENERAL VIEW OF THE WEDDING RECEPTION

6. WEDDING GROUP: EVA AND MICK GILLIES, 3 JANUARY 1970.
ON EVA'S LEFT: MICK'S DAUGHTER SUSIE, AND BEHIND HER, BROTHER-IN-LAW BERNIE INGHAM.
ON MICK'S RIGHT: DAUGHTER JACKIE, AND BEHIND HIM, COLLEAGUE TONY WILKES.

7. WEDDING SNAP: EVA'S MOTHER, WITH EVA ON HER LEFT;
BEHIND, SISTER TRIXIE AND HER HUSBAND BERNIE INGHAM.

8. GABRIEL BAWA AKEREJOLA. THE OLOGORI OF OGORI, PHOTOGRAPHED BY EVA, 1966.

9. EVA AND MICK: TEA-BREAK IN THE GAMBIAN SUN, 1970S.

10. AN ANCIENT MOTOR BIKE: AND SOME BUMPS ALONG THE WAY – AS RECORDED LATER BY MICK IN *MAYFLY ON THE STREAM OF TIME* (PP. 294-95); SEE EVA'S LIST OF PUBLICATIONS, P. 303 BELOW.

11. A BRAND-NEW HOME IN THE BUSH: RELAXING AT WALLI-KUNDA.

12. TREADING GRAPES FOR THE WINE-MAKING: HAMSEY.

13. IN A SUSSEX COUNTRY GARDEN: A RETIREMENT WELL EARNED.

PART FOUR

TOWARDS AFRICA AND ANTHROPOLOGY

Chapter 1

Discovering Nigeria, 1960-62

My first journey to Africa was in 1960, to interpret for the International Labour Organisation in Lagos, then the capital of Nigeria. The ILO had just established a new Field Office for Africa there, in the year of Nigeria's independence. In November of that year they were holding their first conference, and this is where I was invited to interpret. It was an exciting time to be there. Already at the new African Field Office was an old friend from my previous, full-time, job at the ILO, one Hasan Askari, whom I used to meet occasionally over lunch at the staff restaurant.

The conference itself I don't remember well, but I do, very vividly, the pleasure of being in Nigeria at that happy time. The sheer niceness of people, the friendly way you were invited into a modest home; I am remembering a junior staff member at the ILO, whose shy wife said, at parting, what must have been the Yoruba *ekabu*! This was translated to us as "Welcome," but is something which Yoruba people often also say in farewell. Literally: "Greetings for coming!"

I remember also (I suppose at lunchtime) meeting, across the table, a black Kenyan, who began to tell me, as he had been taught it, the history of his country. He was saying: "... Then we were discovered by a man called Captain Krapf." I interrupted: "Ah! Did you get my surname properly, when we first introduced? K, r, a, – p for Peter, f for Freddie?" Of course he hadn't, nobody ever does. So I said: "Well my name *is* Krapf, and I am in fact a relative." At that stage, I wasn't quite sure whether I was saying the right thing, whether I was not confessing to some terrible colonialist past in my ancestry. Instead, the dear man nearly threw the table over in his haste to embrace me as a long-lost sister.

I explained to him that there had been no "Captain" Krapf as such; that was what the man had wanted, but his father had been unable to finance it. He had come to Africa as a missionary, so we talked about this for a bit. At some later stage, the same man said to me (I think a few drinks had been taken): "Of course we wanted Krapf, but in another way, we didn't want Krapf. You understand?" and I said yes, I thought I did.

I also remember being struck, on my wanderings through town, by the number of imposing and very Latin-American-looking buildings in central Lagos. Hasan Askari too was struck by this, and both shocked and amused to find that the mosques, of which there were quite a number, all seemed to resemble Christian churches – to be exact, Latin American colonial churches.

Another thing I remember is my first attempt to dance the highlife at one of several parties. I danced as best I could, first with a very tall broad chiefly figure and then with a short spare one; he was in fact the more effective of the two at pushing my hips the way they should go, and said, encouragingly: "Well, you are trying." Which again, I found out later, is quite a common Nigerian expression.

I moved from the original hotel I had stayed at, recommended by my father (who had been in Nigeria for WHO) to a smaller, older and much pleasanter one, in Ikoyi, a leafy residential suburb of Lagos. This was on the recommendation of my friend Hasan; there were, I suppose already then, the beginnings of a romance between us, which naturally flourished as we began to spend free evenings together.

Back in Geneva with my parents at Christmas, we pulled crackers as usual. Out of the crackers would come little leaden charms; and by family tradition, these were heated with one of my father's matches and dropped into cold water by each of us in turn: the shape they produced was then meant to foretell the coming year. My little bit of lead emerged in an extremely wild and woolly shape, which one couldn't easily relate to anything; but my father said: "Ah. The African jungle! That means you are going to go back there – but you liked it, didn't you?"

Marriage

Hasan and I were married in Geneva, near the end of 1961, in a registry office. I had been to Buenos Aires a bit before that, and had asked my father's friend, Father Carlos Cucchetti, what the Church might think about such a marriage.

My father, as a psychoanalyst in a Catholic country, had, very sensibly, kept a short list of confessors suitable for people of various ages and sexes; Father Cucchetti was clearly what he had regarded as suitable for me when, in my late teens, I had quarrelled with my previous confessor, who did not hold with women going to university. With Father Cucchetti I got on like a house on fire. Now, years later, back in Buenos Aires in 1961 and thinking quite seriously of marrying Hasan, I went to him again and said: "Tell me, what is the Church's view on somebody like me marrying a Muslim?" Father Cucchetti said: "Well I've never seen anything *against* it. Tell me more about this man." So I did, and he said: "Well, you go right ahead, my dear! I'll tell you one thing though, don't marry him in church just yet. Marry him in a registry office, and if your marriage is still going strong a year or two later, I promise I'll come to Europe and marry you properly myself." So Hasan and I got married in a registry office.

He was in Geneva on his way to some home leave. The ILO granted every permanent member of staff home leave every two years, to go back to their own country. It did have to be their country, they couldn't get leave just to swan around; but they were allowed a quite generous couple of months or so. Hasan was also taking some other leave due to him, because he needed to have his tonsils out. So he came to Geneva, had his tonsils out and we got married in a local registry office. My parents held a reception for us.

The first part of our honeymoon we spent in London, where we saw not only various friends, but also Hasan's very nice sister, Maryam Sultana, known to me as Sultani. As the wife of her elder brother, I could address her by her name, which her junior siblings could not. They had to call her Baji, "sister". Sultani was already a widow. She had had an arranged marriage; Hasan told me once she had cried like a baby because she had to be married before finishing her secondary schooling.

Hasan's family, the Naqvis, were Sayeds, in other words they were believed to be descended from the Prophet himself. This means, among other things, that, while it is quite all right for a Sayed man to marry a non-Sayed woman, a Sayed girl *has* to marry a Sayed man. This is not unusual in many societies – we all know that Dukes can marry showgirls, but their sisters simply *cannot* marry mere film stars.

So Sultani had been married off to another Sayed, an accountant, quite a bit older than herself. They had lived in East Africa and had three children, and had come to London for the sake of those children's education; whereupon her husband had died prematurely. So there she was in London, a widow with three children and not much education, still very concerned that her children should have the best. What could she do?

What she did was go out to work as a cleaner; she managed to hold the family together, and the children went to state schools. There was also a younger brother, Alun, with an English girlfriend – not that that was going very well.

So Hasan had quite a bit of family in London and I myself a few friends: we spent several days there. Then came the honeymoon proper. For this, we used Hasan's home leave, to which I too was now entitled; this meant travelling to his country, Pakistan.

First we took a boat to Bombay. There, we stayed at the Taj Mahal Hotel right opposite the Gateway to India: I think Hasan was being specially extravagant on his honeymoon. I was much impressed by the hotel, though a little annoyed that the rather large band played nothing but Western dance music. From there, we visited the Ajanta and Ellora Caves. How I wish I'd looked at them more searchingly.

I did notice that Hasan was pretty scared all our time in India: he kept thinking someone was going to attack him. I only later came to see why.

Then came the obligatory journey to Pakistan, and this was where our problems started.

If Hasan did not use his distinguished surname, Naqvi, but called himself simply by his given names, Hasan Askari, it was in order to distance himself from his father. This father was indeed a formidable old gentleman. The family had originally come from Amroha, a town in former British India. Hasan once told me that as a small boy there, he remembered, at the Muslim festival celebrating the end of Eid, sitting on an elephant and scattering sweets and small coins among the populace, as a Sayed boy should. Amroha remained in post-Independence India after Partition in 1947, but the family had to leave for Pakistan in a hurry, fortunately all safely. When they got to Karachi, there was no longer much money around, so Dad opened a petrol station, which enabled the family to live in reasonable comfort. They were, of course, still widely respected in the local community because of their Sayed descent.

Now the formidable Mr Naqvi felt very strongly that, when we came to Pakistan, we should live with them in their house; which I was very willing to do, in fact, I would quite have enjoyed it. Hasan, however, said: "*No*, no way!" I tried to persuade him. My father, who liked Hasan very much, also tried to persuade him, but he just went on saying: "No." When I asked his reason, he said: "Well, – we'd never be able to have a drink." I said: "But, Hasan, for heaven's sake! I could manage perfectly well without a drink for three weeks, and I'm sure you can." "No – definitely not!" Clearly, this was part of his general very difficult relationship with a somewhat tyrannical father.

However, we were still obliged, by those ILO home-leave rules, to spend three weeks in Pakistan; but Hasan had so arranged our travel that it need not be one day longer.

From Bombay we flew across to Karachi, to stay at the airport hotel. We were welcomed there by another younger brother, Shaman, who came along with a garland of flowers to place around my neck. He told us he and his mother were trying to negotiate with the old man so that we could get together in an amicable way without our actually living in the household. But they hadn't yet succeeded; meanwhile, we had perhaps best take ourselves off elsewhere for ten days or so, or maybe a fortnight, and then come back. So we duly took ourselves elsewhere. While we were planning all these journeys upcountry to get ourselves out of Karachi, I said jestingly to Hasan: "You know, we *could* stay in Karachi." He wasn't very tall, not much taller than I, all he would need to do was wear a *burqa*! Because the women of the house, of course, never went anywhere without a *burqa*. But this of course was not on.

We went first to the valley of Swat; we even went a little way up the Khyber Pass, not very far, but we did see men with rifles. Most of the journey was by train, but for the Khyber Pass we hired a car with a driver. We also went to Taxila, and Mohenjo-Daro, and in general saw a lot of very interesting things, which I probably would never have seen if Hasan hadn't had this difference with his father.

Eventually we did have to return to Karachi – and now, things seemed to have righted themselves. We were asked to ring up the family home, and promptly did so. First, Hasan spoke with his father in Urdu and then he passed the telephone to me, and I heard, in mellifluous tones: "My dear, dear daughter, what a pleasure it is to hear your sweet voice!" And this was the terrible old man. You see, although I was clearly not descended from the Prophet, nor even a Muslim, it does say somewhere in the Koran that if a man's wife, or his concubine, is a Jew or a Christian, he should leave her to say her own prayers to the one God. This is not generally known, and the issue does not even arise the other way round since Muslim women are not permitted, in principle, to marry non-Muslims. So the fact that I was Christian (and, had they but known it, Jewish as well) was well counterbalanced by my being an Oxford graduate, which was regarded as very, very, posh and desirable. So the marriage, as such, had their approval.

It was now duly arranged that Hasan and I were to go to their house for dinner, which we did – I wearing the wonderful red-and-gold wedding sari, which I had not worn at my Geneva wedding. We were very well received, and I took it upon myself to sit beside the old gentleman and charm him to the best of my ability, which I think we both quite enjoyed. With my mother-in-law I had no language in common, so we just smiled sweetly at one other. Hasan, meanwhile, was in a corner giggling with his two still-at-home younger sisters. When we eventually got home, he told me what they had been talking about. One of them had been betrothed to yet another proper Sayed, quite a young man; and her Mamma, herself the daughter of a learned divine, had found another useful text in the Koran, which said that although not necessary, it might perhaps not be a bad idea, if people who were going to marry each other actually *met* before the marriage. Thus fortified by the Scriptures, she had arranged for her daughter (I think possibly escorted by Shaman) to visit Hasan and me at our airport hotel when we weren't there. So, of course, she had a cup of coffee in the hotel coffee bar and, funnily enough, the young man was there too! So they met, and they quite liked each other and both of them were happy about the forthcoming marriage. This of course was a great conspiracy which Dad was not supposed to know anything about (I don't think he ever did).

Shortly after that dinner party, Hasan and I left Pakistan to go back to his job in Nigeria. We stopped over awhile in Egypt: a few days in Cairo, a city I like, and then on down to Luxor, where we stayed at the hotel. We could afford a fairly modest upstairs room, where we could look down on an open terrace – definitely larger than a balcony – attached to one of the better rooms; and who should be there enjoying the sunshine but Marshall Tito and his much taller wife Jovanka – quite unmistakable!

The other thing that struck me about Egypt (coming from Pakistan) was that the women were not wearing *burqa*s. This was a still a Muslim country, but they seemed to be walking around freely; I was also struck by this when we got back to Lagos.

Life in Lagos

Lagos was at that time probably about half-Christian, half-Muslim. Certainly there were a lot of Muslims around, and they behaved just like other people. Also, of course, there were a lot of quite wealthy women who couldn't read or write. But they knew to a penny what they had in their bank accounts when these were read out to them (I suppose they must have trusted the bank tellers) and they would sign the accounts with a thumb print. On the streets, women walked around carrying vast loads on their heads, but holding themselves free and proud. I found I liked this a lot better than Pakistan.

There was, of course, a slight problem when Hasan took me to open a bank account of my own; but this was not related to gender. We had agreed it would be simpler if I kept any interpreting earnings separate from Hasan's ILO salary; but at the bank, we were told this could not be authorised except by the head of his office. Hasan was in fact quite junior – third in rank at the Field Office; but as it happened both the men above him were away at the time. I wanted Hasan to write to the bank saying "I, Hasan Askari, at present Head of the ILO Field Office, hereby authorise the wife of my subordinate Hasan Askari to open an account at your bank." But he wouldn't quite do that, and instead just wrote an indignant letter. In any case, my account was eventually authorised.

Later that year, Hasan once again found himself, for the same reasons, Head of that ILO Office, at just the time Jawaharlal Nehru and his daughter Indira were visiting Lagos. In that situation, we were of course invited to the great reception – as were the many well-to-do Indians then resident in the city. I intended to get personally presented, which meant I had to stand out: easiest done by wearing a cotton sari and *choli*, and putting my long hair up in a knot. During our honeymoon, I had been far enough north to see local women no darker in hair or complexion than I. Thus impersonating, among all that silk and brocade, a very high-caste lady of austere Ghandian principles, and accompanied by my husband in (borrowed) Indian formal dress, I managed to slip into the right queue to be presented, first to the great man himself and then to his daughter Indira. I then had the pleasure of explaining to her that many years ago, in Buenos Aires, my own father had made me read the letters *her* father had written her from prison, on world history from an Indian point of view.

For everyday living, Hasan and I had a little house assigned to us by the ILO, in another leafy suburb of Lagos called Apapa, slightly less posh than Ikoyi. Hasan had already lived there as a bachelor, with an Igbo servant Paul, but had decided we might now need two house-servants, to support our married social life. He had consulted with Paul, who had said he could not quite guarantee anyone else to act as "small boy". Hasan interpreted this, I think correctly, as "I haven't any nephews or cousins the right age at the moment."

So Paul continued to do the work by himself, occasionally getting in a little help, if required for a dinner party. He did it very well: every morning there was a new little flower arrangement in an ashtray on the breakfast table. There was also a so-called "garden-boy"; Hasan flouted all local conventions by occasionally digging himself, but most of the work was done by the garden-boy.

The bedroom had air conditioning at night, and there was another small sitting room that had it in the daytime, and there I would sit with my books or trying to write stories; but my attention was constantly distracted by the gardener going about his business outside, wondering what on earth was going through his mind. I was also very interested in the archaeological museum of Lagos, a very good one, then still run by Raymond Apthorpe, later of the Museum of Mankind in London. All this, naturally, brought my mind back to the idea of anthropology, so that I was happy, a little later, when Raymond introduced me to Peter Lloyd, at that time working at the University of Ibadan.

Meanwhile in Lagos, Hasan and I had joined, as I had been advised to do by an Englishwoman in London, something called the Island Club, at that time *the* Nigerian élite club, with both local and expatriate members. We never in fact made very much use of it, but by joining it did meet its secretary, a delightful Yoruba man, named Jedi. Jedi was a builder, clearly an extremely prosperous one, who had trained in Scotland. He always wore Yoruba dress, of the most immaculate kind: his *agbada* robe worn over an impeccably laundered shirt with beautiful cufflinks; and on his head, although a Muslim, he did not wear the semi-Islamic cap that so many Nigerians already favoured – a sort of fez – but the truly traditional Yoruba male head covering, a sort of bobble-cap, rather like the one worn in our images of Father Christmas (which went well with his beard). He was a wonderfully friendly man, and at one point invited us to lunch in a restaurant with his wife; this was quite interesting, because the wife was either professionally or commercially active on her own (as Yoruba women, and indeed Igbo women, often were even then). She drove her own car to the restaurant, but spoke not a word of English, beyond hello and goodbye. So conversation between her and us was slight, but Jedi had done the proper thing and introduced us to her, and I knew something more about one section of Nigerian society.

On the financial side (very fortunately) I did in fact have quite a lot of interpreting earnings to put into that separate account we had managed to set up in Lagos, acquired simply by working in the newly independent African countries. The main English-speaking ones were Nigeria and Ghana, the main French-speaking ones Senegal and Guinea (known in those days as Guinea-Sekou-Touré, to distinguish it from what was still Portuguese colonial Guinea).

Now Guinea-Sekou-Touré was left-wing, and so was Ghana. Nigeria and Senegal were right-of-centre; and, clearly, these pairs of countries were at loggerheads with each other. For that very reason, Nigeria and Senegal quite often needed to talk, as did Ghana and Guinea-Sekou-Touré; so I got quite a bit of interpreting work, some in Lagos itself, and some elsewhere – once, as far away as Uganda. I went to Cameroon and, of course, to Dakar for conferences on a number of occasions.

In Dakar I made use of something I had already learnt, which is if you come from *outside* a country it is possible to ask for an interview with quite exalted people within it, whom you wouldn't dare approach if you lived there! In this case, it was some high up in IFAN (initials which then still stood for Institut Français de l'Afrique Noire); I asked him about something which had been intriguing me in Lagos – the unmistakable resemblance between the older buildings I saw there and the Spanish Colonial architecture I knew from my childhood. And he said there had indeed been interesting contacts between West Africa and South America, and that there was a man who knew a lot about it – a Frenchman called Pierre Verger, who sometimes lived in Lagos, and was then available to be interviewed. So, still in Dakar, I bought Pierre Verger's books, and learned a good deal more about the Afro-Brazilian connection.

I used to do my shopping in the centre of Lagos. Hasan had arranged himself a lift to the ILO Field Office on the other side of the island; so our small car was at my disposal. I used to drive into Lagos, park somewhere and do my shopping in the markets. I found this very much more amusing than Apapa supermarket. If I bought a new vegetable, the next woman in sight would say: "You know how to cook that, do you?" – probably in pidgin English since I had no Yoruba, and this got us into conversation of kinds. In one of these small old streets, I came upon a kindergarten, run by a middle-aged-to-elderly woman for a dozen or so small children, who were being taught English, essentially so they could then go to a good primary school. The kids were made to stand up and greet me and we would have a bit of conversation. And in the course of all this, I got more and more interested in Lagos itself, in its markets, its people, and its architecture.

Eventually I did visit Pierre Verger; an austere-looking old man, who received me in a very bare room. It contained a small table, a stool on which he sat, and a hard chair which he offered me. We spoke about the connections between Brazil and that part of Nigeria. Pierre Verger confirmed my impression: the Brazilian freed slaves who had come across to re-join their ancestors had usually learnt a trade in Brazil; with the women, it was generally dressmaking, with the men quite often building. It was they who had put up these older buildings in Lagos, and for a fee were quite happy to build a mosque, if a mosque was what was required – though they of course were Christian.

The reason all this was possible was that, although slavery continued to exist in Brazil for quite a long time, house slaves (as distinct from plantation slaves) quite often got tips from their masters and from visitors; they were allowed to save these tips.

Occasionally they saved enough to buy their freedom, and would then take themselves and their families back home – to places known from handed-down tradition.

Pierre Verger had started in life as a photographer; at first he had photographed Afro-Brazilian cults in Brazil, and then crossed the ocean as the subjects of his pictures had done, and was now photographing things from the African end. A scrupulously honourable man, he had been initiated into all sorts of secret societies and, unlike many anthropologists, had kept their secrets. The best of his work is still in his photographs, of which I own two volumes.

Despite all these amusements, my mind was turning more and more to my earlier ideas about going back to university to study anthropology.

One major motive for this was that my marriage was, for various reasons probably mostly related to cultural incompatibility, not going too well. Hasan was aware of this too, and we were able to talk about it. He had been married before, and been divorced from his first wife, who had treated him basically as a means of getting a favourable divorce settlement, so that she would have the capital to start a beauty shop, preferably in Europe, but if not, in Pakistan. Hasan was both surprised and pleased when he found out that I was not the same sort of person, but simply wanted us to part in as decent and friendly a manner as possible. We thought that my going to Britain for a year to start graduate studies in Anthropology would do very nicely, giving us time to think about it all and keep our plans quiet from the rest of the world. We also decided that, before we got too serious about things, I would try to find out what would be the least traumatic, the friendliest and most civilised way to be divorced from one another.

So, having between the two of us decided upon a trial separation of a year or so, I began to make inquiries, from Peter Lloyd and others, and discovered that, very conveniently, my own old University of Oxford offered a Diploma in anthropology that could be gained in a single academic year. I wrote to the Institute of Social Anthropology; yes, they would accept me if a College did. So I wrote to LMH; and yes, *they* would accept me if the Institute did.

When I began to make noises about going to Oxford to study anthropology, Jedi at the Island Club said: "Oh but that's wonderful. You must come back here and anthropologise my family, they can really do with it!" A joke, no doubt; but I think in a way he meant it. And indeed, though later at Oxford I kept being told to be tactful about "studying people" during my fieldwork in Nigeria, I found that most of my "anthropologees" agreed with Jedi. And the more intellectual they were, the more they did so. First in Kabba and later in Ogori, I met a number of young students; in fact ran a sort of salon for them; initially I would say things like "I am interested in your history," or "your traditions", but what they actually *liked* to hear was that I was interested in their customs, and was an anthropologist. Indeed, when

I was in Ogori, I used to get deputations from other villages to say that they too had very interesting customs and why didn't I come and spend time with them? I did find that for the villagers, having a resident anthropologist was something of a mark of prestige, though not quite as good as a secondary school.

Having saved most of my interpreting earnings, I fortunately did not have to ask Hasan (or my parents) for funding for my year away. Once I was back in Europe, but before I moved to Oxford, Hasan and I had agreed that I would try to find out about the least traumatic way of our getting a divorce. In Switzerland there were bureaucratic problems: a divorce between two non-Swiss citizens, married as we had been in a Swiss registry office, would require the approval of both their countries. And, although in Pakistan there was such a thing as divorce, at that time in Argentina there wasn't; so the whole thing could not arise.

A friend had recommended me to a solicitor in London, whom I went to see. This man advised that the easiest way, not involving accusations of adultery or mental cruelty or anything else disagreeable, would be to agree with each other that the marriage had not been consummated. In that situation, in English law as well as Roman Catholic custom, it could be regarded as a marriage that had never existed. "But," said the lawyer, "such an agreement between you would of course break the law, because it would amount to 'collusion between the parties'. You must therefore put nothing in writing; but when your husband is next in Europe, talk to him, and if he agrees verbally, you can try this method."

So I simply wrote to Hasan: "When you next come on leave, I want to talk to you about our plans."

Chapter 2
A Post-Graduate at Oxford, 1962-64

I arrived back in Oxford in the autumn of 1962, feeling that at thirty-two years of age, I was really rather old to be doing this sort of thing all over again.

One of the first things I needed to do was find somewhere to live: as a graduate student, I could no longer live in College. I went first to the University Lodgings Committee, which was no use; they did in fact find me a room, but it was far, far away at the other end of the Banbury Road, and involved a long bus ride into Oxford. I then went to a commercial firm, which gave me two addresses; and I thought, since I only had limited money, that I would look at the cheaper one first. This was at 29 Warnborough Road, a converted family house, top floor; it looked like a nice room in a nice flat and there seemed a pleasant woman in charge of things, so I said cheerfully: "All right, I like this, I'll be staying." The pleasant woman, whose name was June Stephenson, was by no means certain she wanted me to stay; she had had bad luck with her previous tenant and was feeling extra cautious. But she was too English and polite to say she didn't want me, and thought she would get rid of me later.

She still hasn't managed it.

So I now had a room in somebody's flat. June, who worked for an International Marketing Organisation, had decided that what she needed by way of a tenant was a woman graduate student, who would work late into the night and sleep late in the mornings; by the time the student got up, she, June, would have had breakfast and gone off to the office. This worked out quite nicely; only at weekends did we have to coincide with one another.

During that first term of my Diploma year, I worked quite hard, but would occasionally go for a Sunday morning walk. On one of these I crossed Port Meadow, towards Binsey Church, trying to find something I'd been told about, St Frideswide's Well.

I was having trouble locating it, when there appeared, seemingly out of nowhere, a small slender elderly lady, wearing a long skirt (by the standard of those days), a cloak, her hands in a muff, rather as if she'd come from another age. I asked her about St Frideswide's: "Oh, yes indeed!" she said, and showed me where it was. She also told me her personal legend of St Frideswide, not so much about the saint having been the first to convert Oxford, as about an intending suitor of hers, who (since she wanted to hang on to her virginity) was struck blind, whether by Providence or through her intervention I don't remember. Whereupon he promptly repented, and fell on his knees. She held out her hand and found the well, whose water cured his blindness. (I think he must have entered holy orders after that.)

At any rate my little lady showed me the well. She told me also that a few centuries later, Charles Lutwidge Dodgson, also known as Lewis Carroll, had come there with those three little girls and their governess, and seen this well. Apparently in his Greek the word for "treacle" and that for "healing" were the same word, so the well of healing became the "treacle well" in *Alice in Wonderland*. "Yes indeed," she said, "the church is very old. The last time we had royalty here," she added, "it was Henry VIII, he was married to Ann Boleyn at the time. I do so wish I'd seen him, he must have been so handsome then." It sounded as though she had unfortunately been called away to a friend on just the weekend of this unexpected visit from royalty. After I thanked her, she wished me well and walked up the little path into the cottage adjoining the church. I never saw her again.

The Institute

The Institute of Social Anthropology in those days was housed in a building just opposite Keble College, famous chiefly for having been the home of Dr Spooner, the inventor of "Spoonerisms", whereby the first letter of two words is exchanged, to comic effect – as in "Must get my luggage, two bugs and a rag". This too had at one time been a family house. The various anthropology dons, most of them, had studies somewhere inside; certainly Professor Evans-Pritchard himself had. Godfrey Lienhardt already operated from Queen Elizabeth House; while I was sent for tutorials, that first term, to Nuffield College – to one Ruth Finnegan (herself working on her doctoral thesis, but already taking on Diploma students). I remember the first essay she ever set me had the title: "Why am I doing this Diploma?", which did indeed make me think about my reasons. So useful did I find this that when, a few years later, I was myself teaching first year undergraduates at SOAS in London, I used the same title for their first essay assignments. One also learns quite a bit about one's students in this way.

For the rest of the time, Ruth Finnegan taught me, essentially, the basic theories of structure, function and politics. At the end of term, she asked me who I would most want to teach me next. "Well if at all possible," said I, "Professor Evans-Pritchard", and she did duly deposit me on his doorstep.

I had, of course, visited the Institute before, on the first day of that Michaelmas Term 1962. Almost the first thing we had to do was leave it again, to walk into the centre of Oxford to register as Diploma students. When I did so, I found myself walking between two priests, both in their dog collars. The constitution of the Institute at that time said that a Diploma student had to have a previous degree (subject not mentioned), or equivalent experience. "Equivalent experience" was put there precisely for people like missionary priests and District Officers – people whose duties might have made them familiar with particular "remote" parts of the world, but who wanted to understand better the theoretical frameworks that anthropologists might bring to this kind of knowledge.

Keeping up with Aunt Ann

Living with June in her apartment in Oxford, I already had a problem that would come to dog me the rest of my life, namely too many books and not enough space to put them. June used to joke, I think semi-seriously, about them being a bit much for the attic floor of an elderly house, and we thought that perhaps my Aunt Ann could store some for us. Aunt Ann and her husband Billy, having sold their Isle of Wight property, had bought an enormous house on the mainland (from Charles Clore, no less) – not so much for sake of the house, as for the grounds, which were 300 acres. The grounds, of course, were for the cattle. By this time Aunt Ann didn't only have Dexters, but some other breed as well, I forget what they were. She looked after the cattle and Billy looked after the rest as usual; the house was looked after by an Italian couple. Aunt Ann was never domestic: she was quite prepared to get up at six in the morning to mix feed for the calves, but not to get up at any time at all to make breakfast for her husband or herself. They had Tina and Tony for that. And on this basis, June and I used to be invited to stay.

We broached the subject of these books and my Aunt Ann said: "Yes, yes, of course. But – Oh dear! Where? It's going to be a bit difficult in this house – the floors might well give." June and I managed not to catch each other's eye. In the end a place was found. The books were lodged in the West Wing, while we were in the East Wing, or it may have been the other way round. At any rate that was the books taken care of, fine.

But then over the years Tina and Tony had been saving their money, as good Italians should, to buy their own land in their own bit of Italy; so they wanted to leave. Total collapse of civilisation! What were Ann and Billy going to do now?

It wasn't that there was nothing else on the estate. There were, as far as I remember, eight pairs of cottages (it may only have been six) for the staff, not all of which were occupied, and Aunt Ann said: "Well it's quite simple. We'll knock two of the cottages together and live in that." But Billy said: "No! I'm fed-up with old houses. I want something clean and modern and spanking new. Why don't we send to Scandinavia, for one of those do-it-yourself kits and build ourselves a bungalow?" June and I wondered, over several visits, which of them going to win. The answer was, they both did. My Aunt Ann duly converted a couple of cottages. Uncle Billy duly sent for this build-yourself-a-bungalow kit, and built himself indeed a very nice bungalow, right next door to hers. But then came complications.

The faithful cowman Ken, who had been with them a good many years, said he could not possibly allow Madam to live all by herself, and moved in with my

Aunt. Whereupon the faithful cowman's wife, Mrs Ken – I have never known her by any other name – moved in with my Uncle next door. What the neighbours can have thought, I do not know. My mother's main worry about the whole thing initially was that Ann and Billy had a joint bank account; and supposing Mrs Ken took or inveigled money out of that to get herself a fur coat? However, none of this happened. Mrs Ken was a perfectly decent person and did not want to get a fur coat out of the situation.

The only person in all this whose emotions were really involved was Ken; I could see by the way he looked at my aunt. She was no beauty, nor did she take care of herself. But she did have charm, and Ken quite clearly adored her. I don't think she adored him back particularly. She was fond of him of course; but whether things ever went further than that, I have no idea, nor has anyone. She was rather straight-laced, so perhaps they never did.

All four were on quite reasonable terms. I think Ken grew the vegetables for the whole community and Billy the flowers – though it could have been the other way round. If I went to stay with Aunt Ann, Billy would send a message round saying: "And do come and have coffee with the opposition afterwards."

I remember thinking at the time – this is *Lady Chatterley's Lover* as re-written by Iris Murdoch.

Christmas vacation: in Lagos again - The Afro-Brazilians

In the Christmas vacation of that academic year, 1962, I had a chance to return to Lagos. Since I still needed to earn money, someone had found me a week's interpreting job in Accra, at a West African Studies congress to be held in Legon University in the city. This got me to West Africa, and earned me enough money to let me travel on to Nigeria, where I might talk to Hasan about our impending separation, and how to be divorced in as civilised a manner as possible.

When I got to Lagos, as Hasan was still working during office hours, I pursued my Afro-Brazilian enquiries. Pierre Verger had advised me to go and see an old lady, Donha Rumana da Conceição, living in the old part of central Lagos.

I found Donha Rumana in quite reasonable health, and very lively. I started our conversation in Portuguese, but my Portuguese was clearly not good enough for her, so we switched to English. I said, politely but truthfully: "But you, Donha Rumana, still speak wonderful Portuguese!" (She had already explained to me that she had come to Lagos with her family at the age of four or five.) "But *niña,*" she answered, "you don't expect me to forget my native language." We spoke of this and that; she told me about her journey and about growing up in Lagos. Suddenly, she asked (it happened to be Christmas Eve): "What are you doing tonight?" and I said: "Well, I'm here with my husband, I don't think we have any particular plans." "Oh good!" she said: "We Brazilians are having a Christmas Eve Party, and you and your husband, I'm sure, would be very welcome. If you'll just wait a little, my daughters will arrive, then they can take you to the house of the lady who is actually giving the party, so she can invite you herself."

Eventually the daughters arrived – great big strapping Yoruba wenches, without a word of Portuguese. After a fond farewell embrace from Donha Rumana, they took me to a rather smart flat in Central Lagos. From the interior of the flat (we were in the sitting room) there appeared a man, white, who kissed hands all round, and then went off with the two girls, presumably to shop for the party. Then there emerged a young woman, very good looking, also white, wearing shorts. I introduced myself rather diffidently, and explained I had come from Donha Rumana da Concepição and that I had heard that there was a Christmas Eve party. "Oh yes," she said "and you *must* come!" I found out that their name was Da Rocha – an aristocratic name in Brazil; one of them was a painter and the other a poet, though I've now forgotten which was which. They were, anyway, aristocratic Brazilian intellectuals, who, like others of the sort, were fascinated by the Afro-Brazilian heritage; so they had used their connections to get him appointed Cultural Secretary to the Brazilian Embassy in Lagos. Once there, they took their job eccentrically but very seriously – that is, they managed to get acquainted with all "Afro-Brazilians" in Lagos. This was what the party was going to be all about.

That evening, Hasan and I showed up at the flat. Mrs Da Rocha had organised a lovely tropical "Christmas tree" – not an imitation fir, but simply some bare branches on which she had hung baubles; beneath this was a heap of presents. It was quite a large party, consisting partly of smooth young men from Latin American Embassies, but mostly of Donha Rumana and her contemporaries, their children and grandchildren. First, the youngest child toddled up to the tree to get its present; then we went roughly by order of age. There were even presents for Hasan and me! – I still have them, a book of poetry and one of paintings by our hosts. Then the party began to hum and I noticed with interest that all these people, black and white, addressed each other as "aunt" and "cousin". It seemed that, from the point of view of the Lagos Brazilians, what they had nowadays, very usefully, was a cousin in the Brazilian Embassy. This says a good deal about the relationship that must have existed, even in the days of slavery, between the Brazilian white slave owners and their house slaves.

Eventually there was a very good Afro-Brazilian supper – Bahian cooking is among the best in the world. I don't know who the Da Rochas had got to do it, but it was delectable. Then there was a fair amount of rhumba-ing. Shortly before midnight the party ended: we all went off to Lagos Cathedral for Midnight Mass, like the good Catholics we all were (with the possible exception of Hasan!)

I believe that what I've said, about the relationship between Brazilian slave owners and their slaves, is part of a more general difference between Latin Americans, including those of Spanish descent, and their French and English counterparts further north. And, among the Spanish-speakers, this extended also, to some degree, to relationships with the autochthons, with American "Indians". I have found out since that much of Argentine high society is descended from one particular minor *conquistador,* Irala, who acknowledged the children he had by one or two Indian concubines. He fathered quite a number of children, to all of whom he gave a start in life: the boys got some sort of primary education, and were inducted into the army; the girls got dowries.

This was not unusual; there is a classic Latin American author called Inca Garcilaso de la Vega who was indeed descended on the one side from the Incas, the rulers of Quechua Peru, and on the other from the Garcilasos, one of the first families in Spain.

This sort of thing seems to have happened quite a bit. Usually, the Spaniards who came could not, in any case, marry their concubines, even had they wished to, because each already had a wife living in Spain (though sometimes, as in the case of Garcilaso, there *was* a marriage). But the point is, these relationships were between high class Indians and the noblest houses in Spain. The conquerors killed the men, often with the utmost cruelty, but treated the women with honour, very different from the attitude in Northern America.

The Argentine author Lucio Victorio Mansilla, whose work I was later to translate (see Part 6, Chapter 5) attributed this, probably correctly, to the fact that the Spaniards at first brought practically no women to their newly conquered lands, unlike the English and the French, who imported prostitutes (as is clear from the novel and, later, opera, *Manon Lescaut.*) This made a very considerable difference, and has altered the relationships between the races in the different parts of the American continent; the Portuguese and Spaniards were basically similar in this respect. Initially, there was, of course, considerable rivalry between the two European countries as to who owned which bits of this new continent, supposed to be so full of gold and silver. This was resolved in 1494 by Pope Alexander VI, in what may have been the first international agreement to be respected by both sides. The Pope chose a particular meridian (running down through the middle of the Atlantic, and cutting through what is now the north-eastern chunk of Brazil) and decided that everything west of that meridian was Spanish, and everything east of it Portuguese. This helps to account for the eventual distribution of Portuguese colonies in Africa and Asia. Both sides, as I say, more or less respected this; the interior of Brazil in any case was totally unexplored. There were a few scuffles; by 1828 it was seen as necessary to create the country of Uruguay, much desired by the British merchants, because it was on the frontier between the two, so as to avoid too many border problems!

Academic and personal events: the first half of 1963

Returning to Oxford for the Hilary Term of 1963, where now I had Evans-Pritchard himself as my tutor, I was returning also to one of the coldest winters England had ever had. Everything was covered in ice, and June Stephenson and I, living as we did at the top of this converted family house, got even less heat than those below us; I remember our friendship maturing as we spent time, down on our knees, pouring salt down the lavatory pan, so it shouldn't freeze up.

The Easter vacation I spent largely in Geneva, where my father was by now rather ill with pulmonary emphysema, and would soon have to stop work. My brother Tommy had been suffering from a mysterious illness which was also getting worse – the idea was being discussed of sending him to a specialised Institute in Germany, where they might at least find effective ways of delaying his symptoms.

For the summer term of 1963, I returned to Oxford. The Institute of Social Anthropology was not only a nest of Catholics, but also a nest of East Africanists, with the exception of David Pocock, a specialist on India. And there was another man, not at that stage very prominent in the Institute; in fact he wasn't there all the time. His name was Edwin Ardener, and he was a West Africanist, specialising in the Cameroons. Since I was still interested essentially in West Africa, I began to go to Edwin's seminars which took place late in the afternoon once a week.

Meanwhile, and towards the end of that first academic year, Evans-Pritchard suggested that I apply for a Nuffield Junior Fellowship; this would finance a further year for me to write my B.Litt. thesis, and might possibly be extended later to cover field work. For this purpose, I went down to London and faced the Nuffield Scholarship Committee, of which E-P himself was a member; the only anthropologist there. (At a later stage he once said to me: "They tell me anthropology should be better represented on this Committee, but I don't see why – if there are other anthropologists there, they will want the fellowships for their own students; I want to keep them for mine!") Other members of the Committee asked me various questions as to what I had done. I confessed somewhat shamefacedly to all the years I thought I had wasted by interpreting for a living, but they didn't seem at all unhappy about that. They asked me about my time in Lagos, and I told them. Then I left, and to relax my nerves got on a boat on one of the canals in London and spent the afternoon there, and only took a train back to Oxford in the evening. It happened to be the same train E-P was on, so that when we got down at Oxford we ran into each other at the railway station. "Well", said he, "you got it! – but don't tell anybody." I asked his permission to tell, at least, my parents, and he said yes, yes, I could do that, but should not tell anyone else. So I duly wrote a letter to my mother (my father was now already in hospital with what was to be his terminal illness). The next day, when I arrived at the Institute, everybody – but everybody

– was congratulating me on my Nuffield Junior Fellowship – E-P himself hadn't been able to keep his mouth shut!

Hasan's death

Not long after this, I got a telephone call from Geneva, from the International Labour Office. Hasan, who had been due to come on leave shortly, and for whom I had already booked a hotel room in Geneva, had been asked by the Office to fly on one more short mission before his leave. His plane had crashed in Cameroon. It was from this phone call from the ILO that I heard the news of Hasan's death. They had attempted to inform me more gently, by ringing my father (to whom it was quite a shock, he had been fond of Hasan), but for some reason my father had not been able to get in touch with me. So I got it, cold, from the ILO.

One has curious reactions to these things. The first one, emotionally, is: *Oh dear, I wish I'd been nicer to him!* Immediately after that, you think: *Yes, and if I had been, I would have been on that plane, wouldn't I? I'd be dead now.*

The next reaction after that was, for me: *Oh Lord, and I've got people coming for drinks the day after tomorrow. I'd better ring them up and tell them they can't.*

So I rang up my friends – my old friend from undergraduate days, Brigitte Heinsheimer (now Pring-Mill) and her husband Robert. I forget which of them I got on the phone; I think it was Robert, who said: "Right. So now you pack your toothbrush and your nightie; you are coming to and stay with us." I was extremely glad to be told what to do. I packed my toothbrush and my nightie, left a note for my landlady June and off I went to the Pring-Mills, who got me blind drunk that evening and put me to bed.

The following morning I woke up feeling able to cope, and said so to Brigitte and Robert. Brigitte said: "Right, well, if that's how you feel, go back and cope. But I'm leaving your bed made up for a few nights, in case you want to come back."

So I went off, and one thing that saved me was that I had my Diploma examination about three weeks from then, so I *had* to do something, namely work. My other salvation was the attitude of all the people I knew in Oxford.

I now know, which I didn't then, that they had heard about Hasan's death quite independently of me: Edwin and Shirley Ardener, in Cameroon at the time, had in fact seen "Hasan's pyre" when the plane fell. At the time I didn't even think about it. Nobody paid me formal visits of condolence, but everybody, from my former moral tutor at LMH, Katie Lea, to Godfrey Lienhardt to Michael Dummett, saw to it that I never spent an hour alone unless I wanted to. (Some of the time I did want to, because of having to study for that exam.) But the combination of the silent, but real sympathy from my Oxford friends, and the fact that I had something very specific to work for, probably kept me going during that very difficult time.

The following autumn, I began work on my B.Litt. thesis. I had spent most of the summer vacation largely reading around the relevant literature on Yoruba life, and the long history of their well-organised towns – and finding out in the process that composing a thesis was really very different from sitting for exams. I've always been good at regurgitating information; I found I was much less so at building something from it.

Also during that summer vacation, I discovered that Hasan's tragic death had solved my financial problems for years to come. Unlike most international civil servants, Hasan had died, not in his own time on sick leave, but in the Director-General's time, while on a mission for the ILO. As a result I got a very substantial pension, during all my widowhood, with the promise of a dowry of two years' pension, should I wish to marry again. I had to have my continued widow's status certified every so often; this was done by E-P, who used to ask me suspiciously every time: "You haven't been and got married without telling me, have you?" but then he would always duly certify me, so I was financially stable for the time being.

Official widowhood

My bureaucratic troubles, however, were far from over. At the time of my birth in Munich, my parents got me registered at the Argentine Consulate within a few weeks. I've never quite understood why – whether they had extraordinary prescience or just wanted to keep all options open for me – I suspect the latter. It meant that up to the age of eighteen I would have, not dual nationality, but *no* nationality. This hadn't mattered much, because up to then, I'd always travelled with parents, or other adults with my parents' written authorisation.

When I reached eighteen I had a choice: technically I could opt for my nationality. In 1948, there was no way I was going to opt for being German. My father, always extremely good at defeating bureaucracy, had it all very well organised: he had already made copies of my birth certificates and had all the paperwork done. He got all this translated and rubber stamped; and on my Argentine passport, which I still have, it says that I'm Argentine "by option", which is a small but extant legal category. It means that I am the equivalent to being born Argentine, as my father, a naturalised citizen, never was. In theory, I could have run for President of the country, which he could not have done.

By 1963 my Argentine passport recorded me as a married woman, but now, after Hasan's death, I wished to be classified as a widow, in case I ever wanted to marry again. I had been sent several somewhat faint carbon copies of Hasan's Cameroonian death certificate, signed by a Cameroonian official who rejoiced in the name of Faustin Happy Happy, which did not make for great seriousness. Having all my life known about bureaucratic problems, I had got this document stamped by every possible authority and, with this in my hand, went to the Argentine Consulate.

"We can't accept this," they said. "This is not a proper death certificate." I said: "Look, if the President of Argentina were to ask the President of Cameroon for a death certificate he wouldn't get any other. This is the way they do them in French-speaking lands; it is also the way they do certificates in French Switzerland where I got married." "Ah yes! You got married in French Switzerland, didn't you? Has that marriage been certified by our embassy in Berne?" So I said: "No, that was not required at the time." "Have you still got anyone living in Switzerland?" "Yes... my mother is still there..." "So will you ask your mother, then, to get your marriage certificate registered in our Embassy in Berne and stamped accordingly, and send it to you, and then we can see our way to accepting this death certificate." Or, as my friend June put it: "Prove you were married to him, dear, and he *must* be dead."

My father's death

It was late that autumn, not long before Christmas, that my father became very ill indeed. I went to Geneva, and saw him in his hospital bed. Soon afterwards I had to go back again for his funeral. My mother was at the time receiving formal visits of condolence, which I thought were pretty dreadful, but probably meant something to her. I was tidying up my father's library and used to emerge rather dusty, shake hands as required and remove myself to the library again. But once those visits were over, my mother was dropped out of the Geneva social scene like a hot stone. By sheer bad luck the two close women friends she had had in Geneva had already left, following their husbands' retirements – in one case to Scotland and the other to America. Without these close friends, she was with one or two exceptions left strictly on her tod after my father's death. What a contrast to the way I had been treated in Oxford!

These frequent, though short, trips to Geneva meant that I was occasionally away from Oxford during term, when by University regulations I should not have been. When I told Edwin Ardener about this, he said "Don't worry; I am sure we can all swear to having seen you in Oxford."

Chapter 3
Summer Vacation, 1964

My young brother Tommy had been born in 1944 – late in my mother's reproductive life (she knew my father wanted a son and was trying to give him one). At first he seemed a perfectly normal, though somewhat bad-tempered, baby. A special room had been built for him at our weekend house in San Miguel, with his own door, so that at a later stage he could go out on his lawful, or less lawful, occasions, without crashing through his sisters' bedroom.

When Tommy was about five or six, he began to get very fat, and then, about the time my family came to Geneva in 1953, extremely thin: it became obvious that something was seriously wrong. I couldn't work out what it was. He was, so far, being treated as though he were a normal boy; he was attending the International School in Geneva and walking there. He was always obstinate and there was a shortcut he liked which he was not supposed to take, so he habitually took it. The school then closed the gate with some barbed wire, so he bought a wire cutter with his pocket money, and simply cut his way in. He also had considerable intellectual interests, concerning mostly ancient Egypt, but also ancient Rome; I remember his writing a five-act tragedy about Julius Caesar. He was also, already, a considerable collector, both of Orthodox icons and of semi-precious stones.

But it was becoming increasingly obvious that Tommy was far from well. At some point in the late 1950s, thinking my father (never mind my mother) didn't want to recognise this, I went to another psychiatrist, a friend of my father's, and explained the situation. Dr Ajuriaguerra said: "Yes, I can tell you what's wrong with your brother, he has Muscular Dystrophy" – a disease more frequent in boys than in girls, which tends to declare itself in childhood; such patients seldom live beyond the age of twenty-one.

I asked Dr Ajuriaguerra: "Well, isn't there any way that you can perhaps tell my father." He answered: "Your father knows." "Oh! So why does he never talk about it?" "That," said Dr Ajuriaguerra "I don't know. Your father has a very difficult row to hoe, and he doesn't perhaps know what to do about it. I think he hasn't told your mother. But he does know exactly what the problem is."

Then in 1962, when I was living with Hasan in Nigeria, Tommy came to spend some of his summer holiday with us. At the time he was still coping fairly well and I think rather enjoyed his stay (he would always enjoy something exotic). I remember we went to what was then still Dahomey, to one of those fishing villages built over water. He had to be lifted into the boat, but enjoyed seeing the houses on stilts and people calling to him. But he already had considerable difficulty walking, and fell once or twice. The local people passing had this wonderful African habit of saying "Sorry", meaning not that they thought it was their fault, which it clearly wasn't, but that they were sorry it was happening. I think this stay was a happy time for Tommy. Hasan was very good with him.

Tommy wanted to study law. I used to tease him about his politics, which I said were those of an elderly *rentier*; they were certainly well to the right of mine. On the other hand he was interesting on this, as on so many other subjects. This was about the time that Hammarskjold's plane was shot down in Africa, and people like me blamed the Belgian *Union Minière*. Tommy said: "It's all very well; the *Union Minière* may be guilty at bottom, but Africans are not going to fight for that – they will fight for their tribes. It's a question of knowing which tribes are on which side. Oh yes! That's what is interesting." And by the next time I saw Tommy, he had made a list from his reading as to which tribes were on which side. (I also went with him to see the film *Citizen Kane*; altogether, Tommy was very much an intellectual companion to me.)

But now, after my father's death in 1963, the bad news was out. I don't know whether he told my mother on his deathbed or not, but we did by then all know what was the matter with Tommy. And now the secret was out, it was decided that Tommy should, for the time being, go to an Institute in Germany, where cases like his were treated according to the latest techniques, to afford at least symptomatic relief; he could be cared for there while my mother made further plans. She had already decided to re-structure her life around her ailing son. So she now had to make plans, for Tommy and for herself. She decided not to stay in Geneva, where as a widow she had been so promptly dropped from the social calendar; but to return to her native Buenos Aires, and find somewhere to live there. Tommy still wanted to study law, and my mother thought it should also be possible to arrange for some financially strapped boy of his own age to push his wheelchair and help him with notes, in return for his own education being paid. Meanwhile, however, she came to pay me a visit in Oxford.

My mother had always had an eye for interesting intellectuals, and she took an immediate shine to E-P. E-P on the other hand, as soon as he got me alone, said: "Eva, tell me, has your mother got enough to live on?" I said yes, she had plenty enough. I am sure that if I had said no, E-P would have organised some sinecure or other for her, for no student of his – never mind their widowed mothers – was ever going to be in want.

I also wanted to give a party for my mother. This could not happen in Warnborough Road – the flat was too small – but Godfrey Lienhardt very kindly offered his rooms and some other space in Queen Elizabeth House and said he would deal with the drink; my friend Wendy James said she would deal with the food. So June and I took my mother around the gardens of Oxford and the surrounding countryside, and only arrived at Godfrey's rooms about half an hour before the party was due to begin. There was nobody there just yet, but very soon after that, there arrived two Nigerian guests – one of whom I had actually invited – and June exercised her considerable social talents by making conversation with them. I had meanwhile found the food, which Wendy had stowed away beneath the table in the common room, and set my mother to work making cheese sandwiches – which I think she quite enjoyed. I fortunately had some money on me, so I went outside, and, equally fortunately, the next two guests were people I knew well, so I stuffed two ten-pound notes into their hands, and said "For heaven's sake go and get something to drink!" The original drink was later found, well before the party was over, in the gents' loo, where Godfrey had put it for safe keeping, and where I had not thought to look for it (nor could I have done so).

An unexpected journey

Although I had transferred myself from interpreting to anthropology, a return to my previous occupation was offered me during the summer of 1964. My B.Litt. examination had been quite short – my internal examiner, Godfrey, when asked if he had any further questions, had said "No; I hope the formal part of the proceedings is now over, as I wish to smoke." So that was that. Soon after, E-P said to me "Eva: I have just the holiday job for you."

It seemed the Wenner-Gren Foundation wanted him to recommend them an advanced anthropology student, perfectly bilingual in English and Russian, as a sort of "guide, philosopher and friend" to accompany the American delegation on their way to a vast anthropological congress about to take place in Moscow. Now, the object of their desires was a purely notional category; you might get advanced students in Slavonic studies being perfectly bilingual in English and Russian, but not anthropology students.

I explained to E-P that my languages did not include Russian. "Nonsense, nonsense, Eva – you speak all these foreign languages!" "I'm sorry, but not Russian." "Well," he said, "What are these Americans going to want? They'll want to know where to get a whisky and how to get a girl, surely you can manage that?" "No E-P, I don't think I can." "Well," he said, "by the time they find that out, you'll be there, won't you? I am told Moscow is a very interesting place."

I don't like to argue with my professor. At his behest, I went away and wrote myself a letter of recommendation for him to sign, in which I said, truthfully enough, that I could read, write, and speak Russian. (My entire vocabulary was fifty words, but I didn't mention that.) It is true that from early Russian lessons, way back in Geneva, I can read the Cyrillic alphabet, which is quite useful for words like *telefon*, and I can also write the Cyrillic alphabet if I have to. I said that I had spent time in the Soviet Union the previous summer, perfectly true – four whole days in what was then still Leningrad, living on board a Finnish ship and visiting the Hermitage and other things during the daytime.

And, when I gave this letter to the Institute's Secretary, Barbara, to type for E-P's signature, she said to me afterwards "I hope you don't mind, Eva, but I've added your age, because you'd made yourself sound about seventy." (I had also said, again with truth, that I was a Conference Interpreter of many years' experience. Perfectly true, just neither to nor from Russian.)

It turned out E-P was quite right. When I got to Moscow, they had lots of English-speaking Russians, to do all the interpreting and guiding necessary. I did arrive a couple of days early and picked up some useful information, such as how one got to the Kremlin by public transport – things like that – and I had in fact done a bit of Russian revision before I went. And indeed, on the first day of the Congress I did meet two elderly ladies who wanted to go to the Kremlin! I would have been happy to take them, only unfortunately I never found them again in the crowd...

As I was finding my way around, at one point I asked a young Russian man – he must have been good at languages, because he immediately spotted that my linguistic behaviour in an unfamiliar language was that of a Spanish speaker; so he replied in very decent Spanish. (He was studying the language at university.) He told me how to get wherever I was going and then said would I like to meet him at such and such a place the following evening, which I did. He took me off to some friends of his, a couple who were living in one of the few surviving *izbas* in town – small one-storey wooden houses which I believe no longer exist in Moscow.

We had a pleasant evening, I forget exactly what we talked about, but my young man, whose name was Sasha, interpreted between his friends and me. By the end of the long evening, all the subways were closed! There was no way to get back to the Congress hotel, the Gostinitza Ukraina. So I spent the night at Sasha's friends' house – very chastely I may say, though on a shared sofa. The following morning I went back to the hotel, thinking all hell was now going to break loose. However, nobody had even noticed my absence.

Some wonderful trips had been planned for delegates after the Congress. I yearned romantically for Samarkand, but I'd left it too late to put my name on the list for that trip, so I thought, Oh well, I'll go to Tashkent and see what happens. So I went to Tashkent, the next best thing. Most people on this trip were either couples or pairs of friends and were therefore given rooms together. There were two lone women, one Caroline Svetland, a Norwegian/American ethnographic film-maker, and me.

So Caroline and I were put in a room together and, as we unpacked and on about half-an-hour of acquaintance, she said "Say honey, would you like to go

Samarkand?" "Yes," I said. "And I guess you're not the kind that would mind sitting up all night in a train if we had to?" "No" I said. "Well honey, you speak a little Russian don't you? Come on!" So the next day, having, rather classically, left a note pinned to a pillow to say what we were doing, Caroline and I set off rather early in the afternoon. Our passports, of course, had remained in the hands of Intourist at Tashkent. However, I knew from that trip to Communist Poland that the secret is to spend one's night in public transport, where nobody asks for your papers. So we went, and I asked in my best Russian for two tickets to Samarkand. "Certainly, Comrade, I suppose you want first class sleeper, here you are" – very much cheaper than Intourist, I may say. We found our carriage, got in, took the two bottom bunks. It was a fairly slow, stopping, train and at some point in the night two male Russian engineers got in and, in gentlemanly style, took the two top bunks, and in the morning we arrived in Samarkand.

We had a superb breakfast in the market, and then brushed our teeth at the town pump, greatly to the amusement of the local population. We visited Tamberlaine's tomb, and the various other wonders of Samarkand. And then we thought we would push our luck, having got that far, and we'd try and go to Bokhara on our way back to Tashkent.

So once again to the station: "Two tickets to Bokhara." But this time my Russian let us down: we got to Bokhara all right, but in the middle of the night! We would have made ourselves very conspicuous, two foreigners hanging about the streets in the middle of the night; so there was nothing for it, but to go to a hotel. The other useful bit of information I had picked up (and passed on to Caroline) was that you must always have with you an identity document with your photograph on it. She had a somewhat out-of-date Norwegian Youth Hostel ticket, and I a United Nations *laisser passer* to say that I was (had been) the wife of an International Civil Servant, and please be nice to me. Caroline's was in Norwegian, mine was in English and French.

We asked our way to a hotel (I suspect the only one in town), found it, gave our papers to the lady at the desk, who was fluent in Russian and Uzbeki, and accepted our papers without question (she returned them the following morning, without even a stamp). That night, she said "Well, as long as it's for one night that's fine, but I'm expecting a lot of tourists tomorrow." So we reassured her it was only for one night, and got a perfectly decent twin-bedded room with a shower.

The following morning we left and went around Bokhara. This was interesting, because Bokhara had escaped the fate of Samarkand. At Samarkand, they had left the historic monuments, indeed restored them, but the rest of town had become simply a Soviet "Warm Climate City" with a Park of Rest and Culture and all the rest of it – a near-carbon-copy of all the others. But by the time the authorities got around to Bokhara they had began to realise that this was no longer the thing to do, so the place was untouched. Well, when I say untouched, everything had been so cleaned up and tidied, it looked like a Hollywood film set. Not the dropping of a donkey on any street!

So we walked around Bokhara, visiting, among other things, what had been Avicenna's library, now rather nicely transformed into a museum *and* public library. Towards afternoon, we thought we had better confess our sins to Intourist, since we were due back at Tashkent that evening, and back to Moscow the following day. I explained the situation at their Bokhara office, and the young woman behind the desk said "Yes, well, I suppose that means you would like to catch the late afternoon plane. It leaves at 4 o'clock, so if you come here at 3:30?" and then I heard her telephoning her colleague at the airport. "Tanya, I'm sending you two foreigners, so you will look after them for me, won't you. One of them speaks Russian, but *plohoi-plohoi*, very badly."

So we returned, we were shepherded on to this bus. We got to the airport. Tanya looked after us. We got into the plane. The plane didn't quite run to seatbelts, but was otherwise OK. It stopped somewhere on the way to Tashkent, and there was a very polite young man in uniform who asked who we were and what we were doing; and we explained; then we got back to Tashkent.

Where, meanwhile, our disappearance had made us a nine days' – or rather three days' – wonder: our note hadn't been found for 24 hours, nobody wishing to invade our privacy. The one person seriously angry was Margaret Mead, a member of our post-Congress tourist party who was used to being herself the centre of attention. She read us the riot act: We had spoilt the name of Western tourists in the Soviet Union for ever and ever! Our young Intourist guide would undoubtedly be sent to Siberia! What did we mean by such behaviour?

Margaret Mead's scolding didn't bother me much; but when Caroline and I were alone again I did say "Do you suppose we've really caused trouble for that nice girl?" Caroline replied, "Well, I don't think so, honey, but if you're worried, let's go see her." When we did, the girl said "Oh no! At any other time of year I might have got a scolding – no worse than that – from the local Intourist boss; but just now, he's entirely too busy. Of course, there would have been serious trouble if you *hadn't* got back in time to join our plane to Moscow; but you have, so that's all right. And you needn't think," she added, that you're the first tourists who've ever done this! It's far too easy – quite popular in fact. Mind you, I am a bit cross with you – I've never been to Bokhara in my life, you might really have taken me along!"

But what was really bothering her wasn't that: it was that we had paid for two nights at that Tashkent hotel and not slept there – how was she going to compensate us for that? We said for Heaven's sake don't worry, that's neither your fault nor Intourist's, entirely our own doing and it doesn't worry us. "Well, I don't like it." And the wretched girl got up next morning, at Heaven only knows what hour, and went to market to buy Caroline and me melons and grapes to make up for that night we hadn't spent at the hotel.

Also, before our party left Tashkent, the local Intourist office asked for signatures in their Book of Honour – not from all of us, but only from the most senior and distinguished people there, who they decided were Margaret Mead and my friend Caroline.

My last day in Moscow was a sunny one, and as I went for a last walk I saw a young father proudly accompanying his son. The boy was tricked out in a sailor-suit of the sort that had not been seen in Western Europe since before the First World War; and on the cap was written, in Cyrillic characters, ASTRONAUT.

Altogether a wonderful trip; and, while I was enjoying it, my brother Tommy died, quite alone, at that expensive Institute in Germany. My mother was already in Buenos Aires, finding a place to settle, which she did indeed in the end. But now the light rather went out in her. She continued to keep up a good front, and to look remarkably young, but now, Tommy having died, she had nobody left to live for. There was some notion of her doing translations, which she would have done quite well, for the World Federation of Mental Health, of which my father had at one point been President. But she decided after a while that they didn't write her enough thank you letters, that she was not being properly appreciated, so she stopped doing it, and for the considerable rest of her life lived in a very nice flat in Buenos Aires, occasionally coming to Europe, otherwise not doing anything very much. I remember my sister Trixie later complaining she was an absolutely useless grandmother: "Can't so much as take the kids to the cinema, once in a while." I dare say that here too she felt underappreciated.

But now, in the summer of 1964, with both my finances and my personal papers in order, I paid a brief family visit to Buenos Aires on my way to Nigeria; and thence, as a budding anthropologist, to my fieldwork.

INTERLUDE 4

On Anthropology, and Anthropologists

Margaret Mead was the one anthropologist I had come across before taking up the subject myself; even before the encounter in Moscow, I had met her. She was already something of a legendary figure – whose books I had read as an adolescent in my father's library. In Geneva he began inviting such people to his WHO Mental Health meetings – clearly, if you are dealing with the world's mental health, an anthropologist is a useful person to have around. I once dined with her and my parents in a Geneva restaurant, and heard her attempting to order her food in French! Now, considering she goes on quite a bit in her writings about how easy it is to pick up a new language, I thought "Well, her idea of picking up a language cannot possibly be the same as mine." The anthropologists I came to know later, first in Oxford and later in London, appeared to belong to a totally different species.

I remember her too as the worst conference delegate I ever came across. It was at a small meeting on some psychological subject. The head of our interpreting team was one Louise O'Brien, the French widow of an Irishman. Margaret Mead said to her, with considerable arrogance, that she did so hope that what she, Mead, had to say would be interpreted by a woman, because she didn't want to be heard in a male voice. Now if you are running a team of interpreters, you do not run it according to gender, but rather, according to their various language skills and the combinations that can be made between them. Louise was furious, as well she might have been.

By the time our paths crossed again at that Moscow Congress in 1964 from which a couple of us had absconded by taking a train to Bokhara, I don't know that she remembered me; I had changed my name since then, and in any case was by now well beneath her notice. Now in her old age, Margaret Mead was always walking around with a tall stick – she probably *needed* a stick – but *hers* was more like a sceptre – quite as tall as she was, and she wasn't tiny. We used to say this was her antenna for Heaven, for divine inspiration. At that Congress we heard quite a lot of her divine inspiration.

When in later life I found that an American anthropologist, Derek Freeman, had been to the Pacific regions of the world and had found that, surprise, surprise! – the locals had told Margaret Mead exactly what they thought she had wanted to hear, thereby invalidating not just her ethnography but the world-shaking conclusions that had impressed so many people, including my father, I was absolutely delighted. Later, based in Hamsey, I gave a lecture based on this for the University of the Third Age in Sussex, called something like "Anthropology Revisited". I did, in my day, read her autobiography *Blackberry Winter*, or at any rate skim through it, thinking

I had never come across a more firmly emphasised matriline. She talks about her grandmother, her mother, her daughter and her granddaughter; husbands are purely incidental – as they seem to have been in her own life. I suppose, in her youth, she must have been attractive; by the time I met her this was difficult to imagine.

A Different Species

"All quite mad," people said about the rather different species of anthropologists in Oxford; "brilliant of course – and Roman Catholics the lot of them!" In Michaelmas Term 1962, this was very nearly true. Even before hearing such remarks I had actually rumbled the Catholicism of at least the Lienhardt brothers, Godfrey and Peter. Having sat near me at a public lecture, they invited me for a drink at the Mitre Hotel; there was something indefinable in their chivalrous manner towards me, and when Peter said "We're Catholics, you know" I responded with "I'd rather guessed that." At which elder brother Godfrey turned to look at me before saying "Yes – you'll make an anthropologist!"

At the Institute of Social Anthropology, Maltese Ken Burridge may well have been a cradle Catholic; but Professor Evans-Pritchard, the Lienhardts and David Pocock – that expert on all things Hindu – were all converts. There was indeed one Anglican, John Beattie, but he fitted in quite well.

The real exception was Rodney Needham, who worshipped at a totally different shrine: the god of his idolatry was abstract – the complex mathematics of descent-and-alliance theory. This would, after the Professor's official retirement a few years later, cause serious problems; but at that early stage the Institute was still held together by personal devotion to E-P.

The general nest-of-Catholics atmosphere did have one curious and useful spin-off: the Oxford Institute seemed then to be the one anthropology department in the country to take *pagan* beliefs seriously. Elsewhere, someone like Lucy Mair could write intelligently about livelihood, politics, marriage – but the moment she approached religion it became obvious she felt she was describing "the unfortunate superstitions of the natives". Whereas, here, E-P and Godfrey had each written a serious and respectful book about the beliefs of, respectively, the Nuer and the Dinka.

Godfrey indeed never wrote another book about his Dinka; but E-P had by then written a good many, not only about the Nuer but, perhaps more importantly, about the Azande, also of the southern Sudan. I have been told he managed this through his habit of very early rising. The one time, years later, when I was living in London and he had asked me for a night's hospitality, he was certainly up long before I was and – having by some mysterious instinct already found his way to Mass at the nearest Catholic church in the area, woke me with a big bunch of flowers! For breakfast, he had told me the previous night he wanted wine; getting up, I duly produced this, as well as some bread and butter and a slice of ham; I can't remember whether he partook of the solids.

Not that the two priests flanking me on that first walk from the Institute building to the central University offices where we would register as post-graduate students had been drawn by the Catholic atmosphere. Their presence was due to an unusual feature of the rules governing the Diploma in Social Anthropology: these stated that the Diploma could be taken by anyone with a previous degree (in any subject whatsoever) *or equivalent experience.* It meant in practice that the Head of the Institute was totally free to decide whom he considered to be a suitable Diploma candidate, even beyond the usual mssionaries and colonial officers. One curious instance of this freedom occurred during my own Diploma year. A young countrywoman of mine, Hebe D'Alessio, very recently married, had looked around in Oxford for something interesting to do while her philosopher husband worked for his D.Phil; and had decided on social anthropology. Hebe's "equivalent experience" (after completing her Argentine secondary studies) had consisted of a few months spent as agony aunt on a lowbrow women's magazine. But E-P, having duly interviewed her, said "Mrs D'Alessio, I can't promise you'll succeed in getting your Diploma in Social Anthropology: but if you want to have a try, by all means do so" – and took her on as his own personal pupil. As it turned out, this may not have been only because he could not resist those huge black eyes: Hebe, a highly intelligent young woman, worked very hard. She not only got her Diploma but the following academic year completed her B.Litt thesis, before it was time to return to Argentina with her husband.

Tutors and Friends

At the Institute (then at the Parks end of Keble Road) most of us, staff and students alike (though not Rodney Needham), did tend to get together with E-P and each other at 11 am for coffee after the main lecture and later for beer at the Lamb and Flag. The weekly Friday afternoon seminar with an outside speaker was also followed up in the pub, though E-P tended to go home early (along with the reputation of getting up early too, in order to write).

After an initial term being given tutorials by Ruth Finnegan, who had her study at Nuffield College, I was transferred to E-P for tutorials in his room at the Institute. How I wish now I had made better use of my time with him! Though I do remember the time when, having earlier disagreed over whether there was in people's minds any real boundary between the sacred and the profane, he happened to mention that he must now make his Lenten confession. "Blackfriars?" I asked. "Oh no, they all know me socially there! For confession I go to St Aloysius up the road." "Ah – profane and sacred, I see." He grinned and said "I think you win that one!"

One serious problem was that I never did work out how to discuss his work with him: whether one said "You say in *Witchcraft, Oracles and Magic among the Azande*" or "Evans-Pritchard says in his book *Witchcraft* etc"; and he himself was clearly reluctant to cite his own work. We therefore conducted tutorials as if there had never been such an anthropologist as Evans-Pritchard. I do wish, though, that I had taken notes of the scandals he produced about the private lives of the French scholars associated with the classic journal *L'Année Sociologique* – who was found in whose bed by whom...

But at the end of that Hilary term, I did feel that if I was going to get ready for the Diploma examinations I would need to be taught by somebody else; so I actually asked E-P whether I shouldn't be transferred to Godfrey Lienhardt, to which our modest Professor agreed. Godfrey himself seemed quite happy to have me, as long as I arrived at his Queen Elizabeth House study at 5 p.m., so that the pubs would be open when the tutorial ended. I also remember a seminar class during that winter term in 1963 with Godfrey Lienhardt, suddenly interrupted by Godfrey himself, who said "Come on, let's go out into the Parks. If anthropologists can't celebrate the return of Spring, I don't know who can!" So we all went into the Parks, and I was particularly struck by the fish lying around – because winter had flooded and frozen the river, and the fish had not got back in, and had been frozen alive – only by this time they were no longer alive, and rather stank.

I felt closer to Godfrey and his contemporaries than to most of my fellow Diploma students, who seemed so much younger and with less experience of the wider world. The main exception was Mark Holmström. Closer to me in age, he had also worked for the United Nations – in New York in his case, and as a translator not an interpreter: his first degree had been in Modern Languages. He had met his South Indian wife, Lakshmi, more generally known as Lakku, while both were undergraduates; she was at the time reading English Literature and Language, having managed to persuade the University authorities that the literary Tamil she had studied at home was just as much a classical language as the Virgilian Latin the rest of us had to know. During Mark's years in New York, Lakku had worked for the Indian Permanent Delegation there; now, like me, he had decided to become an anthropologist, and had returned to Oxford to study under David Pocock. I soon found I had to read *The Guardian* very attentively every morning, before meeting Mark at the Institute's morning-coffee time: he was, and has remained, a person of hugely sensitive social conscience, and I did have to know what he was going to be indignant about that particular morning! He and Lakku then set up house not far from the Institute; so I often dropped in on them.

One of the times I did so, during our B.Litt. year, Mark and Lakku looked at one another, and one of them said: "Shall we tell her?" "Yes, let's tell her."

"All right," says Lakku, "My pains are coming rather often by now! But the thing is, I've made some very good curry, and I know Mark, he'll never eat it once I'm in hospital, so I think we'd better have a meal now." So we ate Lakku's curry (which was, as always, excellent); and by now the pains were coming really very frequently. We all three felt she should go across to the Radcliffe Hospital as soon as possible. So off we went: very pretty, very pregnant young Indian woman; husband beside her carrying small suitcase; friend on her other side carrying coats and things. It was perfectly obvious where we were going, and why, and the lorries passing by issued friendly hoots and cat-calls to us. I left the couple at the Radcliffe.

I rang up the following morning, was asked whether I was a relative and rather foolishly said no, I wasn't, so only later did I learn that Lakku had been taken straight to the delivery room. She had felt – I have never had a baby so I don't know the sensation – something that caused her to say to the attendant nurse: "Nurse, I need a bedpan." And the nurse said: "No dear, what you need to do is to have that baby!" Whereupon Lakku laughed so much, that out popped the baby.

Mark and Lakku later went off on field work, obviously in South India, where as a couple, they were ideally placed to get to know *everyone* in any community they studied. Lakku later told me about some evening ceremony at which an Indian academic saw her in the half-darkness and said, in English: "You're very Indianised, aren't you?"

Old Fellow-Students Meet Again

Some time during my Diploma year, my friends Robert and Brigitte Pring-Mill asked me to dinner. Robert was by now a recognised expert on Spanish-language literature, not only in the Iberian Peninsula but also in South America. On this occasion they had asked me to meet a house-guest of theirs, one Victor Haya de la Torre – a Bolivian politician of partly Amerindian origin, who had achieved considerable fame as leader of a non-communist but left-wing political movement in his country. He later had to leave Bolivia in something of a hurry, and was now on a visit to England.

When we were introduced to one another, he got very excited: "You're an anthropologist! Do you happen to know a man called Evans-Pritchard?" "Quite well," I replied; "he's head of the Institute of Social Anthropology where I study." "Oh! Oh, I should so *love* to meet him again!" "Well," said I, "that's not difficult. Let's see, tomorrow's Friday, there's a pub at which we usually get together, and E-P is nearly always there. So if you'd like to come between twelve-thirty and one, I'm sure it can be arranged."

Next day, there we were at the pub. I told E-P an old friend of his was coming, and may even have mentioned the name. He disclaimed any knowledge and kept looking nervously at his watch, saying he really must get away to fetch his children from – I think – a language lesson, but it could have been dancing class. Haya de la Torre, like a good South American, was late. Nothing was happening; nothing went on happening; I was getting increasingly nervous myself. Then, just as E-P had risen to go, the other man appeared at the door. After which the two embraced very warmly, made a date to meet the next day, and E-P went off on his lawful occupations.

Haya de la Torre joined the rest of us for a drink, after which he gratefully asked me out to lunch. And said "Isn't it wonderful, Evans-Pritchard hasn't changed at all! He still has the same wonderful blue eyes as forty years ago." Next day I saw E-P, who said "Do you know my old friend Haya de la Torre?" "Yes, I've recently met him." "Ah, it's amazing how he hasn't changed in all these years – still that mane of jet-black hair!" – I learned only later that when Haya de la Torre had been in danger of his life in his native country and had taken refuge in the British Embassy, E-P had been instrumental in securing this.

The two had originally met when both were attending Malinowski's lectures in the 1920s. During the latter's tenure at the London School of Economics, it seems to have been rather the fashion for politicians and other potential leaders from what were still colonial countries to come to these lectures, and then to apply what they had learnt there: Haya de la Torre was by no means the only one. The most famous was Jomo Kenyatta, whose *Facing Mount Kenya* became quite well-known, especially after he embarked on his political career.

And I know of a third example, one Chief Thomas Marealle, who became Paramount among the Chagga people living on the slopes of Mount Kilimanjaro – very shrewd, commercially able people, who grew and as far as I know still grow coffee there. Chief Tom Marealle, having learned about sacred kings, decided it would be a good idea to turn himself into a sacred king, and attempted to do so. This was not a success, because people were entirely too shrewd and he was, peaceably enough, deposed. I actually met him at a bed-and-breakfast near the FAO building in Rome once, where I was doing a brief conference on my way to Nigeria. The first morning, there was just one breakfast table with a spare seat. So I went up and asked the other guest there whether I might join him. "Yes, of course." We had breakfast and made conversation; I asked him where he came from and he said, he was a Chagga, from Tanzania. "Oh," said I, "how interesting! Do you know, I was once told a very interesting story about a Chagga Chief called Chief Tom Marealle – I suppose you must have known him?" I told him the story. He gave a little grin and he said: "I *am* Chief Tom Marealle! The FAO nowadays employs me as an expert on agricultural co-operatives." I was amused by this story, the more so because of my Krapf ancestry and connections with that part of the world.

Entertaining Visitors

I have to confess that E-P got into the habit of entrusting French anthropologist visitors to me, with instructions to take them out to lunch and conversation. Thus I got to know Denise Paulme-Scheffner, a specialist in African folk-tales whose husband ran the *Musée de l'Homme*'s collection of musical instruments. It also got me the job of looking after Claude Lévi-Strauss's ten-year-old son Matthieu while his parents were attending various functions prior to the ceremony at the Sheldonian Theatre, where the great man was to be awarded an honorary doctorate.

The Lévi-Strausses were staying at the Randolph Hotel; my instructions were to give young Matthieu lunch in the hotel restaurant before getting him into a clean shirt – duly laid out by his mother – and taking him to her at the Sheldonian just before the ceremony. Easier said than done. Matthieu was genuinely a handful: it was all I could do to prevent him pelting other luncheon guests with bread-rolls! I was (only just) able to stop him by diverting his attention: I did know French schools gave pupils Thursday afternoons off, and that little boys like Matthieu would then be taken to various educational museums, so I managed to ask questions about what interesting things he had seen on Thursdays.

All this was nothing to the after-lunch job of getting him into that clean shirt: I remember squeezing him between my knees to keep him standing still. But I did manage it in the end, and even got him to the Sheldonian on time.

Lévi-Strauss had, naturally, offered to pay for my services; I had declined this, saying that what I really wanted was one of his books with a personal hand-written dedication. The great man said sternly that a parcel containing such a book was ready for me, but *only* on condition I also accepted a certain envelope accompanying it. The envelope contained a £10 note (quite a lot of money in 1964); the book *La pensée sauvage* – a first edition complete with wild pansy on the dust-cover – I still cherish it, especially for the generous *dédicace* in which the author hopes that a few hours spent with *un éxotique petit sauvage* would not have put me off "field work" (the one English phrase he used).

A West Africanist Supervisor

Having secured from the Nuffield Foundation the money to finance the academic year I would need to write my B.Litt. thesis, my next problem would be to find someone to supervise me for this: the Institute did not seem to contain anybody much interested in West Africa at large, though Godfrey did have some ties with Ghana. Fortunately, towards the end of that academic year a new Africanist appeared on the scene, Edwin Ardener, an anthropologist who, with his sociologist wife Shirley, was doing field research in the Cameroons. I attended Edwin's afternoon lectures, without initially understanding much of what he had to say about the uses of statistics; but it became clear to me that when I came to work on the Yoruba, Edwin would be my supervisor. And indeed, in Michaelmas Term 1963 Edwin was given a permanent appointment at the Institute; he even now had a room in Dr Spooner's house.

The first time I went there, he said, "You've changed. You look more *indigenous* somehow," And when I commented on this to his wife Shirley, she said "Yes! more of an English rose." I still don't quite see myself as an English rose, but it was a kind thought.

Edwin proved an admirable supervisor. At first I was a little alarmed at his habit of casually flipping over the pages of my typescript, but soon came to appreciate his robust good sense and total lack of pomposity. Quite typical of this was his answer when a couple of years later, still in Nigeria, I wrote to ask him as my supervisor whether I should accept a temporary post in London even though I still had my doctoral thesis to write: "If I can supervise you in Nigeria I can certainly supervise you in London – and there are trains, you know." (Of course, if I'd given the matter a minute's thought I'd have realised that I would never have been offered that job without my supervisor's recommendation!)

Also, he had asked me, before I ever departed on that fieldwork, to call in London on his and Shirley's friend Phyllis Kaberry at University College. Having done so and been warmly received, I had recalled myself to her memory by a few cards during my two years' absence; which meant that, if and when I began work at SOAS, I already had a friend round the corner at UCL.

London in prospect

The junior lectureship I had been offered on my return from Nigeria was at the small Department of Sociology and Anthropology at SOAS which, like University College, was part of the much-scattered University of London. First, I had to be interviewed by its Director, Professor Christoph von Fürer-Haimendorf, who was – very unfairly but I suppose inevitably – nicknamed "the Führer". (In real life, Christoph, who was of Austrian origin, was not only a particularly gentle person but also an honourable anti-Nazi refugee.)

Before this interview actually took place E-P, himself an endearingly old-fashioned snob, had told me "I think you'll find Christoph von Fürer-Haimendorf a gentleman"; and at the interview itself I actually guessed from his manner that in his Viennese boyhood he had attended the Theresianum – a school founded by, or for, the Empress Maria Theresa, Marie-Antoinette's mother. I had only once before met a product of the Theresianum, a Sicilian prince with an Austrian mother, Antonio Trigona di Calveruso, who had, as a refugee in later life gone to a rather less exalted school in Buenos Aires with my brother-in-law Bernard Ingham. Nonetheless, I felt I recognised that manner and, towards the end of an interview that seemed to be going well, actually asked my new boss whether he'd been to the Theresianum? I had guessed right, and he seemed quite pleased about it.

It's never easy to explain why a particular "manner" – as distinct from conventional manners – should be unmistakeable; but I do know an English equivalent: the Winchester manner, as exemplified in E-P himself and in the man I later married, Mick Gillies. E-P was, like Christoph, quite pleased to have the manner instilled by his school; Mick, left-wing in his leanings and a bit embarassed by his posh background, was not.

In anticipation, to draw some contrasts between my experience of the Oxford anthropologists and those I would join in London after my fieldwork: the one real problem for me at SOAS was obligatory participation in the Friday Staff Seminar each week. Friday seminars were not in themselves a new idea to me: we had had them at the Oxford Institute too. But these seemed much more formal, and there was no socialising afterwards. What a relief, therefore, when Phyllis Kaberry encouraged me also to attend seminars at University College round the corner! Daryll Forde, who presided over these, may not have been E-P's equal in groundbreaking ideas; but he was certainly a marvellous talent scout. Among the many interesting anthropologists I met at these UCL seminars was Mary Douglas, whose *Purity and Danger* was just then turning upside down everyone's ideas on ritual pollution. Mary was always, then and later, very kind to me; I have never been able to work out why the normally gentle Phyllis so detested her! Perhaps Mary's "Establishment" manner annoyed or even scared her: tiny Australian-born Phyllis perceived both her stature and her country of origin as making her vulnerable, unless protected by somebody like Sally Chilver (then Head of Bedford College), the historian with whom she had worked together in Cameroon. I too came to protect Phyllis, often against her own guests. We came to live conveniently near each other in London; every time Phyllis gave a party, I would see to it that I was there half-an-hour beforehand. Phyllis, out of sheer nerves, would have had a bit too much to drink and have become very confused about how to arrange glasses and small eats – something I could easily do for her.

My own sense of what researching and writing anthropology might be was to be shaken up a little in London. The first time I ever entered – as a member of staff – the premises of the Department of Sociology and Anthropology at SOAS, a young man, a somewhat more mature student than most, Indian, obviously very well educated, speaking admirable English, said to me: "Are you a structuralist?" I'd never heard of structuralism! I had read some Lévi-Strauss, certainly, but structural*ism?* However, I kept a straight face, and replied: "Yes, I think so," to which he said "Good! We *need* structuralists here."

I suspect I never did live up to his expectations. My own focus remained rather firmly on ethnography and the realities of "the field".

PART FIVE
NIGERIA IN FOCUS

Chapter 1
Fieldwork: Kabba

It had been decided that my "academic umbrella" in Nigeria should be the Institute of African Studies at the University of Ibadan, at that time one of the two leading universities of the country. So I didn't stop in Lagos, but went straight to Ibadan, where the University put me up in a lodging they had for visiting scholars. At the time, the anthropologist G. I. Jones and his wife, and also a medic called Gilles (without the second "i" in my own married surname – so not related in any way to the man I was later to marry) were also staying there. Herbert Gilles saw to it I got all the shots and other precautions that he thought necessary for my fieldwork.

The Institute of African Studies had a distinguished Director, an Igbo historian, Professor Dike; but, in the usual way, the distinguished Director didn't do the nitty-gritty of running the place. This was done by a young recent graduate, another Igbo, Elochukwu Amucheazi, known to his friends as Elo.

Elo was extremely efficient at his job. He dealt, for instance, with the complications of my Argentine passport. The Nigerian authorities were none too pleased at the idea of a foreign woman travelling by herself, even though it now said on my passport, perfectly properly, that I was a widow; and of course they had never heard of Argentine passports. So Elo had quite a lot to do over that, and did it very competently. He also got me a decent second-hand VW car to travel up-country to my fieldwork; and dealt with a number of other things, but none in a particularly friendly manner. I have a feeling that at this stage Elo was somewhat anti-white.

I also had a few introductions in Ibadan, mostly through Wilfred Whiteley, a friend of the Lienhardt brothers – not an anthropologist but a linguist. Wilfred had introduced me to a colleague of his who was also an anthropologist, the American Robert Armstrong. Bob Armstrong was very kind to me, and helped with various other introductions.

There was also the adult education official Lalage Bown, whom I had in fact already met at that conference in Ghana during the 1963 Christmas vacation. She was on leave when I first arrived at Ibadan, but when she returned we greeted each other warmly; and Elo, having seen me locked in this warm embrace with Lalage Bown, clearly decided that I must be human after all, and thereafter treated me quite differently.

Initially, I spent something like ten days in Ibadan getting sorted out, and then began my drive up country. I had elected to do my field work in Kabba – a northern Yoruba town which, I had been told, was quite untouched by hand of anthropologist, and would therefore offer me opportunities for new research.

I arrived late one morning, having been told to contact the DO there. I had assumed District Officers, here in the North, would still be mostly British; but this one was Nigerian; moreover, he wasn't there, but on some kind of assignment, leaving his wife in charge of things. But she and I had no language in common; she was not Yoruba, but came from somewhere near Lake Chad. Also, she was in the process of having a thorough house-cleaning in her husband's absence. She had half the furniture out on the verandah, with servants beating carpets and fluffing-up pillows. Clearly an extremely competent woman: in no time flat she had me sitting in an armchair on her verandah with a cool drink; and immediately sent to her husband's office for somebody English-speaking, to find out my business.

When she learned that, for whatever reason, I intended to stay in Kabba, she despatched me to the local bush rest house, which contained furniture but no bedding, with some bedding of hers, a towel, and a servant to make up the bed. For the rest of the few days I stayed there, she also sent me over three meals a day, cooked European style, on little trays. She even gave a dinner party for me! – with several of the junior staff, some of whom spoke English. I realised that I must do *something* in return for all this, and hunted desperately in my luggage for what I could possibly give an unknown lady with whom I had no language in common. I found a pair of earrings, which I though might do the trick, and gave them to her. Eventually her husband returned and we got sorted out.

I needed somewhere more permanent to live. Kabba did have an absentee-landlord, a trader, quite well-off; he had a house and offered to rent me the top floor of this, which contained a bedroom, verandah and bathroom. I was very happy to accept, and for my first few months in Kabba that was where I lived.

Now it was true enough that Kabba was "untouched by hand of anthropologist"; but it, and its surroundings, had a quite considerable European population – essentially the staff of its five post-primary schools. There was a Roman Catholic Mission and an Anglican Mission. The Anglican Mission ran a boys' school; the Roman Catholic Mission ran separate boys' and girls' schools. There was also a Teacher Training College, Government-sponsored, a little way out of town, and an equally Government-sponsored Agricultural College; all these were staffed almost entirely by assorted non-Africans. This meant, of course, that by the local population I was instantly categorised as a teacher and treated accordingly. They were none too fond of telling me the kind of things they didn't think white teachers like to hear; such as, for instance, that Kabba still had a considerable slave population. They weren't *poor* slaves, but slaves they were. They lived in a separate quarter, and white people were known not to like this and were therefore not supposed to know.

I soon called upon the Ọba of Kabba, a large stout man also called locally the Ọbaro. Yoruba political units are small kingdoms, some smaller than others, rather similar to ancient Greek city-states in that each consists of a town surrounded by agricultural land; the distinctive feature of the Yoruba, as against other West African peoples, is that they don't live on their land, they live in the towns (except perhaps for a few weeks at harvest time). They might have a hut on their agricultural land, but most of the time they live in towns and are very proud of it, seeing it as proving their innate superiority to "bush people".

The Ọbaro was friendly enough, but (again) not very forthcoming. I didn't greet him in traditional style, which would have involved a deep curtsey on my part, which I didn't know how to do. Men had to prostrate themselves, which must have been even more difficult; they were very good at it, extremely athletic; they could prostrate and up again in no time flat.

Perhaps inevitably, I tended to make friends initially among the European population. When I say European, there were Americans at the Teacher Training College, and indeed, one of them was black. She had decided, quite consciously, that she would sooner marry the first-class citizen of a second-class country, than a second-class citizen in her own. (She had, I think, been previously divorced.) In the end, she got herself a very pleasant Nigerian husband, I think connected with the Agricultural College. She had her problems, though, in that the locals never accepted her as one of themselves. The word for stranger (and they generally mean white-skinned stranger) in that part of the world is *oybo*, and she was always, when she went to market, addressed as Oybo; and didn't like it.

The other American at Teacher Training was a young, very pretty, white woman who had, at College, fallen in love with a black man, a Nigerian. Though he was not around (he was still at College) she had decided that in order to get her parents to understand about this, she had best get herself a job in Nigeria, which, through the Peace Corps, she did. She was very much into doing all things properly, not only learning to cook Nigerian style (as the other American teacher did too) but the white girl would do her curtseys in front of the Ọba and generally behave as she should. As far as I know, her romance came to a happy end.

The head of this Teacher Training College, Winifred, on the other hand was a real old fashioned colonialist. She didn't, of course, ever *say* that she didn't regard Nigerians as having the same intelligence as other people (meaning herself); but she (in fact like most Northern Nigerians) disapproved of the South, full of all these terribly pushy upwardly mobile Igbo, and even Yoruba – well they did have chiefs, *but* – Winifred was for the old North. I remember when there was a *coup*, her comment was: "Well, I do hope this isn't all a Christian-Communist-Igbo plot." Which describes her sentiments exactly.

The Vice-Principal, Muriel, was very different. She was a middle-aged, verging on elderly, woman, who had initially worked for the Missions (she was Roman

Catholic) and had left them, in an understandable huff, when they would not allow her Nigerian adopted son to live with her in their senior quarters. Muriel decided this was not for her, and joined the Government Teacher Training establishment. She was not particularly academic, but was very intelligent, and as you will gather from that adoption, very sympathetic towards Nigerians. She also had a sense of humour. She used to set every new intake of students an essay on The Customs of Foreigners, because she wanted to know what *they* thought of *us*.

She once had a very clever student, who fooled her by talking about the peculiar habits of (I think) the Japanese, people she had read about. But from other essays Muriel and I learned quite a lot about what were regarded as our peculiar habits, such as, for instance Europeans, *oybo*, who don't like to be greeted more than once a day. In Nigerian politeness it is the done thing to come several times a day (this happens in parts of Latin America too) to say: "I've just come by to greet you", and the person greeted is supposed to reply politely and at some length. Europeans tend to "be a bit busy" at these and other times, and this had, of course, been noticed. Also Europeans are very rich, so they can build themselves beautiful houses, but they build them away from anyone else, they don't want to live with other people. Foreigners are indeed very odd!

Then there were the Roman Catholic and Anglican Missions, both quite large, the Catholic being the larger one. In addition to the priests, all Canadians from what was then called the Fellowship of the Holy Ghost, and nowadays would be that of the Holy Spirit, there were some American nuns. The nuns ran the girls' school, and (this was still 1964) I was a bit surprised to see them happily driving motor cars.

The priests were very hospitable. There was a reason for this: they did not allow themselves beer, *except* when they had visitors. So obviously visitors were extremely welcome, because then everybody could have a drink. There was also a large, as yet unfinished Catholic church where we used to go to Mass.

Both missions were very worried about the remaining paganism in Kabba. Kabba was theoretically a Christian town, but there were still the *ẹbọra*. Now, *ẹbọra*, I eventually found out, was simply the local name for *orisha* – a word familiar to me from my reading, as this is the name given by Southern Yoruba to their assorted deities – a large and complicated pantheon, quite as complex as that of the ancient Greeks.

The *ẹbọra* were, I think, somewhat less differentiated local gods, who mostly lived up at the top of the hills at the back of Kabba town; adolescent boys had to be initiated into their cult. This happened on top of the highest hill at a particular time of year – and, I need hardly say, no women were allowed to be present. The *ẹbọra* also made most peculiar sounds; I later found that this was done with the help of a comb and some tissue paper, but it terrified those of the local inhabitants who were not initiated, including all the women; and, while it didn't terrify the Europeans, they profoundly disapproved. Clearly, one of the things I most wanted to do was to witness this initiation. (I never quite managed it, but nearly so.)

There was also, of course, a women's secret society, the *olofoshi*, for followers of the women's deities known as *ofoshi,* and the local witches were supposed to get together to worship them. Now it *was* possible for me to join this society, and I used to go to their meetings, which seemed to me harmless enough though slightly mysterious; we would sit around and there would be a bit of chanting and that was basically it. But it got me considerable fame throughout Kabba. I was known, and am apparently still remembered, as *oybo olofoshi,* the *oybo* who was a member of the *ofoshi* cult.

Since I wore European clothes (though not trousers), drove a car and smoked, I was generally treated as if I were a man (except that I was *olofoshi*), and I decided this had its advantages, but also its disadvantages. I wanted to be able, at least sometimes, to be treated as a woman. Simple; what I needed to do was wear Yoruba dress.

I managed to acquire some material from the market, to get somebody to stitch me up a blouse or top; the skirt was a simple wrap-around, and you wore a head tie round your head and, if you were a proper lady, also a stole.

The first time I got into these clothes and stood at the top of the stairs behind my flat, facing the compound where my landlord's lesser family and servants lived, there was a cry of joy from the surrounding populations. Some of the women came rushing up the stairs, saying things like "You haven't tied your head-tie right", and "Where's your stole?" "Haven't you got a handbag?" and other things of that nature, and, when properly accoutred, I was then escorted, very firmly, to the local photographer to have my photograph taken.

After that, I could and did manipulate my gender. It was quite funny. If I was wearing Yoruba dress and was therefore a woman, the men would occasionally make what could have developed into a pass at me, whereas the women would take the material of my top, feel it and say: "What did you pay for this? Ah, you were cheated!"

Talking of passes, the men of Kabba had a most civilised way to deal with any problems that might be posed by a strange woman from a different culture. I was asked quite early on, at a funeral, "Madame, will you be needing a husband while you are here?" and when I said "No, I wouldn't really," that was that. The rest of the passes were more jokes about my dressing as a woman than anything else.

This funeral had taken place pretty soon after my arrival (I had already realised that a big funeral was the most important event I could possibly attend). I was then still living in my temporary accommodation at the Bush Rest House, and, after following the funeral for many hours, returned rather tired, stumbled across some stones on the steps leading up to my door, and collapsed into a chair. Almost immediately afterwards, I was visited by a tall blond man, wearing only a sarong, who greeted me politely, in Portuguese...

He was a Dane, Harald Hansen, there in some agricultural capacity, I think to do with the growing of bananas, not connected with the Agricultural College. He was married, and lived in a house not very far from the Bush Rest House, with his wife Jeanne, also Danish despite the name, and much younger than he.

Harald had come to see me that evening because he had heard there was a new person from South America; he had spent time as a tropical agriculturalist in Brazil and assumed therefore that I would be Portuguese speaking. The pebbles I had stumbled over on my way in were his message, in Portuguese, to greet me and invite me over to a drink the next evening. As it was, he realised how tired I was and said: "You'd better come over for a drink straight away." So I did, whereafter I saw quite a bit of the Hansens.

Harald was not very well regarded by the rest of the white community. He was not, except to me, particularly sociable; and of course he was undoubtedly an intellectual. He had read, and made me read, all sorts of things. He held heretical views on every subject under the sun, and was altogether not what you would expect the expatriate community in Kabba to like.

I had also made an early friend among the black people of Kabba, Edward Adamu. Now Edward was not in fact a Yoruba, he was from Ekiti, a little further south. He was a teacher at the Anglican Mission primary school, spoke very good English and was exceedingly helpful. He understood what I was trying to do, and whenever necessary (which, in the beginning, was just about all the time) would come and interpret for me. Once at a gathering of people (I think they were local minor chiefs), I had asked a number of questions and he had interpreted my questions and then their answers. And then he said, unprompted: "Now have you got any questions you would like to ask the anthropologist?"

And they did! They wanted to know who was paying for me, and I started to explain about Lord Nuffield who manufactured all these motor cars and made a great deal of money. I didn't have to finish: "Ah yes, and therefore he has left money for the advancement of learning. Good!" They were on to that straight away. But they also wanted to know what, other than money, was in it for me: "Well," I said, "here you men 'take title' (when you have reached a certain age and status), by giving feasts to the existing holders of titles. We do it a different way. We have to write a book, which has to be about something that nobody's ever written a book about before, and that's what I'm learning about among you; and why I get financed and that is what's in it for me." It all made complete sense to them.

I did have my considerable problems with the Yoruba language. During my B.Litt. year at Oxford, knowing already that I was going to Yoruba country, I had gone to London once a week to have Yoruba lessons from an English retired missionary, who did his level best to teach me Yoruba. I learned how to read it, no problem, nor was the grammar too difficult. My trouble was pronunciation, because of the tones. If I said something I thought quite harmless, it quite often came out as either obscene or ridiculous. So I soon decided that, aside from the immediate greetings such as: "*Ojú re!*" literally "Your eyes!" – which means "fancy meeting you here", I had better not try. Edwin Ardener had told me that if the English of my informants was better than my command of their language, I was not to be puritanical about it. That was my excuse.

Came the time of year when the Catholic Mission ran its Corpus Christi Procession. It was, for Nigeria, a very curious procession, held in complete silence and preceded by a lot of banners showing pink and white images of Jesus and of the Virgin Mary; at the end, the Fathers invited me to a beer, and asked me what I had thought of their procession. I told them I thought very poorly of it – first, because all those banners, no doubt embroidered by some kind ladies in Canada, could have meant very little, if anything, to the local population; and secondly, because at a real Nigerian procession there would be, not only people talking, but people drumming, which would mean that others would join the procession. Altogether, I didn't like the way they'd done it at all.

They took this with their usual charity. By this time I had parted brass rags with my previous landlord and was in fact living in one of the mission houses, which had been standing empty at the time. A few days later in came the head of the Holy Ghost Fathers of Kabba, with a strange priest who was introduced as "Father So and-So. He's our spiritual superior, and if you don't like the way we run our services, he's the man to tell."

"Oh!"

So I offered the spiritual superior some coffee, and repeated, in rather more detail, what I had said earlier. I may have also have added that, contrary to what might have been thought in Canada, missionaries were not inscribing Christianity onto a blank slate; that pagans had beliefs of their own, which deserved respect. Then, after a while, I thought: "Oh dear! I'm shocking this poor man to no avail." So I stopped and offered him some more coffee.

He accepted the coffee, and then said: "That's very interesting! Now, we are about to hold a retreat here in three weeks' time. Would you like to give us a couple of talks on this?"

The moment he left, I went straight to the wife of one of the teachers at the school, one Moira, and told her the situation. Moira, intelligent and skilful, had already started creating a new lot of banners for people to carry at processions (and very good they were, African patchwork like the hangings in the Palace in Dahomey, which I had described to her). "Moira," I said, "I've been asked to preach at a retreat!"

And when that retreat came around, I did indeed give them two talks expanding what I had said to the "spiritual superior". The Canadian priests all took my strange views in very good part, and said they had really learned something, thanked me and more or less promised to mend their ways. The only one who really suffered was the sole Nigerian priest, who had had to abandon all his pagan beliefs and here I was bringing back the bathwater with the baby... He was not liking it!

Talking of this kind of thing, men, I noticed, were far easier to convert than women. Women are, I believe in every culture, religiously conservative. Here, they were the ones, the wives and mothers, who continued to think that one did have to take notice of the *ẹbọra* and of other things, just to be on the safe side.

I also remember saying to the Canadian Fathers, when they were cross at one of their students wearing some kind of amulet around his neck: "Look, don't punish him! What you are objecting to is not paganism, it is a lack of scientific education. He thinks this amulet is going to *cure* him. This is not about religion. It's about prophylactics." I don't know whether they took any notice.

But then came the time of the *ẹbọra* festivities. All the women indoors! I had been cultivating the *ẹbọra* elders as much as I could, including presents of kola nuts and money and heaven knows what else. But I was still not allowed up! However, I was waiting for them when they came down from the hills, and no other woman was out; and this they took in good part. I danced with the *ẹbọra* procession. Being a man for the purpose of this exercise, I wasn't wearing Yoruba dress. But in my ordinary clothes, I danced with them all up and down Kabba, no doubt driving away the evil spirits. Anyway I was *oybo olofoshi*, so perhaps doubly immune.

And then there was the wedding!

The wealthiest man in Kabba was one of the subordinate chiefs, Fadille. Chief Fadille was a tall, good looking and highly intelligent man. He was also possibly the most prominent supporter of the Catholic Mission, although he was not in fact a communicant, because, although monogamous, either he or his wife (or both) had been divorced before their marriage. This did not prevent him from contributing very generously towards the building of the big church, or from giving his children a "good Catholic education".

Chief Fadille had a daughter, whom he had not only seen through primary and secondary school, but who had been given a nurse's training at Ibadan. And during my time in Kabba, her wedding took place. Three weddings in fact. One took place at the Catholic Church, with the girl in white bridal dress and all the rest of it; but this had been preceded by a small gathering at Chief Fadille's house; to which he invited me, because he was one of the few local people who *did* understand what I was doing. So I was able to witness the traditional handing over of kola nuts as bridewealth for his daughter. He did not accept money; it was clear that he had more than enough already.

After that came the church wedding; and then there was a big reception at what I think must have been the Town Hall, with bride and bridegroom in Yoruba dress in matching cloth (as was local custom), where all the other Europeans had also been invited, and where we listened to a number of speeches, some of them in English. I remember particularly one speech in which the bridegroom (who was not from Kabba itself) was described as having "undergone engineering" in London. I kept a straight face, but only just.

This new son-in-law of Chief Fadille's, and also his wife, became good friends of mine. He, despite having undergone engineering, went on to teach mathematics, at the nearby Igbirra town of Okene.

Now one of my interests, which I kept trying to pursue, was the local blacksmith community. Neither free nor slave, they were a community unto themselves, and had little to do with the rest of the population. I met one or two of them and began asking questions. Finally one of them said: "Look, if you are so interested, we blacksmiths have a town of our own, you ought to go and ask our chief there."

Right.

I enlisted the help of Fadille's son-in-law, teaching at Okene, collected him in my car, and we drove towards this town of the blacksmiths, just south of the border between the Northern and Southern Regions of Nigeria, as things then were. On the way we passed a rather prettily situated village among hills, looking a little like a central European village; there was a large church half-way up the hill, as if it might be Switzerland. And my guide said: "You know, you ought to come here sometime. This is Ogori. They have the highest educational standard of any village in the province" (he was in a position to know) "and moreover they speak a very curious language among themselves, not one of the local languages." I thanked him. We went on to the blacksmiths. I asked the questions. Didn't get anything very interesting, but was asked to come again.

The next time, I went by myself, and thought: *Well I'll just go and have a look at this village of Ogori.* I had been issued, by the Ibadan Institute of African Studies, with several copies of a quite long vocabulary in case I came across any strange dialects or languages in my fieldwork area. After the usual kinship terms, the vocabulary went on to 1, 2, 3, 4, 5 etc, and terms for such natural objects as star, moon, earth. Quite a large thing, several pages long, for me to fill in. I also had, of course, a tape recorder. I went to call on the Ologori, the chief of Ogori, who I had also been told spoke good English. He received me amiably. I explained that I was from the University of Ibadan, and that I understood that in his village they had a different language from the surrounding ones; he gave a little grin and said: "Yes, we have our own." "Well," I said: "I also understand that you have the highest educational standard of any place in the province, so perhaps you could ask one of your English-speaking subjects to assist me for a couple of hours, so he can speak these words into my tape recorder and help me to write them down." "No," he said, "I think I'd like to do that myself. I will just go and tell my people I shall be busy, so we won't be disturbed. Meanwhile, you might like to look at this." And he produced a large ledger-like book, which I thought was going to be his photograph album, one of which Nigerian chiefs always seemed to have. And he was off, and I opened it.

It was not a photograph album.

It was a history of his people, written by himself, in English, in an educated longhand. Complete with Acknowledgements, Table of Contents and quite a number of illustrations of musical instruments and the like!

Well, the Ologori came back. (He styled himself as would a Yoruba king, Ologori meaning something like the Lord of Ogori, and he dressed as an Ọba, when he wasn't actually farming.) He came back and duly spoke his words into my microphone and we wrote them down. I was spending the night near there, somewhere in a Bush Rest House. He very generously lent me his manuscript, which I read by the light of a kerosene lamp that night. In reading it I began to realise that I had stumbled upon a completely different people, and not only in terms of language: they had a form of bridal choice entirely new to me.

They too were divided into a landowning or noble class and a class of what they called servants: Ikọtoro, plural of *okọtoro*, which comes from *okọto*, service.

Now Ikọtoro could marry whoever they liked. On the other hand, if you were upper class, you had to marry within the ruling class of course, preferably within your own patriline. These people were of course polygamous, but their incest taboo extended to those of the same maternal origin. A half-brother and sister could get married as long as they were not from the same mother. If, at the apex of their shared genealogy, there was a mother and two daughters, none of their descendants through any links, male or female, could marry one another.

I returned the next day, asked whether I could borrow the manuscript some more, to which he very kindly consented. Back in Kabba, one of my friends from the Agricultural College helped me to reproduce it. Which in those days was a complicated business, certainly up where we were, involving a bathtub and various kinds of acid. I can't remember details of the process, but I do recall it was complicated, and that you had to hang the sheets up to dry for a long time and that my friend Bill and I spent most of one night doing it.

I returned the manuscript to the Ologori of Ogori and told him I was extremely interested in what he had written. I also explained that I was an anthropologist and described what this was. I didn't have too much explaining to do; he had once been sent to England by the British Council.

Chapter 2
Fieldwork: Ogori

At this point I decided to go back to England for a short spell, partly for personal reasons, but partly also because I wanted permission from my supervisor, Edwin Ardener, to change horses in midstream. And not only that; what would the Nuffield Foundation think of a change of both topic and area? For I was now planning to research an unfamiliar pattern of bride selection and in order to do this intended to move outside Yoruba-speaking country; and the money I had been given was to enable me to do research in Yoruba country. But also, the author of the *History of Ogori* that had inspired me – the Ologori himself – had, in the best style of the English books he had read, put in Acknowledgements. Prominent among these was the name of R. E. Bradbury, the man who had been the external examiner for my B.Litt. thesis! So I thought: *"This is probably Brad's territory, I mustn't muscle in on it, not without his permission."*

So I went to see Brad in Birmingham, carrying my (by now) rather tatty copy of the manuscript and showed it to him, including the Acknowledgements, and he said: "Oh dear. Don't tell him, he sounds *such* a nice chap. But do you know, I have no recollection of ever having been in that village!"

I think I can reconstruct what happened. My senior colleague, on his way from X to Y, had stopped at the village, politely paid his respects to the Ọba, been shown the work in progress and said something like: "That's very good! Do carry on." And to this very lonely born-intellectual, sitting there in his village, this had been quite enough encouragement to rate a written acknowledgement. As for my supervisor Edwin, he simply told me to avoid scrupulosity. "The Nuffield are very lucky to be getting any work out of you at all," he added.

So I happily returned to Nigeria, and moved from Kabba to Ogori, where I was – at last – the only white stranger for many miles around. I was not even addressed as *oybo* any longer, but had become *Oviya*, a courteous form of address, both intimate and formal, which felt like the Russian use of baptismal name and patronymic. Also, a girl was said to become *Oviya*, become a grown-up lady perhaps, at her initiation in adolescence, and the Ologori told me that he habitually addressed his wives as *Oviya* – something like Ma'am.

Gabriel Bawa Akerejola was a most remarkable man. Gabriel was the Ologori's baptismal name, Akerejola his surname. The second name, Bawa, means "slave" in Hausa. He had been one of those children who are believed to have died and come back several times, and who are therefore both marked with a knife and given a derogatory name, so that the spirits shouldn't want to grab them again. He still had the scars on his temple to show me.

As a boy he had been to the excellent local Anglican primary school, and had then spent several years as a clerk in the Provincial Office at Lokoja. This was the full extent of his formal education, but he was the sort of person who reads absolutely everything that falls into his hands; so he had educated himself quite extensively.

I remember seeing in his office, where then and later he usually received me, piles of ancient *Reader's Digests*, in which every word he didn't know he had underlined and then looked it up in the dictionary; and he had an amazing memory. I was able to add a few technical terms to his vocabulary. He was delighted to discover the English term "sibling", which corresponded to a word in his own language; he hadn't realised before that there was an English word that could mean either brother or sister.

His "History of Ogori" he had written for political reasons: he wanted to make it quite clear that the people of Ogori and Magongo were *not* part of the Igbirra; the Igbirra being the quite numerous people (though not as numerous as the Yoruba) who held the town of Okene nearby. All of this area was more or less the "shatter zone" of pre-colonial days, which had faced slave-raiders from the Muslim North. I believe that, for Ogori and Magongo at least, the Brits had genuinely come as saviours and were still very favourably regarded. The Igbirra were Muslims. This naturally counted against them in local terms, though I suspect the reason they felt able to be Muslims was that they had been the only people in the area to have resisted the Northern slave-raiders; so they did not need to demonstrate their non-Northernness by becoming Christian.

Ogori was very largely Christian, either Anglican or Catholic, depending a little on how near you lived to which church; there were indeed some half-dozen Muslims, who were not persecuted, but neither could they be people of any importance. However, Christianity was, as so often in that part of the world, a young man's game (in the case of Ogori including young women): it was what you did in order to gain an education. When you reached maturer years, and especially if you belonged to the local land-owning class, you might nevertheless have to take on a number of traditional family duties, even as a priest of your family shrine.

This, then, is the background to what to Gabriel Bawa Akerejola was doing. He himself was, of course, very much pro-education. He had, at this time, five wives. But before becoming Chief he had had only the one, Dorothy, who, no longer very young, was still quite clearly his favourite. He had taken on the others in order to ally himself with the other principal families of the area.

They all went on Sundays to the handsome Anglican church across from the house where I lived, the men on separate pews from the women, as was usual in Nigeria. The five wives would sit together on the women's side. He sat on the men's side, and (I happen to know) had folded (inside his prayer book or his hymn book) whatever he was reading at the time – a little like a Voltairean nobleman in pre-revolutionary France. The wives would come and visit me on their way home, under the sponsorship of Dorothy, and I would offer them tea and kola nuts.

In a way, I was a kind of honorary wife. I don't mean this in the least sexually, but whenever Gabriel had an important call to make, or was himself receiving important visitors, he rather liked having me around.

But I did not live in the Palace compound, so called. When it became known that I was coming to Ogori, a town meeting was held, at which the three "quarters" rather quarrelled over which of them was going to have me; an anthropologist of one's own was a very desirable thing to have – not quite as good as a Post Office, never mind a secondary school, but prestigious all the same.

The competition for my presence was won by a man not from Gabriel's quarter, an absentee landlord whom in fact I never met. He had built himself quite a handsome small house, but was in fact away in Kaduna, working in the Northern Civil Service. Like quite a number of people, he had built himself this house for his retirement, and was very glad to have this prestigious anthropologist living there. His poorer kinsmen used to come and collect a really ridiculous peppercorn rent from me once a month and I would be given a return present of something like a few eggs – so it was a very friendly arrangement. It was a nice house, and my one and only complaint during my time in Ogori was that the young man whose job it was to ring the gong for services at the Anglican church across the way absolutely *loved* his job, and used to ring it as often as possible and very loudly.

I also had two "maids of honour", as I called them to myself, nieces of the Ologori, who were assigned to me essentially for the improvement of their English! I was told I needn't pay them anything, but did in fact pay them a little. At night I would see them studying improbable things like the geography of Sweden or Canada by the light of the kerosene lamp, because they were preparing for exams.

The village, or the quarter, had also built me a little bathroom outside the house, with the luxury of a cement floor so that I would not be trampling about in the mud; and I had borrowed, from my friend Muriel in Kabba, a baby bath. My two girls would go, every evening, with empty kerosene tins to get water from next door, as I didn't have a well; they would heat one lot and leave the other cool, and then the two tins would be placed side-by-side on the bathroom floor. I had a bowl, and I would stand in my baby bath and mix the water in this bowl to an appropriate temperature and give myself a shower. It worked extremely well.

So I was really well dug-in and very happy to be in Ogori. Thence I later returned to Buenos Aires, I think a little earlier than I should have done; but I did remain in Ogori for the best part of a year.

The language situation was no better than it had been among the Yoruba; Ogori too was a tone language and I learned, in the usual way, a few greetings ... "*Wayna monne – o*" which is what you said of an evening, and not really very much else; for, of course, with the local high educational standard, most people spoke English; at least the men did. When, later, I began to collect songs, my farmer neighbours, who had had no more formal education than their king, would kindly offer to write down the words for me. The next time I saw His Highness – I always addressed him as "Your Highness", never as "Gabriel" until later in correspondence; he addressed me as "Ma'am", as if I were the Queen or a senior officer in the women's services. The next time I went to see His Highness, I asked how come my neighbours could write down things in Ogori?" He answered: "Well I don't know what happens nowadays, but when I was a boy at school, we would be kept in an hour or so after official classes, to be taught to write our own language." And I said: "Yes, yes, but who worked out the spelling?" He looked at me as if my brains needed examining and said: "Well *we* did, of course! If you can write Yoruba in European characters, why can't you write Ogori?"

So there had been *no* missionary translators; this was because, while Ogori had been pretty thoroughly missionised into Anglican Christianity, this had not been done by white people, but by Yoruba. The story was (and I'm prepared to believe it) that, in the early days, some young man from Ogori went further south to trade, was given hospitality in a Yoruba compound, where he saw somebody reading, probably moving his lips. Fascinated by this, he returned to Ogori once his business was done, told other people and they thought: "Ah! This we must find out about." So he sent back south for Yoruba teachers and reading-matter. Thus, Ogori people learned to read and write and were, at the same time, Christianised.

They learned other things from the Yoruba too; indeed they imitated the Yoruba in every way they could. One item was growing cocoa. They had initially no idea what it was for, but if the Yoruba were growing these new cocoa trees, there must be something to it, so let us do it too.

The Scriptures as used in Ogori, and the church services, were all in the Yoruba language, and the resident chaplain, the Anglican priest in charge of the church, was himself a Yoruba. The Holy Ghost Fathers from Kabba used to come approximately one week in three to say Mass at the smaller Catholic church. The Yoruba language was so used not only in Ogori, but also in Akoko-Ekiti, further south – where my Kabba friend Edward Adamu had come from. It was used among all these people, who spoke languages different from each other. It functioned, in fact, a bit like Latin in medieval Europe: the language of church and school, and also the language which people of different linguistic communities communicated with each other. Yoruba, *never* Igbirra! His Highness obviously spoke Yoruba, and Ogori, and Igbirra, and rather good English, and moreover Hausa, and a couple of other languages; but then he was a superior person. The two little nieces staying with me spoke only four languages; their own Ogori, of course Igbirra, Yoruba and some English – which I was supposed to improve, and indeed it could have done with improvement.

The general population was, I'm pretty certain, at least trilingual, and it was then I first realised something for which I have since had much confirmation in Europe: it is the small tribes that are multilingual! The English, the French, and (once upon a time) the Spaniards don't bother; the Dutch, Swiss, and the Danes do, and you can quite see why.

The Ogori-speaking community, which comprised also the village of Magongo, had, like most peoples in the area, a four-day "market week". In other words, there was a market every four days. For Ogori, however, the four-day market week was divided into two sets of days, in which "service days" alternated with something rather more like Sabbaths.

Service days were those on which those people who were "servants", *ikọtoro,* had to work for their masters – that is as tenant serfs, owing labour to the owners of the land. On non-service days they could work for themselves. Those were also the days on which, if you had a problem that you might wish to consult an oracle about, you would seek out the *isíyaro. Isíya* is the local version of the Yoruba divination system *Ifa*, based on multiples of four in a similar way to the market week. *Isíyaro* were venerated elderly men expert at this; you might consult an *isíyaro* if you had genuine health problems, or even simply a run of bad luck. Now, Ogori being a small community, the expert knew quite a lot about you in the first place; so he would ask you questions like: "Now, have you resolved that inheritance problem with your brother?" or "Is there still jealousy between your wives?" and a few other things of that nature. You might also tell him your dreams, or he would ask about them, and interpret them. So much so, that when I once described to Gabriel what my father the psychoanalyst had done for a living, we agreed that it was not so very different.

Normally, when the consultation ended, the *isíyaro* would prescribe, first of all, as in the New Testament, that you made it up with your brother, or whatever; and also that you made a small sacrifice to the ancestors you had offended. Ancestors were still very much present, even in this predominantly Christian community. There were also little local spirit shrines; but ancestors were, for most people most of the time, more important as the guardians of morality.

I once witnessed one of these ancestor sacrifices, and indeed in a sense took part in it, because once the cockerel was killed, it was barbecued and I was given some for myself by the old man who was making the sacrifice; and, as with every pagan ceremony I have ever witnessed, whether in Kabba or Ogori, it all ended with a prayer for the anthropologist: "May she return to her own country in peace! May her work be successful!" which I found very moving.

I have spoken earlier on the form of address *Oviya*, meaning something like Lady or Madam; as a term of reference I only came across it in talk about a girl "becoming *Oviya*" at puberty. Earlier on, before the coming of Christianity, I was told that becoming *Oviya* took most of a year. The girl in question would be secluded for approximately three months, perhaps longer, while the proper scarifications were made on her stomach and had time to heal (I even saw these scarifications on the stomachs of some elderly women). The young girl who was telling me about these "primitive customs" said: "It must have been *horrible*, can you imagine the pain?" And I looked at the child's wrist, on which she had had a little wristwatch tattooed, and thought: "Well *that* can't have been entirely painless either!"

By the time I was in Ogori, the whole *Oviya* initiation had been telescoped into a single long weekend, firmly affixed within the Christian calendar: two weeks after Easter for Anglicans, three for Catholics, because one does have to mark the difference somehow, doesn't one? In both cases, from the Friday evening onwards, people would come to greet the new *Oviya* in her own compound; or, if she wasn't there because she was away at school or university, it would have to be her photograph, proudly, and perhaps a little sadly, displayed; and her parents, or elder brother or whoever, would obviously entertain guests to the local beer and a kola nut or so. This would go on, through Friday and Saturday, while everyone sang all the old *Oviya* songs – because they were not allowing the songs to get lost, even if the ceremony itself had been shortened and Christianised. It would end on the Sunday, with a church service in each case, thanking God for the successful conclusion of the *Oviya* festival. And even those people who might not be able to be there for Easter certainly saw to it they came home for the *Oviya* festival – it was very important in everyone's life.

The word for "mother" was *iya,* and I suspect, though I don't know, that *oviya* was related to it. The matrifocal group was known as the *iyagben*, "children of the same mother", and the descent groups based on mothers were called *iya ukúba*. This was most clearly spelled in their views on incest. A man was allowed – indeed encouraged, if he belonged to the upper class – to marry within his patriline, his *ẹdẹda ukúba*; even a half-sister, if she was not by the same mother. But if the relationship was through mothers, then descendants (in whatever line and for however many generations) of two sisters born of the same mother, could never marry – at any rate for as long as the relationship was remembered. (The *History of Ogori* contained a number of genealogical trees to assist memory.)

The people of Ogori believed that in the making of a child, an embryo in the womb, blood came from the father and water from the mother. And it was the water, in other words the maternal descent, that determined who you could, or could not marry. Their word for "incest" was *iwúro* which was also the name of a very large container kept in every compound and used to store water, at which the women of that compound would fill their water jugs for washing and cooking. Marrying someone related to you through two ancestral sisters born of the same mother was interpreted as meaning that you had "returned to the common water-storage jar" – something seen as the perfect metaphor for incest.

Members of the serf class, *ikọtoro,* belonged to matrifocal groups like anyone else: they too had mothers. But they could not belong to an *ẹdẹda ukúba,* a patriline. For a young man of the upper class, his first wife undoubtedly had to be a woman from his own patriline, what was called an *Ọwẹ* bride. This first wife was generally found for him by his father. After that, however, he was on his own; and, as in most societies, upper-class men tended to grab the prettier girls from the lower class, so minor wives were quite likely to be *ikọtoro* by birth. They need not, however, always remain so.

If and when the husband died, his widows naturally underwent a period of mourning, fairly severe in terms of shaved heads and abstinence from this and that – two years for an *Ọwẹ* widow, one for a widow from the *ikọtoro* class. However, if the latter chose to observe mourning for two years, she became classed as *Ọwẹ* – because "she had loved her husband as if she were his kinswoman". She was then "inherited", in the usual way, by her late husband's nearest male relative, and she and her children absorbed into the upper class. The children thus acquired a patriline, an *ẹdẹda ukúba,* and were thus in the running for land, title or whatever else ran in that lineage.

This curious form of social promotion explains why the number of *ikọtoro* was, at any given time, quite small. They did exist, of course; only some women could join a patrilineage through marriage and longer widowhood. Not all were given the chance, and no man could, in the nature of things, ever have such a possibility of promotion. It is also quite possible (though I don't know this for certain) that a childless young widow might not consider the longer mourning worth her while; this remained a personal decision.

As was apt to be the case in rural Nigeria – perhaps in rural Africa on the whole – the standard of manners for the young was very high indeed. At first, every time I left my house, I was a bit disconcerted at the nearest boy snatching my expensive tape recorder, and another my camera, until I noted that a third one had taken my notebook and a fourth one my ballpoint pen, and realised it was part of the old code of manners, whereby no decently brought-up child allows its elders or betters to carry *anything.* Actually, I was regarded as pretty tough: their previous notion of white women was that they were terribly delicate creatures, who had to spend all their time indoors, would shrivel up if the sun touched them and probably melt in the rain. Whereas I was capable of climbing a (really rather gentle, and not very high) hill, and actually sit there and use my tape recorder; they thought this was pretty tough for a white woman.

Also, boys in the upper forms of the big Anglican primary school attached to the church opposite my house, and probably also those in the smaller Catholic one in the central part of the village, had a duty to keep the paths to the fields and terraces clean and clear. As there was not quite enough land, Ogori people did quite a lot of terracing, unusual in that part of the world; such things require frequent maintainance work, and this was a job for these boys.

Girls were not expected to do this job, but they too had high standards of courtesy. If I was sitting on my verandah, it was the proper thing for a passing girl to curtsey to me. The daughter of my across-the-way farmer neighbour was already old enough to be wearing grown-up clothes, but she didn't have a great many. For some reason, one evening when she passed me sitting on the verandah writing up my notes, she was wearing a top, a kind of blouse, but nothing below the waist; probably her only wrap-around skirt was being washed and dried. But, though you may or may or not be wearing something below the waist, manners is manners: the child curtseyed. This was part of the general attitude.

When I first arrived, within a few days of my settling into the house, I was interested to see quite a large group of women, between a dozen and twenty, coming from house to house, including mine. At each house they would stop, and they would shout and sing – none of which I understood – and raise their fists, not in a menacing way, but as if in greeting. So I raised mine and smiled at them. What was I to do? The next time I saw His Highness, I told him about this. He said: "Ah yes! A woman will have had her first baby in your quarter, that is what women do when one of them has her first baby." "Well, I shook my fist at them too!" "In that case," His Highness said, "they'll now believe that you have had children. Because women who have never borne a child run away and hide from these situations. But you have now officially had a child, and if I'm asked I shall tell them yes indeed, and that you have left it with your sister to be looked after, if that's all right?"

There were two religious primary schools in Ogori, a large Anglican and a smaller Catholic one. There was also a state primary school between the villages of Ogori and Magongo, to which His Highness sent his own children – I think essentially because he had rather a lot of them, and this was free, whereas at the religious schools you had to pay. But the remarkable thing, to me, was that each of the two religious schools had a kindergarten, where, very much as in modern Western society, children were looked after when their mothers were away buying and selling at market, or busy at other work, perhaps a little horticulture; although women did not actually grow yams, that was for men. But women did attend other markets around the area, which also took time; so children too young for school were left at those kindergartens, for which the European term was used by most people. (I don't even know whether there was an Ogori word for these facilities!)

And when I asked who had had this idea, I was told, "Oh well, somebody read it somewhere, it seemed like a good idea" – maybe in one of those *Reader's Digests?*

When I first arrived in the autumn, much of the younger population was elsewhere. The young adults were at college or university. There was even one young man – not related to the Ologori – who was "eating his dinners in London", preparing for a career in the law; sadly, he later died there in a motor accident.

More mature adults like my landlord would be at jobs, in Kaduna or elsewhere in the North; for, although Ogori had genuinely been unknown to anthropologists and other scholars, the little town was known all over the Northern Region: Ogori people were employed everywhere, both in the Civil Service and in private firms. You had only to say the words "from Ogori" for people to know you were talking about an educated person, efficient and not too involved in major tribal politics; so Ogori people went all over the shop.

Not all those employed in that largely Muslim Northern Region got Christmas off; but students could and did come home at that time of year, and in my day organised a concert of old songs in the market square – to which my tape-recorder and I were most cordially invited.

For Ogori had kept its old songs, and not only the *Oviya* ones. When the village converted to Christianity, the locals, a generation or so above Gabriel's, had decided it was a pity to throw out the baby with the bathwater, so the old songs were kept; and the students were delighted to have recordings of them. Other than that, I found myself running a kind of *salon* for these young people, who all used to come and visit me, and ask me what I was doing, and about anthropology. I remember some of them were rather worried: "What did I do for clean water?" So I explained that my girls got it from this neighbour's well, and then boiled it, and I showed my guests the water filter. (Because, while they knew that Europeans' stomachs are very sensitive to water, they had always hitherto seen "clean water" brought out from a fridge – and I didn't have one.)

What held these geographically scattered people together as a culture were, precisely, the songs they had kept. They were well aware of this. There was of course an Ogori Students' Union – indeed I think it was they who organised this concert. I asked them about their other activities: "Oh, well, we get together at Ahmadu Bello University or wherever we are, and we sing." I asked what they sang. "Well, we sing Ogori songs. No we don't have an anthem of our own, we don't do anything political. We just sing our own Ogori songs! Then of course we come back here and sing them again."

Titles, ceremonies, and events in Ogori

My friend the Ologori, who styled himself, dressed, and generally behaved like a Yoruba Ọba, was not, of course, the only titled chief in the place. On the contrary, his role was a comparatively recent one: there had only been an Ologori or an Ọba for a couple of generations, though each of the various quarters of the settlement had its own chief with his own title. Titled men, who in fact constituted a kind of governing council, each had two sceptres: a carved wooden staff symbolising peace and good will, and an iron spear for war. Whenever they met together, they had to leave the latter outside the house and enter only with their wooden staffs.

Interestingly, in Ogori tradition there were also titled women. These had their own sceptres, smaller wooden staffs rather like large thick walking sticks, to be carried on special occasions. The carving on these was quite non-representational, nothing particularly feminine, sexual or maternal; but, like the men's wooden staffs, they seemed to represent peaceful, gentle, "feminine" values. Quite how women succeeded to title I was never able to find out; perhaps through the matrifocal group. No actual political power seemed to be involved, it was more a question of influence through prestige. But this set of ideas and values was certainly very useful to me as a woman anthropologist working on her own.

The important and socially mobile matrifocal group, *iyagben*, also had a very sinister side, relating to the causes of death. The deaths of small babies, as had been the case with His Highness, were attributed to their having been taken by spirits who might, with luck, be persuaded to return them. The demise of old people was regarded as in the course of things, natural enough; indeed, if a man lived to a very ripe old age, he was given a sort of funeral before his death, one he could himself enjoy. He was carried about the village; after that he gave up all responsibility, his titles if any, and all the rest of it, and was carefully looked after until his physical death.

What was felt to need explanation, understandably, were the deaths of young adults, who should not be dying. Here, it was felt that this could only be from witchcraft, and the witchcraft could only have come from somebody within their own matrifocal group – the only category of person close enough to them to bewitch them to their deaths.

As the owner of the local shrine against witchcraft said to me: "We are all good Christians here, but you've got to do *something* about witches!" This anti-witchcraft shrine was a little way outside town. Whoever was suspected of being a witch, or whom the oracle had declared might be a witch, would go there with a sacrifice (usually a fowl), would present it and say to the priest of the shrine: "If I am a witch, may my share in this meat kill me." And of course normally her share, or his, didn't kill them, and therefore – well, there must be some mistake! They were not necessarily drummed out of town (though I did see this happen once during a brief smallpox scare), and after a while the thing was forgotten. (Who did rather nicely out of it, of course, were the priests at the anti-witchcraft shrine, who got a lot more animal protein than other people.)

Aside from Christmas and the *Oviya* festival, there was a third very important time of year, the New Yam Festival. The local people grew yams and guinea corn, but the yams were the main nutrition crop and the digging out of the first yam a matter of enormous ritual importance.

However, when I went to ask His Highness about this, he said: "I'm sorry, there I can't help you. The priest in charge of digging up the first new yam, is Chief so-and-so of such-and-such a quarter, and you will have to go and ask him." So I did go and ask this elderly chief, who was very good about it. He said, well, he didn't do the digging up himself any more, he was too old, he sent his sons to do it. But it did have to be done at night, so if I didn't mind being woken by his sons at two in the morning? So I said I didn't mind at all. And at two in the morning several young men came and woke me up, and we all proceeded over rather humpy hillocky ground – full of yam heaps, the other new yams which would soon be dug up; we chatted on the way and one of them said: "Well, we did consult the oracle! You know, some years the oracle doesn't allow us to speak when we go to dig up the first new yam." So I said: "Well, I'm very glad *Isíya* allowed you to speak this year, because otherwise you couldn't warn me about these irregularities of the ground and I'd fall down." "Well, this year the oracle must have known that there was an *oybo* coming with our party." Clearly the oracle was well informed.

So we got to the place, a little way outside the village, the first new yam was duly dug up, and *immediately,* in the same piece of ground, in the same hole, were placed a few seeds of guinea corn, their other crop, which grows during the other half of the year. So that the harvesting of one and the sowing of the other were part of the same rite. Then there were the prayers, including the usual prayer for the anthropologist to return to her own country in peace, etc.

Then, dawn already breaking, we made our way back to the village. Waiting for us by the path were a number of women who wanted to touch the new yam we were bringing: if you touched the new yam, you just might conceive and successfully give birth to a new child.

Back in the compound of the New Yam Priest, we found the old boy standing erect, leaning on his spear, to keep bad spirits away. As the young men and I came in, he greeted us; then the new yam was cut up into quite a lot of pieces, some larger than others. The larger ones were anointed with palm oil, the smaller left bare; and these were placed in pairs and then thrown out, by the old man himself, to rather more than the four cardinal points, in every direction from the compound. It was explained to me that these pieces of yam symbolised male and female. The "male" bit of new yam was the un-oiled piece, and the "female" the one anointed with palm oil, which made it symbolically gentler; and if they had made that one bigger, it was because they hoped that feminine qualities of gentleness and peace would prevail in the coming year.

The New Yam Priest himself (speaking through one of his sons) added that, in the past, all the shrines towards which he had thrown the pieces of yam had been within his compound. "But I don't keep them here any more, because, you see, my sons are all Christians, and the silly lads might, when the mood is on them, jump over these shrines or insult them in some other way. I don't want harm to come to my sons!" – the young men kept becomingly silent and grave – "so I've placed the shrines out in the bush and the boys don't know exactly where they are." I was allowed to take photographs, but these came to nothing in the still poor light of early morning.

When next I saw His Highness, I thanked him for his good advice and told him more or less what had happened. He shook his head sadly: "Oh, you Europeans are so lucky. All my life I have wanted to see the new yam ceremony, but do you suppose they'd let me? No. Never!"

I had by now been in Ogori for some time, the year was 1966.

One day I heard my two little maids of honour, His Highness's nieces, talking together rather excitedly. I asked them what it was about. "Well, we don't know for sure, but they say that the Sardauna is dead, and Sir Abubakar is dead, and the Army has taken over the country."

Oh.

This was early in the evening, just before supper time. They brought me my supper and as I ate it, I thought, "Well, maybe after supper I'll go and see His Highness and see what he knows about it;" so I did.

I found him sitting out of doors, inside his compound, surrounded by his wives and with his radio on his lap. (I could not afford a radio myself, so I had to get my information from somewhere else.) I asked him about this *coup*. He said: "Well, Radio Nigeria denies it, but the BBC says it's so, and so does the Voice of America, and personally I believe *them*."

At this point, or maybe the following day, we confessed to each other verbally, something which he had probably guessed about me, and I had certainly guessed about him, that we had both been against the much unlamented Sardauna of Sokoto, who had been the tyrant (there's no other word for it) of the Northern Region. The reason I had guessed it about Gabriel was that in his study where he received visitors, he had a large and handsome official portrait of Her Majesty the Queen; which of course nobody could fault him for, Head of the Commonwealth and all that; but other people had a portrait of the Sardauna. I had grown up politically very much aware of who has and who hasn't "Our Leader's" portrait on the wall.

The day following the first radio news, I reflected a bit more and thought: "Well there are going to be problems; I had better go and see that I have enough money to meet any unforeseen expenses."

My money I got, as needed, from some institution, an educational institution, I think, in Okene, the nearest town of any size; the University of Ibadan had made arrangements for money to be sent there. I thought I'd better go now and draw out quite a lot, so as to survive any *coups* there might be. I did so, quite successfully (and a good thing too); and then I thought I had better let my mother know I'm all right, just in case she hears about all this in Argentina! This was a little silly of me; my mother, a sensible woman who'd lived through quite a number of *coups* in Buenos Aires, knew perfectly well they're harmless, unless you happen to be in the line of fire. However, I'd forgotten that; I had now long lived in England, where people are rather more scared of *coups*. So I went to the Okene Post Office and said, "I want to send a telegram to Buenos Aires."

The Post Office was run by two young men, both Igbo. They said "Well, we'll do our best, but we can't guarantee it gets there." So I gave them a brief text: "Quite OK here, love Eva", that kind of thing, paid for it, and drove back to Ogori.

Eventually I got a letter from my mother thanking me for my nice telegram, saying she didn't quite see why I had bothered to tell her all this, and what on earth was I doing in Ibadan? Looking back upon it, I think that one or both of the young men must have decided he'd be happier in Ibadan than in what was still, technically, the Northern Region. At any rate, the telegram had been sent from Ibadan, and this was more or less all I found out about the *coup* just then.

For some time after that, every time I wanted to go to Ibadan for a rest, a change and some shopping, people would say: "Will you be all right? I mean, Ibadan is so *restless*." I would say I thought I would be all right, and would drive there and stay at Lalage Bown's. When I wanted to leave again, Ibadan academics would say: "Going up North again? Oh you *are* brave!" or words to that effect.

The only time something happened, or rather didn't happen, was once when I was going back up North and was actually stopped by a tree trunk placed across the road for just that purpose. I didn't in fact have any money on me, having spent all I had for the journey, but I did have an expensive camera and tape recording equipment in the car, so I wasn't best pleased to be stopped. I did a very silly thing: I started winding up my window, fat lot of good that would have done! So the men who were stopping me said: "Don't do that, we like you too much, lady." And then, I must say, I had some quite other fears! However, I was mistaken. I happened to know – as I say, I have grown up politically aware – what the correct hand signal was in that particular bit of Nigeria at that time. Two fingers up: "V for Victory" kind of thing; I made it, they laughed, and motioned me to the side of the road, and on I went, perfectly happily, to Ogori.

As regards safety on the road during this period, my friend Muriel Halligan, who worked at the Teacher Training College in Kabba, had this adopted African son, whom at this stage she was sending to boarding school in Ibadan. Muriel found it was best if she travelled with Johnny and the driver because, if she was in there with her white face, they were safe. The one thing all Nigerians knew was that we whites were not involved in this lot of political quarrels. Whereas if Johnny had been sent alone with the driver, they would both have been in danger simply through being black.

That was really all I ever knew then about the *coup*, except that some time later, as I was leaving Nigeria and was already back in Ibadan, somebody told me about an Igbo lady who had been offered a very well paid job, teaching something or other at Ahmadu Bello University in the North. I never met this lady, but I sent her a message saying: "For heavens sake don't take it! Scrub floors in Ibadan if you have to, sooner than go to that well-paid job in the North. There's going to be trouble." I still hope she took my advice.

While I was still living in Ogori, a little after the *coup*, I found a letter awaiting me on one of my visits to Ibadan. I was being offered a job at the School of Oriental and African Studies (SOAS), part of the University of London – a lecturer's job, to be held initially for one year, with the implication that after that we'd see... I couldn't believe my eyes. Here I was, still in the field doing my doctoral fieldwork, being offered a job on the basis of my existing B.Litt.! I think it was still supposed to be subject to an interview, but this didn't worry me – I'd always been good at them.

When I got back to Ogori and told His Highness, he actually got up and danced for joy. This is something I had seen other Nigerians do before – even, delightfully, a vicar's wife thus expressing her delight at the amount of a church collection. But the joyful dance of so tall and regal a man as His Highness was something else again – he had not done so, for instance, when I had told him the University of Ibadan intended to publish his *History of Ogori* – as indeed they have done since.

Sometime after this, I decided on what I meant to be a brief visit to my mother in Buenos Aires, intending to return to England via Nigeria and spend a little more time in Ogori. In the end I didn't, but travelled straight to England, something I now regret; but at the time I was anxious to attend that interview and secure my new job.

Years later, after the Biafran war, I did return to Nigeria, on a visit to my friend Elo (Elochukwu Amucheazi), now Professor of Political Science at the University of Nigeria, married, and the father of my god-daughter Onamma. I also went to visit Lalage Bown, now teaching at Ahmadu Bello University in the north. When I got there, Lalage took me out to lunch at the Senior Staff Club. We were joined by a pair of youngish Nigerian academics, who asked me politely whether I'd been in Nigeria before and what had I done there; I said I'd done field work as an anthropologist.

"Oh!" said they "Where?" and I said "Well, a small place called Ogori." "Oh! We have someone from Ogori here, in the Veterinary Science Department, name of Akerejola." Then I remembered that I had never met the eldest son of His Highness Gabriel Bawa Akerejola, Ologori of Ogori, and I said: "Lead me to this Akerejola!" Which they did.

It must have been a weekend, because he was at home, and very pleased to see me, as was his delightful young wife, who already had two small children. They asked me to dinner with them the following night, and when I came, we spoke of course mostly about his late father the Ologori, and the young man said: "You know, you obviously knew my father much better than I was ever able to. Because, in this country, there is such distance between father and son, that I never learned all these things about him."

His young wife, on the other hand, said: "You don't remember me, but I remember you quite well. You came to my granny's funeral." I forbore to tell her that in Ogori I'd been to everybody's granny's funeral – because that, of course, is where you find out the most about the community. She herself had, some time ago, taken a first degree in Sociology. She then had these two kids and was now wondering, just like any young woman in the West, whether she should go back to her career straight away, or wait until the children were a little older.

By now I do know that Akerejola junior became a Professor and has now duly retired from Ahmadu Bello University. His father would have been very proud of him

Chapter 3
A Base in London

The interview with my new boss, Christoph von Fürer-Haimendorf, did indeed go well; the lecturer's job at SOAS was mine for a year.

Now, I had to find myself somewhere to live in London. I didn't want to do anything as binding as *buying* a flat, or taking a long lease, because I didn't know what was going to happen at the end of that academic year. I was fortunate in finding a small flat, available only for a year, at 66 Vicarage Court, a building put up in the 'thirties somewhere off Kensington High Street. It must have been very "modern" when it was first built; it consisted of small flats for single people. I had one of these, consisting of one fine large room, one small kitchen, and one small bathroom – just enough for my needs. The kitchen was somewhat primitive: the cooking facilities consisted of a cooker with a single plate, which knew only two positions, "off" and "on", so it was a little difficult to produce anything very nice for a dinner party, but I did manage once in a while to have close friends there. Anyway, the flat did me quite well.

The SOAS atmosphere

It was rather more difficult to get used to the job conditions at SOAS. My actual duties were quite light; it was taken into account that I was still writing a thesis. But I had never before worked in a place where there wasn't anywhere for staff and students to get together socially. SOAS was in those days an enormously hierarchical place. There was a Senior Common Room; there may have been a Junior Common Room also. There were certainly senior and junior dining halls, and the etiquette was such that Christoph's wife, who worked as a draftswoman in the administrative section, was not allowed into her husband's common room or dining hall, because she was so inferior to him in station.

My office I shared with another staff member, which meant I had to do my own writing at home. Also, if I wanted to see a student, just the two of us, often the only way to do so was to take him or her round the corner to the nearest café. Which was all right, if it was a girl; if it was a boy, it could be a bit embarrassing, because in those days young men still felt they had to pay for the coffee, and I would try to fight this, because obviously I had more money than they had – it wasn't easy. Also, there was no equivalent, no real equivalent, to all of us going to the pub on a Friday evening. There *was* a pub and most did go to it; but London is London, people lived in different directions at considerable distances, and were expected back home to supper, so that at most, we had half-an-hour together. It was altogether not quite the cosy atmosphere I had been used to in Oxford.

Work from home

There was quite a lot to do from home; not only preparing lectures and writing that fieldwork-based doctoral thesis that Edwin Ardener was supervising from Oxford. There was also the flattering fact that the OUP had decided to publish my B.Litt. thesis, "Yoruba Towns and Cities" (which had itself been part of my prepration for fieldwork); this too, clearly, needed work done on it, and here, Edwin decreed that publication came first – well before the doctorate. "You can live without a doctorate," he said. "After all, I do." (True; but he must have been one of the last reputable academics to manage this.) "What you can't live without is publications! So put that first and get your MS ready for the OUP as soon as you can." Who was I to argue with my supervisor? And indeed, *Yoruba Towns and Cities* was published by the Clarendon Press in 1969.

Meanwhile, during this academic year 1966-67, thesis writing was relegated to the back burner: Edwin had also told me it was just plain silly *not* to write down one's teaching material, since one never knew when *that* might come in useful for publication.

Teaching anthropology

My main teaching duty at SOAS was a rather curious one: I was to take a group of students, somewhat over a dozen, and teach them anything I liked – but *no* anthropology please! The reason being, that there were two courses in anthropology, one took four years, and the other three; and if my little lot, who were the four-year students, knew too much anthropology before they started to work with the others, they would have an unfair advantage.

What next? I tried to think of all the things that I wished I had learnt before I started anthropology myself; it became, I suppose, a kind of history-of-ideas course. I put in a few unnecessary things; for instance I taught them a certain amount of genetics, little realising that they would have had this at their secondary schools (as I had not). But – history of ideas? We talked about Marx, we talked about Freud, we talked about Durkheim. But first, I made them write the essay I had myself been made to write in my first Diploma term, "Why I am doing this degree." I did this partly, of course, in order to get to know *whom* I was teaching.

I can now only remember one of them – a small scrawny young woman who came, she explained in her essay, from the absolute bottom of the working class. *She* was doing this degree, she wrote, largely in order to be in London, where it was all happening. And indeed she was later, in 1968, much involved in all the various sit-ins and other demonstrations. She was perfectly upfront about this; it was her version of Rousseau's *Confessions*. I also remember her writing that when she was at school (I don't know whether on a scholarship), she had begun to make friends with another girl, until she went over to this new friend's house, and that girl's mother had not allowed her to come in, saying (and now I quote from that essay) "Stultitia (I lend her that name) has her own friends."

Seminars

My new department at SOAS, just like the Institute in Oxford, held a weekly seminar; but I found the one in SOAS rather harder work. For one thing it was compulsory. I was staff, I had to attend the seminar, like it or not. For another thing, the papers were often on a subject that did not actually interest me very much at the time: the politics of tribal societies. Who is a "big man"? Who has power? How does he get it? How does he lose it? All these things. Such matters had not been a feature of my fieldwork, nor indeed very much of my previous studies. On the other hand, not only did I have to attend; I had been warned, probably correctly, that it was essential that I took part in the discussion. How was I supposed to do this?

Seminars have never been very useful to me because, while I listen to what people are saying (and quite often understand it) I can never think what to say in reply, because that used not in earlier life to be my business. My business as an interpreter had always been just to listen and understand, and then reproduce. This didn't worry me too much at Oxford, where seminars were a form of entertainment, but here at SOAS it was part of my weekly duties to attend the Friday seminar *and* participate! But I quickly worked out how to do this. Harking back to Oxford, at one of the philosophical societies there you also had to participate; in order to do so you scratched your head, looked puzzled and then said "Would the speaker be so kind as to repeat his *third* point?" I adapted this, quite nicely, to seminar questions, and was careful never to ask the first question. Somebody else asked the first question, and then I would ask the seminar speaker to repeat that third point; then, having done my duty, I went back to examining the ties of all the men present – in those days men still wore ties to work – wondering how these had come to be chosen. This lasted for an hour-and-a-half, and kept von Fürer-Haimendorf happy, so that was all right.

However, at London University there was also a far more interesting weekly seminar, not in our department, but round the corner at University College, where Anthropology was still presided over by Daryll Forde – not, I think, in the first rank as a published anthropologist, but a marvellous talent scout. He could elicit interesting papers from colleagues and students as nobody else could. To these seminars I was invited by somebody to whom I had had an introduction through Edwin and Shirley, namely Phyllis Kaberry.

Towards the end of that first academic year in London, in mid-1967, Christoph called me into his office to tell me of a good job going at the University of Newcastle-upon-Tyne; did I want him to recommend me for it? I said well, I would prefer to stay in London; but he did not know yet whether the finances would be available, and so he thought he should tell me about this job. After a very quick think I asked: "Christoph, can you *imagine* me in Newcastle-upon-Tyne?" and he laughed and said no, he couldn't. So I took the little risk and it worked out; a few weeks later the powers that be decided that my lectureship was to be extended, despite the fact that, as I say, my duties were still light and that I was still only half-way, if that, through my doctoral thesis.

My duties had been increased to the extent of my running a small seminar of my own, I've forgotten on what subject, for some half-dozen more mature students. One of them was a somewhat aggressive young man; at one point, I found it necessary to rap my fists upon the table and say: "In that case Mr Smith, let us agree to differ." Which got me a general laugh and a suggestion (from one of the girls) that perhaps I ought to have a speakers' mallet or something? I did own a small bronze bell I had bought in Dahomey a long time before, so I brought that along, but never had to use it.

Some time after this, the same young man asked me whether I thought it would irreparably damage the student-teacher relationship if he asked me out to a meal one evening? I said I didn't think so; so he took me to a cheapish restaurant, one he could afford, and afterwards back to his digs. On the way there, we passed a more expensive eating-place (which didn't actually look very nice to me), at which he said, "Oh dear, this is really the sort of place one *should* take a woman like you to, but I just can't afford it!" So I said "there, there" or something else soothing. Once at his digs, coffee was produced; and a succession of young men, three or four of them, came in, were introduced and greeted, maybe got a sip of coffee and then left. I suspect Mr Smith had bet his flatmates he was going to take his formidable tutor out to dinner, and was now showing he had done so.

A permanent home?

Now that I was staying on in London, I had to find myself somewhere more permanent to live. My friend Kenneth Syers gave me a very good tip. He said "What you need to do is, buy the *Evening Standard* when it comes out – late morning; take it straight home and read the Apartments for Sale/Properties for Sale bit. You won't want to live all over London; on any given day, there will only be two or three in which you have the faintest interest, so you go and see those, *then and there*, before anybody else does." I followed his advice, and in fact took the second place I saw. This was called, rather quaintly, a maisonette – Americans would call it a duplex, I think; in other words it was on two floors. It was part of a converted family house of fairly modest proportions; I was getting the bottom half. The "garden floor", in other words the basement, did indeed lead out into a small patch of garden; otherwise it consisted of a living room and dining room which had been run into one, and at the back a kitchen. Up some stairs there were two bedrooms, and a bathroom above the kitchen. On first seeing all this, I did something which I've since been told one should never do – I said: "I like this, I think I'm going to buy it." And I found the price within my means, especially as I thought I could get a mortgage.

I started to arrange this with my solicitor, but found I did have a problem; not because I didn't have a steady job – I did – but because I was a woman and with women you never knew! But my solicitor, Jack Gaster, was able to find me a bank that was prepared to lend me money.

Jack Gaster was an interesting man, one of the nine children (I believe) of a certain Rabbi Gaster, by then long dead, who had been the main authority in London on the folk tales of Rumania, which was where the family originally came from. Jack himself was a card-carrying communist, which did not prevent him from being the most delightfully old-fashioned solicitor it is possible to imagine – in his dress, his vocabulary and the way he dealt with things. His youngest sister, Bertha, was a good friend of mine, through Kenneth Syers; she too was very left-wing, though not I believe an actual communist. She told me once that between the Gaster children, they had represented every possible shade of political opinion, but they were agreed on things like upping the pension of their old Nanny, and going to see her from time to time. She also said that she had learnt all about revolution when they were fighting against porridge in the nursery, when direct action had consisted of throwing the porridge out of the window!

I had previously arranged, that summer vacation, to go with Phyllis to Italy and then join June in Greece, and I thought I could still go and do these things, having first made the necessary banking and mortgage arrangements, so that it would all work out in my absence. I remember the vendor and myself saying to each other – I don't know which of us started it: "Now you're not going to welsh out on this are you? Because I shall be stuck if you are." But no, we were neither of us going to welsh. So off I went with Phyllis to Italy, later joining June as planned.

When I got back, the first thing I did was try to get into this new flat of mine, because I wanted central heating installed; but I did not yet own it apparently; the key was still in the hands of the vendor. So I rang him up at work and asked whether he was still living there. He said "No I'm staying with my brother," so I explained about the central heating and said it would be terribly useful if I could have a key, and he said: "Yes, by all means. Come along any evening." So I duly went along and got the key. I opened up; the central heating engineers came. They were very uncomfortable about producing central heating in my bathroom and said my husband would surely not like this, to which I answered: "I'm between husbands at the moment, and *I* would like it!"

So for the first few weeks of that 1967 autumn term, I stayed on with June in Oxford, coming down every few days to see how the work was getting on. One day the workmen said: "Ah! Your lawyer's just rung." So I rang up Jack, who said: "*Where* are you ringing from?" and I said: "6a Redcliffe Place" and he laughed and said: "Right! Well, I was just ringing up to tell you, you're now legally there, you own it."

The heating engineers finished their work. The electricity hadn't yet been turned on for some reason, so June and I had a somewhat curious weekend trying to arrange things while there was daylight. Come evening, I took her out to the local Greek restaurant and then we went back and slept in the dark flat.

1968: The student rebellion

While I was swanning around Italy with Phyllis Kaberry, and later around Greece with June, Christoph von Fürer-Haimendorf was taking off for a well-earned sabbatical. At least part of this he was spending in Nepal, his field speciality. He may have spent some time in Vienna too, but in any case was away for all that summer vacation, and quite a bit of the following academic year. He returned only in the summer of 1968, by which time all sorts of things were beginning to happen.

For in 1968 we had, like every other university in Western Europe, our own student ructions. The ones at SOAS, I realise with hindsight, were not very bad. After all, our Department of Sociology and Anthropology was the only one that was actually concerned with society and its workings. People studying some lesser-known Tibetan language are less likely to revolt in this climate, any rate in England. In France, of course, the Sorbonne was occupied by everyone and life got very exciting indeed.

Ours was only moderately so, but we did have a bit of disturbance and it took different people different ways. Dear Phyllis Kaberry was terrified of the students: she kept thinking that they would knock her down, which nobody ever tried to do as far as I know.

The historian Sally Chilver, tall, broad and full of self-confidence, dealt with matters quite differently. Then head of Bedford College, she called the ringleaders to her. (She has told me since, it was even then quite obvious which of them was later going to run which Government department, or which major firm. She's been proved right, too!) With a Gauloise dangling from one corner of her mouth, she would say something like: "Look chums, I've got a problem you've got to help me with." This worked wonders. They addressed her as "Granny", offered her another Gauloise and helped her with her "problem", to the extent that Bedford didn't have any particular troubles.

I thought I could manage my own few students quite nicely, since they had all eaten my bread and salt, or at any rate my wine and cheese, at my own house, and were therefore less likely to attack me. Also (this was a matter of personal vanity), in those days it was still usual for women lecturers to be rather dowdy and (what was at the time deeply unfashionable) long-skirted. So I wore my own skirts as short as I dared, and saw to it that I did not look like the average student's idea of a female academic; which worked among my own students. But the person who really solved the problem for the whole department was the boss, Professor Christoph von Fürer-Haimendorf, who had just come back, possibly a little prematurely, from his sabbatical. And what Christoph did was use his "Theresianum manner": he lay in wait in the corridors of our small building, and every time a clearly new student showed up, Christoph would say: "I don't think we have met before. My name is Christoph von Fürer-Haimendorf and I have been on sabbatical, er – I wonder if you would care to come into my office, I do so want to get to know you properly." No student, however revolutionary, can really resist being invited into the Head of Department's office and have the Theresianum spell cast over them; ours most certainly couldn't.

After some three weeks of this, our own little rebellion was over; Christoph told me, and probably other people, that he was absolutely exhausted. But it had worked! One thing changed in our department – suddenly it was found *possible* to devote one room (and a new coffee machine) as a place where staff and students could all get together and perhaps even talk to each other.

The room required a little decorating. I seem to remember being in charge of this. I delegated, as usual. I had a very nice graduate student, a black American, who confessed to having had her own problems in finding lodgings. I got her to take charge of choosing the paint and what was going be applied where. At any rate it got done rather nicely and we then had a sort of Common Room, at least in the Department of Sociology and Anthropology.

Elsewhere, there were meetings, and meetings about meetings. I remember one of these, on a particular topic, it may even have been Common Rooms or Dining Rooms open to all. I suggested there be a committee, and my Mr Smith, the same one who'd asked me out to that evening meal, said: "This is the thing about Mrs Krapf-Askari. She always thinks everything is solved by committees", which got him a laugh. I can't remember whether that committee was ever formed.

Working on Nigerian studies

Meanwhile, at my new residence, I could at last install a study of my own. I decided to sleep downstairs, near my radio and non-professional books; of the two upper-floor bedrooms, one could be a guest-room; in the other, I set up a big table with paper, typewriter, field notes and other working materials. Bliss! Here in my own space, well away from university politics and social life (I had even finished preparing *Yoruba Towns and Cities* for the Clarendon Press), I could at last get on with that doctoral thesis on Ogori.

During my early months in London, I was still in correspondence with His Highness; though by this time we had actually begun to address one another as "Dear Gabriel" and "Dear Eva". But to my horror, not long after I had moved to my new flat, Gabriel was overthrown by his "quarter chiefs", who I think had grown increasingly jealous of what they saw as his overweening power – something which, to my shame, I had not properly picked up during my own stay in Ogori. He did not live to see the University of Ibadan's publication of his *History*, but died, in Okene, quite soon after his political downfall, I think of a heart broken by failure at what he had seen as his main vocation; he was not much past fifty years old.

Meanwhile, other things were hotting up in Nigeria; I was increasingly glad I had advised that unknown Igbo lady *not* to accept that job at Ahmadu Bello University.

Biafra was coming into being; my friend Elo's increasingly fierce Christmas cards were only one indication that the (ultimately unsuccessful) struggle for Biafran independence from Nigeria would be coming quite soon.

The summer vacation of 1968 was entirely devoted to finishing that D.Phil. thesis: if I wanted to be examined on it during the following Michaelmas term I had a clear deadline for producing three properly typed and bound copies. The arrangements for binding I had already made; and (my own typing being distinctly erratic) had also contacted an excellent typist from University College. But then, everything nearly fell apart when she contracted a fluey cold! I remember sitting up all night at her flat – where she had kindly offered me hospitality – giving the stuff she'd done a last proof-read; it was in my mind that if she still found me at work when she got up in the morning it might well act upon her professional conscience. And that bit of moral blackmail actually worked: she did finish the job on time, I was able to get it bound quickly, and, when the poor girl finally felt well again I treated her to a really good lunch at which I handed her a very well-deserved cheque.

A visit between sisters

So, a date having been fixed for my Oxford viva in Michaelmas Term, I prepared for a visit from my mother. As ever, she did not stay with me (she had, possibly with good reason, absolutely *no* trust in my housekeeping), but at a nearby hotel, from which she would come over to see me.

I duly invited my Aunt Ann up to London and gave them both lunch at the maisonette; but then, as time passed, my mother began to say, "You'd really think Ann, my only sister, could invite me down to see her new place! It's not so far away, I could perfectly well do it by train. Nobody's asking her to put me up, but she could at least show me the place and then we could lunch at a pub, couldn't we?"

Eventually I got bored with hearing this, rang up Aunt Ann and said, "I'm getting a bit tired of my mother complaining about how her only sister never asks her down to lunch – and moreover, she's got a point. Why don't you?" And then the reason for this neglect had to be openly admitted. My Aunt Ann, by now in her 50s, was terrified of her elder sister finding out that she was no longer with Billy, but had moved in with Ken the cowman. How on earth would Nena react to this situation? Perhaps I could break it to her tactfully? So the next time I saw my mother, I said "I've been asked to break it to you tactfully that your sister Ann is living in her new cottage with Ken the cowman."

My mother laughed heartily, and said she'd always regarded Ken as a most attractive man. (I didn't agree, I still think Billy was far the more attractive of the two.) I reassured Aunt Ann, and my mother duly took the train and went down to lunch there. When she returned, she said to me, "You know, in the unlikely event of my having my cowman or other manservant living with me, and I then asked my sister to lunch, I do think I would have us all eating at the same table, not leaving poor Ken in the kitchen." As, of course, Ann had done in deference to what she saw as Nena's class consciousness.

Later, I told June the whole story; thenceforth, when she and I went down to see Aunt Ann, we would insist on eating in the kitchen – "so nice and warm and homely" – which solved that little social problem.

A change of lifestyle

A little after my mother's visit, the London term began, and a week later Oxford Michaelmas term. My thesis having been handed in on time, a date was fixed for my *viva*. I travelled up to Oxford the previous night and appeared, properly dolled up in academicals, at the Institute on the appointed morning.

I was met by our secretary, Barbara Alloway. "E-P sends his greetings, Eva, and says he'll be expecting you for lunch at the little French restaurant." So I was reasonably certain of the outcome before I even entered the examination room; and indeed, I was let off very easily indeed. Quite a bit of the conversation revolved around what changes I might have to make to the text for publication (something which never did happen!); and then one of the examiners said he understood I had a luncheon appointment and I really mustn't keep my host waiting... So one of them carried the heavy thesis down the stairs for me, and I sallied forth to the little French restaurant to join E-P.

Not long after this, however, there was a rather more difficult hurdle. My boss Christoph had, all this time, been very considerate in keeping my teaching duties light, so as to allow me time to write that doctoral thesis. Now that I had my doctorate, he may well have hoped to get a bit more work out of me. Instead, I had to tell him that I had, a few days before, accepted a proposal of marriage from an entomologist who worked at the new University of Sussex – just too far from central London for me to be able to continue as a lecturer at SOAS. (I suppose I could have used an accommodation address, but as I was also inheriting two teenage stepdaughters, I had decided this was not really possible.)

Christoph was extremely good about it – he accepted my news with polite regret, before offering congratulations and good wishes. E-P, by contrast, took the line that it was just plain stupid to lose all that International Labour Office Widow's Pension money, why couldn't I just live in sin with the chap? I think I muttered something about country neighbours; and by way of cheering him up said I was marrying another Wykehamist. But Mick, with his left-of-centre political leanings, was all his life rather embarrassed by his public-school upbringing, so Winchester School was not a possible conversational subject between them. I arranged for the three of us to dine together one evening, during the meetings of the Association of Social Anthropologists at the University of Sussex. This turned out to be a mistake. Both men were extremely shy; not even entomology seemed to generate conversation. E-P's sole contribution here was that he knew nothing whatsoever about mosquitoes. It all made for rather a long evening, by the end of which I had decided that it would not be a good idea to ask E-P to give me away at the wedding.

PART SIX
REFLECTIONS AND CONNECTIONS

Chapter 1
New Life in Hamsey

Descent and alliance

"I'm going to feel a bit out of this," said my mother. "Here I am, having personally given birth to you; now, you're going to acquire two stepdaughters and, from what you tell me, every other woman in this family you're marrying into either is or has a stepmother!"

"Both, in one case" I replied, thinking of "Sam", my future mother-in-law.

"Well, you'll just have to make me a sort of family tree of these Gillieses."

She was in fact delighted at my forthcoming marriage. A neighbour of her own, on being told her daughter Eva was now engaged to the son of a well-known English plastic surgeon, had exclaimed "*Not Sir Harold Gillies*!" My mother had not been aware that, in December 1941, Sir Harold had indeed spent time in Buenos Aires, lecturing on and demonstrating his surgical techniques – many, such as the tube pedicle, of his own devising and still in use today – and had, by his mischievous humour and English-eccentric behaviour, attracted considerable popularity.

My mother had happily spread the story. But now, a few months before the planned London wedding, I was paying a last solo visit to the family in Buenos Aires. Mick, a medical entomologist I had met at a scientific conference where I was interpreting, was at this time pursuing his profession in The Gambia; I intended to call on him and his team on my way back to England.

My mother's request for a family tree of the Gillieses did not come as a complete surprise: Mick had already done one for my own family of birth. How fortunate – thought I – that during my Diploma year in Anthropology I had been taught how to draw up genealogical tables!

When I came to do so, I couldn't help being struck by the similarity of backgrounds apparently so far apart. In each case, a father eminent in his own branch of medicine: Sir Harold the plastic surgeon, my father the psychiatrist and psychoanalyst. On each side, one genuinely famous collateral ancestor – though, I had to admit, Mick's Edward Lear was rather more amusing than my nineteenth-century missionary and East African linguist, Johann Ludwig Krapf. Mick a widower, I a widow, both distinctly in love with Africa. After this, things did begin to differ, though still within the same framework: Mick's Cambridge to my Oxford, his passion for natural science to mine for the humanities.

Mick was the youngest of four. His brother John and his elder sister Margaret had both gone to live in their father's native New Zealand: I was not to meet them until well after our marriage. But very soon after our engagement, I did come to know his stay-at-home younger sister Joanna and her children, as well Lorna Townend and Liza Picard, sisters of his late wife Agnes Sleigh.

Mick also had two daughters by his first marriage, Susie and Jackie – it was to them I was now to become stepmother. My future mother-in-law Sam was herself the second Lady Gillies; it was she who had a stepmother of her own, to whom she was much attached. Moreover, the girls' maternal grandmother having died, their grandfather on that side had also re-married – this was the Swiss lady known as Didy who now, widowed herself, again spent most of her time in her childhood home near Lucerne, with her two sisters. During Mick's absences in The Gambia, she had looked after his teenage daughters in Sussex.

On my side in England, there was only my Aunt Ann, now living with Ken the cowman; in Argentina – aside from my mother, my sister Trixie and her husband Bernie with their two children Alex and Veronica – only remote cousins and rather closer school friends. In Germany, my first cousin Heino (son of my father's Nazi younger brother Fred) with his wife and two children; and, mostly but not entirely in England, a fair number of friends.

So now in Buenos Aires, I explained to my mother as best I could about Mick's various families and stepfamilies, meanwhile instructing my brother-in-law Bernie (a very shy man, but he had at least met and liked Mick) on the art of acting "bride's father" at a church wedding.

Then, on my way back to England, I did indeed visit Mick and his small team in The Gambia, where his employer, the Medical Research Council, had a large regional station in Fajara, near the country's capital Banjul. Mick and his team, however, worked up-country at a subsidiary station, Keneba. After spending a few days with them there, I returned to the coast to catch my flight back to England.

In the plane, I took a look at my passport – still an Argentine one, with a rubber-stamped UK residence permit. These permits had, during the several years I worked at SOAS, been renewed for me every summer; SOAS were quite used to this, I was by no means the only foreign scholar they employed. But this permit, I now noticed, was due to expire before the planned wedding date of 3rd January, 1970. Resignedly, I asked for the relevant form and, on it, requested a renewal.

At Heathrow, I handed all this to the Immigration Officer, whereupon the following dialogue took place:

"Your residence permit is still valid – why are you asking for another one?"

"This residence permit is in respect of a job I no longer hold, so I do need another."

"Ah! You no longer hold this job – and you want another residence permit. Will you be looking for a job?"

"No."

"You have no job, will not be looking for one, and want us to give you a six months' further residence permit! Why?"

"Because I'm about to get married."

"Ah! And is your future husband a British subject?"

"Yes."

"And is he in this country now?"

"No."

"So where is he?"

"In Africa," said I, leaving the colour of Mick's skin to the man's imagination.

"Ah! And when is this – er – this *marriage* going to take place?"

"On the 3rd of January – and if you think it over very *very* carefully, I think you will find that is just over the three months; which is why I am asking for six."

"Ah! And how do you propose to occupy your time between now and the 3rd of January?"

"Looking after my future stepdaughters – if it's any business of yours!" Which was naughty of me, since I suppose it *was* his business – but I had lost my temper by that time. Some poor shy African or West Indian woman, in exactly the same legal position as mine, would have been reduced to tears by this time.

I duly took the next train to Lewes, and a taxi from the station to Hamsey; where I found Didy with her little suitcase packed ready to return to Switzerland. Now, I did look after my future stepdaughters for the next three weeks or so: time enough for us to get to know each other a little, but not much more; then, with Mick back from The Gambia, my mother arrived from Buenos Aires and it was time to begin organising church and reception, whom to invite and what to wear.

We got married at St John's, Notting Hill – I being at that time a member of the Anglican communion, and Mick a polite agnostic who didn't object to a church marriage – by the extremely nice Vicar of that parish, who had got up from his bed of sickness to do so. Then, having entrusted the girls to our Hamsey neighbours Patrick and Anita Bolshaw, Mick and I set off for a fortnight's honeymoon in Morocco.

The best way to do this, I had learnt, was to fly to Gibraltar and there hire a car to take us across on the ferry; then, once in Morocco, we could plan our travel to suit ourselves. This seemed, at first, to work out beautifully; but once we were well down south in Marrakesh, it began to rain. And rain. And rain. And flood roads and bridges the whole width of the country. Was it, I now wonder, an early manifestation of climate change? At any rate, we spent quite a lot of time pushing our rented car out of thick mud. I can think of a lot of honeymoons that might have been ruined by this; fortunately, we had both of us lived quite a while in up-country Africa during the rainy season.

Fortunate, too, that Mick had French colleagues in Rabat; who very kindly lent us the wherewithal to buy air tickets straight back to England: we could not, after all, expect the Bolshaws to look after our teenagers forever. So a telegram was dispatched to the car-hire firm, telling them of the car's whereabouts in Marrakesh and that its keys were with Thomas Cook in that city; and we flew home.

Sometime along the way, Mick had asked me what I intended to do when we got there. "Pursue my new passport and nationality," said I. He may have thought I was being a trifle neurotic; an innocent Englishman, he had never lived with an Argentine passport, and didn't know about such things. I did, and intended to get my British passport as soon as possible. The Argentine Consulate was OK this time; the Passport Office was not. They looked at my marriage certificate and said "This is not valid."

"Not valid?" said I – "but *why*?"

"Because the vicar who married you hasn't signed it." True enough: kind John Livingstone, who had got up from his sick-bed to marry us, had indeed forgotten to sign his name.

"Well – what do I do about that?"

"You go back to this vicar and ask him to issue you with another certificate, properly signed this time; and to certify his own signature."

"And how does he do that?"

"Well, he takes a sheet of vicarage notepaper and writes on it: "I, John Livingstone, certify that what appears below is my signature. John Livingstone."

"Are you sure?"

"Yes". So I took a taxi to St John's Notting Hill vicarage. A young man opened the door, to whom I stated my business.

"John! Here's a woman who says you married her to somebody three weeks ago but you didn't make a proper job of it."

So I was ushered into the presence, where I stated my business all over again. The vicar said, not unreasonably, "But anybody could *steal* a sheet of vicarage writing paper!" – I agreed, but reminded him we were here dealing with bureaucracy – and told him of my encounter with that immigration officer; which did indeed resemble some of the experiences of his own parishioners in that racially variegated part of London. He duly wrote what was asked of him; and back I went to the Passport Office, which this time accepted my marriage certificate.

Which did not prevent a Lewes district policeman coming to our house in Hamsey the following Sunday. Mick and I had gone for a walk on the Downs, and got back only after dark – it was still January – to find Susie and Jackie in a high state of excitement: "A *policeman* is here to ask about Eva – and oh, isn't he handsome!" The Home Office was presumably following normal procedure.

The pursuit of a British passport involved quite a number of further negotiations. When I finally came to swear allegiance to Her Majesty before my solicitor, Jack Gaster, that atheistical Jew and card-carrying Communist, said, "*Mazel tov!* Now, what would you like to swear on – Old Testament? New Testament? Koran?"

Usually Jack Gaster, always immaculate in dark suitings and snowy shirtings, liked doing things rather more formally. That summer, when Mick and I were in The Gambia, Jack wrote him a letter about the new Will he was drafting for him, stating that, whatever else, Mick would have to leave me a "messuage". Mick was tempted to reply by telegram: "Messuage Received But Not Understood" – but feared the telegraphists would take "messuage" for a spelling mistake, and spoil the joke by correcting it. Jack later explained "messuage" was an old legal term for something like "dower house" or even "roof over one's head", which he liked using. We liked it too and ever afterwards, between ourselves, referred to our house Whitfeld as "the Messuage". And years later, after Mick's death, when it fell to me to edit and publish his autobiography, I did so under the imprint of "Messuage Books".

Village or hamlet?

"I've found your Hamsey on the map!" my friend June announced triumphantly, soon after I had told her where I would live when I married Mick.

"Well done – but locating it in real life, you'll find, is another matter."

This remains true. There are, in these east Sussex lanes, several signposts indicating the direction to Hamsey; but never one announcing you've arrived there.

There are reasons for this. The name Hamsey is used, not only for the small grouping of houses in which I still live, but also for "Hamsey Parish" – and this not just "parish" in the ecclesiastical sense (though it is that) but also in the meaning given to that term in local administration – the smallest sub-division of a District; consisting in fact of three small centres of population: Offham, Cooksbridge, and Hamsey proper. Cooksbridge has a little railway station and (nowadays) a Community Hall that serves the whole parish; Offham, a pub and a Victorian church; Hamsey only its small Norman church, not much used now except for weddings. Both this and the Victorian church at Offham are dedicated to St Peter; this is confusing for outsiders, but to local people they are simply St Peter's Offham and St Peter's Hamsey – both served by the same Rector, whose Rectory is in Offham.

Hamsey proper was once a much larger place; not all the buildings once surrounding its Norman church have yet been excavated. But during the 17th century Great Plague, most of its inhabitants died, and the few survivors moved on to higher and more salubrious ground at what is now Offham. After that, nothing much happened around the little church for about 150 years, when the Reverend Sir George Shiffner, Bart., had a large Rectory built for himself a little below the upward slope of the hill. This, still the largest and handsomest house in the neighbourhood, was long known as the Old Rectory. The Reverend Sir George – known locally as "the Squarson" because he was both the Squire and the Parson – was a wealthy man; moreover, he knew what he wanted. His Rectory, built early in the 19th century, was already designed in a purposely retrospective style, to look more like a Georgian building. Alongside it ran an earth road, just wide enough for the carriages of the local gentry, who now lived at Offham or even further afield, to get to church on Sundays. However, the wealthier parishioners got tired of having their carriages splashed with mud: they wanted that road paved. This idea did not suit the Squarson at all – what? a horrid clatter of hooves past his garden windows? Not if he could help it.

But could he? A Parish Council meeting had been requested. The Squarson, who was, of course, the Council chairman, looked up the regulations and found that, if he had been asked to call such a meeting, he was obliged to do so. But nothing was said about his having any obligation to declare the meeting open for business... So he didn't.

He and his parishioners sat in solemn silence for quite some time before the penny dropped: the meeting would never be called to order! Disgruntled, the gentry left; a new church was built at Offham, and the paving of the road from there to Hamsey proper did not happen until after the Squarson's death.

By this time, people had begun moving into the neighbourhood again. Two old houses in fact had survived the long break; one of them was a farmhouse, and a few cottages were built, along the newly-paved road, for its workers. Then, halfway through the 19th century, a Lewes private banker named Whitfeld had a large family house built on the other side of the road from the Rectory; he named it Hamsey House.

Sometime in the 1970s, I was asked to present a paper at an Oxford anthropology seminar; I had rather run out of African material by that time, so I thought I'd try my hand at an ethnography of my little Hamsey. At the time I described it as an "age village", though not quite in the traditional African sense: what I meant was that it was inhabited almost entirely by people between the ages of 35 and 70 – no *really* old people, no young children. I explained this by expense: people came to live in Hamsey when they could afford to buy a house there, by which time they were well past their first youth; and left when they could no longer cope with the garden. Nowadays, I am almost certainly The Oldest Inhabitant (in terms, not of biological age but seniority of residence – though my stepdaughter Susie disputes this, since she lived here as a young girl, well before I joined the family). I now find that Hamsey is no longer in any sense an "age village".

It is still an expensive place, and it is still the truth that those farmworkers' cottages are not occupied by manual workers of any sort. But there are now at least two three-generation households; there may even be more than two! As the Oldest

Inhabitant, I no longer know quite everybody in the village... But can it even properly be called a village? Thinking about Nigerian centres of population – where the concepts of city, town, and village are subject to considerations quite other than size – has sensitised me to the proper nomenclature for centres of population elsewhere in the world. In England until quite recently a city required a cathedral of its own, otherwise it was a mere town – and even as I write there are only two exceptions. And, to me, a village is something that has, in addition to its own church, at least a pub and/or shop – somewhere for people to meet socially outside each other's houses.

By these criteria, the scattering of houses I have been calling Hamsey proper is quite definitely a hamlet not a village. The considerable grounds of Hamsey House, which had already changed hands several times, had been bought up by a developer, and divided into four. He lived in the big house while the stables and coachman's house were converted into a dwelling for sale; this was named Whitfeld, after the original owner of Hamsey House, and is where we now live. Agnes, Mick's first wife, was extremely lucky to be shown this house (which had only that morning been entrusted to the estate agent she consulted) – and very sensible to seize the chance at once. The family needed a house near the (then quite new) University of Sussex, where Mick was just beginning to work; and neither of them wanted to live in noisy Brighton. Whitfeld has a sizeable garden of its own, once the vegetable garden of the whole property, and a huge greenhouse in which cucumbers and tomatoes were grown. My husband grew grapes there for wine making; it is now converted into a two-part conservatory, the "business" end furthest from the house and the nearer end providing a pleasant extra sitting-room adorned with tropical flowering plants. This procedure has, over time, been typical of the house as a whole – a patchwork combination of different rooms with varying uses.

From the beginning of life in Hamsey, it was clear to me that I was going to have to learn a great many things all at once. Most importantly, how to relate to two teenage girls who were visibly none too pleased at someone taking what had been their mother's place in the household. But also, the household itself: I had never run a house that size. And the garden – all I had ever done in that line was pull up a few weeds (under June's supervision) in her Oxford garden. Then, cookery – I had, over the years, learnt quite reasonable "bachelor cooking", that is, I knew how to make several dinner-party dishes (mostly involving a fair amount of garlic); but this was not much use for a family devoted to rice pudding and suet pastry. And over and above all these, I had to learn to live in a hamlet where one was on some kind of visiting terms with all the neighbours, when all I had ever really known, outside academe, were big cities and the West African bush.

I also wanted to know other things I had never learnt, such as the names of the local wild flowers, not to mention birds! My mother was rather puzzled by this curious desire of mine.

My mother had given me a generous wedding present of money: mine, she said, to spend as I liked, but personally she advised me to have a little study built on, "because you've had your own study up to the age of nearly forty – you'd miss having a space of your own." Good advice, I decided; Mick had his own study-lab in what had originally been designed as the dressing-room to our bedroom upstairs; mine could be downstairs, just behind the utility room, where there was already a suitable little rectangular space. "Opposite ends of the house", we joked, "for when we really need to get away from each other!" Mick's little study was made into an extra bathroom a year or so after his 1999 death; mine still contains my father's bookshelves and the huge old desk from his Buenos Aires consulting rooms.

At the time of our wedding in 1970, Susie was just 15, her sister Jackie two years younger. Just a few years later, Susie became engaged to Richard Winter from nearby Barcombe; they were lucky enough to be married at Hamsey St Peter's, where Mick had not wanted us to be wed because he so cordially disliked the Rector of that period. Susie and Richard then began to build an extension to the house, in due course to become 'Whitfeld Annexe', their own home.

Aunt Ann: end of a long story

Aunt Ann never came to our wedding; and now, in the early 1970s, further changes began in her life. Her husband, Billy Tanner, decided he wanted to return to his native Isle of Wight and find himself somewhere to live. "Mrs Ken", for her part, decided not to accompany him: she wanted more time with her grandchildren. So they parted amicably, and Billy duly went down to his Isle of Wight and bought himself a small flat near the sea.

Whereupon Aunt Ann decides she too wants to return to the Island! Not, indeed to join Billy, but will he please buy her and Ken a house there? – any house, sight unseen. Billy obediently does so; then she and Ken live in this house for a few years – I remember visiting them there with Mick – until she decides the Isle of Wight climate is not good for Ken's health (or was it her own health?) and wants to return to the mainland.

She and Ken now set up home on a farm near Reading; until one day Ken dies, unforeseeably, of a heart attack. Billy then feels Ann should not be living by herself: he'd better find her a place in a retirement home on the Isle of Wight, somewhere near him so he can keep an eye on her.

About this time, I remember asking him whether I could help in any way, which I would have been glad to do. He answered, unforgettably: "Thank you, no. Ann *is* still my wife and I'm responsible for her." However, she never did get to that Isle of Wight retirement home; at this point Billy died, of old age. (He did still have a few bits of shrapnel in him from Dunkirk, but they don't seem to have bothered him much.)

So then Aunt Ann moved from home to home, finally to one a little beyond Petworth Park in West Sussex, not too far from Hamsey – an oldish brick house, rather tatty outside, but inside impeccable and, more importantly, staffed by extremely nice and caring people. I went to see her there quite a number of times, until the moment came when she no longer recognised me; after that, I kept tabs on her once a week by telephone, though I do know she was visited by people living nearby, including a nephew of Ken's with his wife. She died not long after, leaving her money to some society for the welfare of dogs, which both my sister Trixie and I were happy to accept.

The big mainland house she had shared with Billy had been sold to a pop group – quite a wealthy pop group it must have been! Once in Hamsey, looking at a calendar, I said "That looks just like my Aunt Ann's house." The girls must have thought I was putting it on rather: the calendar photograph was of Chequers.

To-ings and fro-ings

During those first few years, Mick and I paid a couple of very short visits to Buenos Aires; it was my mother who came several times to Sussex to see us, staying several weeks. Still lacking confidence in my housekeeping, she would not actually stay at Whitfeld, but made her home in an excellent small hotel in Lewes, The Shelleys, which had once been the local residence of the family of that name. Having installed her there, it was then my job to persuade her to come and dine with us as often as possible. She was, she said, anxious not to outstay her welcome with her son-in-law; moreover, having had servants all her life, she was much concerned about my having to do all this cooking, never mind "ruining my hands" in the garden! "Take advantage," she advised "of the annual honeymoon you can have every summer in The Gambia."

Mick was employed by the Medical Research Council (MRC) to head a small research unit into the behaviour of malaria-transmitting mosquitoes: the idea was to find some way of diverting the insects from centres of human population. For eight months of the year, this Mosquito Behaviour Unit (its initials quite fortuitously formed the Swahili word MBU, which translates as "mosquito"!) worked at the University of Sussex; for the remaining four – summer in Britain but, more to the point, mosquito season in West Africa – Mick and his team worked from the MRC's large field station on the coast at Fajara. Initially, the "Gambian honeymoon" had to fit in with the girls' summer holidays from school: both were at that time going to the comprehensive secondary school in Lewes – not at all a bad one, since it had resulted from the fusion of the local Secondary Modern with two Grammar Schools. So I would wait until the end of term, and only then could the three of us take a plane to Banjul Airport. Once there, Susie and Jackie were parked as paying guests with an English family at Fajara, while Mick and I went up river.

The first year we went to a place called Sapu, some 200 miles upstream, where there was an Agricultural Research Centre. This had, during the dreaded mosquito-and-rains season, a few living quarters available; it was even possible for Susie and Jackie to visit us for a few days. We acquired a cook, Ousman Jawara, who was to return to us every working season until Mick's retirement from The Gambia. Microscope studies, that first year, had to be conducted in a caravan. These studies normally took all morning; during the evening, Mick was often out trapping night-flying insects in a series of devices he thought up for the purpose. This left us the late afternoon for exploring the countryside, both by Landrover and, for shorter distances, on foot. Sapu, like other centres of population on the River Gambia, was in fact built on a ledge quite high above the stream: there was no agreeable paddling to be had from there. But we did find, slightly downstream, a place where we could get our feet wet: a tiny port called Walli-Kunda, with its own jetty for the transport of the local cash crop – variously called peanuts or groundnuts. But groundnuts, like mosquitoes, only happened in their own season; now during the rains, Walli-Kunda seemed to be home only to a few fishermen. I still remember the first time we came out of the river there with wet feet (it must have been high tide). Out of nowhere appeared a middle-aged woman, who smilingly dried my feet, then Mick's, and found our footwear for us. It gave us an excellent first impression of Walli-Kunda and its few inhabitants.

The following year, Mick's up-country work took him to Kabba (a total coincidence of name with the Kabba in Nigeria where I had lived). This was meant to be more comfortable; I hated it on sight. The village/town, nowhere near the river, was run by fanatical Muslims – very un-Gambian this – who refused to let their own fellow-inhabitants play music of any kind. And alongside this gloomy and silent centre of population, the MRC had – with the consent of those Muslim elders, who no doubt had an eye out for the main chance as much as anyone else – built quite a large walled compound, with several dwelling houses, a good-sized lab, servants' quarters, a chicken-run – and such utterly meaningless luxuries as glass in the windows instead of mosquito-netting. But Mick only worked from Kabba for two or three summers.

The river – when you could get to it – was well downstream from Sapu: the tidal water was still salty, or at any rate brackish; and he now needed to work with freshwater mosquitoes. Then we remembered that charming place Walli-Kunda – wasn't there a groundnut trader's house there, right on the river and almost certainly empty during our own working season? Didn't it belong to the Lebanese Mahdi firm, with which the MRC might negotiate?

Also, I was now no longer tied down by the girls' school dates. Susie had already left school, and was studying at Bournemouth Art College. Our younger, Jackie, was now off to study architecture at Liverpool University. Our Walli-Kunda summers could begin.

Elementary science

In England, I found soon enough I couldn't follow Mick's conversations with his colleagues in the pub, my lengthy and extensive education never having included much by way of science. But surely, at my age and already a D.Phil. (Oxon), I wasn't going to embark upon yet another course of academic study! I consulted one of Mick's lab technicians at Sussex MBU, and learned I could obtain a similar qualification to hers at Brighton Technical College (now part of Brighton University).

At an initial interview, I explained that I, a middle-aged housewife, did not intend to start a career as a lab technician, but... My interviewer asked about my previous knowledge of maths, physics, biology, chemistry; and I had to tell him it was for all practical purposes nil. So, would I not feel insulted if they asked me first to sit for the equivalent of O-levels in these subjects? Far from it, I'd be grateful to be taught. But, while I would be quite happy to attend classes all day Thursday as per timetable, could I be excused the "general education" session on Thursday evenings? Because my husband might want my company then, and if I wasn't generally educated by now I never would be.

Indeed I didn't need any Thursday evening general education, he agreed; but would I do him a favour? In fact, two favours: first, to fill in one of those Thursday evenings for him with a talk – on any subject I liked. And second, one of the requirements was to write an account of one's life story – would I care to do mine? "You shouldn't really have to – but I confess, I'm curious."

Slightly to my own surprise, I quite enjoyed that first experiment in autobiography. When it came to filling in that general slot, I simply waffled on a bit to my fellow students on what it had felt like to live alone in a Nigerian village; I can only hope it amused them.

These fellow students were, of course, much younger than I; as indeed were several of those who taught us. The kids were lab technicians on their first lowly job, under-educated but bright; trade union rules required their employers to give them one day a week free to improve their qualifications. I was, I suppose, a slight puzzle to them; and, in my own inexperience, was fool enough that first year not to insist on being called by my first name. So I was "Mrs Gillies" to everyone, which made for social distance.

We had different teachers for the four subjects – maths, physics, chemistry and biology. The maths syllabus commenced with vulgar fractions, which even I remembered from school, and then moved on to higher things; and I found, to my mingled delight and fury, that I was actually rather good at this new language. So much so that I tended to be able to finish our teacher's reasoning for him; and – shades of that long-ago convent school! – stupidly did so aloud once or twice. He didn't like it! But our dislike was mutual.

About the physics and chemistry teachers I remember little. Physics I found I could just about do by creating my own simplified "textbook"; chemistry has remained a total mystery, and got worse when we were supposed to do experiments. In biology, of course, I was far more at home – helped also by a brilliant and amusing teacher, who remained a friend for the rest of his life. Towards the end of my three years (two for those O-levels, one for an elementary proficiency qualification as a lab technician), Dave said "Tell me, Eva, are you scared of these exams?" "Yes!" "Well, don't worry! I'm one of your examiners – and if I have to forswear my immortal soul, I'll see you through!"

So I am now the proud holder of a certificate proclaiming me to be a qualified junior lab technician and – between this and a few years' experience at home – found I could understand most of my husband's conversation.

Chapter 2
Back to West Africa: Walli-Kunda

"Are the cutlasses in the lab, Tony?"

"Certainly, Supremo – right next to the Tampax boxes!"

Mick and I, together with his assistant Tony Wilkes, were all sitting on our wide low basketwork *bantaba* in front of the house, contemplating the wide brown River Gambia, its bird-haunted islands and the north bank beyond. I've now forgotten what the Tampax boxes may have contained – certainly not Tampax – but still remember thinking, even then, that this particular piece of dialogue could only have occurred in Walli-Kunda.

Mick, always embarrassed by his posh background and his "officer-and-gentleman" manner, had spent much of his adult life trying, unsuccessfully, to stop other men calling him Sir; but Tony Wilkes addressing him as Supremo bothered him not at all. Tony, unashamedly working-class, with a yen for beer, betting and similar pursuits, was, in fact Sancho Panza to Mick's Don Quixote; and – exactly as in the tale told by Cervantes – a deep and solid friendship had united the two for many years.

Mick's early working life as an entomologist had taken him and his wife Agnes to Tanganyika, which was to become Tanzania, where both their daughters had been born. At Independence in 1961, he had received a substantial golden farewell from the Colonial Office. Returning to England, he and his wife initially bought a house near Cambridge, whence, for the first few years he updated a major work of reference, *Anopheline Mosquitoes South of the Sahara*. That finished, he was in the market for a job, preferably researching the behaviour of mosquitoes.

The MRC were prepared to employ him to do this; and the University of Sussex, then quite new, actually *wanted* biologists to fill up its corridors and was especially welcoming to a small unit that didn't require lab space. All Mick needed was a couple of microscopes (which he had, or soon acquired), one or two mosquito-netting cages in which to breed the creatures, and one typewriter. His team, varying a little over the years but never amounting to as many as six, consisted of Tony Wilkes, one or two other assistants and one typist – who, having worked with Mick in Tanganyika, immediately gave up his existing job to join him again.

The University would in fact have preferred somebody who would teach as well as do research; but Mick, who hated teaching, got away with two non-specialised talks a year.

One of the nice things about marrying Mick was that I could now be married without being *settled*: that annual Gambian honeymoon kept me very much in touch with West Africa. The Gambia, a tiny English-speaking country sandwiched between the two halves of Senegal, was well suited to Mick's field research, not only by the excellence of its mosquitoes (*Anopheles gambiae*) but also by the fact that the MRC, his employers, had (and still have) that huge field station at Fajara. Here were a number of labs and a small hospital, workshops and garages; and here Mick could get all sorts of mosquito-traps made, as well as acquire a Landrover or two for the season. Mbemba Sisseh, his driver and senior mosquito-catcher, was employed at Fajara all the year round.

Nearby Banjul, moreover, offered shopping opportunities – essential for those of us planning to spend a couple of months up-country. Moreover, The Gambia's independent government regarded the MRC as a ministry of its own: if Mick, or any other researcher, needed to import equipment from Britain, it came in completely free of customs duty. Altogether, The Gambia was the place to go!

So to The Gambia we went.

If the country is called "The Gambia" and nor just "Gambia", it is because it is simply the valley of the wide river of that name. Mick used to say, I think correctly, that it had been a British colony because it extended over exactly the space that could be controlled by a British gunboat going up the river. The country is 300 miles long and about 30 miles wide.

The tiny village of Walli-Kunda is about two hundred miles up-river, where the water is still tidal, but no longer salty, or even brackish. We used to go swimming in it and I had to work out when the tide was going to be high, because otherwise there would be more mud than water. But for other reasons too it was very convenient living by the river: not only did we wash ourselves and our clothes in it, but our drinking water came from it – as did that of Mick's Gambian assistants, who lived in Brikama Ba, a bigger village nearer the main road. They said, no doubt correctly, that the river water was better than what they could get from their wells.

We boiled ours and then filtered it – basically, as Mick used to say, for aesthetic reasons, because we were not used to filmy, muddy water. But certainly nothing bad ever happened to us from the water of the great River Gambia. Any other natural necessities I used to perform in the bush, taking with me some lavatory paper and a box of matches to set light to it. Preferably not setting light to the surrounding bush – I did once, but Mick fortunately saw, and put it out in time.

Walli-Kunda was, like Hamsey, more a hamlet than a village. It was more active in the winter – the groundnut season – because it was a port for exporting groundnuts. But the house used by the main groundnut merchant stood empty during the summer, and we were allowed to use it. I've forgotten whether we'd paid a peppercorn rent or whether the firm was so pleased to have it looked after, we didn't pay anything. But in any case we had this quite large house, not in itself very wonderful, but with a glorious view of the river.

Mick and I used the bedroom; when Tony was also there, he slept on a camp-bed in the other, slightly larger room. Also within the compound, there stood a little kitchen; outside it but quite near by, a small generator for part-time electricity, and a fair-sized laboratory building.

An interesting pet

One day, Mick introduced a new housemate – a Royal Python! He had rescued it from his Gambian staff and, finding it to be a non-poisonous snake that killed its prey by strangling and would never grow longer than a man's forearm – totally harmless, therefore, to mankind – had decided it would make an interesting pet. I agreed, so initially we placed the creature inside a big empty crate in the living-room, together with a laboratory rat in case it felt peckish during the night, and covered the whole thing with the crate's wooden lid weighted down by a heavy earthenware jug.

Mick was going out for his night's work; I told him he could turn the generator off, I wanted an early bed and would, as always, go to sleep at once.

But when he returned couple of hours later, he found me out of doors, wandering up and down in my nightie (to the puzzlement of the night watchman), the Voice of America going full blast from indoors but not quite drowning out loud bumps from that crate. And then I was weeping in his arms, stammering that I had no objection in the world to the Python, but I really didn't want that rat – and the *noise!*

Mick calmed me down, cautiously shifted one corner of the crate lid – and found the poor snake tightly curled up on itself in one corner, while the rat was noisily trying to shift lid and pot and escape. He and the night watchman removed the pot to a safe place and then carried the crate and its inhabitants out into the lab, where the rat was at last given its freedom. It had, of course, been far too big for the python even to dream of catching and strangling it; so the snake curled up as tight as it could and pretended it wasn't there (Gambians, we later found, also nicknamed it the "shame-snake" from this bashful behaviour). Its real name in Mandinka was *minyango*, which we shortened to Minnie, thereby assigning it a gender. We never did find out what sex it was; but did learn that a cold-blooded animal (in fact, ambient temperature to the touch) did not need or want to eat at all frequently; so we kept Minnie happy on little experimental mice occasionally harvested from the big labs in Fajara.

She made a pleasant pet, eventually quite affectionate in her own way – allowing herself to be picked up from her normal home behind the bookshelves and waving her little head about, tongue out "to taste the air" as Tony put it. Also, quite useful in shortening some local visits that seemed to go on forever – "Have you met our pet *minyango*?" But after a few years, we gave Minnie her freedom back.

Moving house

And then, one year, the old groundnut merchant, who had always used that house during his trading season, died. He was replaced by a new man, who seems to have been obsessed with security: he had the whole compound fenced in with corrugated iron, completely shutting out the view of the river.

Now, I declared myself on strike.

I didn't mind, I told Mick, not having a bathroom; I could well do without much electricity, or indeed any at all. But, if I was to be deprived of my daily view of the River Gambia, I would renounce Walli-Kunda and all its works!

Mick, as ever, calmed me down. His MRC budget allowed for the building of an experimental mosquito-trapping hut; he would now get one built, and we would live in it. So a very little further down river, and with the local Chief's permission, a fine *rondavel* was erected: on a cement base, but with locally sun-fired mud bricks and palm thatch over palm rafters (it leaked a little, but in well-defined places). Mud and thatch are both good insulators, so who needed unhealthy air-conditioning? Especially as the one large window had mosquito-netting instead of glass, so even the lightest breeze from the river could blow in.

Perfect! And at that time, the cheapest form of housing ever built in the country for Europeans. (Nowadays, I'm told there is no halfway decent tourist hotel in The Gambia that does *not* offer "mud huts".)

Towards the end of our stay in The Gambia, one of the times Mick and I were both down at the big MRC compound in Fajara, came the news that "the Hatchet Lady" was arriving from London – the Hatchet Lady being a high MRC official, come to see that MRC Gambia was not spending too much money uneconomically!

Mick hated dinner parties. People had learnt this, and tended not to ask him. I, on the other hand, was asked to the dinner party at which somebody had the courage to entertain the Hatchet Lady; and I found myself sitting very near her at one of the tables.

I was introduced to her as "Eva Gillies, who spends most of her time up river in Walli-Kunda." "Ah, yes." says the Hatchet Lady, "Walli-Kunda! Now that was the place that was built up, but never appeared on the budget." So I said: "Well, what *was* on the budget, for my husband's research, was a mosquito-trap hut, and that indeed is what we had built; only we're living in it. In fact, it is fairly small and quite primitive. The difficult bit was getting our furniture from the trader's house, where we no longer wanted to live, to this new place, over land. In the end, we did it by boat. We even had to dismantle the chest-of-drawers and carry it, drawer by drawer, on this boat, to the new place."

I went on about this a bit, and about being just like the Water Gypsies, until she said, with obvious disapproval: "When I think of the wonderful holidays we finance for people like you." At this I lost my cool, and replied: "I beg your pardon! I go to work in order to earn my fare to The Gambia. It is true that we live, rather modestly, on my husband's generous allowance, during his time here; but I do not feel I personally owe the MRC one penny." I got no more flak out of the Hatchet Lady.

The following year, a smaller *rondavel* was built to one side of our hut, to serve as our bedroom; later, another for Tony, or in his absence for any visitors we might have. Visitors unused to our ways might also welcome a small WC building; and Ousman needed a kitchen.

Visitors from the coast came, in the nature of things, unannounced; usually they brought fresh fruit and vegetables with them, and also letters. It was thus that I learned, in a letter from Trixie in 1977, of our mother's fairly sudden, but entirely peaceful, death in Buenos Aires. I was too late even for the funeral, but wanting to be near my sister at such a time, travelled down to the coast, took the next plane to Dakar and thence south across the Atlantic, to spend a few weeks with Trixie, sharing memories as well as the sad tasks of dividing up furniture, ornaments and jewellery.

Jumaa Maneh and her family

Because of its tiny size, Walli-Kunda shared a chief with Brikama Ba, the much larger village near the main road, where our own Alhaji Kuliba was also responsible for one ward. There, he kept his main residence, and his two seniormost wives; his third wife, Jumaa Maneh, had her own little house in Walli-Kunda, where Alhaji Kuliba spent two or three nights a week. In his case, "Alhaji" was a given name, not a title (as with the common honorific "Al Hajj" referring to a Muslim who has completed the pilgrimage to Mecca). Jumaa's given name means Friday, the Muslim holy day; Maneh was her maiden name, which among the Mandinka, as in old-fashioned Argentina, women keep all their lives.

Jumaa was a most interesting person. She came from a well-to-do, Western-educated family; her brother, down on the coast, was a surgeon. She was illiterate, or should I say pre-literate, purely because in her childhood it had not yet been the custom to send girls to school; nonetheless she was who she was and the whole world knew it. She had been married to somebody else before Alhaji, but she didn't like him, so she left him.

One has to assume that she did like Alhaji, for she stayed with him. She had some money of her own I think, and certainly some land of her own, and was able to hire other women to help her work it; she did so herself, but mostly she bossed the other women about. But above all, she ran Walli-Kunda when her husband was not there – not of course officially, but, curiously enough, whenever there was a palaver between two of the other inhabitants, Jumaa would be called upon and would, in a gentle and ladylike manner, settle the question, and that was all right by everyone.

The reason I learned some Mandinka, I think, was that I wanted to hear what Jumaa was saying about me to her other friends. She was also the reason why I first began to wear proper African dress. I had had what they called in Ibadan an "up and down", but I heard her describing it to a friend of hers, and what she was saying would be in English "Yes, Hawa is a good friend of mine" – Hawa is the local version of Eva – "and I love taking her to naming ceremonies and other things." "But what does she *wear?*" "Well she does have a *sort* of African dress, but frankly it's not much, I wish I could see her in something decent." Well, I thought, I cannot have Jumaa ashamed of me every time we go out together! The next time we go to town I will get myself something decent. Which I did; I kept it, I wore it at Susie's wedding reception, and I still have it.

Jumaa had tried, all of her married life with Alhaji, to have children, and it had never worked. She had tried Western medicine, through the *aegis* of her brother, and she had tried native medicine; neither had been successful. She *had* managed to become pregnant a couple of times, but there had always been a miscarriage. So she dealt with this problem by adoption (informal adoption of course – there was no such thing as full legal adoption). She "adopted" girls of two sorts. First were the children of relatives; perhaps her own, perhaps Alhaji's, from families less well off than she was. Then, there were girls of slave origin.

While, of course, The Gambia officially had given up slavery long ago, everybody still knew – probably still knows – perfectly well who comes from a slave family and who doesn't. At home, Jumaa treated them all equally. They all addressed her as "mother", and did the housework. But she could not quite afford to send them all to school. So the freeborn girls went to school and the others didn't. However, they still did quite nicely out of it. There was one girl called Jonsaba, a name meaning "third slave". Now Jumaa found everybody a husband of course, it was her duty; she found Jonsaba an extremely nice husband, of her own class but very much better looking and more intelligent than the extremely plain Jonsaba could possibly have got on her own. And then Jonsaba became pregnant and gave birth to a boy. This little boy was put to the breast, both by his biological mother and by Jumaa – who is to me living proof of what I had heard before: that a woman who has been pregnant can, on demand, produce milk even if not pregnant at the time. And Jumaa then took over the little boy. I don't think Jonsaba minded very much; it was a good future for this child and she herself was obviously going to have several more children.

The little boy eventually became a toddler, walked about and was in body-shape tall and slender, with rather a big nose by local standards; and was therefore nicknamed "Little Doctor Gillies" after my husband. This made him a *tomaa* of Mick's, even if only by nickname; *tomaa* means namesake – an important relationship in those parts. I have met, in the nature of things, several "Hawas", and they were all *tomaa* to me; we would give each other little presents, and so on. So Mick was this little boy's *tomaa*, which made him something like a kind of godfather. And many years later, when Mick was no longer working there, we went back to The Gambia on a visit and hired a car to drive us up country. We got to Brikama Ba, where by this time Jumaa was now living; immediately the cry went up: "Gillies, Gillies, your *tomaa*'s come. Come and greet him!" They go in very much for nicknames in that part of the world.

A fourth wife

At one stage, fairly late on in our time in Walli-Kunda, Jumaa's husband came on a visit; I suspect she was very much his favourite wife. On this occasion, I went to call on her in her small house; she was sitting on the bed and I sat there beside her. Alhaji sat facing us in a chair and said, "I have some news for you. I am going to take a fourth wife. So you must be nice to her, you must love her for my sake." Jumaa (sitting beside me) put an arm around me and squeezed a bit, saying: "Yes, but not as much as you love *me*." This was the only mark of jealousy Jumaa allowed herself to show over the whole business.

Alhaji having gone back to his other wives in Brikama Ba, Jumaa and I spent the next week or so being driven around (I must admit the MRC Landrover got used for such things as well as other social occasions) to Jumaa's fairly large number of women friends in the area, where the conversation was always: "And you may or may not have heard, but Alhaji's taking another wife. I'm absolutely delighted! It's high time we had some new young blood in the compound, in the family; no, I don't yet know her of course, she's still in her father's compound. Her father's Chief Something Something of Somewhere Else, and I'm looking forward to meeting her very much." And she went around and made this little speech at everyone. She was meanwhile getting her own clothes and the necessary presents together. When she was good and ready, she and I, and our cook Ousman Jawara – who could not be left out of these things – and of course the driver, went off to this other village where there resided the Chief who was the father of the new bride.

We stopped a little before we got there, at the house of yet another of Jumaa's women friends, in order to be given a chance to refresh ourselves and have something to drink and do our hair properly and so on. We then proceeded in state to the compound where the bride still lived. She, poor thing, was a tall girl (I imagine in her teens), very shy, very embarrassed by the whole situation, but she bravely did her stuff, and greeted us. And then we went into the large reception room and were asked to sit down. Jumaa and I were the only women present. Speeches were made of course. When it came to the speech made by the father of the bride, he welcomed everybody, saying how happy he was to see us. He was very happy about this marriage, not only because he was giving one of his daughters as a wife to his old friend Alhaji Kuliba, but also because of Jumaa Maneh. It was not that he was unaware that his friend Alhaji Kuliba had two other wives senior to Jumaa, but they had not honoured his daughter by a visit to her compound. Jumaa Maneh had done so, and therefore it was to her he entrusted the happiness of his child. She was to look after this new young wife, to tell her what Alhaji liked and disliked and generally introduce her to her new life. The whole thing resolved itself into a paean of praise for my friend Jumaa, who said absolutely nothing, just sat there looking modestly downwards and looking extremely beautiful.

The next bit of the story I didn't witness. It was a name-giving ceremony, one of the big occasions thereabouts, to which I was told (by a witness) Alhaji Kuliba went with a wife on each arm; on one arm he had the new young bride and on the other Jumaa, who was wearing a very large and handsome pair of earrings no-one had ever seen on her before. Jumaa spent quite a bit of money on herself, but on clothes not jewellery, so I assume the earrings were a present from her husband in reward for her understanding.

A year later we returned to The Gambia. The unfortunate new bride was in the big compound in Brikama Ba with the two old So-and-so's, having had her baby; while Jumaa continued to reside in her own little house in Walli-Kunda, where she ran things the way she wanted them. It made me realise that being a third wife, and childless at that, need not, even in Africa, exclude one from human society – not if you are good looking and highly intelligent, and moreover everybody knows you come from a good family. You *can* manage such a situation, and she did.

Several years later, the MRC decided to send a team of nutritionists to The Gambia. The word had got around that I spoke Mandinka, so they wanted me to give these nutritionists a one-day immersion course beforehand in the Mandinka language. You can't do much in that time. But I thought: Oh well, a few greetings will do no harm and perhaps to know how the verbs work, and so on. At the last moment I got cold feet, and said: "If you can possibly find me a native Mandinka speaker to back me up and tell me when I'm going wrong...?"

All this took place in Cambridge. I started out, of course, with something which is not Mandinka any more than it's English: *Salaam alekum*, *alekum salaam*, which is the initial greeting and response in any Muslim country. Then we went into Mandinka greetings, and a few other things. To illustrate verbs, I had a sentence I *knew* was all right, because I hadn't made it up, I'd heard it – from our night watchman, who was much amused on some occasion when Jumaa and I were going somewhere, and she was as usual late, taking so long to get ready. The night watchman said: *"Hawa parêta, moto be lorin, Jumaa mam pareh"* – Hawa is ready, the motor is standing there, and Jumaa is not ready. (*Moto* is of course from "motor", and less obviously *parêta* and *pareh* from the French, *prête* and *prêt* – Senegal is only a few miles away!) He thought this very funny and repeated it several times, and it gave you three different useful variations, so I produced it.

Now came the coffee break and the young Gambian who had been asked to come and help me – he was "eating his dinners" in London for the law – said to me: "You probably don't know this, but Jumaa Maneh is my aunt." That is The Gambia for you! Everybody is related to everybody else; and even if they aren't, they all have a junior wife or a brother, or a sister or somebody, who works for the MRC. That made us part of the family too, a link of a peculiarly lasting kind.

The coup

For nearly all the years during which we spent the mosquito season in the Gambia, its president was Sir Dauda Jawara. The surname "Jawara", which he shared with our cook Ousman, is one which, in that caste society, belongs principally to blacksmiths and their wives the potters, whose occupation also needs hot fires. In The Gambia, blacksmiths and potters stood low in the social hierarchy. And in those days at least, the landowning class to which such people as Jumaa belonged, did not bother with politics. Sir Dauda was originally a vet, living in or near Banjul, and dealing mainly with the pets of Europeans living there. (The MRC had the usual drunken Scots engineer that everybody in the tropics seems to have; this one said that he was occasionally asked what the government of The Gambia was like. He would say: Well I don't know, but my dog's bitten the President and I'm still alive!")

Sir Dauda was at that stage a Christian. He'd been trained in Scotland, as quite a number of medical people in West Africa seem to be. Then, when he went into politics he acquired a couple of wives more, for the same sort of reason as His Highness the Ologori of Ogori had done, for political reasons, and by the same token became Muslim – but in a thoroughly unfanatical way.

During one of those years a German, whose name I can't remember, started a brewery on the coast near Banjul. They made something called Joyful Julbrew – JUL from "Banjul" and BREW, all one word. Joyful Julbrew was not the best beer you've ever drunk, but good enough, and cheaper than the imported stuff; we used to drink it. The brewery also made various forms of so-called fruit drinks. Then Libya offered The Gambia, a poor country, a rather large present: a fleet of buses for its empty roads – on condition this evil factory making alcohol was closed. Sir Dauda, to his eternal honour, said: "Sorry! The Gambia is just a republic not an Islamic Republic. Herr whatever-his-name has broken no law, moreover has given employment to quite a large number of our people. I have no intention whatsoever of closing this factory!"

But now, with independence well in the past, new political forces were at work. That summer of 1981, Sir Dauda being away in London for the wedding of the Prince of Wales to Lady Diana, a Marxist coup was launched. The conspirators had planned to kill Sir Dauda the moment he got off the plane on his return; but quite innocently he had decided to spend an extra week or so in England playing golf near Haywards Heath. So he was not on that plane! But when he heard of the events, he sensibly rang up his Senegalese opposite number and said: "Would you be so kind as to invade my country?" Which they were very happy to do, since the last thing they wanted was to have a Marxist take-over in their own backyard.

Now all this Mick and I found out only very gradually, because we were out there in the bush. Our radio had been borrowed by someone; and this being our last year, Mick and I had decided we didn't really need a new one. So we only heard the news from our driver and senior mosquito catcher, Mbemba Sisseh, who came along roaring with laughter, pointing at our cook, Ousman Jawara and saying: "This man, he no be President no more!" And indeed, that man no was president no more.

We had Susie and Richard staying, that was the only complication; and Susie was meant to be back in England quite soon, being at that time pregnant with Andrew. Jessica was a toddler, on the whole quite well behaved. But Susie was due back in England, her doctor said – and how was this going to happen when there was a battle all over the airfield, or so we heard. Mick and I used to go for long walks in the bush to work out how this was going to happen, but in the end we decided it could be solved. Mbemba Sisseh had a wife the other side of the border too; so he could always cross over into Senegal, and take them into that country. Once there they were on their own; but surely they could find *something* to take them back to England.

In the end all this turned out to be unnecessary, because this entire war did not last very long, ten days I think. This, we heard about when people came up from the coast, from the MRC, partly to see whether we were alive, but mostly, I think, to buy food. Because the MRC compound was full of refugees whom they needed to feed, and we had rice, fish and groundnuts, if nothing else, so they bought quite a lot of those and I managed to give them lunch too. Yes, the airport was going to be all right! So we drove down to the coast with Richard and Susie. Richard, an English innocent in Africa, had to be told not to take photographs, but the rest of us knew, thank you! So they took the plane they were always were going to take back to England, and I did a little bit of shopping, and then we returned to Walli-Kunda. As I've said before, it's quite all right being in a country with a *coup*, as long as you're in the bush, you're safe there.

Back in Lewes, a little before Mick's death, it was announced that the daughter of one of my fellow parishioners was getting married, and was moreover getting married to a Muslim. This was all taking place at the ecumenical Chapel in the grounds of the University of Sussex, and we were all cordially invited. I didn't take too much notice, until I met the priest who was going to marry them, a good friend of mine, one Father Pat Shanihan.

Pat Shanihan had started a charity in Ghana, which is only now self-running, called Street Child Africa. This does exactly what it says on the label, it looks after street children without being judgmental about them; indeed they are very often the children of streetchildren. He was going to perform this wedding ceremony. When we met at a dinner party, Pat told me who the bridegroom was: a son of Sir Dauda Jawara! The former President of The Gambia was by now retired and living, naturally, in Haywards Heath, practising his golf, along with – among others – Susie's doctor. And I said to Mick: "I'm sorry, dear, but this is one wedding we are going to. We don't need to go to the reception, but we are most certainly going to the service."

So we did go to the service in the beautiful chapel, and were placed on the bride's side. Here, we were mostly Christians of one denomination or another, mainly Catholic. At other side, the bridegroom's side, Sir Dauda duly arrived – not a tall man, but magnificent in green brocade, with a little gold cap and a wife on each arm, and a number of other wonderfully dressed people. Pat started out by giving, I suppose a sort of sermon – certainly a talk. Which he started by saying: "*Salaam alekum*" and those of us who knew on our side – I think only Mick and I, went: "*Alekum salaam*"! And Pat then went on about how happy he was to be performing this marriage, blah, blah, blah. And phrased it in such a way as to make it quite clear to the Catholics that it was not they who were taking a great step in tolerance, it was the Muslims who were doing that. Because one of their sons was marrying one of our daughters, and eventually the children would be brought up Catholic. He managed to introduce into this a number of complimentary references to the Prophet. And generally made a very good job of it. Now when I was young, if you so much as married an Anglican you didn't get a nuptial Mass. But this wedding had a nuptial Mass – and how!

On the way out – I'm quite good at getting myself into the right queue – I got myself into the queue that went past Sir Dauda in his green robes, and shook his hand and said: "You won't remember me, Sir, but we last met on the jetty in Walli-Kunda when you were President of The Gambia! My husband was working for the MRC, and at that time you were wearing one of those wonderful flowered African shirts; you're looking even more wonderful now," or words to that effect. He was really pleased! I think Mick and I were the only people there, aside from Father Pat, who knew who on earth he was.

Chapter 3
Visits Abroad

Following my mother's death, although I had come into a fair amount of money, I continued to accept conference duties. One day, interpreting in London, I was sitting in the booth alone and bored, wishing myself anywhere else. Suddenly I thought "Why? Why I am doing this to myself? I no longer need these jobs – and there are people out there who do. I don't have to do this any more, ever. OK, I'll just keep the contracts I've already signed, and never take on another."

I kept my word, and have since then done only the most amateur interpreting. I now had enough money to live as I wished; and although Mick around this time retired from working in The Gambia, I realised I need not, even now, give up travelling and settle down.

On one of her last visits to England, my mother had asked me why we never went to New Zealand, Mick's father's home country where he still had a sister and brother – when we had more than once visited Argentina. I had answered that going all the way to New Zealand was very expensive; my mother's view was that it would be well worth it. Now, I suggested to Mick that we should honour her memory by a journey to New Zealand.

A scattered family

We were indeed far from the first Gillieses of our generation to return to Sir Harold's homeland. Mick's elder brother John, a chartered accountant turned RAF pilot, had spent much of the Second World War in an officers' prisoner-of-war camp. His work there was later recognised with the award of an OBE; this was thanks to his excellent German, which helped him find out a good deal (from boastful prison guards) about the Führer's "new secret weapons" – later known in Britain as "doodle-bugs". He had communicated this information, in code, through the Red Cross letters he was allowed to write to his wife in England. While in the camp, he met a fellow-prisoner from New Zealand who happened to be an accountant too; and this colleague had suggested that "when all this is over" John should "come out to New Zealand and join our family firm."

So after the war John Gillies came to England just long enough to pick up his wife Eileen, and then moved with her to Invercargill in New Zealand. Eventually they had three children, Jinny, David and Christopher; by the time Mick and I paid our first visit, all three were more or less grown up, even Christopher having already turned eighteen.

Of Mick's two sisters, Joanna was the stay-at-home; she still lives in Cambridge, where she has recently celebrated a 90th birthday; her elder son Gavin, however, having fallen in love with a New Zealand girl, emigrated there. Only Joanna's daughter Clare and her son Nigel remained in England. In our immediate family, Mick's younger daughter Jackie has also married a Kiwi and lives in New Zealand; to be followed later by Susie's daughter Jessica, who has also acquired a New Zealand husband – and it looks as if her brother Andrew might be going to settle there too. In the end, it seems all Sir Harold's descendants may well return to his country of origin.

The elder sister, Margaret, was a different matter. Mick used to say I resembled her. After an adventurous and much travelled youth (she had accompanied her father to Buenos Aires in 1941) she had married one Joe Divers who – having already fought in the First World War – had entered the Second as a Sergeant and ended up a Brigadier. Joe was also, by then, an insurance expert, and a close friend to several of the men who were to form the Labour Government in 1945; he entered the Civil Service at a high level and was said – at least by his wife Margaret – to have been the main author of Britain's National Insurance system.

By the time the two met in Kathmandu, Joe was with the UN, helping the governments of some of the new countries set up their own Social Security systems. After Nepal, it was the turn of Saudi Arabia; at this stage Margaret, now married to him, began to worry about overwork and health; and decided, she told us later, to "butter his paws". And where better to do so than New Zealand, where her brother and his family were already living?

Not, however, boring Invercargill! – or indeed any urban area. Countryside was what she wanted – somewhere they could have a really big garden for Joe to organise, and enough woodland to indulge her own passion for birdwatching. Trouble was, local legislation did not allow people to buy land in the countryside unless they intended to farm – farm *properly*, not just grow a few vegetables and enough fruit for the household. This was – and is – because the government did not want precious New Zealand to become one enormous garden suburb: in urban areas (again by law) every dwelling house must have its own quarter-acre, but the countryside – or its flatter areas unsuitable for sheep pasture – is for serious agriculture.

Margaret and Joe were fortunate in finding a corner of land between two big farms in Southland Province, which neither of the neighbours wanted. They called it "Northwest Corner" after the prevailing wind, though "Southeast Corner" would have been geographically more accurate. About half the land was wooded, sloping down to a stream which some years overflowed its banks; on the other half, they built themselves a sizeable house, and still had plenty of room for orchard, vegetable garden, fruit garden and Margaret's special collection of roses. So "the Brig" had plenty to organise, and as for Margaret, she was in paradise. She and Joe remained childless; but she was a devoted and welcome aunt to John's offspring (then still living with their parents in Invercargill); and, when our Susie turned eighteen, Mick and I encouraged her to spend a generous money present from her godmother on a voyage to New Zealand rather than a first car – despite the fact that she was already going out with Richard, into whose arms she fell again the moment she got back.

John and Eileen, Margaret and Joe, all lived on the South Island, and indeed in its southernmost parts. New Zealand consists of two main islands; and being, like my own Argentina, a long country from north to south, has more than one climate. Simplifying broadly, the North Island is subtropical, South Island temperate to cold. Most of the country's inhabitants prefer to live on the warmer North Island; its main town, Auckland, which lies on the sea, is internationally known as a yachting centre. The South Island is inhabited largely by sheep, plus a few farming families, mainly of Scots descent, among whom were the original New Zealand Gillieses. Maoris live on both islands; they too prefer the North for its climate; though on the South Island, increasingly, the tourist industry is partly – and quite profitably – run by them.

Tourists in New Zealand

On that first visit after my mother's death, Mick and I landed, like most tourists, in Auckland. Our plane journey had taken an almost uninterrupted 28 hours; we arrived totally exhausted, with feet so swollen we could hardly squeeze them into our shoes. (This taught us, for later trips, always to plan for at least a two-day stop along the way, generally in Bangkok.) We took refuge in the hotel room we'd booked in advance, but our sleep was soon interrupted by the telephone: sociable Margaret had arranged for some distant connections of hers in Auckland to ring us up, bid us welcome, ask us to lunch... Whoever they were, they got short shrift from Mick, who was never too fond of the telephone anyway; and his much-loved sister in Southland soon got instructions *never* to set us up with new acquaintances – related or otherwise – again.

On recovering from jet-lag, we did telephone both Margaret and John, and then spent a pleasant few days in the neighbourhood of Auckland. The town itself, despite its beautiful situation, we found rather boring – miles upon miles of the garden suburb required by law, with all the gardens prissily un-exotic; no central open space and nothing much by way of public buildings. There were, however, some agreeable beaches beyond (described by our hotel waitress as "out in the wopwops") and, having hired a car, we enjoyed exploring these.

Then we set off on our journey down the North Island. This took several days, because – even avoiding all those distant cousins – we did stop to visit a huge volcanic lake and an area of hot springs. Eventually arriving at the strait between the North and South Islands, we took the ferry: a couple of hours of brisk sea breezes and much dodging of ravenous gulls that wanted our sandwiches. Once on the South Island, we boarded the train.

Margaret had told us about this train, already then one of the last in the South Island; travel within the islands is mostly by road, nowadays also by plane. The train was mainly for tourists like us; I hope it still exists. It meandered gently down the South Island, stopping at wayside stations, once for a full hour to enable passengers and crew to buy lunch at a tiny station restaurant. One really saw the rural landscape as it slowly passed, before reaching the period magnificence of the end station, Dunedin, where Margaret was expecting us.

Dunedin is the greatest possible contrast to Auckland. Built by moneyed immigrant Scots at the end of the 19th century as an "Edinburgh of the South" (the name Dunedin translates Edinburgh into Scots Gaelic), it is carefully planned, with wide well-spaced tree-lined avenues and a large central area known as the Octagon. It also has the best university in New Zealand, with the attendant amenities of hospital and bookshop. If the capital of the whole country is Wellington (on a site clearly more appropriate to a fishing village than to a capital city) this is because this was the only way the Auckland/Dunedin rivalry could be peacefully resolved.

All this, of course, we did not learn on that first visit. Margaret happily drove us away from Dunedin, first to Invercargill to lunch with John and Eileen at their house, then on to her own Northwest Corner, where the Brig awaited us. There we largely stayed for the rest of the six weeks our tourist visa allowed, enjoying garden and woodland (Mick took particular delight in the little stream with its mayflies), and sometimes taken by Margaret in her car to see at least some of the mountain-and-lake wonderland that is the southern part of the South Island. Glow-worm caves, snow-capped mountains, waterfalls rushing into the abyss – I still find it a shame that the English Romantic poets never had a chance to glimpse those South Island landscapes! Nor can I understand why so many New Zealanders prefer to live on the infinitely duller North Island. Most of the South Island is very sparsely populated, except by sheep.

People do congregate round the lakes, which indeed sustain a considerable tourist industry, one of the country's main sources of income. Most important of the tourist towns is Queenstown on vast Lake Wakatipu, near which our daughter Jackie now lives with her family. A smaller, but to my eye still more beautiful, lake is Wanaka, where John and Eileen had, already then, a holiday home which later became their place of retirement; they invited Mick and me there for two unforgettable week-ends, during which we once motor-boated up-river to the foot of the well-named Southern Alps.

This was only the first of many trips to New Zealand: my mother's advice, and her legacy, really did result in closer ties with those fragments of our scattered family. Also, we found that the expensive fare from England to New Zealand – literally at the opposite end of the world – became slightly cheaper if one made the flight part of a round-the-world-tour, which in turn increased visits to Buenos Aires.

On belonging to Argentina

In 1982, the year after Mick retired from work in The Gambia, came the idiotic conflict known in England as the Falklands War, which I still name (to myself) "the Malvinas War". This is a matter of long-ago politics. The real ownership of the islands is, apparently, a matter on which international jurists can spend many days of research and debate; but during my Buenos Aires childhood in the 1930s *Las Malvinas Son Argentinas*, "The Falklands are Argentine" was a slogan much in vogue among nationalists, a name itself code for pro-Franco and, later, pro-Axis sympathies. I was therefore firmly brought up to believe that the Falklands were British: my views were not originally those of a typical Argentine.

This has changed.

When the war started, in May 1982, I felt very gloomy about it all; just as gloomy, if anything gloomier, was my sister Trixie in Buenos Aires who, in addition, felt very isolated. She could not ring me up, because she would have to go through a telephonist, and our two countries were at war. I, however, could simply dial her number, and not even Mrs Thatcher could stop me (though she might, in theory, listen in). So I would phone Trixie fairly often to make comforting noises; at one point we said to each other, "When this whole bloody stupid thing is over, let's spend the next Christmas together!" She added "You and Mick can come out here", and I gladly agreed.

Other than those telephone calls, living out the Falklands war here in Sussex was distinctly odd. For one thing, it changed my view of the world and of my place in it. I had started out just feeling "A plague on both their houses!" I well knew that Galtieri, the dictatorial President of Argentina, had invaded the islands because his popularity was waning; and also that Mrs Thatcher needed to win the next election. A plague on both their houses therefore – until the sinking, well outside Falklands territorial waters, of the *Belgrano*. It was then I realised that, however long and happily I may live in England, I remain at heart Argentine. Not that I was exposed to any trouble locally – Mick and I simply didn't *know* anyone pro-Thatcher.

A young Argentine lad, a friend of Trixie's, was then doing a postgraduate degree in agronomy at the University of Reading. During one of our chats, Trixie told me about him, adding "He must be feeling very lonely in England… couldn't you have him over for a week-end?" I contacted the young man, who did indeed come over; he and I spent most of that week-end sitting in front of the television and weeping, Mick I think feeding us at intervals.

The lad told me how kind people had been to him at Reading. His supervisor had asked him whether he wanted to stay – this would surely be a very short war – "and about money, don't worry. I realise your father can't send you anything just now; I'll gladly be your banker here. Or, if you'd sooner transfer to the US, I could arrange for some really good institute to recognise the research you've done here."

The young man stayed to complete his degree at Reading.

Then again, once the war was over, I was able to talk to the one member of the Argentine Embassy who had remained in London throughout: the Commercial Attaché, who had been representing his country's business interests from the Brazilian Embassy. When we met, at the International Sugar Organisation, we swapped stories. He told me he too had been extremely well treated, as had his children at the International School in London – not the tiniest bit of flak from their school-mates, which he assumed (I think rightly) must have been due to very firm instructions from teachers. He himself and his wife had received flower arrangements and invitations to dinner from people they were hardly aware that they knew.

On the other side, both the British Hurlingham Club just outside Buenos Aires and the descendants of the Bridges family who had originally opened up Tierra del Fuego, had also been well treated, and indeed protected, by the authorities. Trixie told me, too that her daughter Veronica (who, in her teens, was earning pocket money by teaching Scottish dancing) had not lost a single student.

Tourists in the New World

Arranging travel to Argentina for the Christmas after that Falklands war was not in fact simple. We could not, yet, travel there on our British passports – but had to use my Argentine one, which I had always kept and got renewed – and now I knew why. In addition, Trixie had to write "TO WHOM IT MAY CONCERN" that Michael Thomas Gillies, holder of British Passport Number Whatever-it-was, was genuinely married to her sister, and she really did wish to see him.

For this journey we had to pass through the USA for some reason, and thus also needed an American visa on my Argentine passport, as I would not have done on my British one; so I went to the American Embassy in London. In those days, if you were from an English-speaking country you simply handed in your passport, went out for a coffee – maybe two or three coffees – returned and collected your (now visa'd) document again; but it was not so with the "lesser breeds without the law" of whom I was now, once again, one.

As a member of this category, you waited – waited for rather a long time, among all the other members of the lesser breeds, all huddled together in one large room. When my turn finally came and I handed in that Argentine passport, the woman behind the guichet was, understandably, a bit suspicious. "You're Argentine and you live in *England*? Why's that?" "Because I'm married to an Englishman." "You're Argentine and married to an *Englishman*. Where did you meet your husband?" "In *Africa!*"

said I – implying, where does *anybody* meet their husbands? She was so totally gobsmacked that I promptly got my visa, with indefinite entries and exits for the USA.

Then Mick and I were actually able to travel, not initially to Buenos Aires, though we did have to change planes there, but to Punta del Este – East Point, which is indeed the easternmost point of the Uruguayan south coast. I will, for once, call the country by its official name, The Oriental Republic of Uruguay.

This Oriental Republic had once been the Oriental, i.e. Eastern, strip of the United Provinces of the River Plate. In the mid to late 19th century, with a rather more successful strongman than most other provinces, it had achieved independence. A delightful land, not particularly rich but friendly and welcoming, it lives to a considerable extent on the tourism of wealthy Argentines and others who've heard of it: it does have the best beaches I know of throughout the globe – and I have been to beaches in Italy and India, Japan and Australia; but the Uruguayan ones are best. Trixie and Bernie had acquired a little house on the outskirts of Punta del Este, which was where we were going to spend Christmas with her and her family.

Mick of course had to find some mayflies to amuse himself, so he began exploring the local freshwater streams. He found plenty there – New World mayflies that had never been studied before! So he was often doing that while I idled on the beach or enjoyed Trixie's parties.

In the New Year of 1983, we did get to Argentina. We couldn't have gone there first: Mick only had permission for one entry into that country, not two or three, so it had to be Uruguay first. Just outside Buenos Aires lay the Hurlingham Club, where Trixie (to spare Mick the horrors of big-city life) had made us temporary members: a large comfortable club house where there somehow still lingered a very English smell of lavender-scented furniture polish, set in huge grounds that included facilities for both cricket and polo. The Club restaurant closed at week-ends, so we had to find somewhere else to eat – a little local restaurant, Italian, did us very well. We later found out it was co-operatively owned, so the waiter who attended us felt able, as part-owner, to say to Mick (in Spanish, which Mick understood quite well by then) "I suppose the *Señor* would like a whisky?" – and to produce, on the house, an Argentine whisky – not half bad in fact, though Argentine gin is best avoided.

Naturally, we also went travelling up and down the country, an English husband giving me the best possible excuse to explore regions most people from Buenos Aires never bother with. In the old northern Andean provinces of Salta and Jujuy – their cities founded by the Spaniards less than a century after the arrival of Christopher Columbus – we visited both these cities and the spectacular surrounding landscape by hired car, before turning south to the central province of Tucumán, whence we were to travel by fast train back to the capital. This train, however, we managed (through a misunderstanding of a.m. and p.m. railway timetables) to miss, and thus had to take a very slow and ancient train, complete with antediluvian English silver teapots and other such delights. The train, of course, stopped everywhere, but we did eventually reach Buenos Aires. "I know these things happen" was Trixie's comment; "but why do they always happen to my sister?"

Patagonia

Now for the South. In the first instance, we flew to Río Gallegos, an Atlantic airport by the river of that name. There, we hired a car to drive across Patagonia, to reach the very beautiful lake district at the foot of the southern Andes, where we stayed for a while in the small town of Cafayate, well off the normal tourist track. The one available hotel was very simple, indeed not quite finished – we had to be careful piling up clothes on the still splintery shelves of our bedroom. For a couple of days, we went away to have a look at Mt. Fitzroy, so named after the captain of the Beagle. On the way back, I was driving when the car slipped on pebbles, tumbling deep into the adjacent river gorge. Mick and I were quite unharmed, but our camera was a write-off and so was the hired car.

So we waited – just waited by the roadside to see whether anything would happen. Those roads are pretty much deserted; so the wait lasted several hours until there came a man driving a lorry. He was, I believe, South African; what he was doing in Patagonia I know not. He was, however, going in our direction, kindly picked us up and drove us, not just to Cafayate, but to our actual hotel; where he said to the manager at his desk, "Hi, chum! I've brought you these two, they've smashed their car, but they're all right." He refused our offer of a drink, saying no, he had to go and see his mother-in-law, of whom he was clearly in awe.

The hotel manager greeted us, adding "Your room awaits you", so we retired to consider what to do next. We *had* intended to drive back to Rio Gallegos, and thence catch our reserved flight to Tierra del Fuego; but without a car this no longer seemed possible. Returning to the hotel desk, I explained our plight to the manager.

"All those problems, *Señora*, are already solved. Have you any others? "

I must have stared a bit. He continued, "I have taken the liberty to book you two seats on an army plane that leaves for Río Gallegos tomorrow morning at 10 o'clock; it should get you there in plenty of time for your connection. You will have to find your own way to our little airport, but there is a taxi rank across the road from the hotel, and the distance is not great. I have also got in touch with the brother-in-law of the man you hired the car from in Río Gallegos; he will wait on you at your breakfast table tomorrow, so you can deal with insurance matters then. Any other problems, *Señora*?"

I must have said something like "You're wonderful, you're marvellous, how do you do it?" To which he answered, "*Señora*, you're here on holiday! You're not here to have problems. The problems are for us."

When we later told this story in Buenos Aires, nobody would believe it – but then Patagonia is Patagonia. As a Frenchman we had met at some point in our travels very neatly put it, "The nice thing about Patagonia is, here we're all friends. If we're meeting for the second time, why then we're *old* friends."

So we flew, as arranged, to Ushuaia, the capital of Tierra del Fuego; but our luggage didn't. Mick, seeing our bags on the tarmac of Río Gallegos airport, remarked "If I were Bernie (my brother-in-law being a notorious pessimist) I'd say that was *our* luggage," I looked out past him and said, "I am not Bernie, and that *is* our luggage!" The engines not having started yet, I rang for the stewardess and explained the situation. "No no, all luggage for this flight is on board already, the plane will just follow its schedule." So we arrived at Ushuaia minus the luggage.

There, I went straight to the man who appeared to be in charge of the airport – a good-looking young man with quite a lot of unshaven twelve o'clock shadow on his face – and explained the situation, adding "You see that stewardess over there, yes the one with all that eye make up, *may she get irredeemably fat* – she told us..." (Mick was meanwhile hiring us another car, so I was able to let fly without embarrassing my poor husband) – "*she* told us our luggage was on board that flight and as you can see it was not." "Well *Señora*, can I have a look at your tickets. I produced these, one of which had the usual bits about luggage attached. "OK" said he, "I'll telephone Río Gallegos." I heard him do so, and quoting all the relevant numbers. "Oh, so you've sent those bags to Buenos Aires, have you? I can only congratulate you. The lady who owns them is here, absolutely furious and quite right too. You will send that luggage *at once* to my office in Ushuaia." He then turned to me, saying "Well, I've done what I could. I'm afraid your bags won't be here for a day or two – I hope you and your husband can manage for a day or two on what you have in your carry-on-luggage." I said I thought we could.

He gave us the address of his office, also that of a pleasant hotel a bit inland from Ushuaia. Thence, we explored the local countryside, enjoying wilderness and wild life but occasionally wishing no one had thought of importing cuddly Old World otters, whose dam-building was messing up both woodland and small streams. I also remember a conversation with the hotel barman.

"*Señora*, is your husband English?"

"Yes, he is."

"You mean *English* English? *Real* English?"

"Yes" I repeated, now somewhat apprehensively.

"Ah, well, in that case" – extending his right hand towards Mick – "Welcome, *Señor*!"

On the third day, back to Ushuaia, to the Aerolíneas Argentinas office. Our young man was behind his desk; I asked for our luggage.

"Luggage? What luggage, *Señora*?"

Just before exploding, I noticed the look in his eye: he was having me on. Our modest bags were concealed behind his desk. I accepted them gratefully, adding "And to think there are people who don't believe Aerolíneas to be the most efficient airline in the world!"

He replied with the much stronger, local version of "*Señora*, there's no accounting for tastes."

We spent a few further days in and around Ushuaia, one of them on a visit to the *estancia* which had, so long ago, been allocated by a grateful Argentine government to the English Bridges medical-missionary family, and which still belonged to their last descendants. We got ourselves invited for the day on some pretext involving a box of chocolates from Buenos Aires; and were received, beneath the two huge shark's teeth that formed the gateway to the sea, by an old lady whom I still remember twisting a length of thick wire in strong freckled hands. She vividly recalled entering Tierra del Fuego on horseback as a little girl; now she lived here with her grandson – not present, out on *estancia* business – and his American wife, Natalie Goodall, a naturalist interested in the evolution of the whale family, cetaceans. A quite unforgettable meal beneath a canopy of vast Leviathan skeletons attached to their dining-room ceiling.

More prosaic, but memorable in its own way, was dining in Ushuaia on *centolla*, a delectable local crustacean which, for conservation reasons, is unavailable anywhere else. Altogether, Patagonia and its southern extension are not easy to forget.

North to Londres

Rather bravely, Mick and I hired another car and took ourselves off to spectacular northern Argentina, to the old northern Andean provinces of Salta and Jujuy. We visited their capital cities, and also explored some of the spectacular landscapes surrounding them.

My most vivid memory, though, of that northern journey is of our stay with the Mayor of Londres – the Spanish version of London, a town originally founded still further north during Spain's colonial era, in honour of the marriage of their King Philip II to English Mary Tudor. True, by the time this New World Londres was founded, the lady had already died; but then, news took a long time to reach distant colonies on the Pacific coast. Later, Londres was moved south, to what is now northern Argentina; and it was with the Mayor of this Londres that Bernie's brother Harry had become acquainted and whom he had advised us to visit.

The Mayor of Londres was very proud of his post and most generous in his hospitality. Speaking no English, he still took great pleasure in displaying what he called "my Tower of London" – *mi Torre de Londres* – a particularly tall water tower;

he thought this a splendid joke. He had spent some time in England courtesy of the British Council – but all that, of course, was before the Falklands War. During that war, he had had his troubles locally, but had refused to be ashamed of being Mayor of Londres.

His children were grown-up and living in Buenos Aires, as provincial people's children so often do. He himself lived with his wife and sister (or was it *her* sister?) in a big old house built around a central courtyard, rather like an African compound. All three were what in Argentina are, rather charmingly, known as "Turks", *Turcos*, by which we mean people from the Middle East – people who might be from Syria, from the Lebanon, or even (but not very often) from Turkey: all are known as Turks.

When they arrive they are usually Muslim, but this doesn't last very long. Typically, a first-generation *Turco* will start out as a "snapper-up of unconsidered trifles", hawking ribbon, buttons, press-studs and the like. But *Turcos* are very good at business: in the next generation, that man's son will have a small corner shop. Then the corner shop increases in size, and soon comes the time when the children are going to secondary school. Then, naturally, the next thing that happens is the girls marry a best friend's brother, the boys a best friend's sister – all of whom are of course good Catholics! So the "Turks" become good Catholics too, or at least their children do. So well do *Turcos* fare in Argentina that we have even had a President from among their number – the first of his family to go to University; Carlos Menem, who on the whole did more good than harm.

The Turks of Londres had not got quite that far; but they took great pride in the local *Colegio de los Turcos* – the Turks' school, a secondary school facing the central Plaza of Londres – a well-reputed one, teaching both English and French – of which all three of them had, in due turn, been head.

Tourists no longer

Meanwhile, our younger daughter Jackie, now qualified as an architect, had been, not very happily, pursuing her career in England. Part of her problem was, she told us, that a degree course in architecture tended to indoctrinate you with the need to put up state-of-the-art modern buildings. Not what came naturally to her antique-loving aesthetic. Nor were things going too well in her personal life. We reminded her that she, too, like her sister Susie, had an Aunt Margaret in New Zealand, with whom she might stay to sort herself out.

Margaret, now widowed, had been making alterations to the Northwest Corner house, and duly introduced Jackie to her architect; who promptly offered her a part-time job. She loved this and, after considerable to-ing and fro-ing, ended up in charge of a new branch of his business in Queenstown – an increasingly prosperous tourist resort where people often bought land and needed houses built on it. When, not long after that, her boss decided he'd had enough of little New Zealand and was now moving to Canada, or maybe South Africa, Jackie was stuck with a quarter of a table in a Queenstown office, unsure whether she even owned the T-square she was using – and certainly without a work permit as an independent professional. In local law, being granddaughter to Sir Harold Gillies entitled her to nothing. A good lawyer, however, helped her resolve these bureaucratic problems and she began to work successfully in Queenstown. In the course of this, she met another New Zealand lawyer – this one, Warwick Goldsmith, specialised in helping people buy Queenstown property – and the two were now, in 1992, proposing to get married.

We English Gillieses were far from the only family members attending what turned out to be a very picturesque wedding – even Trixie decided to come from Buenos Aires. New Zealand law allows marriage, under a properly appointed official, to take place wherever those concerned might wish – at their favourite restaurant or halfway down a mountain slope; Warwick had decided it would be best to marry on board the *Earnslaw*, the small steamship which was then still allowed to pollute the pure air above Lake Wakatipu, and which held some 50 people. A wonderful day was had by all, and most of us remember the hilarious moment when Mick, speaking after dinner, followed his father's example by proceeding to remove his (outer) trousers as a preliminary to presenting his new son-in-law with the polished-wood gentleman's suit hanger devised by Sir Harold, which made private undressing easier but was not popular with tailoring shops because it did not display suits to their best advantage.

One last visit

For a few years after this wedding, we went to visit Jackie and Warwick, and later also their children, quite a number of times, pausing always in Bangkok for a mid-flight rest. But then came the time when, just as we were about to depart from Bangkok Airport, Mick had a stroke. He was admirably looked after by a big Thai hospital, where I was allowed to share his private room. As soon as possible, I cabled Jackie and, when Mick began slowly to recover, she flew out to Bangkok to help me convey him to New Zealand. We were able to stay for several weeks and visit most of our surviving kin; but then decided to return to England, where Susie and Richard had already built themselves an annexe to Whitfeld so as to be able to live immediately next door to us. This return journey too we managed, but it was obvious to all concerned that this had been our last visit together to New Zealand.

Chapter 4

Visitors from Abroad

From a Mayfly Conference

After Mick stopped going to The Gambia every European summer, he felt able at last to allow himself an extra luxury: attendance at Mayfly Conferences. These took place every three years, during northern-hemisphere university long vacations, each time in a different country. Mayflies having remained, for nearly everyone, a "hobby insect", there were not vast numbers of these specialists scattered around the world (though there were, interestingly, two in China), but they did feel the need to share research and exchange ideas at regular intervals. Organising a conference is, however, an expensive business even without interpreters; so the "mayflopterists" as Mick called them, had decided to share expenses and time with the enthusiasts for the zoologically closest insects to their own, the Stoneflies or *Plecoptera.*

The first such meeting we attended took place in Czechoslovakia, then, in the early 1980s, still one country under Communist governance. Czech entomologists seemed, however, to be quite relaxed in their politics; they welcomed us to a fine big castle owned by their Faculty of Biology, standing on its own sizeable grounds at a considerable distance from Prague. Most mayflopterists had arrived with their wives, some even with small children; each couple or small family was therefore allocated their own little apartment within the converted castle, heated by a tiled wood-burning stove that, on its other side, also warmed the corridor.

We wives were not expected to sit in on the scientific meetings, but had a Ladies' Programme arranged for us, consisting essentially of visits by coach to nearby places of interest, with a guide speaking several West European languages. Mick told me, early on, to look out among my fellow-passengers for a young East German wife, Michaela Jakob, and told me why.

She and her mayflopterist husband Udo had arrived without permission from their government to join the conference, though there was no law to prevent them from taking a camping holiday in Czechoslovakia – "our Switzerland" Michaela later explained to me. So they had simply stuffed all their camping gear into their car and set off, leaving their two small daughters in the care of Udo's mother. Once arrived at the castle, they had asked the Czech organisers for permission to camp on the grounds, and for Udo to attend meetings and be allowed to buy copies of his colleagues' scientific papers; to which the Czechs had replied, more or less, "Don't be silly – you can be our guests at the castle, there's plenty of room; and *of course* Udo can attend meetings and take away all the papers he likes. As for Michaela, she can just join the Ladies' Programme and enjoy her holiday."

"But she won't know anybody," Mick pointed out to me; "and she may not speak any language other than German, and anyway she'll feel very shy. So you'd best talk to her and make friends."

This was easy: Michaela, or Michi for short, was young, pretty and charming. Initial shyness soon wore off, as she explained about Udo's and her decision to come. "Oh they'd have allowed *some* people, but Udo's never been on good terms with his bosses. He's not a Communist, you see; but he's so good at his job they don't want to sack him, just keep him under control. We've even got West German friends, and *that's* all his doing; he met them first in Peru. Before sending him there on some research job or other – it was long before we knew each other – our authorities had tried to make him promise he'd never speak to any West Germans he might meet abroad; but he'd refused, simply saying *of course* he'd talk to compatriots. So when he met this couple who spoke no Spanish – he'd taken good care to learn some – he helped them out a bit; they invited him to a few meals, and we've always kept up. We manage to meet them sometimes at the Frankfurt Book Fair, and she quite often sends me clothes."

Only towards the end of a week during which we spent many hours sitting beside each other in the Ladies' Programme coach did Michi feel able to confide in me about their future plans. I then learned that, at that time, the prosperous Federal Republic of Germany made, every few years, a large, very low-interest loan to the less well-off Democratic Republic to the east – low-interest but with non-financial strings attached. These strings consisted, essentially, of the eastern Republic granting, within the next three months, a certain number of permits for emigration westwards. And, Michi added, "if you have, like us, two children and an elderly mother you don't really want to leap over the Wall!"

She and Udo had consulted their West German friends about whether life would be better for their family in the Federal Republic; and had been told that – while the West was hardly a capitalist paradise and would not suit everyone – their friends felt that both the Jakobs were young enough and adaptable enough to make their lives anew there. So they were waiting for the next of those low-interest loans, and had meanwhile as far as possible got themselves ready to move fast when occasion arose.

The following spring, we heard from the Jakobs again, this time from a West German address. They had made the transition, successfully but with some difficulty: thus, having already sold their car and prepared to leave their flat, they were on the very last day summoned at 6 a.m. to the relevant government office, where they were deprived of their Democratic Republic nationality and told they were legally entitled to stay in that country until noon that day, after which they would be arrested for treason.

The Jakobs, however, were prepared. They had been living out of suitcases for weeks, and Udo's scientific papers, that would eventually enable him to find a job in the West, were packed up in a separate briefcase; Michi's brother stood ready with his car to drive them to the East Berlin railway station.

Once in the Federal Republic, life at once became easier; the authorities there were by then used to receiving such new aspirants to citizenship. Transition camps were prepared to receive them; their papers, including those entitling them to various state benefits, were ready within 48 hours. The religious authorities also stepped in (Udo and Michi had both by now been devout Lutherans for several years), found the whole family a currently vacant parsonage to live in and arranged schools for the girls.

Here, however, a difficulty arose: Renate, the eldest Jakob daughter, was at just the right age to move up into secondary schooling; and here in the West, just as much as in the East, some knowledge of a foreign language was required. Only, in the East that language had been Russian; here it was English, of which Renate had no notion. So might she come with Michi and stay with us for some three weeks, to learn an acceptable minimum?

We were, naturally, delighted; and a very pleasant three weeks we spent with them here at Whitfeld – though there was initially a language problem between Michi and myself relating to our different exposure to the German language, which I have mentioned in Interlude 2, on language, above. Renate, bright like both her parents, picked up English fast; after their return to Germany, she fitted quite well into the nearest secondary school. As for Michi, she found a job well before Udo did: he, sensibly enough, waited for an academic vacancy. Michi, however, had an East German qualification, half in theoretical botany and half in very practical gardening; looking like a flower herself, she was promptly snapped up by a posh flower-and-plant shop, where an excellent salary enabled the family to live quite well until Udo got the sort of job his qualifications warranted.

Whitfeld Academy?

After Michi's and Renate's stay, word seemed somehow to spread. At one point Mick and I wondered whether, below the name of our house on one of the gate-posts, we shouldn't display a small notice calling ourselves something like "Academy for Perfecting Young Ladies in the English Language". The teaching fell mostly to me, since Mick did still go to the University of Sussex on weekdays; when at home, however, he gladly welcomed them into his small study-cum-lab. The young creatures – from France and Switzerland as well as Germany – generally seemed to me to emerge from our Academy with an excellent vocabulary in entomology and cookery, but not necessarily in any other subject.

They were, indeed, nearly all girls; though at one stage we had, for several weeks, Stefan Krapf, my cousin Heino's young son; but this was quite a while after his elder sister Susanne had spent time with us. By the time Stefan came, it was because his parents had, at last, got the chance of a trip to Thailand – but where to leave their children? Fortunately, by then Richard and Susie, with their children Jessica and Andrew, were living in Uckfield, only fifteen minutes away from us; so Susanne went to them as a kind of guest-cum-baby-sitter and Stefan stayed with us. In his case, Mick's biological teaching seemed to have some effect: Stefan is now a medical doctor.

Other Visitors from Abroad

Heino and his Heidi also came several times by themselves. They had developed a yen for holidays in the west of Ireland ("the last wild country in Europe") and took in England, and Whitfeld, on their way there. We had visits, too from other members of our scattered families: from Trixie and Bernie (whom we once took on a motor trip to the west of England), Bernie's brother Harry and his wife Isabel, and also from New Zealand: John and Eileen, and more often Margaret and the Brig, who advised me knowledgeably on growing vegetables.

Margaret herself would volunteer to weed; in the course of this, she once rediscovered an old well which none of us had known about. Long before Mick and Agnes had bought Whitfeld in the 1960s, the well had been covered over with a large stone slab, and over that with a thin layer of soil – over which we had been walking for a number of years. We oldies were, naturally, unable to move the heavier covering materials: this had to await the arrival of Richard, our strong and practical son-in-law, and his (by then teenage) son Andrew, who used brute force as well as an iron lever. Later, we had a well-head built; there is still no working pump, but the depth or height of the well-water does serve to measure the degree of drought or possible flooding.

The Jakobs came again, the whole family this time; so did various former colleagues of mine, including Daniel Waissbein who was later to give me invaluable help in translating the Argentine nineteenth-century classic *A Visit to the Ranquel Indians*.

So, indeed, did my old friend from undergraduate days, Donald Nicholl – now between jobs, having resigned from his California (Santa Cruz) chair during his mother's last illness, and not yet appointed Rector of the Tantur Ecumenical Institute for Theological Research near Bethlehem. I had recently, on trips to London, begun seeing Donald again; he now asked me for a night's hospitality, having someone to see in Brighton the next morning. I had told Donald my husband was an agnostic; I had not told Mick that I considered our coming guest to be a saint. The three of us spent a pleasant evening together; religion went unmentioned, but Donald, a superb mimic, told a number of very funny dialect stories. In the morning, six-foot-six Donald scrunched himself with some difficulty into our small car, and I drove him to Lewes railway station. When I returned home, Mick said:

"Odd chap, that friend of yours."

"Oh?"

"I've never in my life felt such an unmistakable aura of sheer *goodness* coming out from anybody!"

"Oh, so you've noticed, have you?"

After which Mick and I always referred to Donald Nicholl as "St Donald" – he'd have had a fit if he'd known.

A Guest from Nigeria

My old friend Elochukwu Amucheazi, who had been teaching at the University of Nigeria since the end of the Biafran War, had asked me to be godmother to his eldest daughter Onamma. When she reached adolescence – the age when girls always seem to want pen-friends – Onamma realised she actually had a built-in one, in the shape of a godmother in England. So she began to write to me. Her letters were so amusing I decided I really had to meet their author, and invited her to come and stay a fortnight or so with "Uncle Mick" and me in Hamsey.

Her father, now a Professor, decreed this could not happen until she had, at 18, completed secondary studies; but soon after that, I was able to collect her at Heathrow. Everything amazed and delighted her, from the length of our twilights to the sheer antiquity of our churches: "You keep old things in this country – I do like that!" (She fell in love with, among other things, Gothic architecture.) And when the time came for her to go, and we couldn't change her reservations, both of us were close to weeping.

She would have liked to study world history or something similar; but her father very firmly advised a first qualification in accountancy – "It's no longer what it was like when I was a young man: I've done quite nicely, but nowadays there are historians and political scientists crawling out from behind every stone in this country. At least as an accountant you'll always be able to earn a good living." He may well have been right. In the 21st century Onamma, understandably, no longer likes to call herself "a banker", preferring the less invidious term "financial adviser" – but she does earn enough money to take the odd holiday in England and visit me here in Hamsey.

Major moves

During the second half of the 1990s, Susie and Richard, then living at Ardingly College where she was already teaching, asked our permission to get themselves an annexe built to our house, so that they could move in next door to us – permission we very gladly gave. The building took six months to complete; in 1998 were they able to move in part-time and a year later Whitfeld became their full-time home. We decided to celebrate the event, together with several family anniversaries, with a big party in the garden. Jackie came for that, with her children; she told me then how tired her father was looking.

And indeed, in December that same year, Mick suffered another stroke. This time he didn't recover as he had done in Bangkok, but died a few days later in hospital. Susie, her daughter Jessica and I were able to be with him; poor Jackie was still on her way to say goodbye, and Susie had the unenviable task of meeting her sister's plane and telling her she was already too late.

One of the people I rang with the sad news was Heino in Germany. He said very little on the phone, but rang back an hour later to ask my permission to attend the funeral. I told him, naturally, that his presence would be a great comfort to me. Yes, but – it turned out that in order to get a cheap ticket he would have to stay in the UK for five nights. Could he possibly stay here?

Thus it came about that, after funeral and wake – during both of which my cousin was the greatest possible help – he and I were, for the first time in our lives, alone together – without uncles, aunts, spouses, children... And then, out of a clear blue sky –

"My father was a Nazi, you know."

"Yes, Heino. I did know."

"And I've had to live with that.... It hasn't been easy."

We spoke a little about it that night; but not until a few years later did Heino really get it off his chest. He had by that time joined a creative-writing course – unnecessarily I thought, as Heino had always written very well; but Heidi was spending quite a lot of time singing in choirs and he felt the need for a semi-professional retirement occupation of his own.

The course seems to have consisted of three terms. During the first, members were (I suppose) taught to write grammatical German; during the second, a short story for which they were prescribed a first sentence and a fixed number of words. The third and most difficult demanded a non-fiction piece, and Heino used it to write up his father, my uncle Fred.

He later sent me the piece. The first sentence read "The man was very short." There followed a brief, more or less reasoned, biography, ending in that death in a Russian labour camp. The final paragraph consisted of a single explanatory sentence:

"I am his son."

Chapter 5
Working from Hamsey

Witchcraft Abridged

Having decided, when I first moved to Hamsey, against another university job that might leave me without enough time or energy for my new duties, I quite soon found, however, other kinds of academic work – more easily done from home – coming my way. One of the first such tasks was abridging Evans-Pritchard's *Witchcraft, Oracles and Magic among the Azande* for the Oxford University Press.

E-P had first published this work in 1937 – a time when 550-page monographs were still entirely acceptable to the Press. The book turned out to be of absolutely central importance; it became, indeed, impossible to write, not merely about magic or witchcraft, but about beliefs concerning causation, the expression of social tensions in mystical idiom, or even the general sociology of knowledge, without reference to it. But by the early seventies, this weighty tome had priced itself out of the market; the OUP wanted to re-publish it in paperback, but its sheer size made this materially impossible. It would have to be abridged.

E-P, however, was reluctant; a number of possible abridgers had been suggested, but he wanted nothing to do with any of them. Until my name was mentioned, and he decreed that "if Eva did it, it would be all right."

A tremendous honour for me; a tremendous responsibility also, and, I realised, a job of some urgency: E-P was almost certainly not long for this world, and to me it seemed vital that he should be able to see and (if possible) approve of what I had done. So I set to work with a will.

I soon found, however, that the original work, though long, was carefully structured: I must not impede its general line of argument. Moreover, I could no more bear to cut into E-P's admirably limpid prose than into living flesh. So what to do? Only one possible answer: leave out nearly all the many case histories with which the author illustrates his theory! An evil still, but (I thought) the lesser one.

I did manage to finish my task in time to take a complete typescript to E-P; whom I found already lying on his bed, though still perfectly alert mentally. "Well, Teds, here it is!"– laying it on the bed beside him.

He leafed it over absent-mindedly. "Oh Eva, I'm sure it's perfectly all right... Now, what I wanted to tell you is, the real reason why I like Tennyson's poetry so much is...." And he was off again on his current favourite reading. This was the last time I ever saw him.

Returning home, I now had an Introduction to write; after which the OUP published the desired paperback. This, now at a price most students can afford, has sold amazingly, both in the original English and in its many foreign translations: the Press quite recently sent me two complimentary copies of my abridged *Witchcraft* in what was described as "simplified Chinese"; and every year I get a welcome contribution to my income from what still seems to be an indispensable read for anyone doing anthropology.

Interpreting Argentine Indians

The worst of trips to New Zealand remained those long flights to get there. To alleviate the boredom, I used to save up unread copies of the *Times Literary Supplement*; and on one such journey, in 1980, read a longish article by Malcolm Deas, in praise of a book I had known about all my life, ever since it had formed part of the Argentine literature curriculum which I had not bothered much with while studying for those secondary exams in Buenos Aires. (I was to remember later that my father had said then, "That's a very good book; you really should translate it into English sometime!" and that I had shied away from the very thought of so long and boring a task.)

Malcolm Deas appeared to agree with my father. His article reminded me that *Una Excursión a los Indios Ranqueles*, written in 1870, narrated a visit paid that year to the Ranquel Indians of the book's title, by one Lucio Victorio Mansilla, who had been a nephew of the Argentine dictator of a slightly earlier period, Juan Manuel de Rosas. This Mansilla sounded an interesting character in his own right, and the (translated) quotes from the book with which Deas had larded his article were also enticing – giving the impression almost of passages from an early work of South American ethnography.

I seldom had much to do during these New Zealand visits; so I actually wrote to Deas, c/o the TLS, saying how much I'd enjoyed his article and asking whether he was engaged in translating a book he clearly knew and loved so well. Eventually, he answered: no, he was not translating "the Ranqueles", but he did wish somebody would.

This really made me think. Here was I, an out-of-work antropologist, totally bilingual in English and Spanish, with considerable experience in interpreting between these languages; moreover, a middle-aged woman of leisure. If not I, then who? Once back in England, I shared these concerns with my friend Daniel Waissbein, at that time living in Oxford.

Daniel and I had met some years earlier in an interpreting booth. Not much work at that conference, thus plenty of time to get to know each other. He, very young at the time, had come to England with his new wife for three weeks; they liked it so much, he told me, that they stayed. I found him amusing: on the one hand, a recognizably typical Buenos Aires Jewish intellectual, but on the other somebody who could say,

"My mother would never let me go to school on days when there was a revolution – so I never did have much education!" This was a barefaced lie (he had just emerged from the Sorbonne, where he had met his Portuguese wife); but it amused me sufficiently to make me decide I wouldn't mind meeting this young man again.

By now in Oxford, he was supposed to be working for a D.Phil. (which he has never completed) under the supervision of Robert Pring-Mill, who had long ago married my college friend Brigitte Heinsheimer. And now, being informed of my thoughts about the Ranqueles, said he knew Malcolm Deas and would be glad to invite us to dinner together whenever I was next in Oxford.

Deas, although very encouraging about my project itself, advised me not to put pen to paper until I had a publisher for the translation; and volunteered to find me one. Then, once I was back in Hamsey, the weeks passed endlessly. Nothing from Malcolm Deas, despite a few timid telephonic reminders. I was also phoning Daniel, who finally said: "Look, if you're going to wait for Deas to do something, make sure you're sitting comfortably. It's not a short book; it will take you a long time to translate it properly. If you really intend to do this, then start now! And we'll start looking seriously for publishers when you're at least a third of the way through. Meanwhile, I'll help you in any way I can."

And, bless the man, he meant it.

From then on, I sent Daniel every page I wrote, and he returned them heavily scored with stern blue pencilled comments, including things like "Don't try to improve on your author's style" and "You're getting tired at this point – clearly you're at the end of your half-hour" – reminding me that, in simultaneous interpreting, one is never supposed to work for longer than half an hour at a time.

Although we had met in an interpreting booth, Daniel is very much a translator by temperament – a perfectionist, somebody quite prepared to work slowly to get it absolutely right; the perfect complement to my own rapid and somewhat impressionistic style. Between us, we have, I think, managed to produce quite a good English version of *Una Excursión a los Indios Ranqueles.*

Both of us, however, were puzzled by many aspects of the book – often matters of specialised or out-of-date vocabulary. Initially, I began to consult Harry Ingham, the brother of my own brother-in-law Bernie, who knows the interior of the country and many of its customs and sayings; but when I came to the end of Harry's knowledge, he passed me on to his lawyer and friend, Martín Villagrán San Millán – "from a good provincial family" explained Harry: "he'll know these things."

Martín did indeed "know these things"; he helped out with the military ranks of the period, as well as the meaning of various games of chance still played in the countryside. (Later, I would turn to him for assistance with the detailed endnotes that would be required for the full edition.)

There was still, of course, the matter of finding a publisher. Clearly, this would need to be an academic one – it was increasingly obvious that the book would need copious notes. My preference would have been for the OUP; after that, I tried Cambridge, then London. None of these publishers had ever so much as heard of Mansilla, and they were certainly not going to bother reading his book. Lesser university presses, I suspected, would be even less interested. I would have to look further afield.

My old friend from Oxford, Romy Davidson, was by now living in Cambridge, where she worked for the CUP. When I told her my troubles, she offered to introduce me to David Lehmann, at that time heading the Cambridge Centre for Latin American Studies. This sounded hopeful; so to Cambridge I went, clutching beneath my arm the edition I was using as my text. Mansilla's classic has never been out of print in Spanish; at that time, a very scholarly new edition had just been brought out in Venezuela by one Saul Sosnowski.

I showed this to David Lehmann, who acknowledged sadly that he'd never heard of Mansilla either. But, said he, why didn't I ask Saul Sosnowski for help?

"Why on earth would Sosnowski want to help me?" I wondered. "He's never heard of me."

"I can think of three reasons," replied David. "One, he's Argentine too, which might put him on your side. Two, he now lives in America and is much involved in academic publishing there, so he should know his way around. Three, I happen to have his address, which I should be delighted to give you."

Sosnowski wrote a very kind letter back, suggesting three academic publishers I might like to write to, and generously allowing me to mention his name. Two never replied; the third, a woman Professor of Modern Languages from California, eventually did, apologising for having been absent on a sabbatical. (Years later, I found out she was in fact Argentine, and had spent that sabbatical in Buenos Aires.) She suggested I should write to the University of Nebraska Press, which she believed might have an interest in my translation.

She was right. At Nebraska, improbably, they had not only heard of *Una Excursión a los Indios Ranqueles*, they actually wanted to publish an English-language edition. Not only that, but they had actually commissioned one; and, best of all, they had rejected it on grounds of insufficient quality! Clearly, these were the people I wanted to work for; I could only hope my own translation would pass muster.

As publishers will, they asked me initially for a couple of sample chapters and an Introduction. This I had seen coming; and had, indeed, already very nearly written one, in the form of a lecture I had been invited to give in Lewes, to which I had given the title "The Colonel and the Indians"; in this, I had enjoyed tracing the much-travelled life of my author, who, by 1870, was indeed a colonel, serving out a year or so on the frontier of Indian country by way of a punishment station. This lecture, slightly adapted, I sent to Nebraska with my sample chapters.

They in turn consulted two peer reviewers, whose opinions they passed on to me. One, a Professor whose name I can't remember, clearly didn't think much of the whole idea of publishing Mansilla anyway; the other was no less than Sosnowski himself.

Sosnowski approved of my translation, but about my attempted introduction wrote that, while what I had said was well enough as far as it went, if we were going to introduce this author to a 20th century English-speaking readership, we would need to place him, in both space and time. "This need not" he added "take her more than a few pages."

I replied that while I entirely agreed with Dr Sosnowski about the need for a much wider historical introduction, and would be happy to research and write it, this would take me considerably more than a few pages. Nebraska told me to go ahead.

Thus I embarked on what was to be a condensed history of the native populations of Argentina, from the beginning of the Spanish Viceroyalty of the Rio de la Plata in 1776 to 1870, when Mansilla paid his visit to the confederation of the Ranqueles and wrote it up, serially, in the main weekly newspaper of the period. Some of the information I acquired in the Taylorian library at Oxford; much more came from a book about "our Indian countrymen" then just published in Buenos Aires, which I asked my family there to find for me.

The expanded Introduction done and approved, I returned to the translation itself; and here, soon found I had to ask my sister in Buenos Aires for another book – this time, a scientific one on local zoology and botany. Daniel Ross, my editor at Nebraska, was (not unreasonably) objecting to my having left too many words of my translation in the original Spanish. I agreed it was a translator's business to translate, but pointed out that Mansilla's terms for the local fauna and flora were, nearly always, completely inaccurate: the first Spaniards had, like the first Englishmen further north, named what they found in the new country after what it most reminded them of in their native one, and an *algarrobo* was no more like a Mediterranean carob tree than an American robin was like an English one. I therefore proposed to keep Mansilla's terms in the text, but referring each, on its first appearance, to an endnote giving its scientific identity. Ross agreed to this, and in return I promised to translate all terms relating to human identities and man-made artefacts.

A promise I promptly had to break. A word pair that occurred frequently, generally in important contexts, was *compadre/comadre* – literally, "co-father/co-mother". This refers to the relationship between a child's biological parents and its godparents – a relationship of immense importance in Mansilla's day, particularly within the framework of Indian-Hispanic contacts. Some Indians were beginning to convert to Christianity, and one motive, undoubtedly, was to secure for one's children a powerful godfather, and for oneself a powerful *compadre*, who might be expected to feel obliged to help his co-parent in situations of difficulty. Clearly, *compadre* and *comadre* would have to stay in the original, though here too their first appearance would require an explanatory endnote.

To this, Nebraska readily agreed. A thornier problem was the translation of Mansilla's term *lenguaraz*, which he uses for the person attached to a Ranquel "delegation or embassy" to himself in his capacity as frontier commander, in order to render the greetings, questions and requests, of the Indian plenipotentiary. Mansilla notes that this functionary's work "is arduous, even in the most insignificant parley. It requires an excellent memory, outstanding vocal chords, and a great deal of calm and patience." I had been pleased to find, in Rattray's *Ashanti*, a description of an exactly similar functionary, whom Rattray calls the chief's "linguist"; and had therefore used that term to render *lenguaraz*. But when Nebraska's professional readers objected to "linguist", as being a term referring to modern knowledge or study of languages, and suggested "interpreter" for *lenguaraz*, I had to point out that, elsewhere in the book, Mansilla explicitly contrasts the skills of a *lenguaraz* with the ignorance of a mere interpreter, *intérprete*. I had rendered the latter term (however reluctantly with regard to my own long-standing profession!) as "interpreter"; and therefore had to point out to my editors that "interpreter" could not be used for *lenguaraz*. I wrote that I was aware the choice was between two evils, but considered that it was up to me, the translator, to make that choice. This, they accepted.

Then there was the question of style. Mansilla wrote extremely well, in a literate yet informal idiom. I did not feel I could translate his prose into slangily modern English; but my text did have to be easily accessible to 20th century readers. I decided a diction and syntax from his own late 19th century would be my best bet. Fennimore Cooper, surely, had also written about Indians? But, I very soon found out, not nearly as well as my Mansilla! I next gave myself a revision course on the writings of Robert Louis Stevenson, and found here exactly what I needed – a writer, moreover, who also did equally well on action and reflection. So RLS-style it had to be.

The next problem would be completing the endnotes. These would have to be of two kinds. Mansilla, a well-read man, was quite fond of showing off his learning: his text is larded with quotes, not merely from Latin, but also from the literatures of England, France, Italy... quite aside from the fashionable Parisian cabaret songs of his youth. (Thank God, I would occasionally mutter to myself, he never learned German or Russian.) I asked Daniel Ross what to do about all these literary references, adding tactfully that while everyone knew who Shakespeare was, and quite a few people had heard of Byron, we would not here in Britain expect Spanish-culture students to know about Madame de Stäel or *The Imitation of Christ.* Notes on everybody, Ross requested – literary or historical: "We want this to be the Mansilla in English for all time."

This was not in fact too difficult in the literary sphere: most of the authors cited appear, complete with dates, in the old *Nouveau Petit Larousse Illustré* of my schooldays; and the rest I could find somewhere in the twenty volumes of that admirable lexicographer's unabridged dictionary in Oxford's Bodleian.

Matters were far more difficult with Mansilla's many topical references to persons or events of his own day. His is a very political book; some of these references are to important matters of a period in Argentine history about which I had long forgotten what little I ever knew. Here, once again, I turned to Martín Villagrán. Martín, by profession a lawyer, is by vocation an historian, specialising in Argentine military history; but, even though my request lay a little outside his sphere, he thenceforth spent hours and days in the specialised libraries of Buenos Aires, sending me photocopies of anything he found that could be even remotely relevant! A debt of gratitude I can never hope to repay, even though his wife rang me, halfway through the process, to *thank* me for having given Martín this absorbing new hobby which (she said) made him so much easier to live with!

And then, just when I thought the worst was over, Nebraska University Press started sending me page-proofs! I remembered from past experience the near-impossibility of perfect proof reading; and tried to wangle out of it by asking them whether they didn't have their own professional proof-readers? "You best know your own work," replied Daniel Ross austerely; and I had to admit he was right. All this godfathering throughout Mansilla's narrative, just like biological fathering, produced recurring names -- often of both first name and surname. It meant there could be as many as three people of the same name on a single page, and only I was in a position to know which was which.

For the few maps required, I did manage to get Nebraska to employ professionals. But it was clearly my job to pick illustrations, including a frontispiece portrait of Mansilla himself at approximately the right age. He looked very handsome; one could quite see how my husband had, over the years, often jestingly accused me of being in love with my Argentine colonel – so different, indeed, from one's usual notion of men in that category. But then, this was one subject on which I disagreed with my hero: he thought of himself as a professional soldier, whereas I see him more as a very high class journalist, morphing into an anthropologist *avant la léttre*: he had really studied his Ranquel Indians, even including a somewhat simplistic but rational attempt at analysing their language.

My first idea for this translation had come, I think, in 1970; it was eventually published, with the title *A Visit to the Ranquel Indians*, in 1997. This publication, unlike that of the abridged *Witchcraft, Oracles and Magic among the Azande*, has never earned me much in royalties, partly because the University of Texas brought out, at much the same time, the translation Nebraska had so long ago rejected ("We must hope" wrote Daniel Ross piously "with some improvements"). It has, however, brought me a number of new friends, as over the years I discovered that Daniel Waissbein and I were far from alone in our enthusiasm for Mansilla.

Prominent among these is María Rosa Lojo, an Argentine novelist who, while I was still halfway through my translation, had published a book my sister Trixie gave me that Christmas: *La pasión de los nómades* (The Passion of Nomads) in which she brings Lucio Victorio Mansilla back to life in the 20th century and has him meet, among others, many of the characters who people his *Visit to the Ranqueles.* I managed to get in touch, initially on the telephone; we became firm friends, and María Rosa organised several book-launches in the course of my 1998 visit to Buenos Aires.

The largest of these, at one of that city's many newish universities, was attended, not only by women who had last met me in primary school (in our "Great Village" rumours spread fast) but by a Ranquel woman who appeared nowadays to be the main spokesperson of her people. She too had been first approached by me on the telephone (she lived in a Buenos Aires working-class suburb). I had invited her to this launch, and she had answered: "Yes! Some of us think we should never talk to the *winca* (white people) who've stolen our land, but I don't agree. I'll come."

And there she was, clad from top to toe in Ranquel costume of her own making, from spinning and dyeing the vegetable fibres on upwards (she earned her living teaching such skills), her greying hair in a long thick braid down her back. It was pretty to see the flower of the Buenos Aires intellectual élite queuing up for the honour of shaking her hand; neither tall nor beautiful, she received them like a queen. Meanwhile her husband, a Ranquel in ordinary Western working-man's clothes, was thanking me for having done this translation. "You've done a great thing for us, *Señora*, though you may not know it – because, now that this book about us exists in English, people will take a lot more notice of us, and of our claims for our own land and language!" And, knowing the foreign-languages snobbery of my countrymen, he may well have been right.

Also in the audience was Daniel Waissbein, who had managed to engineer a filial visit of his own so as to coincide with these events. Beside him sat a young man, clearly, at least in part, of Indian origin; Daniel, ever curious, asked the boy his name. "Alejandro Linconao" – lineally descended from one of the Ranquel characters in Mansilla's book! The lad had a minor clerical job at this university, had seen a poster up about the launch, and thought it sounded interesting. "But come and meet the translator!" "O Sir; you *know* her?" – and up on stage they both came.

But neither these brief moments of glory (there were a few in England too) nor even my new Mansilla-fan friends quite suffice to explain the satisfaction I still feel at having done this job. Perhaps Mick was right and I was a little in love with "my Colonel"? But not just with his good looks – perhaps even more because he remains, as far as I know, the only white man in the Americas, north or south, to have written and published, in the year 1870, that he felt shame at what his society was doing to the native inhabitants of the land.

Editing a Mayfly

Not long before Mick's death he had, at all our requests, begun writing an autobiography. He had even found a title for it: "Mayfly on the Stream of Time" – a quotation from Eric Linklater's novel *Magnus Merriman*, which I had not been aware he'd ever read. He had completed his narrative, and been in contact with a small firm called The Better Book Company Ltd., which specialised in helping people to self-publish their writings. Taking over the role of publisher for this project, I decided to call myself "Messuage Books", in memory of our long-ago correspondence with our solicitor about Mick leaving me "a messuage" in his Will.

What he had also left me was a thick pile of typescript; and it was now my job to edit this, to choose illustrations, create an index and (with the help of friends) to proof-read. Friends also added two separate bibliographies of Mick's writings, one containing his publications on mosquitoes, the other those on mayflies.

As he was working, Mick and I often argued about this autobiography of his, he maintaining that it could only ever be of interest to his family and close friends, I arguing it would interest a considerably wider public. Here, I turn out to have been right: I have since sold this book – which contains a good deal about both mosquitoes and mayflies, all in Mick's relaxed, readable style – to quite a number of perfect strangers on several different continents.

Quest for an Ancestor

In the year 2000, a few months after Mick's death in December of the previous year, I realised that the Association of Social Anthropologists, of which I was still a lifetime member, was holding its next Conference at the University of Sussex. I had not gone to ASA meetings for several years, but felt that, this one being so to speak in my own back yard, it would be positively rude not to attend; also, that this would be a pleasant opportunity to catch up with old friends.

One of these old friends was Wendy James, who had been a fellow-student during those 1962-1964 post-graduate years in Oxford. Wendy had, in the intervening years, made a huge career in anthropology; it now emerged that she would be co-convening the next ASA Conference, and that she intended this to take place at Arusha in Tanzania. Before becoming an anthropologist, she had once taught at a girls' secondary school on the nearby slopes of Kilimanjaro. Wendy wanted this

Conference to include scholars based in African universities and museums, and thought it should be focused on both anthropology and history. E-P, of course, had brought us up to believe these were closely related disciplines. She strongly felt the concept of history should include oral traditions, which many African scholars might not have learnt to regard as proper, i.e. written, history; the dread word "history" would therefore have to be severely qualified in the official title, which became "Time and Society: Perspectives from Anthropology and History".

All this gave me an idea! I had, after all, a perfectly genuine oral tradition of my own, in my father's tales about our collateral ancestor the missionary and linguist Johann Ludwig Krapf – who had, moreover, in the 1840s, done his stuff in just that part of East Africa. Might I perhaps produce a paper on him?

Wendy already knew of the existence of this ancestral Krapf. And over the years, even before starting on the anthropology Diploma in 1962, I had found out a little more about him – including his astonishing facial resemblance, in a portrait, to my father – and had, indeed, been rather inclined to brag at Oxford about this connection. And – before marrying Mick and acquiring a new, pronounceable, spellable surname, I had used the hyphenated form Krapf-Askari as my professional signature. After all, thought I, if I was so fortunate as to have a maiden name celebrated in Africanist studies, why waste it?

Wendy received my proposal for a Krapf paper with enthusiasm, and encouraged me to go ahead. I was enormously helped with this when her husband, the historian Douglas Johnson, put me in touch with one Clemens Guetl in Vienna, who was actually in the process of writing a book about this ancestor of mine. Guetl, a young Tyrolese, had become interested in Krapf because he had an aunt who was a missionary nun in Kenya. He very kindly sent me large sections of his almost completed manuscript; these, and the ensuing correspondence, were enormously useful to me in composing my paper.

A few years earlier, I had managed to buy a first edition of Krapf's *Suahili-English Dictionary*, and had been told that it had still been regarded as authoritative on the Swahili language in the 1950s; moreover, a friend had once sent me another first edition: the same author's *Elements of the Kisuahili Language*. I was now able to acquire facsimile editions of both the German and the English versions of his *Travels, Researches and Missionary Labours*, each text actually written by the man himself (the English version rather shorter), further displaying his truly phenomenal gift for languages. At the CMS archives in London, I was also able to see the original letter of 1837 in which Krapf, already an ordained Lutheran clergyman, had offered his services to the English Church Missionary Society – a letter he was already then able to write in very nearly perfect English.

Johann Ludwig Krapf had been born in 1810, to a farming family in Württemberg, at that time – before the unification of Germany – a small largely Protestant kingdom (only recently elevated from the status of duchy) sandwiched between two much larger Roman Catholic ones. This made for a zealous Protestantism, influenced moreover by a more recent religious movement, Pietism, which contained strong millenarian expectations: the world would quite soon end, so it behoved good Christians to save as many souls as possible before that came to pass.

From his autobiographical writings, we know that the boy Krapf had pored over a world atlas his father had bought him, and also over an odd volume of Bruce's *Travels*, lent him by a local bookseller. He was fascinated by the vast expanses of East Africa left almost bare of place-names – could there be a desert there, inhabited by hyenas? He wanted to grow up to be a ship's captain and explore these unknown lands; alas, his father could not afford to buy him a ship. Perhaps he could become a missionary?

Much of this I had already gathered from stories my own father told, in our San Miguel *quinta* during my teens. More puzzling was the fact that a German Lutheran should have been employed as a missionary by the English Church Missionary Society. True, the Missionary Seminary at Basle, where Krapf had trained, had links both with his native Württemberg and with the CMS in England. More concretely, the CMS, founded in 1799 during a period of Evangelical revival, had for its first fifty years considerable trouble recruiting British missionaries: its Low Church aims and methods were suspect to many Anglicans, including originally all bishops. Therefore, during this period the Society recruited quite a few missionaries from continental Europe; these had to be Protestant, but not necessarily Anglican. Krapf was one of these.

Initially, he was sent to join the Abyssinian (Ethiopian) mission. The languages, Aethiopic (ie., Ge'ez) and Amharic, he had already mastered; but the ill-judged Abyssinian mission was not a success. Ethiopia had long been a largely Christian country; a French Catholic Franciscan mission, already there, was attracting some converts to its own different brand of Christianity; so was another monotheistic religion, Islam. By 1843, Krapf (now married to Rosine, "a maiden lady of Basel") was paying his respects to the Sultan of Zanzibar and learning Swahili from a local teacher, in preparation for establishing a settled mission on the East African mainland – meanwhile embarking on a translation into Swahili of the First Book of Moses.

By July 1844, however, Krapf, his wife and the baby daughter she had just borne all caught malaria; only Krapf himself survived. Rosine and the child were buried "opposite to Mombaz on the main-land"; Krapf later wrote to the CMS Committee that they should "see in her grave the pledge and token of the possession of East Africa for Christ." In August, he himself made his first sortie to Rabai Mpia, a mainland settlement of the Wanyika, a people with no clear centres of political authority but subject to some control by Arabs and coastal Swahili. Here Krapf, now joined by another Württemberg CMS missionary, Rebmann, began to set up a permanent mission.

The Wanyika were friendly but, their missionaries soon found, had no proper sense of sin, and could not see why they should give up their familiar customs for incomprehensible European ones. Krapf and Rebmann, hoping for better success in the interior, began to plan a chain of missions starting at Rabai and stretching across all equatorial Africa to the west coast. Thus began their journeys further into the continent, where all previous European attempts at exploration had failed. They travelled in turns, one always remaining at Rabai.

Rebmann went first, and it was he who first discerned, on 11 May 1848, the snows of Kilimanjaro. My father had attributed this momentous discovery to our own ancestor; but Krapf did not travel beyond Rabai until the second half of the same year. Then, in 1849, it was Rebmann's turn again.

Krapf meanwhile was having to care for two further missionaries who had promptly succumbed to malaria. Just after noting in his journal that their arrival made his burden heavier rather than lighter, he adds quite as a matter of course "It seems to me necessary, for the sake of future missionaries, that I must learn the Kikamba, Kiteita, Jagga and Kisambara languages," to which he then applied himself.

As a missionary, Krapf was never a great success – his one convert, "the cripple Mringe", did not live long. However, snow-capped Mount Kenya became an explorer's prize; on 3 December 1849, he did see "the Kegnia most distinctly... an enormous mountain... covered with a white substance". Sadly, neither his nor Rebmann's geographical discoveries earned either man the fame they deserved.

Krapf's real and enduring legacy was in linguistic scholarship. He learned – in addition to the Aethiopic and Amharic of his earlier days – some ten African languages, most of them previously unknown to the West. (It is difficult to be certain of the exact number, since this depends on different classifications of language and dialect.) Of these, only Swahili was already a written language; but it had previously used Arabic characters.

In the course of his missionary years and later, he produced in all some 25 linguistic works – translations, grammars, dictionaries and vocabularies, including my "Suahili grammar and a comparative vocabulary of six East African languages". It is in these works that he first advances the theory that Swahili is one of "a family of languages, ramified and scattered all over South Africa". He initially called this family "Hamitic", later "Nilotic", later still "Orphno-Hamitic"; we know it as "Bantu".

Krapf's scholarship was certainly, as he intended, of practical use to both himself and the missionaries that were to follow him into various parts of Africa; but he also opened up the field of language studies in a totally new way. It fed, too, into the nascent discipline of ethnography, which increasingly used language as a framework for the classification of peoples; indeed, Krapf himself attempted to match his observation of linguistic affinities and contrasts to different physical types.

The bulk of this work was done in a very few years – essentially the late 1840s. In the spring of 1850 Krapf travelled to Europe, partly for health reasons and partly to advance with the CMS Committee his scheme for that chain of missions across Africa. After brief visits to Basle and Württemberg, he reached London in June. Here, in addition to missionary business, he attempted to defend, to armchair geographers at the Royal Geographical Society, his and Rebmann's sightings of equatorial snow. Moreover, both his linguistic labours and his grand missionary scheme had also attracted the attention of the Prince Consort, who expressed great interest in his plans.

A very little later in Germany, where he was overseeing the printing of some of his linguistic writings, he was introduced to the (by then 84-year-old) naturalist and explorer Wilhelm von Humboldt. Humboldt, after close questioning, accepted the snow story and indeed incorporated equatorial snows into his own ongoing great work on the Cosmos. Krapf was also asked to dinner by the King of Prussia, Frederick William IV, who at parting conferred upon his visitor the coveted order *Pour le mérite.*

Krapf returned several times to Africa; but that great chain of missions was never built. One final journey in 1867 to the continent of his boyhood dreams had him acting as interpreter to Sir Robert Napier's military expedition against the Ethiopian King Theodore. But his health was no longer up to it, and he was forced to return to Germany, where he eventually died by his own bedside on 26th November, 1881.

Beside the grave of Krapf's wife and daughter "opposite Mombaz on the main-land", there now stands a tall white obelisk, with commemorative inscriptions in English and German. The English text describes Krapf as a man of God who died on his knees in prayer; the German one hails him as the father of African studies, who opened up languages and cultures to scholarship. Both are perfectly true.

More than enough material here for a conference paper, which I duly wrote. Having, by an oversight, missed the plane on which I was supposed to join my ASA colleagues, I was rescued by Wendy from a later flight and was thus able to present my work in Arusha on my 73rd birthday. I took good care to let the audience know this, hoping it might deflect any adverse criticism; and indeed cannot remember that there was any, but only that, by a happy coincidence, that very evening was the Conference party, so that I was, on that birthday, danced off my feet...

Then, after a blissful few days in Zanzibar, I returned home to find young Clemens Guetl wanted me to come to Vienna for the launching of his Krapf book, now just published. Highly honoured, I demurred (quite ineffectively) at the idea of my trip and hotel expenses being paid by the Vienna Institute of African Studies; gave in – and only then realised that I would presumably have to speak in German.

Fortunately, I had already invited my Krapf cousin Heino to this Krapf occasion in Vienna. A duty visit to his wife's old mother made it impossible for Heino to visit Vienna on just those dates, but he had suggested that I pay a visit to him and

Heidi in Grünstadt on my way. So, having attempted to write a suitable talk in German, I was able to ask Heino to correct it, which he kindly and efficiently did. He also saw me on my train to Vienna and emailed Clemens my time of arrival; so that when the train did stop there I saw a large panel bearing my name (as "Doktor Krapf Gillies") – and carrying it was a young man who thereupon devoted himself to my welfare for the few days I spent in Vienna, only leaving me, at my own request, one evening to visit my childhood friend Iris, now divorced from the pianist Alfred Brendel, but still bearing his name and living in the flat they had shared.

And – come the launching of Clemens's book – I found nobody wanted me to give my little talk in German. I suppose English was perceived as more international? But then, it was also the language of the other speaker, an Englishman resident in Basel and in charge of its holdings of Krapf papers. A man of great distinction, but a man; so he did not get, as I did at the end of the meeting, an armful of flowers so huge that my little hotel had no vase large enough and I had to make do with a bucket.... Clearly, the Viennese still had their own views on how to treat a lady.

I have never been back to Vienna since, and wish now that I had spent a day or so ringing up the several pages of Krapfs I found in the telephone directory. At the time, it just seemed too big a job to undertake.

Third Age Teaching

The University of the Third Age (an idea which I believe originated in France) started up in Lewes sometime in the mid-1970s. Lewes was, and remains, an excellent centre for this notionally national but in fact extremely local, academic skill-swap between older people. While not actually a university town, it is close to the Universities of Sussex and Brighton, and also has a number of residents retired from work in other institutions of higher education throughout the country. When we started, it was with only two courses, one in Philosophy and my own in Social Anthropology.

It was wonderful being able to teach again – something I had missed rather more than I had my own research. And, I now discovered, it was even better teaching adults. I had something over a dozen students, with quite varying degrees of intelligence, and also of previous education; but what they had in common was a genuine desire to learn. Nobody was there because they had an exam to pass, or a career to further – they just wanted to know something about anthropology.

Their enthusiasm helped when I found we were soon to depart for The Gambia and that I was running out of time to complete the syllabus I had dreamt up. I asked rather timidly whether, since I'd have to stop soon, they would mind the course stretching on for a further year or part thereof? They were absolutely delighted with the idea; and however abstract I got during that two-year course, I never lost a single student.

Indeed, a couple of years later – Lewes U3A activities having meanwhile increased exponentially – I was asked to teach a further short course. Feeling the anthropology I had originally taught had already then been rather old-fashioned, I selected as my new topic "Anthropology Revisited"; sparing, as I have noted already, no sympathy for Margaret Mead in the face of Freeman's revisit to her islands and subsequent devastating criticism of her findings.

Later still, I was asked to run a five-session seminar on some anthropology-related topic of my choice. So, partly on the principle of trying to teach something I knew very little about, I chose as my topic Comparative Religion.

Five sessions, which I knew would be attended by all my former students and quite possibly a few new ones. We would need a larger room, and as for speakers? The first session should, I thought, be on paganism, and that paper I would present myself: I probably knew more about paganism than any other local speaker – not just about Greco-Roman and Nordic, but also about many little local paganisms all over the world. And I should also, I thought, chair a final pulling-it-all-together session. That left three in the middle for world religions.

For these, I decided to try out my heresy theory on the subject: namely that there are just two truly ancient world religions (Confucianism, it had long been agreed, does not count): Hinduism and Judaism. The other important ones – Buddhism, Christianity and Islam – are "heresies" on these two: what I called in my mind "Yes, but" religions. So we could devote one session to Hinduism and Buddhism, and the other two to Judaism and its two "heresies", Christianity and Islam.

Hinduism and Buddhism, clearly, belonged together. On Hinduism it was, at least in theory, easy enough to find a speaker: David Pocock, once lecturer in Indian Anthropology at the Oxford Institute, now lived more or less locally. Greatly daring, I wrote to him: would he consider giving half-an-hour's very generalised overview of Hinduism for a U3A seminar? He answered by telephone: "Eva: what you have asked me to do is *completely impossible*. I'll do it!"

A Buddhist speaker was rather more difficult; in the end I had to ask a nice little English girl from Brighton, a recent convert to Buddhism. Hearing David, she immediately realised she was well out of her depth, but kept up her end valiantly. The meeting ended with questions from the audience, and afterwards David Pocock rang me up again, this time to tell me he had never had such intelligent questions from any lay audience. I felt truly proud of my U3A students, and told them so.

Now came Judaism and its heresies, Christianity and Islam. Here, chronological order – i.e. Christianity before Islam – would avoid the possible embarrassment of a Rabbi and an Imam in the same room; I decided therefore to divide Christianity into two parts, pre- and post-Reformation.

A Rabbi was not hard to find; one need look no further than Hove; and, to speak about pre-reformation Christianity, somebody recommended a learned Anglican cleric, from Brighton. This turned out to be an excellent arrangement: the two were good friends and had already spoken together several times on local radio programmes.

How Jewish am I?

At the coffee break – remembering my not very successful efforts, during a trip to Israel a little earlier, to learn more about my own Jewish roots – I asked the rabbi whether I was correct in supposing that, having had a Jewish mother, I was myself Jewish. He replied:

"A truly Orthodox rabbi would certainly say so! But I myself belong to the Reformed tendency of our faith and, should you wish to join it, would expect you to undergo a course of instruction... though in your case it might not be very long, since you seem to know quite a bit about it already."

I should here probably say something about my own relationship to Judaism, or perhaps Judaism's relationship to me. The fact that I have always had a statistically improbable number of Jewish friends need not mean much beyond my having a liking for Jews, as my gentile father had before me.

I resemble him physically as well as mentally, so it's rather puzzling that every Jew I have ever met has immediately classified me as Jewish, and is indeed somewhat surprised and disappointed to find I am not fully so; whereas no gentile I know has ever spotted me. This has led to one or two rather dramatic encounters, such as the one with a girl of 19 in Germany who had somehow managed to live through the Nazi era and was telling me about her experiences; when I said I was honoured by her confidence and was in part Jewish-descended myself, she answered "Oh, *that* I knew! That's why I told you."

I began to ask Jewish friends and acquaintances what it was about me that made them so certain I too was Jewish. Most of them said, not very helpfully, "Oh well, it's obvious, isn't it?" But I did get one more sensible answer – somebody who said it was nothing in my features, but something in the way I moved my mouth. This I find believable, since it could well have been a childhood imitation of my mother; and it is something which gentiles would not have been likely to notice.

The end of the affair?

Next came the late-Christianity/Islam session. No mosque hereabouts, but I did know a theologian from my own Catholic congregation, Marion Smith, who had done scholarly work on Islam; and for post-Reformation Christianity I was in luck: my friend Jeremy Goring, whom I had known when we were both undergraduates and who was now pastor to our local Unitarian chapel, had actually written a book on the post-Reformation religious history of Lewes! Another successful meeting ensued.

And now at last, in concluding a Seminar which had indeed enabled me to learn quite a lot about comparative religion, I held a session which I decided to chair myself. In the usual way of concluding meetings, all sorts of people said all kinds of things – and I suddenly heard myself saying, “People who disapprove of Roman Catholicism often describe it as being, of all forms of Christianity, the closest to paganism. I believe this to be true – and personally, it’s one of the things I like best about Catholicism: I don’t want my religious life to distance me more than necessary from the vast majority of human beings in both space and time.”

This was something I had never consciously thought about; but once I had said it I knew it was true. I did already know that I found it easier to be a Catholic in (moderately) good standing here in England than ever I would have done in Argentina, where it continues to be the religion of all proper “society” people, the kind that might well, during my childhood, have approved of Franco.

Epilogue

I no longer teach at Lewes U3A; but I still study there. Our Ancient Greek class – from Homer to the dramatists (like other languages it not only has several dialects but evolved over the centuries before classical Athens) – has enabled me to read the Odyssey in the original. This now allows me – having arrived at my own Ithaca – to heed the call of the modern Greek poet C.P. Cavafy and rejoice at the sheer length and variety of the voyage that has brought me here.

My Ithaca is in Sussex, and I do feel at home here, as I know I would still do in the "Great Village" of Buenos Aires; but on the continent of Europe the country in which I feel at home is neither Germany nor Spain, but Italy. This is rooted in the history of the country in which I grew up. Argentina is a country of immigrants quite as much as the USA, and the most successful of our immigrants have been Italian. It is said that one Argentine in four bears an Italian surname; I don't quite believe this, but do think it might be true of one in four of the inhabitants of Buenos Aires! And indeed, my sister and I are the only members of our family, in our generation and below, who have *not* married "Tanos", our slang word for Italian-descended people.

My friend Martín Villagrán, born in the north-western city of Salta (which the Spaniards managed to found in 1582), proud as he is of his own descent from two old Spanish families, has, living and working as he does in Buenos Aires, married a "Tana". I vividly remember from my teens the first Italian neo realist films to reach Buenos Aires after the war, in particular *Rome Open City* in which the heroine, Anna Magnani, spoke and moved exactly like people I could see on the streets around our house. Before that, I had only seen English and American films, and had assumed that the world shown in films was quite different from the real world I knew.

I now realise how thoroughly our waves of Italian immigration have affected our culture, and indeed the very Spanish we speak. But this is only one of the connections which now, here in my Ithaca, I detect between episodes of a life which – many years before young people travelled so widely in their gap years or as volunteers – seems to have involved encounters and apprenticeships on every continent. Connections not always apparent at the time have, like roots beneath the earth, nourished even while binding growths together.

I remember purple bougainvillea splashing over the white columns of the San Miguel house of my adolescence; later, over courtyard walls in Hanoi, over the trees in Herb Cahn's São Paulo garden, even (in rather paler colours) in the more adventurous expatriate gardens in The Gambia. Now in peaceful Hamsey, I need only look at the conservatory my daughter Susie keeps as tropical as she can, to see the bougainvillea splashing over its walls in many different colours and relive the memories it brings back.

The Memoirs of Eva Gillies: An Interpreter at Large.

Eva Gillies (née Krapf), 1930-2011: Key Publications

As Eva Krapf-Askari:

1965	'The social organization of the Owe', *African notes* 2 (3): 9-12. Ibadan: Institute of African Studies, University of Ibadan.
1966a	'Time and classification: an ethnographic and historical case-study', *Odu* 2 (2): 3-18. Ile-Ife, Nigeria.
1966b	'Brass objects from the Owé Yoruba, Kabba Province, Northern Nigeria', *Odu* 3 (1): 82-87. Ile-Ife, Nigeria.
1967a	Review of S.A. Babalọla, *The Content and Form of Yoruba* ijálá, Oxford: Clarendon Press, 1966. *Man* n.s. 2 (2): 322.
1967b	Review of Georges Balandier, *Ambiguous Africa: Cultures in Collision*, trans. Helen Weaver, London: Chatto & Windus, 1966. *African Affairs* 66: 254-55.
1969a	'Ogori: The Sociology of an Akoko Village', unpublished D.Phil. thesis, Oxford University.
1969b	*Yoruba Towns and Cities: An Enquiry into the Nature of Urban Social Phenomena*. Oxford: Clarendon Press.
1969c	'African Cities: A Review Article', *African Affairs* 68: 353-57.
1969d	Review of Jürgen Zwernemann, *Die Erde in Vorstellungswelt und Kultpraktiken der sudanischen Völker*, *Africa* 39: 190-191.
1969e	Review of J.S. Boston, *The Igala Kingdom*, London: OUP, 1968. *Africa* 39 (4): 422.
1969f	Review of J.D.Y. Peel, *Aladura: A Religious Movement among the Yoruba*, London: OUP, 1968. *Bulletin of the School of Oriental and African Studies* 32 (3): 661-63.
1970a	'Introduction' (pp. i-iii), to *The History of Ogori*, by Gab. Bawa Akerejọla Eminefo III. Mimeo typescript, Institute of African Studies, Ibadan, 1970 [Occasional Publication 22; printed cover dated 1973].
1970b	Review of Anne Retel-Laurentin, *Oracles et ordalies chez les Nzakara,* Paris, La Haye: Mouton & Co, 1969. *Man* n.s. 5 (1): 147-48.
1972	'Women, spears and the scarce good: a comparison of the sociological function of warfare in two Central African societies', in *Zande Themes: Essays presented to Sir Edward Evans-Pritchard*, edited by Andre Singer and Brian V. Street. Oxford: Blackwell.

As Eva Gillies:

1970	Review of P. Amaury Talbot, *Some Nigerian Fertility Cults*, 2nd edition, London: Frank Cass, 1967. *African Affairs* 69: 409-10.
1971a	Review of William Bascom, *The Yoruba of Southwestern Nigeria*, *Africa* 41: 66-67.
1971b	Review of William Moore, *A History of Itsekiri*, 2nd edition, London: Frank Cass. *Man* n.s. 6 (1): 137.
1971c	Review of Jean-Pierre Olivier de Sardan, *Système des Relations Economiques et Sociales chez les Wogo (Niger)*, Paris: Institut d'Ethnologie, Musée de l'Homme, 1969. *Man* n.s. 6 (2): 315-16.
1971d	Review of Marguerite Dupire, *Organisation Sociale des Peul: Etude d'Ethnographie Comparée*, Paris: Plon, 1970. *Man* n.s. 6 (3): 509-10.
1972a	Review of Denise Paulme (ed*), Classes et Associations d'Age en Afrique de l'Ouest*, Paris: Plon, 1971. *Man* n.s. 7 (1): 162-63.
1972b	Review of Paul Parkin *et al*, *Fürchte deinen Nächsten wie dich selbst: Psychoanalyse und Gesellschaft am Modell der Agnie in Westafrika*, Frankfurt: Suhrkamp, 1971. *Man* n.s. 7 (3): 503.
1975	'Introduction' and editor of *Witchcraft Among the Azande*, the abridged paperback edition of E.E. Evans-Pritchard's *Witchcraft, Oracles and Magic among the Azande* (1937). Oxford: Clarendon Press.
1976	'Causal criteria in African classifications of disease', in *Social Anthropology and Medicine*, ASA Monograph No. 13 (ed. J.B. Loudon). London: Academic Press.
1977a	Review of Tina Esh & Illith Rosenblum, *Tourism in Developing Countries: Trick or Treat? A Report from The Gambia,* Uppsala: Scandinavian Institute of African Studies, 1975. *Africa* 47 (1): 116.
1977b	Review of Jean Pouillon, *Fétiches sans Fétichisme*, Paris: Maspero, 1975. *Africa* 47 (2): 221-22.
1977c	Review of Denise Paulme, *La Mère Dévorante. Essai sur la Morphologie des Contes Africains.* Paris: Editions Gallimard, 1976. *Man* 12 (2): 367-68.
1981	Review of *Gens et paroles d'Afrique: écrits pour Denise Paulme,* Ecole des Hautes Etudes en Sciences Sociales. Paris: Mouton, 1979. *Africa* 51: 875.
1985	Review of John Agnew *et al* (eds), *The City in Cultural Context*, London: Allen & Unwin, 1984. *Man 20* (3): 561-62.

1988	'The coming of Christianity to a Nigerian Middle Belt Community', in *Vernacular Christianity: Essays in the Social Anthropology of Religion presented to Godfrey Lienhardt* (eds. W. James and D.H. Johnson). Oxford & New York: JASO & Lilian Barber Press.
1997	Translator and editor of the Spanish-language classic: Lucio V. Mansilla, *A Visit to the Ranquel Indians.* With a historical Introduction by Eva Gillies, pp. xix-xl. (Lincoln, NE & London: Nebraska University Press, 1997).
2000	Editor, *Mayfly on the Stream of Time: A Medical Naturalist's Life,* by Mick Gillies. Messuage Books. Production co-ordinated by The Better Book Co. Ltd, Warblington, Hampshire.

Index